Real Estate Finance

Real Estate Finance

SIXTH EDITION

John P. Wiedemer

University of Houston

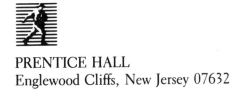

PRENTICE HALL
Englewood Cliffs, New Jersey 07632

Library of Congress Cataloging-in-Publication Data

Wiedemer, John P.
    Real estate finance / John P. Wiedemer. — 6th ed.
        p.   cm.
    ISBN 0-13-762832-1
    1. Mortgage loans — United States.   2. Real property — United
States — Finance.   3. Housing — United States — Finance.   I. Title.
HG2040.5.U5W54   1990
332.7'2'0973 — dc20

89-36256
CIP

*Editorial/production supervision and
    interior design:* Laura Cleveland
Cover design: 20/20 Services, Inc.
Manufacturing buyer: Laura Crossland

©1990, 1987, 1983, 1980, 1977, 1974 by Prentice-Hall, Inc.
A Division of Simon & Schuster
Englewood Cliffs, New Jersey 07632

Printed in the United States of America

10   9   8   7   6   5   4   3   2

ISBN 0-13-762832-3

Prentice-Hall International (UK) Limited, *London*
Prentice-Hall of Australia Pty. Limited, *Sydney*
Prentice-Hall Canada Inc., *Toronto*
Prentice-Hall Hispanoamericana, S.A., *Mexico*
Prentice-Hall of India Private Limited, *New Delhi*
Prentice-Hall of Japan, Inc., *Tokyo*
Simon & Schuster Asia Pte. Ltd., *Singapore*
Editora Prentice-Hall do Brasil, Ltda., *Rio de Janeiro*

Contents

7 *Federal Government Underwriting Programs*   123

8 *Borrower Qualification*   156

9 *Property Analysis*   190

10   *Other Financing Practices*   213

11   *Commercial Loans*   233

12 *Settlement Procedures*   269

Acknowledgments

The author gratefully acknowledges the expert advice, assistance, and encouragement of the following persons who have helped make this book possible.

JAY BIRNBAUM, *College of Continuing Education, Rochester Institute of Technology, Rochester, N.Y.*

RICHARD L. CHUMBLEY, *Richland College, Dallas, Texas*

KEN COMBS, *Del Mar College, Corpus Christi, Texas*

GREG ENHOLM, *Securities Analyst, Salomon Brothers, Inc., New York, N.Y.*

JAMES E. HOWZE, *President Advanced Career Training, Inc., Houston, Texas*

ARTHUR JOHNSTON, *Johnston Associates, Lewisville, N.C.*

PEGGY KARSTEN, *Anoka-Ramsey Community College, Coon Rapids, Minn.*

PATRICIA McAULIFFE, *House Hunters, Inc., Houston, Texas*

DONALD McGREGOR, JR., *Real Estate Investments, Houston, Texas*

ROLAND B. METCALF, JR., *Moseley-Flint Schools of Real Estate, Buckingham, Va.*

PAUL METZGER, *Houston Community College, Houston, Texas*

TOM MOORE, *Supervisor, Single-Family Property Disposition, HUD, Houston, Texas*

KEVIN S. MORRIS, *San Jacinto College, Houston, Texas*

BEN MUSICK, *Valencia Community College, Orlando, Fla.*

WILLIAM ROBERTSON, JR., *Deputy Administrator, HUD/FHA, Houston, Texas*

WILLIAM J. SOWERS, *McLennan Community College, Waco, Texas*

JAMES C. TAYLOR, J.D., *Dean Emeritus, Continuing Education, University of Houston, Houston, Texas*

RICHARD M. WHITE, *Asheville-Buncombe Technical College, Asheville, N.C.*

AVAILABLE VETERANS AFFAIRS CIRCULARS AND INTERIM ISSUES from the Department of Veterans Benefits

GEORGE YOUNG, *In memoriam and grateful remembrance, University of Houston, Houston, Texas*

And a special acknowledgment to my wife, Margaret Ivy Wiedemer, for organization and editing assistance plus her kind patience.

Foreword

Land is a scarce and limited resource. Its availability and use are so basic to human life that they form the foundation upon which societies are organized and function. Inherent in the structure of every society is a system designed to deal with the multitude of relationships concerning land.

In this society, private ownership of real property is an established and guarded right. Here, too, systems have been developed that recognize this right and facilitate the individual's exercise of this right.

The economic importance of real estate transactions is obvious; it is so obvious, in fact, that most people are only vaguely aware of the tremendous impact of real estate transactions on the financial market. The potential size and number of these transactions give the appearance of something too complicated to understand. This appearance is both deceiving and dangerous.

An individual purchasing a home is obligating a large portion of his or her personal income. The real estate salesperson is concerned with the economic well-being of his or her client. Complications notwithstanding, buyers, sellers, brokers, and others are faced with an urgent need to know.

Admittedly, the field of real estate finance is in a state of continuous change: change in practices, methods, clientele, and sources. This circumstance should not be viewed with alarm, for change is inherent in progress. Professionals in real estate, like professionals in every field, must stay abreast of these changes if they are to remain professionals.

Newcomers to the field must gain a solid foundation in the basic principles and terminology of real estate finance. The real estate profession's clientele needs at least a working knowledge of these same principles and terms.

To fulfill these needs, access to accurate, current information is necessary.

The information required is available from many sources. Unfortunately, information of this type is normally presented in an obscure and unimaginative form that makes learning a labor and is of limited educational value to all but the specialist.

In this sense, Wiedemer's book is unique. Not only is the information current and technically accurate, it is presented as an informative discussion. His discussion of methods and elements of real estate finance are objective and complete.

His book contains the information necessary to fulfill the needs of the beginner and is thorough enough to be a valuable resource for the established professional. The book has been written in such a way that the novice can understand the language of the professional.

Mr. Wiedemer has been a lecturer in real estate at the University of Houston since 1970. He has brought to his classroom the knowledge and enthusiasm of a leader in his field. He approaches his teaching duties with a sincere desire for his students to learn. This approach is immediately evident in his book.

A true professional, Wiedemer wants to give back something to the profession that has been good to him. This book and his continuing work in education are overt expressions of this willingness and desire.

James C. Taylor, J.D.
Dean Emeritus, Continuing Education
University of Houston

Preface

Real estate, in its broadest definition, is land and that which is attached to it. Financing of real estate could include farming, mining, drilling, the supporting services for each, as well as surface development. This text focuses on the development of land into various types of buildings, including homes, shopping centers, office buildings, warehouse space, recreational facilities, and factories. Primary emphasis is given to residential financing since this comprises two-thirds of all mortgage lending and has developed a few uniform patterns. Even in the more limited aspects described here, the financing of real estate has long been the largest single demand on our credit system. In 1988, mortgage debt outstanding topped $3,000 billion.

The variety of features that make the mortgage loan system function has resulted from long-term experience in meeting constantly changing needs. Many of the basic credit restraints and lending patterns go back to regulations created during the depression years of the 1930s. Since then, many improvements have been made, reflecting the efforts of men and women working through private industry and government agencies to achieve a more stable and equitable system. It could be said that the mortgage lending industry attempts to match dreams with reality and make them come true.

Any person interested in real estate, whether as an investor or a sales agent, needs a good understanding of the specialized financing procedures that are used. The sources of mortgage money have been enlarged from the limited pool of savings accounts to include the huge securities markets. The variety of mortgage repayment plans has proliferated in an effort to accommodate a changing market. Loan qualification standards, never uniform, have continued to reflect lenders' concerns for full repayment of their loans. Government programs continue to support the goal of providing suitable housing for all qualified persons. A good example is the Government National Mortgage Association, which alone has attracted over $300 billion to the mortgage market, mostly from nontraditional sources, with its guaranteed securities program. And the flurry of consumer protection laws developed in the early 1970s have been improved with experience and provide better information disclosure and some additional sound protection.

The rapid growth period of the 1970s gave way to a more realistic market in the 1980s. Areas of the nation that had suffered depressed conditions, like the Northeast, found new strength in a changing economy. And formerly prosperous areas, such as the Southwest, suffered reversals as energy and agricultural prosperity declined. Changes in the economic health of an area are immediately reflected in the need for housing and other commercial development.

For those unaccustomed to the cyclical nature of the real estate market, it will flourish at times and then languish for awhile. Such ups and downs are the normal workings of a free market system. There is no central government planning authority empowered to set limits on the number of housing units that can be built in any given market area. It is the market that controls. So overbuilding often occurs, providing the necessary check rein. However, the increased tax incentives of the early 1980s added some distortion to the readings of the true market. Even so, overall reading of market needs presents some problems. As one wag recently said, "We had a need for 5,000 new units here, and 10 developers jumped in, each building 5,000 units!" So some are hurt financially, but in the long run, we all benefit from the freedom on which the system is based.

John P. Wiedemer

Real Estate Finance

1

History and Background

KEY WORDS AND PHRASES

Term loan   Common stock
HOLC, FHA, FNMA   Bonds
Gold bonds

The history of real estate financing presents a fascinating record of civilization's learning to live with, and enjoying the benefits of, the land it lives on. While private ownership of land can be traced back to civilizations existing over 2,500 years ago, only in the last several hundred years has it become possible for the average person to own property.

Early Financing Methods

In ancient Rome, citizens of means were most often the hereditary large landlords whose land in the provinces had gained them admission to the Curia. This membership required their residence in the city, allowing them to extend their political, religious, and economic influence throughout Rome. Other members included administrators and shareholders of the tax-gathering societies whose treasuries were assured of capital funds. Of course, these societies were open only to the privileged few, unlike our modern investment institutions.

In medieval times, under the feudal system, land was owned primarily by the king, the nobility, or the church. Thus landownership was restricted to the very few, and those who did possess rights to land could pledge their property rights as security for a loan. In these earlier times there were no savings banks

1

or other lending institutions offering investment capital, and only a few individuals of great wealth were capable of making loans. Besides the severe limitations on investment activity imposed by there being very few property owners, an equally severe limitation was caused by the lack of money—a problem that still exists with many of us today! Historically, the growth of widespread landownership parallels the increase in pools of money available for long-term loans.

With the advent of the Industrial Revolution in the eighteenth century, more individuals became capable of producing wealth with their ideas and their machinery. People began to find that another option was open to them; the life of a serf grubbing an existence from land owned by the nobility was no longer the only way to make a living. With the more widespread wealth came the demand for ways to make better use of accumulated money, and the seeds of our publicly owned savings institutions started to grow.

Colonial America

Prior to the Industrial Revolution, colonial America felt the need for capital to build its new homes and businesses. Many groups began to join together for mutual protection and mutual help. Savings were pooled in informal clubs or fraternal groups to provide lendable funds for members wishing to build a house, to make an addition to their building, or to construct a barn. Organizations were created to provide fire protection for their members. And some groups arranged for periodic payments into the club treasury, which provided for a lump-sum payment to the member's family at his death. The only problem here was that without regulation and accurate reserves based on mortality rates, the groups grew older, failed to attract younger members, and often went broke.

In spite of these setbacks, the desire for economic security and the need for the protection of capital helped to spawn the banks, savings associations, and life insurance companies of the nineteenth century that have become great assets to our nation today. These older institutions, along with many younger ones, plus some growing new pools of money such as pension funds and retirement funds, are now providing us with the funds needed to own and develop our land. Table 1–1 gives a chronological outline of when the major institutions were formed in this country.

Lending Reforms from the Great Depression

In the early 1900s, potential borrowers had several sources from which to seek a mortgage loan: depository institutions (banks, savings associations), life insurance companies, individuals, and some mortgage companies. Regardless of where the

TABLE 1–1
Chronology of Key Agencies and Institutions Associated with Real Estate Finance in the United States

1759 Charter date of the oldest life insurance company in the United States. The Presbyterian Ministers Fund issued its first policy in 1761. The name was changed to Presbyterian Annuity and Life Insurance Company in 1889, thereafter insuring Protestant ministers, their wives, and theological students.

1781 Bank of North America, the oldest commercial bank in this country, opened in Philadelphia. It was chartered by the Pennsylvania legislature and incorporated by the Continental Congress for the purpose of providing money to wage the Revolutionary War against England through pooling of private and public resources.

1791 The First Bank of the United States was established as the initial effort to create a national bank. This institution was promoted by Alexander Hamilton and chartered by the Congressional Federalists. The initial capitalization was $10 million, of which 20 percent was owned by the national government. The bank terminated in 1811 due to considerable opposition in Congress.

1812 The first public life insurance company was formed under the name of Pennsylvania Company for Insurance on Lives and Granting Annuities.

1816 The Second Bank of the United States was established to exert some controls over private banks and to regulate the U.S. monetary system. This second attempt to establish a national banking system was successfully opposed by President Andrew Jackson, and closed down in 1836.

1816 The first mutual savings bank was established and still operates under its original name—Philadelphia Savings Fund Society (although its ownership changed in 1985). The bank was organized to operate for the interests of its shareholders (its depositors), and it encouraged savings by persons of modest means.

1831 The first savings association chartered for the purpose of accumulating capital for building houses was founded by Samuel Pilling and Jeremiah Horrocks under the name of Oxford Provident Building Association in Philadelphia. The first mortgage loan for the purpose of buying a home was made to Comly Rich of Philadelphia in the amount of $375.00. Monthly payments were $4.90.

1835 New England Mutual was chartered as the first of the modern forms of life insurance companies.

1863 The federal government resumed responsibility for the regulation of currency. After the closing of the Second Bank of the United States in 1836, state-chartered banks issued their own bank notes that circulated as currency.

1913 The Federal Reserve Bank System was established by the federal government as a national bank to administer currency and to regulate federally chartered commercial banks and any state-chartered banks that met membership requirements.

1916 The government created the Federal Land Bank as a system to raise money through the sale of bonds for the purpose of making loans to farmers.

1932 Under the administration of Herbert Hoover, the Reconstruction Finance Corporation was established to provide direct government loans to private business.

TABLE 1–1 *(Continued)*

1932   The Federal Home Loan Bank system was created to charter federal savings and loan associations and to regulate their operations.

1933   On March 6, 1933, President Franklin D. Roosevelt closed all depository institutions in the country to halt disastrous runs. Thereafter, those deemed in satisfactory condition could reopen. Within one year, the number of operating banks in this country was reduced from 30,000 to 16,000.

1933   Home Owners Loan Corporation (HOLC) was created to sell bonds and use the proceeds to refinance existing homeowner indebtedness. It was liquidated in 1951 after refinancing over a million homes.

1934   Securities and Exchange Commission (SEC) was established to regulate the issuance and sale of all types of securities to the general public.

1934   Federal Housing Administration (FHA) was created to utilize the credit of the federal government to insure home loans and thus encourage lending from private sources.

1934   Federal Deposit Insurance Corporation (FDIC) was incorporated to insure deposits in commercial banks and mutual savings banks against losses due to bank failure.

1934   Federal Savings and Loan Insurance Corporation (FSLIC) provided a government agency similar to the FDIC to insure deposits in savings associations.

1937   Local Housing Authority (LHA) allowed for the creation of quasi-government agencies for the purpose of developing low-cost housing for lower-income families.

1938   Federal National Mortgage Association (FNMA) was established as a government agency to raise funds for the purpose of buying FHA-insured loans. It became a public issue corporation in 1968.

1944   Veterans Administration (VA), created in 1930, established a home loan guaranty program for veterans during World War II.

1946   Farmers Home Administration (FmHA) was established as a government agency to make and insure loans to farmers and ranchers. It is part of the Department of Agriculture.

1965   Department of Housing and Urban Development (HUD) was created from the reorganization of various government operations intended to coordinate and expand housing programs. It includes the Federal Housing Administration.

1968   Government National Mortgage Association (GNMA) was created from the partitioning of the Federal National Mortgage Association, and is an agency under HUD charged with handling housing assistance programs and loan management functions. Its guaranteed mortgage-backed security program (Ginnie Mae) supports about 10 percent of all outstanding mortgage loans.

1969   Truth-in-Lending Act became effective as a part of the Consumer Credit Protection Act. Its purpose is to require lenders to give meaningful information on the cost of consumer credit.

1970   Federal Home Loan Mortgage Corporation (FHLMC) established by the Federal Home Loan Bank Board to sell securities and use the proceeds to purchase mortgages from member savings associations and other qualified lenders.

TABLE 1–1 *(Continued)*

1970	Environmental Protection Agency (EPA) created to develop rules and procedures for the improvement of our natural heritage and to enforce requirements for proper land development.
1974	Housing and Community Development Act passed by Congress consolidated a number of federal programs such as Urban Renewal, Model Cities, Neighborhood Facilities, Open Space, Water and Sewer Facilities plus some lending authority into a single program. Federal funds are made available to local communities that follow national guidelines and determine how the money is to be spent.
1974	Real Estate Settlement Procedures Act (RESPA), as amended in 1976, was directed toward providing better information on the settlement process to help home buyers make informed decisions.
1974	Equal Credit Opportunity Act (ECOA) prohibits discrimination in consumer credit transactions.
1977	Federally chartered credit unions were authorized to make long-term (up to 30 years) real estate loans.
1978	Community Reinvestment Act (CRA) expands the concept that regulated financial institutions must serve the needs of their local community.
1979	Federal Home Loan Bank first approved alternative mortgage plans for writing by federally chartered savings associations.
1980	Congress passed the Depository Institutions Deregulation and Monetary Control Act. It brought a fundamental change in the operations of depository financial institutions. Greater flexibility was given in the types of loans that can be made, and all covered institutions may offer interest-bearing checking accounts. Reserve requirements were established at uniform levels by the Federal Reserve Board for *all* depository institutions handling transaction accounts (checking accounts).
1986	Interest rate controls on savings deposits in regulated depository institutions were completely phased out.
1989	Homogenization of depository institutions continued with a federal bail-out of savings and loan associations and consolidation of the FSLIC with the FDIC.

money was sought, the rules were quite different then. For example, the standard loan was up to 50 percent of the lender's estimate of property value, repayment might be five years at the most, and there were no escrow account and no amortization payments. The borrower might pay interest only during the term of the loan with the entire principal balance coming due at maturity. It was a system that could cause an instant collapse for the borrower—and added to other loose lending practices, became a part of the causes of the great depression of the 1930s.

The collapse of the real estate loan market in the early 1930s brought a flood of foreclosures with farms, houses, and businesses swept away. It is the now-passing generation who determined that there must be a better way.

Many historic changes were wrought in our economy under the administration of Franklin Delano Roosevelt to prevent future economic disasters. The demand by some economists in those days to "control the economy" or to "eliminate depressions" was the source of many jokes and was not taken too seriously by many people, including much of the business community. But controls were established nonetheless.

The Securities and Exchange Commission was brought into existence to regulate the sale of all types of securities to the general public. The bankruptcy laws were revised to deter one or two creditors from destroying a cash-short business at the expense of all the other creditors.

But the area of change bearing on our special interests encompasses the sweeping reforms made in real estate finance beginning with the closing of all banks in 1933. To start patching up the economy, the Home Owners Loan Corporation (HOLC) was formed that same year to issue government-guaranteed bonds and to use the proceeds to refinance homeowners' indebtedness. Over one million houses were refinanced through this agency, and with the new liquidity in our financial institutions, stability was gradually restored.

To help restore depositors' confidence in the banking system, two deposit insurance agencies were formed: the Federal Deposit Insurance Corporation (FDIC) for commercial bank depositors and the Federal Savings and Loan Insurance Corporation (FSLIC) for savings associations. Also, in 1934, the Federal Housing Administration was created to provide home loan insurance. It did not then, and does not today, make loans. It provides a loan insurance policy, insuring the lender against loss through default, if the FHA qualifications are met. However, many bankers and other lenders, inherently opposed to any government intrusion, especially in an area where character judgment was considered all important, simply refused to recognize a government-insured commitment.

Hence, a few years later, in 1938, the Federal National Mortgage Association, FNMA, or "Fannie Mae," was established to buy FHA-insured mortgage loans and then to resell them as markets could be found. This agency provided the real beginnings of the so-called secondary market for mortgage loans, which may be broadly defined as any purchaser of a mortgage loan who does not participate in its origination. Money to finance FNMA purchases was derived from the sale of bonds.

By 1940, the pressures of a war economy brought an expansion of FHA activities to encourage housing in defense-designated areas and to permit financing of large apartment or multifamily projects. In 1944, Congress passed legislation permitting the Veterans Administration to guarantee mortgage loans made by private lenders to veterans.

Development of Mortgage Banking

In a growing country like the United States, the pools of lendable money were not always readily available where needed or were not always known to a potential borrower. To help bridge the gap, a new industry gradually developed what is now known as *mortgage banking*. The precise date of its origin would be difficult to state because the mortgage banking business has developed from a small service or brokerage facility in the late 1800s into a major banking industry today. Initially, a lawyer, or perhaps a real estate broker with contacts in the investment world, would arrange a loan for a client and charge a service fee. And as some individuals became quite adept at this business, the placement of loans became their principal occupation. Even today, a large number of mortgage bankers come from first- or second-generation family-owned businesses.

The mortgage companies functioned differently before the depression years of the 1930s. Then, many companies raised their own investment money through the sale of securities. The proceeds from the security sales were used to make mortgage loans. The record of repayment was so good that mortgage bonds became known as "gold bonds" and offered sound investment for many small savers. Two problems arose that contributed to the economic collapse of the Great Depression years. One was the short-term nature of mortgage loans—a home loan might be for up to five years with no amortization, just interest payments until the principal balance became due in full. Many farmowners and homeowners were unable to make full payment when this type of loan came due. The other problem was the potential for speculation in the sale of mortgage bonds. With little regulation in the security market, mortgage lenders could easily overestimate the value of a real estate development and raise more money than needed for the project itself. Many of these developments were quick to collapse as the depression years set in. Unable to collect payments due on their loans, mortgage companies were unable to maintain payments to their bondholders. Mortgage companies' ability to sell bonds collapsed—and with it their ability to make loans. The industry suffered traumatic reversals, and since the firms held no deposits, the government saw little need to lend its help as it was doing for depository institutions.

In spite of the industry collapse, mortgage companies had much to offer in their lending expertise. One major path to recovery for them was support of government underwriting programs. While the banking industry in general rejected any government programs, the mortgage companies found them to be a key to their recovery. They promoted both the FHA and VA programs using funds supplied by the purchase of their loans by the Federal National Mortgage Association. (FNMA's origin was a part of the act that created the Federal Housing Administration in 1934.) An interesting point is the pattern created in those depression years—mortgage companies' support of government programs with loan sales to FNMA—that is still a dominant pattern for those loans today.

The Changing Mortgage Market

No other major industry is so dependent on borrowed money as is housing and the construction industry in general. And few industries are as important to the overall health of the economy. Because of this, the federal government has frequently undertaken efforts to stabilize the housing industry and improve the programs that support it. Each year, Congress passes an omnibus housing act to further this purpose. It may change a housing agency's functions, modify or expand an existing program, or offer some new assistance to home buyers. Almost always the changes are directed toward how real estate is financed. How the nature of the market changed and the efforts made to accommodate it are pointed out in the following brief review of the decades of the 1970s and 1980s.

The 1970s

Home Buying Market.   Since two-thirds of all mortgage money is used to finance the acquisition of homes, the nature of this particular market is most important. Two major changes occurred in the 1970s: one demographic, the other economic. First, the post-World War II baby boom reached its peak home buying age of 25 to 34 years old, creating an unprecedented demand for new housing. And second, the increase in two-income families created a greater market for more and larger houses. Both factors were important reasons why the price of houses increased at rates that exceeded the average rate of inflation. By the early 1980s, these particular influences had diminished.

Mortgage Repayment Plans.   To cope with increasing demand and rising costs of both money and construction, both regulators and lenders worked together to give mortgage loans greater flexibility. In the past, there had been only one widely used repayment plan: the fixed-interest, constant-level payment design. In the mid-1970s, two experiments by federal agencies generated some alternative designs. The Federal Housing Administration developed a graduated payment plan that offered lower monthly payments in the early years, permitting easier qualification for borrowers, and at about the same time, the Federal Home Loan Bank Board studied alternative mortgage plans. The FHLBB approved four alternative designs in January, 1979; several allowed lenders to write graduated payment plans, and one set parameters for an adjustable rate design (originally called a "variable rate mortgage"). Lenders learned more about administering the new plans and, after some modifications, the alternative designs became very popular. By 1990, alternative designs accounted for about half of all residential loans.

Sources of Mortgage Money. New mortgage repayment plans by themselves were not of sufficient help to maintain traditional lenders in the home mortgage field. In the mid-1970s, approximately two-thirds of all residential loans were funded by regulated lenders from various savings account sources. At that time, federal law restricted interest paid on savings deposits to 5½ percent, which gave the lenders a fixed cost of their funds. Steps toward the deregulation of depository institutions began in the late-1970s. And by the end of that decade, interest rates began climbing. Indeed, the years 1979, 1980, and 1981 averaged an interest-rate increase of 2 percent each year! Savings institutions holding long-term, fixed-interest mortgages in portfolio while their costs of funds escalated were badly hurt, and many withdrew from the residential mortgage market.

What developed as the replacement for the savings account source was the growth of mortgage-backed securities. This method, described more fully in Chapter 4, opened the huge financial markets up as a source of mortgage money: mortgages could now be sold as securities to a much broader investment market.

Consumer Protection Laws. The decade of the 1970s witnessed a number of new consumer protection laws that affected the mortgage industry. These included fair housing laws, various lender disclosure requirements, and the Equal Credit Opportunity Act (ECOA). Probably the greatest impact on the mortgage market was created by ECOA (described more fully in Chapter 8). Prior to this act, it was a fairly common practice in loan qualification to discount the income of a wife; that is, if a wife reported a $20,000 per year income, the lender might accept half of it as qualifying income. The lender's concern at that time was the potential loss of a wife's income in favor of caring for a child. ECOA, passed in 1974, did away with this concept by requiring the income of both spouses to be treated equally. The result was a substantial boost in borrowing power for home buyers.

The 1980s

After the dramatic changes that occurred throughout the 1970s, the decade of the 1980s was one of accommodation for the mortgage industry. It was a period of learning how to more efficiently handle the new mortgage procedures, and it was a time to cope with a downturn in the economy in many areas of the country.

The New Mortgage Repayment Plans. After a fairly rough start, lenders learned how to handle the new repayment designs; those that were not the long familiar fixed-rate, constant-level plans. After a proliferation of ideas on the many new ways that mortgages might be repaid, the industry settled on two basic plans: (1) adjustable rate mortgages, and (2) graduated payment plans.

When adjustable rate plans were first approved, two impediments cropped up. First, the regulator's efforts to protect consumers/borrowers resulted in adjustment limitations that were simply too tight. Lenders are not required to offer any kind of loan and most lenders declined to offer the severely limited adjustable designs. Once the limitations, or "caps," were lifted, the second problem developed. That was in the pricing of adjustable plans. When offered at about the same interest rates as were fixed-rate loans, borrowers generally opted for the fixed rates. It was not until about 1982–1983 that adjustables became "competitive," offering interest rates at 2 to 3 percent lower than that offered for a fixed-rate mortgage. The lower rate, and lower monthly payments, was the encouragement that borrowers needed to accept the additional risk of interest-rate fluctuations. And adjustables achieved a fair share of the total market.

The graduated payment mortgage, popularized with the HUD's/FHA's Section 245 program, attracted many borrowers in the early years of the decade. It enabled a borrower to acquire housing that might otherwise be out of reach. But the graduated payment concept—reduce the payments in the early years to allow qualification, then increase the amount so as to achieve full amortization later —contained a rather serious flaw. Payments in the early years were insufficient to repay all the interest due with unpaid interest added to the principal balance (called negative amortization). Offsetting the negative aspect, the payment due from the borrower increases each year until a payment sufficient to amortize the loan is reached. The flaw was in the assumption that the borrower's income would increase in roughly the same proportion as did the payment amount each year. When segments of the economy declined in the 1980s, as happened in agricultural and energy fields, the graduated payment design caused hardships for those whose income did not increase. As a result, some changes were made in loan qualification standards.

Nevertheless, the concept of the graduated payment design with its lower initial monthly payments remains intact. The idea was incorporated in a bold new mortgage design suggested in 1989 by HUD called the Price Level Adjusted Mortgage, or PLAM. In this design, the initial monthly payment is calculated at a base rate of interest. The base rate is a theoretical concept that considers the real cost of money as close to 4 percent per annum. The *market rate* is the sum of the base rate plus the going rate of inflation. For instance, in 1988 the rate of inflation was around 4 percent (depending on the statistical source). Add the inflation rate to the 4 percent base rate and the going market rate would be 8 percent; fairly close to longer-term government bond rates for that year. Carrying this idea into the PLAM design mortgage, it would mean an initial monthly payment amount for a typical $100,000 loan to be a little over $400. Then *both* the rate of interest applied *and* the principal balance would be increased each year by the going rate of inflation. Such a concept is best suited to those economies that try to contend with triple-digit inflation rates!

Loan Qualification Standards.   The shake-out of the economy in the 1980s caused a massive re-evaluation of how borrowers might qualify for mortgage loans. Loose lending practices had developed in the boom years of the early 1980s. After all, almost any dumb mistake could be offset by the continuing increase in property values! In these "go-go" years, lenders would fund almost any kind of loan that carried mortgage default insurance. And private mortgage insurers raced to expand their premium income because that was what escalated the value of the insurer's stock (the growth in premium income was more than reflected by the increase in the price of their stock). And loan quality was often overlooked.

Reality returned by the mid-1980s with all participants in mortgage lending tightening their qualification standards. This included lenders, government insurance agencies, federal agency pool underwriters and private mortgage insurers. Principal methods used to limit loan qualification are as follows:

- Lower acceptable loan-to-value ratios—usually by requiring at least 10 percent or more down.
- Tighten the income-ratio requirement for higher ratio loans. Thus, for a 95 percent loan the mortgage payment cannot exceed 25 percent of an applicant's income; for a 90 percent loan, the payment can amount to 28 percent.
- Calculation of the qualifying payment must be the amount that will fully amortize the loan over its term. Thus, excessive buy-downs and tease rates are eliminated as qualification standards.
- Limit qualification of property as collateral to its realistic market value; i.e., not inflated with excessive finance charges.
- Require substantially larger down payments for investor-owned property (meaning houses purchased for the purpose of renting). The highest foreclosure rates occurred in this category of loans.

Sources of Money.   The underlying source of residential mortgage money began to shift away from savings deposits in the mid-1970s. By the 1980s, the shift into mortgage-backed securities as the underlying source of funds grew rapidly. Accelerating this growth was the increased acceptance of federal underwriting of mortgage pools. What this meant was that loan originators could sell their loans into a mortgage pool. The organizer of the pool might be a bank, an investment banker, a federal agency, a finance company, or an insurance company. Loans delivered to the pool must be individually insured against default (VA guaranteed, FHA insured, or private-mortgage insured). Then, a federal agency underwrites the block of loans for a fee—meaning it issues a blanket guarantee for the loan pool. The three federal agencies most actively engaged in mortgage pool underwriting are Fannie Mae, Freddie Mac, and Ginnie Mae (explained in Chapter 4). The effect of mortgage pools and agency underwriting has brought changes to residential lending in the following four areas:

- Adequate funding has been made available to the mortgage industry at competitive market rates.
- Opening mortgage pools has diminished the need for having savings deposits to loan, thus attracting many newcomers to the loan origination market (such as home builders, finance companies, and real estate brokers).
- Loan qualification standards for both the borrower and property offered as collateral have become more uniform.
- Almost all documents used in residential loan processing have become standardized.

Whether or not a loan originator intended to sell the mortgage loan or hold it in portfolio, it seemed sensible to structure the loans in a manner that would make them easy to sell should that become necessary.

As the 1980s decade ended, about 40 percent of all mortgage debt had been converted into securities through various mortgage pools. The other 60 percent was held as investments by depository institutions, finance companies, insurance companies, individuals, and a few government agencies. Because the system of mortgage pooling is funded through the sale of securities in financial markets, the nature of this market is important in any study of real estate finance.

A Review of Corporate Finance

About half the money flowing into mortgage loans is coming from the sale of various kinds of securities rather than from savings deposits. The sale of securities is the business of the financial markets. It is the method by which corporations raise equity money and one way they can borrow money. The student of real estate finance needs to know what kinds of securities are offered for sale and what each represents. Hence, a review of basic corporate finance follows.

Corporations are financed through the sale of securities; paper certificates that represent some kind of an investment in the corporate structure. There are two major classes: (1) *stock* certificates, representing an ownership, or equity, interest in the corporation, and (2) *bonds*, representing a loan to the corporation. Stock evidences ownership; bonds evidence indebtedness.

Stock Certificates

The ownership interest in a corporation is represented by the shares of stock outstanding. *Common stock* is the basic ownership share and entitles its owner to a portion of the corporate profit distributed in the form of a *dividend*. The amount of the dividend is determined periodically by the board of directors of the corporation. There is another class of stock, called *preferred*, which holds a prior claim over common stock to a share of the corporate profit but usually at a not-to-exceed fixed rate of return.

Authorized shares are the number of shares approved by the state charter to the corporation. *Issued* shares are those that have been sold. *Treasury* shares are those acquired and held by the corporation itself.

Stock of the large, publicly held corporations is traded on various exchanges in major cities throughout this country and some foreign countries. The market value of publicly traded stock is only indirectly related to its actual earnings. Corporations seldom pay out the full amount of their profit in dividends, as some of the profit is usually retained to finance company growth. So the price for which a share of stock may be sold depends in part on its earnings record but also on future expectations of the company's profitability; that is, the speculative component of the stock's value.

Bonds

A corporation can borrow money through the sale of bonds to investors. Thus, the corporation has an additional source of funds not generally available to an individual or even to small, less well-known corporations. Bonds are offered in several categories:

Debenture bonds. An unsecured promise to repay, in effect a corporate IOU. The sale of debenture bonds is widely used by the Federal National Mortgage Association to raise part of the money it uses to buy mortgages.

Mortgage bonds. Secured by a pledge of real estate.

Equipment bonds. Secured by a pledge of equipment such as railroad cars or airplanes.

Utility bonds. May be secured by a pledge of certain assets of a regulated utility company.

Government bonds. Federal government promises to pay (no specific assets pledged) with maturity over 10 years.

Municipal bonds. Can be state or municipal issue, may or may not pledge tax or improvement revenue, and offers interest that is exempt from federal income tax with certain limitations.

Mortgage-backed bonds. Secured by the pledge of a large block of mortgage loans, which loans are held by a trustee.

The Securities Market

To qualify for sale in the public markets, all securities must have prior approval by the Securities and Exchange Commission. Approved securities are bought and sold daily on major exchanges throughout the country, but dominated by the New York markets. The exchanges deal in securities that trade in fairly large volume and offer near continuous price quotes. Securities with lesser trading activity may be bought and sold on the "over-the-counter" market that works in occasional trades on a quoted "bid and ask" range of prices. There is a third market that deals in large blocks of securities sold directly to major investors, such as insurance companies and pension funds, bypassing a portion of the trading commissions earned by investment bankers and stock brokerage firms.

Bonds trade freely at fluctuating prices, as do shares of stock. However, most bonds offer a fixed-interest rate of return, rather than the uncertain dividend that may be paid to the stockholder. The fixed interest rate of the bond (the face rate or nominal rate) controls the price for the bond. If market interest rates go up, the bond price falls, which increases the return for the investor based on the fixed-interest rate. Thus, there is an inverse movement in the bond market; if bond prices rise, it means that interest rates are falling, and if bond prices fall, it means that interest rates are rising. Bonds are offered in $1,000 denominations or multiples of $1,000, and the price can be quoted in a dollar amount or a percentage figure.

Example

A $1,000 bond offers an interest rate of 15 percent, paying $150 each year to the holder of the bond. The bond is sold for $925. The party paying $925 still receives an interest payment of $150 each year, which amounts to a return of 16.22 percent on the $925 invested. At maturity, the holder of the bond would pick up an additional $75, which is the difference between the $925 paid and the face amount of $1,000 at which the bond is redeemed by the issuer. Thus, the total return, or yield, on the investment includes both the annual interest and the price differential when the bond is redeemed at maturity. If the bond is sold prior to maturity, the holder could sustain a loss if the market is down.

One other type of corporate borrowing should be mentioned, as it is being used to finance construction by a few large builders. This is the sale of *commercial paper*. Commercial paper is a simple promise to pay that is unsecured (a corporate IOU). The term is generally short, like 30 days to 270 days. The largest issuer of commercial paper is General Motors Acceptance Corporation. Yields offered on commercial paper are generally competitive with the short-term money market rates, running about 2 percent higher than 90-day Treasury bill yields.

There is considerable variety in the securities market. The issuer of a security strives to structure the repayment to the security investor in a way that attracts buyers. It involves more than the interest paid to the holder of the security but that is an important element. The amount of interest demanded by an investor varies with both risk and time—the higher the risk, the greater the demand for higher interest; the longer the term, the higher the interest must be. For a mortgage-backed security, the risk is low. After all, each loan carries some kind of default insurance and, in today's market, most all of these securities are also federally insured, thus, double insured. So, from a risk standpoint, mortgage-backed securities rate slightly higher than government bonds, which classify as zero risk.

The time periods at which principal and interest are paid to a security holder offer a number of variations. Some investors prefer payments each month, some at six-month or one-year intervals. And investors such as pension funds might be willing to wait for years to recover both principal and interest so long as the return justifies the wait. After all, a pension fund is not in need of its cash before its pension obligations become due to its participants. And a pension fund is not subject to income taxes.

Another variation may be in the term of the security. The shorter the investment term, the lower the interest required. In a market where 90-day Treasury bills are paying 7 percent, two-year notes might pay 8½ percent, and 30-year bonds 9½ percent. To take advantage of the lower cost money available on short-term securities, some mortgage-backed securities are structured into several "classes" of bond. The shortest term class might be repaid in two years, another class in five or six years, with an accrual class to handle the balance, each paying interest rates to attract investors. This particular kind of structure is called a "collateralized mortgage obligation" in financial markets. Thus, the expression *mortgage-backed security* is a broad term covering a variety of securities.

Questions for Discussion

1. From whom and under what conditions did people borrow money prior to the Industrial Revolution?

2. How did the predepression methods of financing real estate contribute to the collapse of the economy in the early 1930s?

3. What do you believe is the principal contribution of the Roosevelt administration toward stabilizing the economy in 1933?

4. Why did the Federal Housing Administration find considerable resistance from private lenders to its insured loan program?

5. Describe a mortgage-backed security.

6. What is a bond?

7. Identify at least two kinds of corporate stock.

8. Discuss the effects of risk and term of a bond on the interest rate paid.

2

Money and Interest Rates

KEY WORDS AND PHRASES

Money	Credit market
The monetary system	Interest rate indicators
Federal Reserve System	Treasury bill rate
Money supply measurement	Prime rate
Managing the money supply	Usury
Open market operations	Supply of money
Discount rate of interest	Demand for money
Treasury obligations	

No commodity is more widely used and less understood than money. In a limited sense we know very well what money can do; its value lies primarily in our confidence that other people will accept the money in exchange for their goods and services. A brief reference to history shows that money has been with us in all civilizations as a means to improve the barter system of trading goods and services among people. Commodities of high intrinsic value have always been used in trade, including precious metals, gemstones, furs, and even salt and other spices. In fact, many areas of the world still use such standards today. Our modern business, however, floats on an intangible—the trust and confidence that individuals and nations place in currency and credit lines extended for bonds or other promissory certificates issued under a recognized government's authority. Certainly, the confidence placed in a government and its international trading power is indicated by the relative values placed on a nation's money in the realm of international trade.

The monetary system used in the United States was molded over many years of practical experience generated from trial-and-error methods. It has been shaped by political debates extending through the Civil War during the 1860s, the Great Depression years of the 1930s, on up to the present. In the early years of this country's growth, the control of money was considered a right of each state. The political battles between state's rightists on one hand, and the Federalists on the other, was clearly reflected in how the monetary system developed. Two early efforts to create a central national bank failed, and it was not until the American Civil War that the federal government actually took over the issuance and control of currency. Prior to that time, the individual states authorized their own banks to do this.

Federal Reserve Bank System

The step that firmly established federal control over the nation's money supply was the creation of the Federal Reserve Bank in 1913. The Fed was given the responsibility of handling the country's monetary policies and its seven-member Board of Governors was shielded from political influence. While appointments to the board are made by the president and confirmed by the Senate, the members hold tenure for 14 years and are not subject to removal for political reasons.

The chairman of the Federal Reserve Board is also named by the president and serves a four-year term, but not concurrent with the presidency. While the chairman has only one vote on the board, the authority to influence the selection of the 12 Federal Reserve District Presidents adds to the power of that office. And the chairman's influence is also felt in the selection of which five of the 12 District Presidents sit on the powerful Open Market Committee.

The board is responsible for many other functions, such as overseeing the Truth-in-Lending Act, monitoring the Equal Credit Opportunity Act, and implementing other national credit policies. But it is their monetary policies that most influence the cost and availability of mortgage money.

Monetary Policies

What is it that the Fed controls when charged with making monetary policies? Their underlying mission is to help create a stable and prosperous economy that can provide jobs and better living conditions. However, the nation's monetary policies now affect a global economy, and the monetary policies of other nations directly affect the United States. (About one third of the federal deficit is being financed by foreign investors.) So the Fed must function within global constraints.

The basic tools used by the Fed to influence the monetary system are:

1. Controlling the amount of money in circulation called the money supply.
2. Manipulating the funds available within the commercial banking network, which can be influenced by the Fed's "open market operations."
3. Signaling interest rate movements through changes in their discount rate of interest.

Of the three tools, the money supply decisions have the most influence, as will be discussed next.

MONEY SUPPLY

The difficult task faced by the Fed is to create a balance so that the growth in the nation's money supply is commensurate with the growth in the country's population and its productivity. Too much money can cause destructive inflation, and too little growth in the available money supply can create damaging recessions. Even so, true measures in these areas are quite hard to come by.

The size of our total money supply and of the economy makes the problem appear almost beyond comprehension. For clarification, let us use a simplified example. First, remember that the value of money used today is represented by the goods and services that it can buy. If we have an economy with exactly 10,000 units of goods and services with an amount of money available to purchase these products totaling $1 million, each unit of goods and services would be worth $100. Now by increasing productivity over several years, the economy has 20,000 units of goods and services for sale. But assume that *no increase* has been made in the available money. With twice as much to buy for the same amount of money, the price of each unit of goods and services drops to $50. If a different policy were used so that over the same period of time that our increased productivity supplied 20,000 units of goods and services, the money supply was subsequently increased to $3 million, then each unit would be worth $150. To maintain a stable pricing structure, a balance must be maintained between the money supply and the increase in productivity.

Definition of Money. To make decisions on whether or not to increase the available money, it is first necessary to define what money is. The Fed uses a rather limited definition for this, confining its recognition of money to currency in circulation plus both demand and time deposits within the banking system. This limited definition overlooks other assets that represent immediate purchasing power, such as deposits with nonbank institutions, some money market mutual funds, and some dollar deposits held overseas. To distinguish between some of the differences in the nature of money and to provide a base for its measurement, the Fed identifies four categories of money, using the letter "M" as follows:

M_1 Currency in circulation, nonbank travelers' checks, demand deposits in commercial banks and mutual savings banks, negotiable orders of withdrawal (NOW) accounts and automatic transfer service (ATS) at both banks and thrift institutions, and credit union share draft accounts. As of January, 1989, M_1 totaled $786 billion.

M_2 The total of M_1 plus savings and small-denomination time deposits at all depository institutions, overnight repurchase agreements, and general-purpose money market mutual funds. As of January, 1989, M_2 totaled $3,069 billion.

M_3 The total of M_2 plus large-denomination ($100,000 and over) time deposits at all depository institutions, term repurchase agreements at commercial banks and savings associations, and balances of institutional money market mutual funds. As of January, 1989, M_3 totaled $3,922 billion.

L The total of M_3 plus other liquid assets such as Eurodollars held by U.S. residents, bankers' acceptances, commercial paper, Treasury bills, and U.S. savings bonds. As of December, 1988, L totaled $4,689 billion.

Management of the Money Supply. The amount of money available in this country is controlled by the Federal Reserve Bank Board. It operates through a system of 12 districts, each with some branch Federal Reserve Banks to facilitate local operations. The system works with the approximately 5,000 commercial banks that handle most of the cash transfers in the country.

The Fed's Open Market Committee, comprising the seven Governors and 5 of the 12 Federal Reserve District Presidents, meets each month. At these meetings, the Committee reviews monetary aggregates, examines the influence of current interest rates, and considers the state of the economy. Then it makes a decision on whether or not an increase in the available money supply is justified.

To increase the supply of money, the Fed simply creates additional money and uses it to purchase U.S. Treasury securities. In a sense, the Fed writes "hot checks" to buy government securities. Of course, the checks are not hot because the Fed can clear them through its own bank. In practice, no checks are written; the Fed gives a credit to the U.S. Treasury bank account in exchange for Treasury securities. This authority to create money gives the Fed tremendous influence in financial markets. Obviously, an influx of new money creates an increase in the supply and is expected to lower interest rates and thus give the economy a lift. It works that way some of the time!

OPEN MARKET OPERATIONS

Another tool that the Fed can use to influence the economy is identified as "open market operations." With a large supply of both government bonds and cash in its hands, the Fed can move these two assets in and out of the banking system at any time it deems desirable. If the Fed decides the economy needs slowing down, it can issue an order through a limited group of investment bankers, who must be qualified and capable, to sell some of the Fed's supply of government bonds.

As these bonds are purchased by investors throughout the country, the money to buy them is withdrawn from various banks, sent to the Fed in payment for the bonds, and locked away in the Federal Reserve—not available for the banks to use in making further loans. In the alternative, if the decision is to speed up the economy a bit, then the Fed can buy government bonds, thus increasing the cash in the hands of banks. The increased cash should enhance the banks' ability to make more loans, thus improving business activity.

DISCOUNT RATE OF INTEREST

A third tool that the Fed might use from time to time is to change the discount rate of interest. The discount rate is that interest rate charged by the Fed to those depository institutions eligible to borrow from it. This is probably the most widely publicized influence, because it is the easiest to recognize. Yet, in practice, it is the least effective tool.

Eligibility to borrow at the Fed's "discount window" was broadened by the 1980 Depository Institutions Deregulation Act to include all institutions holding transaction accounts (primarily checking accounts). A further requirement of the act was to extend the reserve rules to all depository institutions. These institutions must maintain certain cash reserves on deposit with the Fed that pay no interest. In effect, this allows the banking system to borrow its own interest-free deposits from the Fed at the discount rate of interest.

Nevertheless, a change in the discount rate is not a critical matter in the banking industry, as it does not represent a cost of funds. Even though an institution is eligible to borrow from the Fed, this money cannot be used as a source of capital. The reserve held by the Fed represents a cushion, a back-up to the banking system for use on short-term loans that allows an eligible institution greater flexibility in meeting unexpected demands for funding. And the money is there to meet emergency needs when deemed necessary by the Fed. All such loans must be fully collateralized by the borrowing institutions.

For these reasons, the Fed's discount rate of interest is more of a signal to the banking community rather than a true cost of funds. If the Fed wants to slow the economy a bit and reduce potential inflationary pressures, it can increase the discount rate. While there is no requirement to do so, most of the banking institutions would follow such an increase with an increase in their own prime rates of interest. The expectation, of course, is that such a move would tend to throttle further borrowing by businesses.

Should a decrease become desirable, the Fed can lower its discount rate, an action that might be followed by similar action from the banking industry. In practice, the more likely scenario has been for the banking system to make its move on interest rates first, and the Fed simply follows the change with an adjustment in the discount rate.

The United States Treasury

While the Federal Reserve Bank Board holds responsibility for the amount of money in the country, it is the United States Treasury that is responsible for raising the money to pay the government's bills. How the Treasury decides to handle this requirement can easily upset the best laid plans of the Fed. In its simplest terms, the money to pay the government's obligations comes from three sources: tax revenues, borrowed funds, and printing money. If the government lives within its income, tax revenues would be sufficient to pay all obligations. When it spends more than it raises in taxes, the additional money must be either borrowed or printed.

This crucial decision (whether or not to borrow rather than print more money), rests primarily with Treasury. However, to pay for overspending through the printing of additional money is a choice that requires the consent of the Federal Reserve's Board of Governors. The reason is that the Fed holds the power to buy government securities issued by the Treasury with its "open-ended checking account." It is this authority to create money based solely on Treasury securities that gives the Fed its tremendous aura of power.

The result is that if Treasury opts to borrow money rather than "print" money to pay for deficit spending, it can do so without approval of the Fed. The only limit on this resource is the national debt ceiling established by Congress. In practice, this is little hindrance, as the ceiling is raised periodically to accommodate such overspending as Congress deems necessary.

The politically less obvious method of covering deficit spending is for the

Fed to agree to an increase in the money supply. By printing more money to cover the deficit (known as monetizing the debt), the need to borrow more money from the general public is reduced. However, an increase in the money supply in excess of the growth rate of the country is certain to cause an increase in the rate of inflation. The reason is that excessive increases in the amount of money debase the value of the currency. But such a result—an increase in inflation— is not an immediate one, and so is much less obvious to the average citizen. Thus, politicians generally prefer that the Fed be more accommodating with its approval of money aggregate increases, particularly in election years.

From the viewpoint of the real estate industry, borrowing by the government to pay its obligations competes directly with the demand for mortgage money. Any increase in demand can easily increase the cost of money. In this sense, increasing the money supply rather than borrowing the money may hold interest costs lower for mortgages, but it is always at the risk of a growing rate of inflation and higher rates later on. It is not an easy trade-off. Some industries have found short-term benefits can be derived from an inflationary trend, real estate being one.

Interest Rates

How are interest rates determined? First, interest is the cost of using another's money, and that cost reflects supply and demand factors somewhat similar to a commodity. However, the effect of the cost of money differs from that of a commodity in that its demand does not always respond to a change in its price.

If sugar, oil, or copper declines in price, the tendency is for demand to increase. If money goes down in price, the demand may not respond at all. This is because other factors influence money. The purpose in borrowing money is for reasons other than obtaining the money itself. For instance, money is borrowed to build a building, buy a car, or expand a business, but if the economy is in a decline, there may be no need for that building, or car, or even the business expansion. So what determines interest rates? It has to be a complex mix of influences, not the least of which is that generated by the government's needs, which are clearly colored by its unique power to create money.

To further explain, there are four major influences on interest rates, which can be summed up as follows:

1. *Supply of Money.* Previously, dependence on savings accounts as a source of mortgage money caused periodic shortages in the availability of funds. This was caused by occasions when savings were withdrawn to invest in higher yielding investments, such as money market funds. As the shift to the use of mortgage-

backed securities developed, the capability of tapping huge financial markets for funds accelerated. Shortage of money became a thing of the past. Now, the supply of money derives from a much broader base of sources, and the influence of supply on mortgage interest rates has lessened.

For these reasons, the "supply of money" is based more on activity in the financial markets than on savings accounts in the thrifts. Also, its cost is more likely to parallel debt instrument rates such as corporate and government bonds.

2. *Demand for Money.*   The demand for money can be put into four categories:

    a. Business borrowing for inventory requirements, capital needs, and longer term investment.
    b. Consumer and personal loans such as auto financing, furniture, appliances, or other personal needs.
    c. Government financing for federal, state, and local governments.
    d. Mortgage loans for housing, construction, industrial and other investment purposes.

A fairly normal balance of the four kinds of demands is that each takes about one quarter of the available supply of funds each year. In some years, one kind of demand will increase and another decline. The underlying problem today is that mortgage money competes with all other demands for credit seeking the same pool of funds. The swing player in the credit market is the federal government, which has the power to absorb all the available supply of funds, and is capable of driving all other demands for credit out of the market. Such action is an extreme scenario and not likely to happen, although it did once happen in 1944 at the peak of World War II when the government took 99 percent of the available credit.

What has allowed all kinds of demand to increase in recent years without adversely affecting interest rates has been the equally substantial increase in available credit. This increase has been provided by both foreign investment in this country and the growth of pension funds seeking investments.

3. *Monetary Policies of the Federal Reserve.*   A major influence on interest rates is the ability of the Fed to increase the money available in this country at any time.

4. *Fiscal Policies of the U.S. Government.*   The way in which the federal government handles its tax and spending policies is called "fiscal policies," and is a

key factor in the competitive markets that control interest rates. If Congress and the president decide to spend more than the income (tax revenues) available, the difference must be made up by either borrowing or printing money.

Interest Rate Indicators

There are a number of interest rates published daily in leading business magazines and newspapers, and all give good clues as to the direction money costs are moving. Following are four rates that represent important indicators for the real estate mortgage business.

Treasury Bill Rate. The cost of short-term borrowing by the federal government is clearly determined each week at the auctions of 3-month and 6-month Treasury bills. The bills are sold by the Federal Reserve banks and can be purchased from the banks or through authorized security dealers. The return on this type of investment is expressed as a *yield* because it is determined by the difference between the purchase price and face value of the bill.

Example

In one auction,* 13-week bills were bought for an average price of 98.405. This means that a T-bill receipt in the face amount of $10,000.00 was purchased for $9,840.50. At maturity, 91 days later, the T-bill is redeemed for $10,000.00. Thus, the investor earns the difference between the purchase price of $9,840.50 and the redemption price of $10,000.00, or $159.50. The return (not an interest rate but expressed as a *yield*) amounts to 6.50 percent based on a $10,000.00 investment. However, since the investment was $9,840.50, rather than $10,000.00, the effective return amounts to 6.84 percent based on a 360-day year. The auctions for Treasury bills are open to anyone with investment cash (they have sold denominations as small as $1,000.00 but generally are limited to $10,000.00 denominations) and reflect the current short-term market accurately. As in all indicators, the trend, up or down, is an important guideline.

Prime Rate. This is defined as the interest rate charged by a commercial bank to its most creditworthy customers. Each bank may set its own prime rate by any method it chooses. Some use complicated formulas, and others depend on the wisdom of their board of directors. In practice, most banks simply follow the lead of one of the major commercial banks. The prime rate is used more as a base upon which to float an interest rate for any class of loans than as an actual lending rate. A good example is a construction loan that may be quoted at two points

*U.S. Treasury bill auction held on May 9, 1988.

over prime—if the prime rate is 10 percent, the construction loan will be 12 percent. If the prime rate moves up to 11 percent, the construction loan automatically will be increased to 13 percent and is calculated from the date the prime change is announced. Another direct effect of the prime rate on the mortgage field is that warehouse lines of credit held by mortgage companies with their commercial banker are usually quoted at prime or a point over prime.

FNMA/FHLMC—Administered Yield Requirements. During the early 1980s, both the Federal National Mortgage Association and the Federal Home Loan Mortgage Corporation phased out their frequent auctions for loan commitments to their sellers/servicers. The auctions have been replaced by daily access to these secondary market purchasers through what FNMA calls its "open window" commitment method. Both use an administered or "negotiated" rate in telephone contacts to their Washington DC offices. While these rates can fluctuate during any one working day, FNMA does issue a weekly news release every Monday reporting its posted yield requirements for the previous Friday.* The yield requirements of both FNMA and FHLMC represent what might be called the "wholesale" market rate for mortgage loans at that time. Loan originators add .25 to .375 percent for servicing the loan, and the cost of private mortgage insurance is often combined as a part of the rate quoted to a borrower. Within the industry, this wholesale rate is called a *net basis* yield, that is, the yield that must be delivered to the purchaser.

U.S. Treasury Security Rates. Shorter-term (one- to five-year) Treasury rates have become more important as an indicator of mortgage rates. Not only do they accurately reflect the short-term money market rates that affect mortgage money, but they also are being used as a major index for setting adjustable rate mortgage loan interest rates. Because the market for Treasuries is constantly changing to reflect the money markets, the rates reported are averages of daily rates for weekly or monthly time periods. All financial publications carry information on Treasury yields, and the Federal Reserve Board now offers a weekly release covering selected interest rates.**

---

*For copies of releases, contact Federal National Mortgage Association, 3900 Wisconsin Avenue, N.W., Washington, DC 20016.
**For further information, contact Publications Services, Mail Stop 138, Board of Governors of the Federal Reserve System, Washington, DC 20551, and ask for "Selected Interest Rates and Bond Prices (Weekly)."

Usury

Usury laws are state laws, not federal statutes, that limit the amount of interest that may be charged to various categories of borrowers. Until the 1970s, market interest rates remained generally below the various state limits, and there was little concern for this particular restriction. But as interest rates continued to climb, lenders in some states found that the restrictive laws made it difficult, if not impossible, to continue orderly lending activities. The rising cost of money for lenders made it more and more difficult to make loans within the statutory limits and retain a safe operating margin. Further, states with higher interest limits were able to attract the big secondary market investors who are able to purchase mortgages anywhere. Many states were simply excluded from the national market for mortgage money by restrictive usury laws. Congress suspended certain state usury limits for the first three months of 1980. Then, on March 31 of that year, Congress pre-empted state usury limits for first-mortgage residential loans.

The historical concept of usury has a religious basis. In earlier societies, charging money for something other than the product of one's labor was considered sinful. Thus, lending money for profit was held to be a violation of religious doctrine by Christians through the Middle Ages. Even today certain Moslem faiths hold this belief and do not permit interest to be charged among the faithful. However, this belief does not apply to lending money to those outside the faith!

The more modern concept supporting usury laws is that the individual borrower should have some protection from the substantial power represented by a lender. In earlier times, and perhaps in some smaller communities today, the protection may be appropriate. But where mortgage loans are concerned, the growth of lending across state lines, coupled with the big national markets for loans, have made restrictive usury laws somewhat counterproductive.

Questions for Discussion

1. Describe the monetary system used in this country.
2. How does the Federal Reserve increase the money supply?
3. How does the Treasury raise money when it has to borrow?
4. Explain the major factors that influence interest rates.
5. Explain what is meant by fiscal policies and by monetary policies.
6. Identify the four major areas of demand for money.

7. How does a change in interest rates affect business borrowing?

8. How do the rates charged by savings associations compare with mortgage company rates in your community?

9. Suggest ways to improve our banking system.

3

Mortgage Money: The Primary Market

KEY WORDS AND PHRASES

Primary market
Mortgage debt outstanding
Mortgage pools
Regulated lenders
Savings and loan associations
Federal Savings and Loan Insurance Corp.
Federal Home Loan Bank
Savings banks
Commercial banks
Comptroller of the Currency
Federal Reserve Bank System
Federal Deposit Insurance Corp.
Federal Savings and Loan Insurance Corp.
State regulatory agencies
Credit unions
Warehouse line of credit
Community Reinvestment Act
Life insurance companies
Premium reserves
Mortgage companies

Mortgage brokers
Mortgage bankers
Loan servicing
Forward commitment
Immediate commitment
Seller/servicer
Correspondent
Application fee
Origination fee
Servicing fee
Farm Credit System
Farm Credit Administration
Federal Land Bank
Federal Intermediary Credit Bank
Banks for Cooperatives
Farmers Home Administration
Pension funds
Real Estate Investment Trust
Individuals as lenders
Endowment funds
Foundations
Fraternal and religious associations

Introduction

The money that funds mortgage loans comes from many sources. Most of it comes from private sources: individual and company savings such as passbook savings accounts, money market accounts, or certificates of deposit. Other major private sources of funds are the premium reserves for policy holders held by life insurance companies; retirement programs such as IRA and Keough accounts; various mutual funds; plus the huge and growing pool of pension funds.

A common misconception is that governments supply much of the mortgage money. Various government agencies do offer underwriting programs that encourage private sources to fund mortgage loans, but there is very little government money in loans. To the contrary, government agencies that underwrite mortgage loans earn money from the fees that are charged and are not normally a burden on the taxpayer.

The Mortgage Credit Market

The demand for mortgage money shares the credit market with all other demands for borrowed funds. While the mortgage share of this market fluctuates, it normally commands 25 to 35 percent of the total credit available. The mortgage debt outstanding at the end of 1988 totaled over $3,000 billion, the largest single class of debt in this country.

Analysis of Mortgage Debt

The term mortgage debt includes all kinds of loans secured by mortgages and all types of lenders handling these loans. To better understand where the money has been used, Table 3–1 identifies the four major categories of mortgage debt by type of loan. Clearly, residential loans dominate the market with nearly two-thirds of the total debt outstanding.

Analysis of Loan Sources

The mortgage loan analyst must distinguish between those *making* mortgage loans and those *holding* mortgage loans. They are not necessarily the same. Loan originators make the loans. Some originators hold these loans *in portfolio*, meaning as their own investment in an income-producing asset. But today most originators sell their loans within a few months to secondary market investors.

Table 3–2 gives the percentage of each major class of loan held by the

TABLE 3–1
Mortgage Debt by Type of Loan in 1988
(In billions of dollars)

Loan Category	Amount	% of Total
Residential (1- to 4-family)	$2,080	66
Apartment (multifamily)	286	9
Commercial	698	22
Farm	87	3
	$3,151	100%

Source: Federal Reserve Bulletin, April 1989, Table 1.54,
Mortgage Debt Outstanding.

principal lender sources. The percentages held in 1979 are compared with 1988 to illustrate how the market has shifted. The largest shift has occurred in the withdrawal of savings institutions from the residential loan market and their replacement by mortgage pools (raising funds through the sale of mortgage-backed securities).

TABLE 3–2
Type of Debt Held by Class of Lender
A Comparison from 1979 to 1988

	Percentage of Mortgage Loans Held							
	Residential		Commercial		Apartment		Farm	
Lender Source	1979	1988	1979	1988	1979	1988	1979	1988
Savings insti.*	54	31	26	22	43	39	0	0
Comm. banks	17	15	32	42	10	12	11	17
Life ins. cos.	2	1	29	25	15	8	14	10
Federal and related	6	7	0	1	10	7	33	47
Mortgage pools	10	36	2	0	5	7	7	0
Individ. and others	11	10	11	10	17	27	35	25
	100%	100%	100%	100%	100%	100%	100%	100%

Source: Federal Reserve Bulletin, April 1989, Table 1.54, Mortgage Debt Outstanding.
*"Savings institutions" now combine the previous separately identified savings associations and mutual savings banks.

The Mortgage Money Market

The market for mortgage money functions at two separate levels; one is the loan origination market called the "primary market," the other the "secondary market" that consists of investors who buy mortgage loans. For the borrower, the source of funds is the primary market where many lending companies compete for business. These include regulated lending institutions, mortgage companies, credit companies such as GMAC and General Electric, finance houses such as Household Finance, home builders, and a newcomer to the loan origination market: real estate brokers working through computerized networks tied into major lending institutions.

The Primary Market

The loan origination market is one of borrowers and lenders. The negotiation for a loan at this level is a discussion of the interest rate and discount. How the requirements for loan qualification are determined depends on who the lender is and whether or not the loan will be sold to secondary market investors. Regulated lenders must adhere to the rules set by their regulatory authority. Nonregulated lenders are not so restricted. If a loan is intended for sale, rather than held by the lender as its own investment (held "in portfolio"), then the loan must meet the secondary market purchaser's requirements.

First, let's examine the nature of the lenders who deal one-on-one with the borrowers—the loan originators. Then next, in the following chapter, we will look at how the secondary market functions as a source of funds for the primary market. The loan originators will be discussed under four categories: (1) regulated lenders, (2) mortgage companies, (3) direct government loan programs, and (4) other primary market lenders.

Regulated Lenders

Regulated lenders are those depository institutions and life insurance companies that are subject to various government regulatory agencies. This class of lender is limited in many ways: in the kind of loans it can make; the percentage of its total assets that can be held in certain types of loans; the kind of mortgage repayment plans it can offer; and the qualifications that can be accepted for both borrowers and property that is pledged as collateral. Because there are a number of different regulatory authorities involved, including separate state and federal chartering systems, there are no uniform standards that can be clearly defined.

In the late 1970s, regulated lenders dominated the mortgage market, particularly that for home loans. This was true since about 75 percent of the money for residential mortgage lending at that time came from savings accounts held by the institutional, or regulated, lenders. This was, and still is, the only class of loan originator that holds deposit assets that can be used to fund long-term mortgage loans. But when the federal limits on interest rates that could be paid to depositors were lifted beginning in the late 1970s, the holding of long-term mortgage loans became much less attractive. As a consequence, this particular source began withdrawing from the mortgage loan market.

Even though regulated lenders have reduced their investment in the mortgage market, they are still major players in the primary market. Some hold loans as sound portfolio investments, and others originate loans that are sold to investors. While most regulated lenders retain the loan servicing function on all their loan originations (meaning the collection of the monthly payments and proper disposition of the money), some now sell even this function to specialized servicing companies.

Following is a discussion of the four major classes of regulated lenders: (1) savings institutions, (2) commercial banks (3) credit unions, and (4) life insurance companies.

Savings Institutions

As now defined, "savings institutions" describes both savings associations and mutual savings banks (now called just savings banks). Because both of these kinds of institution were limited in their deposits to time deposits (savings accounts), they also acquired the combined name of "thrift institutions," or thrifts.

A *time deposit* is one that does not permit withdrawal on demand, usually requiring a waiting period of 14 to 30 days. Besides the obvious time factor in savings certificates and certificates of deposit that give a withdrawal date or time period on their face, all passbook savings accounts are classed as time deposits. Even though the rule on time deposits exists, few institutions attempt to use it under normal conditions. To delay a withdrawal would most likely discourage further deposits by their customers. Nevertheless, it is this access to the more stable time deposits that has provided the justification for savings institutions to make long-term mortgage loans.

SAVINGS ASSOCIATIONS

The origin of savings associations was to provide a source of money for home loans. In earlier years, some were called "building societies" because of this purpose. When Congress established the Federal Home Loan Bank Board in 1934, with authority to charter new savings associations, it required all federal charters to keep at least 80 percent of their deposit assets in "residential loans" (residential loans by this definition includes multifamily housing loans).

A further inducement for savings associations to make residential loans is a special concession in the federal tax code: If savings associations hold no more than 18 percent of their assets in commercial loans, with the rest in residential loans, their income tax can be deferred. The deferral is permitted so long as the income is not distributed but held in a surplus account available for making more home loans. Obviously, the incentive lost its attraction for those associations with income losses to report.

As interest rates began to climb in the late 1970s, savings associations found it difficult to retain their deposits because they were limited by law to paying an interest rate of 5½ percent on passbook savings accounts. To help overcome this problem, new savings certificates were introduced that allowed payment of higher rates for longer-term deposits. The result of this and other factors was a rapid increase in the cost of funds. Indeed, the national average cost of funds for FSLIC-insured savings associations rose from 7.87 percent at the end of 1979 to 11.58 percent at the end of 1981. At that time, savings associations held most of their mortgage loans in portfolio and the fixed income generated by the low interest, long-term mortgage loans failed to keep pace with the rising cost of funds.

In 1980, Congress passed the Depository Institutions Deregulation and Monetary Control Act. The act substantially altered many rules that had formerly distinguished the various kinds of depository institutions from each other. No longer were savings associations firmly committed to making mostly residential loans. New rules allowed them to expand their investment portfolios to many new kinds of loans. In addition, they could now offer their customers checking account services, credit card accounts, and the advice of trust departments; services formerly restricted to only commercial banks. While the intention of Congress was to assist savings associations to recover from the dilemma created by escalating interest rates, they overlooked the role played by federal deposit insurance.

Following the relaxation of rules, some savings associations remained essentially unchanged. They continued to make home loans to local people and hold these loans in their own investment portfolio. Some continued actively in the home loan origination market but shifted their operations to become sellers, rather than holders, of these loans, very similar to the methods used by mortgage companies. And some opted to use the new freedom from regulation to enter the commercial loan market with its larger fees for larger loans than the residential market offered. In retrospect, there is little question that expansion into the riskier commercial loan market created some of the substantial losses suffered by savings associations in the late 1980s.

Regulation of Savings Associations. Savings associations can be chartered by either state authority or by the Federal Home Loan Bank (FHLB) as a federally chartered institution. While state chartered savings associations must abide by their own state regulations, many states pattern their requirements around those made by the FHLB.

The FHLB was established in 1934 to restore some stability to the savings industry and add some support to a nearly collapsed housing industry. Over the years, it has tried to develop sound mortgage lending procedures and has been able to loan funds to associations in time of need. In 1970, the FHLB spawned the Federal Home Loan Mortgage Corporation, popularly known as "Freddie Mac." Its purpose was to add further support to member associations through the *purchase* of their mortgage loans, thus creating greater liquidity in loan portfolios. Freddie Mac, initially a part of the savings association system, has become a major participant in the business of underwriting mortgage pools to enhance the sale of their mortgage-backed securities.

The Federal Home Loan Bank is an agency of the federal government and exercises substantial authority beyond its chartering and regulatory power over federally chartered associations. It is now recognized as a leader in the setting of national housing policies. When the FHLB issues a change in such items as the kinds of loans that federal charters can write, the limits on these loans, the qualifying requirements that must be met, these new rules affect the entire mortgage industry. The rules are met by federally chartered savings associations, many state charters that automatically extend their rules to comply with FHLB, and Freddie Mac, which is controlled by FHLB. In addition, the Federal National Mortgage Association by its charter must adhere to "national housing policies." And what Freddie Mac and Fannie Mae offer to buy as secondary market purchasers becomes a near standard for the industry.

1989 Re-regulation of Savings Associations. Roughly 500 of the 3,000 savings associations chartered in this country have suffered serious financial reverses that have required massive bail-outs by the Federal Savings and Loan Insurance Corporation. To support the government's obligation to depositors covered by this kind of insurance, a combination of taxpayer's money and an increase in fees charged to the institutions for the insurance coverage has been set up. The anticipated cost is estimated at $150 billion spread over a 10-year period. To prevent a recurrence of the problems that caused the losses, new regulations are being phased in that will increase capital requirements and shift the regulatory responsibility to the Treasury Department. The FSLIC has been transferred to the management of the FDIC, although the insuring funds remain separated.

SAVINGS BANKS

Savings banks originated in the early years of this country when most individuals traded in cash and needed a place to deposit their surplus. The "check society" was still a long way off, and there was little need for checking accounts.

For many years thereafter, savings banks (formerly called mutual savings banks), have operated with good success only in the northeast part of the country, particularly in New York and Massachusetts, with a few in the far northwest. In the past they were all state chartered.

Because of the emphasis on savings account deposits, savings banks have looked with favor on the longer-term loans. With their location in generally cash-rich areas of the country, plus the conservative nature of their investment policies, many savings banks favored insured mortgage loans. A special favorite has been the government underwritten HUD/FHA and VA type of loan that they acquired from loan originators all over the country. In recent years, lending policies have shifted away from individual mortgage loans to investing in federally underwritten mortgage-backed securities.

In the late 1970s, the Federal Home Loan Bank Board began experimenting with *federally* chartered savings banks. Then, the 1980 Deregulation Act approved the offering of NOW accounts, which had become popular in the six states of the northeast (a Negotiable Order of Withdrawal is an instrument that functions just like a check). In addition, the door was opened for these institutions to make other kinds of loans. The result of these changes converted this type of institution to functions similar to a commercial bank and they became better known simply as "savings banks."

Deposit insurance for savings banks is carried by the Federal Deposit Insurance Corporation, not the FSLIC.

Mortgages Held.   Even though savings institutions (savings associations and savings banks) have been withdrawing from the mortgage market, as a group they still are the largest holder of mortgage loans of all types. In 1988, savings institutions held 29 percent of all mortgage debt, amounting to $879 billion.

Commercial Banks

The original purpose of commercial banks was to serve the business community and the governments. As such, they were expected to provide the services of checking accounts, including the transfer of money, and the protection of a depository institution.

Initially, states chartered their own banks and, prior to the Civil War, granted commercial banks the authority to issue their own currency. The creation of the Federal Reserve Bank in 1913 brought nationally chartered banks under the credit regulations of the Fed and established lines of cooperation between them. It was, and still is, a separate banking system from that which was created for savings institutions.

Investment Policies.   Because of the business orientation of commercial banks, their lending policies have favored the short-term loan for specific business purposes. Thus, for several reasons, commercial banks have not been very active in the long-term home loan market. One basic reason is that commercial banks hold large demand deposits and have hesitated to allow such money to fund long-term loans. What is changing this situation is the growth of secondary market funding through the sale of mortgage-backed securities. The ability of large commercial banks to originate long-term residential loans, then fund them through the sale of securities, is opening a new market that does not commit their own deposit assets. Indeed, the largest originator of mortgage loans in 1988 was Citicorp of New York, working through their MortgagePower program.

Certain kinds of short-term mortgage loans are more suited to commercial banks, including lines of credit for mortgage companies and construction loans. In addition, commercial banks handle some longer-term mortgage loans as may be needed by their business customers. The four kinds of lending activity that can be found in a commercial bank's mortgage operations are described as follows:

Direct Loans. Mortgage loans made for shorter terms, such as 10 to 15 years for good commercial customers.

Construction Loans. The shorter-term construction loans are attractive to banks due to the higher returns. The larger banks are better able to employ the specialized talent necessary to monitor the disbursement of funds as construction progresses.

Warehouse Lines of Credit. Short-term loans made to mortgage companies for funding of their loans until they can be sold. It is a line of credit for the mortgage company and is listed as a mortgage loan for the bank.

Loan Origination. A fairly new and growing activity in mortgage lending is the origination of home loans, funding with their own deposit assets to create a large block, or pool, of loans, then issuing and selling mortgage-backed securities to recover their cash investment.

Regulation of Commercial Banks.   Commercial banks can be either state or nationally chartered. National charters (not called "federal charters" when commercial banks are involved) are issued by the Comptroller of the Currency, part of the U.S. Treasury Department. National charters must belong, and state charters may or may not be required to belong, to the Federal Deposit Insurance Corporation (FDIC) that insures depositors' funds up to $100,000.

Unlike other classes of regulated institutions, commercial banks face an additional regulatory body. Besides the chartering agency and the deposit insuring agency that normally provides regulation and periodic examination, commercial banks come under the jurisdiction of the Federal Reserve Bank Board as regards their credit policies.

Recent examples of Fed banking regulations are the standards for disclosure to borrowers seeking Adjustable Rate Mortgages that became effective October 1, 1988 (Regulation Z—see Chapter 6). Another important rule being phased in by the Fed increases the capital requirements for depository institutions and introduces a sliding scale that more accurately reflects the level of risk in each institution's loan portfolio.

Mortgages Held.   As holders of mortgage loans, commercial banks rank third in the country, behind savings institutions and mortgage pools. In 1988, commercial banks held 20 percent of all mortgage debt amounting to $622 billion.

Credit Unions

Credit unions may be chartered by any group of people who can show a "common bond." The bond has generally been that of a labor union, a company's employees, or a trade association. However, a recent interpretation of this rule allowed the American Association of Retired Persons (AARP) to form a credit union. With some 28 million members, the common bond would be their age.

There are now over 18,000 credit unions operating in this country. Credit unions offer a special attraction as a depository institution as they pay no income taxes (they are classed as nonprofit organizations).

Most credit unions are relatively small and often managed by nonprofessional personnel. Their primary lending is to their members on small loans for such purposes as buying a car or furniture. However, as savings associations met with highly publicized reverses in the mid-1980s, many individuals transferred their savings to credit unions. By 1987, 55 million people held over $158 billion in credit union deposits. As their resources grew, the credit unions' ability to make the larger mortgage loans increased.

It was not until 1978 that credit unions were authorized to make 30-year mortgage loans—prior to that the limit was 12 years. Also in that year, they were authorized to sell loans to secondary market investors while retaining the loan servicing function. Even then, there was little growth in this particular activity for the smaller unions because of the specialized nature of mortgage lending. The larger unions with professional staff are capable of, and do engage in, the business of making long-term mortgage loans.

Since the deregulation of the banking industry in 1981, some credit unions have expanded their membership to anyone living in their area of trade. Further, there has been an expansion in the services offered, including some formerly available only through their competitors. These include safe-deposit boxes, credit cards, and money market accounts. Also, credit unions are not prohibited from paying interest on checking accounts as are other financial institutions. These extra services and the tax-exempt status of credit unions may not be their only advantages—many identify the intangible item of a closer personal touch to their membership than can be found in other institutions.

Regulation of Credit Unions.   Credit unions can be either state or federally chartered. An independent agency of the federal government, the National Credit Union Administration (NCUA), charters, regulates and supervises activities of federal credit unions. State charters adhere to their own state rules and laws.

Deposits in credit unions can be covered by the same kind of insurance as other regulated depository institutions. The federally chartered National Credit Union Share Insurance Fund, administered by the NCUA, covers deposits up to $100,000. Federal charters must offer this coverage and state charters that qualify are eligible to join.

Reserve Requirements for Depository Institutions

Institutions handling deposits are required to hold a certain percentage of their deposit assets in a reserve account, not available for lending purposes. The reason is to provide a back-up, a source of emergency money should it be needed. Prior to 1980, state chartered institutions operated under their respective state laws governing reserve requirements while national charters adhered to federal re- quirements. They often differed as to the amount of reserves and whether or not the reserves could earn interest. Further, the Federal Reserve Bank Board had authority to alter the reserve requirements for their own member banks, but not nonmember state charters. Changing reserve requirements gave the Fed one more tool in its efforts to stabilize the national economy. But it also created some inequities within the banking system as application of reserve requirements was not uniform.

In 1980, Congress passed the Deregulation and Monetary Control Act that established uniform reserve requirements for all depository institutions offering transaction accounts. A "transaction" account is essentially a checking account that allows withdrawals payable to a third party. Examples include checks, drafts, negotiable orders of withdrawal (NOW accounts), and share drafts. The reserve rules apply to commercial banks, savings associations, savings banks, and credit unions whether they are state or federal charters.

The uniform reserve requirements were phased in over an eight-year time period—from November 13, 1980 to September 2, 1987—to minimize the impact on lending institutions. The requirements called for 3 percent of the first $25 million of transaction balances to be placed on deposit with the Federal Reserve Bank without interest, plus 12 percent on all transaction balances over $25 million. In addition, there is a reserve requirement for time deposits in the amount of 3 percent. A "time deposit" is defined as one allowing the institution at least 14 days' notice prior to withdrawal.

Note that this money does not pay any interest to the institutions that own the reserves, but it does provide a cushion for the industry to draw upon to meet unusual money demands. Thus, any institution holding reserves on deposit with the Fed has the right to borrow from the Fed at the discount rate of interest. In banking terminology, the Fed's "discount window" is open to all who have reserves on deposit—so long as they do not use the money as additional capital for ordinary lending purposes.

Deposit Insurance

Savings associations, savings banks, commercial banks and credit unions are all classed as depository institutions. This means they are specifically authorized by their charters to hold deposits for their customers. Governments treat them as a special kind of trust. When the Great Depression of the 1930s closed about one half of these institutions, savings were lost and depositor confidence was destroyed. To help restore this trust, the federal government created a deposit insurance system. Life insurance companies are not considered depository institutions and are not federally insured.

In 1934, Congress established the Federal Deposit Insurance Corporation (FDIC) to insure deposits in commercial banks and savings banks. At the same time, the Federal Savings and Loan Insurance Corporation was created to insure deposits in savings associations. Later, the National Credit Union Share Insurance Fund was set up for credit union depositors. A few states opted to establish their own deposit insurance funds, and a few permit private insurance companies to underwrite the risk. Due to several failures of state insurance funds in the early 1980s, the federal protection has proved to be more practical.

The insuring agencies charge the insured institutions a fee for deposit insurance coverage. It has been set at 8¢ annually per $100 of the insured's eligible deposits (limit of $100,000 per depositor), paid by the insured institution. The fee is subject to adjustment to cover losses and became necessary in the mid-1980s. The FSLIC was forced to increase its premium charge to 21¢ per $100 of insured deposits applicable to all savings associations. The FDIC charge remained at the initial level throughout this period.

The insuring agency's ability to protect depositors through the 1980s' period of traumatic bank and savings association failures, plus the stock market collapse in October, 1987, has proven its success insofar as depositors are concerned. For the 50 years prior to that time, the agencies operated with few claims and accumulated rather substantial surpluses—about $18 billion for FDIC and $7 billion for the FSLIC. By the end of 1988, the FDIC had managed to pay its losses out of current income and still retain most of its reserves. However, the FSLIC had become deeply indebted and, in early 1989, the federal government instigated a massive bail-out expected to cost up to $150 billion at this writing. In addition, the management of the FSLIC was placed under the control of the FDIC (which is under the U.S. Treasury Department), but the reserve funds of each remain separated.

Operation of the Insuring Agencies. The insured institutions are subject to certain regulatory authority of the insuring agencies and are periodically examined to determine compliance. The insuring agencies are obligated to protect their coverage and have the authority to step into any insured institution if the deposit assets have been placed in jeopardy. The insuring agencies may take such action as they deem necessary to protect the depositor's money. This action includes arranging a sale of the insured's assets to another institution, organizing a merger with a stronger financial group, or simply closing the institution and liquidating its assets. When the federal agency takes over, it accepts no responsibility for any of the insured's obligations except those to the depositors. Thus, even a lease for the bank's facilities can be terminated. However, obligations to insured depositors remain in full, including honoring interest rates to maturity of certificates of deposit and payment of principal and all earned interest on other insured deposits.

Deposits Insured. What sort of deposits are insured? Deposit insurance covers all kinds of deposits, including passbook accounts, savings certificates, individual retirement accounts (IRAs), Keough accounts, and certificates of deposit. The coverage does not include certain repurchase agreements that are classed as loans to the institution, not deposits. The current limit on the amount of deposit coverage is $100,000 for each individual depositor, as set in 1980. If an individual holds more than one account in the same institution with a total exceeding

$100,000, only $100,000 is covered. Husbands, wives, and children are all treated as individuals, and each may hold an insured account up to $100,000.

Community Reinvestment Act (CRA)

The Community Reinvestment Act, which took effect in November 1978, expands the concept that regulated depository institutions must serve the needs of their communities. The purpose of the act is to require regulated institutions to publicize their lending services in their own community and to encourage participation in local lending assistance programs. Enforcement of the requirements is handled by federal regulators—the examiners who regularly review each institution's loan records and procedures. The penalty for failure to comply is a limitation on approvals for expansion that may be required from federal regulatory authorities by the offending institution. The act applies to all federally regulated financial institutions and is subject to interpretation by each of the regulatory authorities. Initially, the guidelines and examination procedures were defined jointly by the Federal Home Loan Bank Board, the Comptroller of the Currency, the Federal Reserve Board, and the Federal Deposit Insurance Corporation.

What the act requires is that each institution undertake four procedures as follows:

1. *Define the lender's community.* Each lender must prepare a map of the area that it serves, which is the neighborhood from which it draws its deposits and into which it makes loans.

2. *List types of credit offered.* A list of credit services available from the institution must be submitted to the regulators and made available to the public. The act is directed toward publicizing methods of borrowing rather than saving money.

3. *Public notice and public comments.* Each institution covered by this act must post a notice in its place of business stating that the institution's credit performance is being evaluated by federal regulators. Further, the notice should state that the public has the right to comment on the institution's performance and to appear at open hearings on any request for expansion.

4. *Report on efforts to meet community needs.* A periodic report must be made on the efforts of the institution to ascertain the credit needs of its community and how it is attempting to meet those needs.

The Community Reinvestment Act has more recently been used to pressure banks seeking approval of mergers to grant additional money for local housing loans. If the bank refuses to cooperate, the penalty could be a protest that would delay, or stop, the proposed merger.

Life Insurance Companies

While life insurance companies are not considered depository institutions, they are fully regulated by the various states that charter them. The cash that life insurance companies hold for investment comes from premium reserves and accumulated earnings. Because these reserves are not necessarily subject to demand withdrawal, life insurance companies have long favored the longer term nature of mortgage loans as investments. At one time, life insurance companies equaled the total investments of savings associations in mortgage loans. But life insurance companies were not organized primarily for the purpose of providing mortgage money as were savings associations. Their primary interest in using their substantial investment funds has been to provide the highest yield possible commensurate with the safety of their policyholder's money. And this has dictated some flexibility in the movement of their investment funds from time to time to achieve better returns.

When a life insurance company sells an ordinary life policy, or certain other kinds of life insurance, regulations normally require that a portion of the premium paid in be set aside as a reserve to protect future obligations to the policyholder. The insurance company pays interest to the policyholder on the reserve amount (depending on the terms of the policy) and invests the money as the company may determine so long as it adheres to the state's regulatory limitations on investments. Over the years, this reserve pool has produced substantial returns for the companies while protecting the future payment of death benefits.

Casualty insurance companies—those that handle fire coverage, automobile insurance, and a host of other types of hazard insurance—have tremendous premium incomes but are not required to maintain the larger permanent reserves demanded for the life insurance companies. Therefore, casualty companies hold their reserves in short-term investments due to the need for liquidity to pay claims. They negotiate practically no mortgage loans and are not a source for our consideration.

In the United States there are over 1,900 life insurance companies, and a few from Canada, selling policy contracts. They range in size from companies with a very few million in assets to the multibillion-dollar giants that have become household words, such as Prudential, Metropolitan Life, and Equitable.

Investment Policies. While insurance companies invest most of their reserves in high-grade securities, they also make mortgage loans. The larger companies have generally confined their real estate activity to making loans for large commercial ventures in which they can also acquire a participating interest. Smaller companies follow a different path and often look upon individual home loans in their local communities as good business and an encouragement to their sale of life insurance. This kind of loan is intended for holding in their own portfolio.

A new trend developed since 1985 that is causing a return of the large insurance companies to the residential mortgage market. This is the process of making individual mortgage loans, committing them to large mortgage loan pools, and selling, or holding in portfolio, the mortgage-backed securities that are backed by the pools. Metropolitan Life Insurance entered this market when they purchased the Century 21 real estate sales franchise operation in 1985 and created their own mortgage company subsidiary. Prudential Life has started its own real estate brokerage franchise operation, and can be expected to pursue the residential mortgage loans that the network generates.

Regulation of Life Insurance Companies. All insurance companies are chartered and operate under the control of state regulatory authorities. There are no federal charters for life insurance companies; consequently, these companies adhere to policies that do vary from state to state, but the regulations are generally directed toward protecting the policyholders. State regulations also apply to out-of-state charters doing business within the state.

The state regulations usually set limits on the types of investment that are permissible, the percentage of total portfolio that may be kept in stock, or bonds, or mortgage loans, or the amount of liquidity that must be maintained for each policy dollar outstanding. And most states establish limits on the maximum amount of any one loan or any one property. Some states have limited their own chartered insurance companies to investments within their own states, and others have placed limits on out-of-state companies selling insurance within their state, unless proportional investments are made within the state.

Mortgages Held. Of total mortgage debt outstanding, life insurance companies held just 7 percent in 1988, amounting to $219 billion.

Mortgage Companies

Historical Background

From its origin as a brokerage-type service arranging loans, the mortgage banking industry has grown to a major business, handling about one-third of the conventional loans and three-fourths of the government-underwritten loans in this country. As early as 1914, the people in this business formed a trade organization, known as the Farm Mortgage Bankers Association, indicating the original emphasis placed on farm loans. The name was changed to its present title of Mortgage Bankers Association of America in 1923, and it now has members from every state and a large permanent staff.

The association serves as a communications and information center for the industry. Educational programs are sponsored to keep the many persons employed by mortgage bankers up-to-date on an ever-changing business. And a constant effort is being made to improve the methods and procedures used in the industry.

In the early years of this century, mortgage bankers arranged for the sale of their own bonds and used these funds to make small home and farm loans. Because of the thrift-conscious nature of farmers and homeowners, mortgages were amazingly free of defaults and provided a widely used medium of investment.

The 1920s brought an increase in mortgage company financing of income properties such as office buildings, apartments, and hotels, perhaps with the firm conviction that a mortgage loan was as secure as gold. And the mortgage companies even referred to the small-denomination bonds that they sold to the general public for mortgage financing as *gold bonds*.

However, the Depression, triggered by the collapse of prices on the nation's largest stock exchange in October 1929, showed up many basic weaknesses in the mortgage loan system. In the next two to three years, most of the mortgage companies that had issued their own bonds as well as those that had guaranteed bonds for other development companies were faced with massive foreclosures. Unable to meet their obligations, many were forced into bankruptcy.

Unlike regulated depository institutions, mortgage companies without depositors were not a concern of the government. The money mortgage companies used for their loans had come from the sale of bonds, considered a business transaction, not a deposit procedure. Hence, mortgage companies were granted no help in recovery from the depression years. One avenue mortgage companies used to re-establish their business was to promote FHA and, later, VA loans. Slowly, the mortgage companies revived.

Mortgage Brokers

There is a significant difference between the services offered by *loan brokers* and those offered by *mortgage bankers* working within the mortgage industry. Brokers limit their activity to serving as an intermediary between the customer-borrower and the client-lender. While brokers are capable of handling all arrangements for the processing, or *packaging*, of the loan, they do no funding, nor do they service the loan once it has been made. There are some loan-wise individuals who prefer to work on their own as brokers and carry their loan applications to a mortgage banker for verification and funding. They earn a portion of the normal one point origination fee plus an application fee.

Other types of mortgage brokers are companies operating on a national scale who primarily arrange purchases and sales of mortgage loans between originators and investors, or between investor and investor. In so doing, they greatly aid the free flow of mortgages across state lines in the private mortgage market. These brokers seldom originate a loan and do not service them. They are part of the secondary market in some of their operations.

Another distinction that may be made between a mortgage broker and a mortgage banker is that a broker works mostly with commercial loans, while a banker is able to handle residential loans in addition to commercial loans. Large commercial loans are normally funded directly by the lending institution, say, an insurance company, and the monthly payments on debt service go directly to the lender. Residential loans require an intermediary, someone who will assemble the smaller loans into larger blocks for easier selling to the big investors. This is a function of the mortgage banker.

Occasionally, a mortgage banker, or even a savings association, will broker a loan for a customer. Money may not be readily available through regular channels, or the loan request may be for something the lender cannot handle with its own funds. The lender may then turn to other sources and earn a brokerage fee for handling the loan. This type of extra service is more commonly found in small communities.

The lines between a broker, a mortgage banker, and a lender are not always clearly drawn, as brokerage service may be handled by any one of them. Brokerage is essentially the service of processing the loan information for the borrower and arranging for a lender to make the loan. Good brokerage work is done by professionals who respect the confidential nature of the information they must obtain and who earn their fees by knowing which lenders are presently seeking certain types of loans.

Mortgage Bankers

The *full service* facility offered by the mortgage banker today developed from both the need for a new approach after the depression collapse, and from the desire of the Federal Housing Administration to conduct its programs in conjunction with private industry. The economic pressures of 1930–31 had dried up lendable funds, construction had been halted, and many banks had closed their doors. The shortage of available funds made the mortgage banker an intermediary for the only remaining sources of cash—cash from insurance companies, from a few large savings banks, and from the Federal National Mortgage Association. The growth of the FHA brought the need for more servicing or loan administration by the mortgage bankers and with a need to fill, mortgage companies aggressively sought an increased share of the mortgage market. So what does it take to become a mortgage company?

QUALIFICATIONS OF A MORTGAGE BANKER

At present, there are no federal requirements regarding the qualifications or licensing of an individual or a company handling mortgage loans. But some states have established requirements, and more are exploring the possible need. In most areas, any individual meriting the confidence of a lending institution could assist in arranging a loan, thereby earning a fee for his or her services.

In practice, qualifications for a mortgage company are set mostly within the industry. However, all the government agencies involved with mortgage lending have standards that must be met to do business with them. This includes HUD/FHA, VA, FNMA, FHLMC, and GNMA. The requirements are similar—a reasonable net worth, experienced personnel, and adequate office facilities. Even so, approval must be obtained from each agency with which a mortgage company wants to do business. And the same is true of any other client-lender of a mortgage company. Each must grant its own approval to do business. Approval by either HUD/FHA or VA in itself is often accepted by conventional lenders as acceptable qualification.

MORTGAGE COMPANY OPERATIONS

Although mortgage companies vary widely in their methods, the business organization common to most operates by means of three basic divisions:

1. Administration.
2. Loan servicing.
3. Loan acquisition.

The administrative group supervises and directs all operations and usually seeks out and maintains contact with its sources of money—the lending institutions and, more recently, the poolers of mortgages for issuance of mortgage-backed securities. The development of stable, continuing relations with a group of investors is a source of pride with the mortgage companies. And there is always more than one investor, since it is not considered good business for either the mortgage company or the lender to maintain an exclusive arrangement. Lenders are in and out of the market as their particular needs fluctuate, while the mortgage company must maintain a steady supply of funds. The mortgage company officers must know which sources are available for loans and what particular type each lender prefers.

Loan servicing includes the record-keeping section that maintains the customers' or borrowers' accounts. Larger companies have converted much of this accounting to computerized methods for more efficient handling. One part of the records involves the escrow section, which holds the required insurance and tax deposits. Escrow personnel must maintain a continuous analysis of taxes and insurance costs for each property to assure the company that sufficient money will be available when needed to pay the taxes and insurance premiums. Another responsibility of the servicing section is to ensure prompt payment of monthly accounts and to send out notifications on delinquencies and in case of a default. All lenders insist on knowing the account status and depend on the mortgage company to use diligence in keeping their accounts current. Laxity in this area could jeopardize a lender's rights in a foreclosure action.

The loan acquisition group, the division best known to outsiders, consists of loan representatives or supervisors who make the contacts with potential borrowers. These are made through real estate agents, banks, accountants, and others to seek out the best loans and to handle the actual application for a loan. A loan processor usually works with one of these representatives to maintain the files and to help collect the information required on both the property and the borrower in putting together the complete loan package.

Mortgage Company Funds

Mortgage companies do not hold deposit assets that can be loaned as do the regulated depository institutions. Therefore, they must use somewhat different procedures to obtain an assurance of funds with which to make loans. Mortgage bankers, dealing with residential loans, generally maintain *forward commitments* (promises of money over a limited period of time) from secondary market sources to assure themselves of funds at a known cost. Other methods are used by mortgage brokers dealing in the larger commercial loans. These are more likely to be placed on a "case-by-case" basis with the most suitable lender. First, let's examine the basic methods used by mortgage bankers, and some brokers, to assure themselves of adequate funding.

Secondary Market Sales. A procedure long used by mortgage companies is to obtain a commitment *in advance* of making any loans. Savings associations, insurance companies, some commercial banks, the FNMA, and FHLMC buy loans from originators. One method used to buy loans is to make commitments of money over periods of 30 days to six months. Mortgage companies maintain contact with loan purchasers and, when the purchasers have surplus money to invest, they may offer to buy up to a certain amount of loans over the next few months. This promise of funds is called a *forward commitment* and generally includes an agreement for the mortgage company to service the loans they make for the loan purchaser. The agreement between originator and purchaser is known as a "sales and servicing contract." Both FNMA and FHLMC identify their approved loan originators as "sellers/servicers."

Large mortgage companies with substantial assets may make loans without a forward loan commitment. They can hold their loans temporarily in their own portfolio or, more likely, pledge them with a commercial bank on a warehouse line of credit. When a suitable buyer is found, the mortgage company can sell these loans that have already been made on an *immediate commitment* basis. "Immediate" means that the loans do exist and can be delivered now. However, industry practice allows up to 60 days for delivery on this basis.

Representative or Correspondent Basis. Insurance companies and other loan purchasers sometimes specialize in handling certain kinds of property loans, such as hotels or shopping centers. Rather than deal with a variety of loan originators, these companies often work through selected representatives throughout the country. These representatives, sometimes identified as agents, and sometimes as correspondents, are commercial loan companies that understand the special requirements of each loan purchaser or investor. If a mortgage company customer is seeking a hotel loan, for example, the mortgage company will handle the contact with the secondary market investor most interested in that particular kind of loan. In a situation such as this, the mortgage company serves as a loan broker, negotiating the loan for an investor. The investor then funds the loan at closing and usually handles the servicing.

Mortgage-Backed Securities. Mortgage companies, particularly the larger ones, have returned to the predepression practice of raising some of their own money through the sale of securities. The most common method is to place a multi-million-dollar block of mortgage loans in the care of a trustee, such as an authorized bank. Then the mortgage company issues a series of certificates backed by the block of loans, which thus becomes the collateral for the securities. The certificates are sold to investors, and the money reimburses the mortgage company. The procedure is often identified as "securitizing mortgages." As the mortgage company that originally made the loans services them, the principal and interest payments are sent each month to the trustee. The trustee then passes these payments on to the holders of the securities. Thus, the expression of "pass-through securities" has developed. Investment bankers have entered the field of mortgage securities with a number of variations that are discussed more fully in the next chapter.

Mortgage Company Income

In the handling of mortgage loans, the profit margin is rather narrow. Mortgage companies make little, if any, money from the discount since that passes to the loan purchaser as part of the money cost. While the borrower measures the discount in a specific number of points, in practice, the mortgage company originator does not receive that precise amount. What the mortgage company is really doing is buying a piece of paper—the mortgage note—when it funds the loan at closing. Then the note is sold to a secondary market purchaser. The difference between what is funded at closing and what the mortgage company sells the note for is what it makes, measured in dollars. If the mortgage company has handled its commitments carefully, the margin covers its origination fee and maybe a small cushion. And if it makes a mistake, or misjudges the secondary market yield requirements, losses can be incurred.

The dependable income for loan originators comes from various fees: application fees, origination fees, and servicing fees. These are more fully explained next.

Application Fee.   Loan originators normally charge a nonrefundable application fee at the time an application is taken. In the jargon of the industry, lenders will "entertain an application" for a loan if it is in general conformance with the kind of loan they make. The application fee covers certain costs involved in screening an application, such as a credit report, a property appraisal, and the time of a loan officer to review the information. The fee is not regulated (except for HUD/FHA and VA) and is charged by almost all originators, not just mortgage companies. For residential loans the fee is in the $150 to $500 range, while commercial loans are often based on the size of the loan rather than on the work involved.

Origination Fee.   An origination fee is sometimes combined with an application fee. However, in most cases, it is a separate charge amounting to 1 to 2 percent of the loan amount payable if and when the loan closes. It is a charge incurred for assembling a loan package and making the decision to accept or reject the loan. The charge is for services rendered and is *not* tax deductible for the borrower. It is a separate charge from a loan discount, which is tax deductible, but the two are not always differentiated when loan costs are quoted.

Mortgage companies usually split the origination fee with about half going to the loan representative who contacts the borrower and takes the loan application. It is considered the "commission" earned by the representative and is not paid if the loan fails to close. In contrast, savings associations and banks pay their loan officers on a salary basis rather than on a commission concept.

Servicing Fee. In mortgage lending, a servicing fee is that charge made for handling the loan *after* it has been funded. The services involve collecting and accounting for periodic loan payments, handling the escrow portion of the payments, and following up on delinquent payments. The fee amounts to ¼ percent to ½ percent of the loan balance and is collected by all servicers—mortgage companies, savings associations, and others. The servicing charge is normally added to the interest rate for the loan and is not distinguishable to the average borrower. In the terminology of secondary market investors, a yield requirement quoted as "net basis" means one that does not include a servicing fee; the loan originator must add that to the rate. Net basis rates are sometimes identified as the "wholesale rate." To illustrate, the rate delivered to a loan purchaser might be 10½ percent, while the charge to the borrower would be 10⅞ percent—the ⅜ percent difference is the service fee.

Because the servicing of large blocks of mortgage loans can be a lucrative business by itself, specialized companies have developed in recent years to do just this. Sometimes a loan originator accumulates several billion dollars in loans to service, and will sell a portion of the block to acquire cash. For example, if a $100 million block of loans is paying ⅜ percent in servicing fees, that amounts to $375,000 per year. The profit potential in this kind of cash flow could make the servicing alone worth $1 to $2 million in a sale. When the servicing function is transferred to another company, borrowers are usually asked to make their payments to the new address. This can cause some confusion for the borrower/consumer, and has attracted government regulation in some instances. This is especially true when the servicing is transferred to an agent in another state.

Government Loan Programs

While most government programs involved with mortgage financing are designed to encourage private lenders to make such loans, there are some programs that handle direct loans to borrowers; that is, the agencies work in the primary market. However, to avoid the appearance of direct competition with private business, many programs require that the loan applicant first attempt to borrow the money from private sources. This is true of the Small Business Administration (not covered in this text) and the Farmers Home Administration (FmHA).

Direct loan programs offered by the federal government are almost all farm related. State-sponsored loan programs are mostly housing related and are usually handled by one or more local housing authorities. Because of its importance in the mortgage credit structure of the country, let's first consider the federal Farm Credit System.

Farm Credit System

Over the years, a number of federal government agencies involved with farm credit have been brought under the supervision of one agency. Today, the Farm Credit System (FCS) is an elaborate cooperative, borrower-owned network of farm lending banks. They are under the supervision, examination, and coordination of the Farm Credit Administration (FCA), an independent federal agency. Administratively, the FCS is composed of 12 regional farm credit districts.

The system makes long-term mortgage loans and short-term production, or crop, loans through different organizations. The distinctions follow:

Federal Land Banks.   There are 12 Federal Land Banks (one in each district) that account for about 68 percent of the total loans within the system. The Land Banks make long-term mortgage loans through more than 400 Federal Land Bank associations. The associations are cooperative credit organizations owned by local borrower-members. It is the local associations that assist farmers in need of a loan, screen and approve acceptable loan applications, and forward the applications to the district Federal Land Bank for funding. Approved loans are guaranteed by the local associations.

Generally, loans are limited to 85 percent of the appraised value of the property, with a maximum term of 35 years. Interest rates are based on the FCS cost of funds.

Federal Intermediary Credit Banks.   There are also 12 Intermediary Credit Banks accounting for about 22 percent of the system's loans. They are the main source of funds for 370 Production Credit associations that make short-term production loans to their members.

Banks for Cooperatives.   One central bank, plus 12 district banks, handle credit for co-ops. They are an important source of funds for agricultural and aquatic cooperatives.

FINANCING FOR THE FCS

Prior to 1979, individual components of the Farm Credit System raised funds independently through the sale of various agency bonds. Since then, the FCS has funded its loans and other assets primarily through the sale of system-wide consolidated securities. Most of the financing is handled through the sale of 6- to 9-month securities, and some with 2- to 5-year coupon notes.

The interest rates charged to borrowers are determined periodically based on the FCS *average cost* of the system's funds. One result of this method is that loans made in the 1970s were at rates considerably below the then-current market. This was because the FCS average cost of funds was determined by securities issued at earlier, lower rates. Then, as the cost of their funds increased, the system was caught with a mismatch between their long-term fixed interest loans and their short-term methods of funding. Later, as interest rates declined in the mid-1980s, the rates charged by the FCS remained fairly high, causing a withdrawal from the system by many borrowers who also withdrew their capital investment from the local banks. Adding to the difficulties of that time was the substantial decline in farmland values. Since land represented a major form of collateral for the FCS, its ability to recover in foreclosure actions was sharply diminished.

GOVERNMENT SUPPORT

Even though the Farm Credit System is supervised and examined by a federal agency, the government offers *no guarantee* to the FCS to assist it in borrowing needed funds. However, in late 1985, the FCS was granted assistance by Congress in the form of a line of credit with the United States Treasury. But Congress stopped short of offering a guarantee for the system's securities. It was expected that the Treasury's line of credit would backstop the system and reassure FCS security holders.

On January 6, 1988, the president signed the Agricultural Credit Act of 1987 establishing a new secondary market entity under the Farm Credit Administration to assist the depressed market for farm loans. The act created the Federal Agricultural Mortgage Corporation (FAMC), which quickly acquired the acronym "Farmer Mac." Farmer Mac began operations in July 1989 as a guarantor for pools of certain farm loans similar to the functions of Ginnie Mae in residential loans. As a secondary market operator, the parameters under which the new agency operates will be further detailed in the next chapter.

Farmers Home Administration (FmHA)

To give perspective, the Farm Credit System just described holds about one-third of the nation's $200 billion in farm debt. The Farmers Home Administration holds another $28 billion of the debt owed by farmers. By the mid-1980s, about half these loans also faced collection problems.

The Farmers Home Administration was established in 1946 as part of the Department of Agriculture for the purpose of making and insuring loans to farmers and ranchers. The program's intent was to provide credit for the purchase and improvement of farms, as well as rural community rehabilitation programs for low-income and elderly persons unable to obtain credit elsewhere. The FmHA is authorized to borrow money from the U.S. Treasury and from the Federal Financing Bank to obtain funds for its loans. Also, the agency can sell participations in mortgage pools to raise additional funds.

The home loan program under Section 502 is limited to rural areas or towns with a population of 10,000 or less and to low- and moderate-income families who are unable to qualify for home financing in the private market. Loans can be made up to 100 percent of the appraised value of a house for a family with an adjusted family income (AFI) of not more than approximately $27,500 per year for a family of four.

The AFI limits vary in different sections of the country recognizing the difference in costs. A typical limit for a single person might be $19,250. For a family of four, it might be $27,500, with higher limits for larger families. Calculation of the qualifying income follows HUD standards generally, with certain additional limitations. The method used to determine income eligibility is to add the family income, then deduct $480 from the total for each dependent child under 18 living in the home. If the result is less than the AFI limit for that area, the family is eligible to make application.

Evaluation of the loan application is handled in a manner similar to other lending agencies and requires a complete financial statement, a history of family income, and a credit report. Each loan is reviewed periodically to determine if the borrower's financial condition has improved to the extent that the loan could be handled by a private lending institution.

For single-family housing, the FmHA will make loans on new or existing structures. However, the living area cannot exceed 1,200 square feet. The maximum amount of a loan permitted for this size house is determined by the applicant's ability to repay the loan, with a ceiling of $43,000.

State and Local Government Programs

Because of the opportunity for assisting home buyers, and perhaps some political advantage for the officials involved, many housing agencies have developed since the mid-1970s. Some offer direct loans to qualified buyers. Many offer secondary market assistance to established mortgage lenders. Almost all programs are funded with lower-cost tax-exempt bonds, which will be considered more fully in the next chapter.

Other Primary Market Lenders

The opening of the secondary market and the wide acceptance of mortgage-backed securities as sound investments have encouraged many newcomers to enter the loan origination market. The major new players are discussed next.

National Credit Companies

Companies with long experience in handling loan qualification and funding for other kinds of consumer-type loans have recently entered the mortgage market. These include such major operators as General Motors Acceptance (now the largest of all mortgage lenders through the acquisition of several large mortgage companies), Ford Motor Acceptance, and General Electric Credit Corp. What these companies do is originate loans, sell them into mortgage pools, and earn the origination and servicing fees.

Home Builders

Several large home builders have entered the origination market through subsidiaries that process the loans and sell them into mortgage pools. By exercising some control over the mortgage money, home builders are able to structure loans that better suit their buyers' needs, thus enhancing sales potentials. Examples are Pulte Homes, U. S. Home, Ryan Homes, and Kaufman and Broad.

National Real Estate Brokerages

Companies that have developed national real estate brokerage operations, through direct acquisitions or franchise networks, have entered the loan origination business. Such companies as Coldwell Banker with its ties to the Sears financial network, and Century 21 with its ties to Metropolitan Life Insurance Company, are able to offer mortgage loan services in their own offices. Southmark Corporation has introduced a mortgage tie-in with their ERA franchisees.

Independent Real Estate Brokers

Probably the most significant new development of all in the loan origination business is the computer network tie-ins of independent agents with major money sources. The concept was originated in 1986 by Citicorp, and is being followed by such other financial giants as Prudential Insurance Company and Chase Manhattan Corporation.

Since starting its network in 1986, Citicorp has strung together over 3,000 real estate brokers, lawyers, insurance agents, and mortgage bankers as contact points for home buyers seeking loans. By the end of 1988, the system, called "MortgagePower," had expanded into 37 states and continues to grow. To tie into the system, the independent agent must pay a fee for its connection to Citicorp, then is entitled to charge the borrower up to a half point for its assistance with each loan. The broker helps the borrower complete a short application form, which is sent by computer directly to Citicorp and acted upon within 15 business days.

Since the Real Estate Settlement Procedures Act (RESPA) prohibits "kick-backs" in loan settlements, there has been a question over the MortgagePower program. In anticipation of this question, Citicorp obtained a letter of approval from HUD (the monitoring agency for RESPA) in 1986. HUD agreed that a payment by the borrower (rather than the lender) directly to a real estate broker in this program did not constitute a kickback so long as the payment was fully disclosed to the borrower. Critics have contended that, regardless of the ruling, the program amounts to "steering" a home buyer to a specific lender who might not be offering the best terms available, which is contrary to the spirit of RESPA.

In 1987 Citicorp's MortgagePower system produced the largest amount of home loan originations in the country at $14.8 billion. Even so, it amounted to only 3.3 percent of the $450 billion in mortgages made by the nation's 20,000 lenders in that year. The "quick loan at a good price" pitch is expected to expand. Prudential Home Mortgage introduced its own program with the name "Mortgage Express," as did several other companies.

By 1989 HUD was prepared to reverse its decision on permitting brokers to earn loan fees for their assistance with the preparation of loan applications. Nevertheless, the idea is likely to continue even without the fees.

Pension Funds

In the past decade, pension funds have become large investors in mortgage loans. By far the most common method is through the purchase of mortgage-backed securities. In this way they avoid the management problems associated with individual mortgage loans and are able to treat such investments as just another kind of security.

However, a few pension groups, particularly those operated by state agencies and by labor unions, offer home loan programs as primary lenders. Some funds restrict participation to their own members, and some offer such loans to the general public if qualifying standards are met. Most of these direct loans are available to middle- and low-income families and offer attractive interest rates.

Real Estate Investment Trusts (REIT)

In 1960, when mortgage money was derived from savings accounts, Congress passed the Real Estate Investment Trust Act. The intent of the act was to make it more profitable for the small investor to enter the real estate market, thus increasing available capital. To achieve this purpose, a REIT must derive most of its income from real estate investments and distribute at least 90 percent of its income to its certificate holders. If these requirements are met, the REIT is not subject to federal income taxes at the corporate level. However, the dividends paid out are treated as taxable income to the recipients.

The concept remained fairly dormant for almost a decade, but by 1970, investment bankers were actively organizing REITs with major banks and insurance companies as the money managers. The sale of interests to investors proved to be lucrative, and between 1969 and 1973 the new industry increased its assets from about $1 billion to over $20 billion. A sharp downturn in the real estate market in 1973–74 caused the trusts to decline and the concept became less attractive as an investment procedure.

The original purpose of the REIT, as envisioned by Congress, was to enable the smaller investor to participate in the ownership, or equity, of real estate. However, two types of REITs developed, one making equity-type investments, the other making mortgage loans primarily for real estate development. The equity REITs made their money from the operation of income-producing properties. Mortgage REITs were attracted to the high yields that could be earned from construction loans in the boom years of 1972–73. But as the industry faltered in 1974, substantial losses were incurred, primarily by the mortgage-lending REITs. And the sale of this kind of security faded from the market.

By the mid-1980s, many of the older organizations had been able to recover, or merge with stronger groups, and a revival of interest occurred. New REITs appeared on the market and successfully raised funds. The idea of setting up a REIT particularly appealed to owners of large real estate properties seeking to cash in their assets. Probably the best known of these property sales was the one initiated by the Rockefeller interests when they sold Rockefeller Center in New York as a Real Estate Investment Trust, raising over $1 billion in cash from investors.

Individuals

Individuals do not come under the legal restrictions and reporting requirements of institutional lenders. Therefore, statistics on individual participation in the mortgage market are not readily available. However, many individuals make mortgage loans, albeit sometimes with considerable reluctance!

As a general rule, the individual lender has motives other than profiting from the loan itself. Most common is when a second mortgage (or a first mortgage) is accepted for the primary purpose of consummating a house sale. In some cases the motivation is to help a member of the family, or perhaps to assist a valued employee to acquire suitable housing.

Another mortgage market that individuals sometimes participate in is the second- and third-mortgage market. The attraction is that junior mortgages offer higher yields than do first mortgages. The high yields are often obtained through substantial discounts. There is, of course, a greater risk in junior mortgages, as prior lienholders must be satisfied first in the event of a foreclosure.

Miscellaneous Other Sources

In different parts of the country, various types of companies and institutions have established themselves as sources of mortgage funds, usually limiting the geographic area in which they will loan money. In the following paragraphs, the most important of these sources are identified.

Title Companies.   Because title companies have a close association with, and considerable knowledge of, the mortgage industry, a few of them have developed direct loan departments or subsidiary companies to handle loans. These affiliated companies act both as primary sources in lending their own funds or those raised from the sale of mortgage bonds and as correspondents or agents for other major lenders.

Endowment Funds, Universities, Colleges, Hospitals.   As a group, endowment funds prefer to maintain their assets in high-grade stocks and bonds that have a good record for security, are considered to be more liquid and, most importantly, require less administrative attention than a portfolio of mortgage loans. However, many endowments are passed on in the form of land and other real property, and these have required more expertise in the mortgage loan field. The endowment funds can, and do, assist in the development of their own land by experienced developers, and they are increasing their activities in mortgage lending with such encouragements as the GNMA mortgage-backed security.

Foundations.   Foundations have been established primarily by corporations or by wealthy families as a means of continuing charitable or other purposes through the use of income earned from the foundation's investments. The attitude of foundations toward mortgage lending is somewhat similar to that of the endowment funds. They are primarily interested in investing in high-grade stocks and bonds but are not adverse to mortgage loans, particularly if a purpose of special interest to the foundation can be served.

Fraternal, Benevolent, and Religious Associations.   Over the years some fraternal, benevolent, and religious organizations have accumulated substantial pools of investment money, which are generally little known and very seldom advertised.

The administration of these funds is usually handled on a sound economic basis with security of the loan of more importance than the yield. Some of these organizations limit their lending to their own members and will provide low-cost loans to qualified members in good standing.

Questions for Discussion

1. Discuss the steps that have been taken to improve the liquidity of a savings association loan portfolio.
2. What role does the Federal Home Loan Bank play in the banking system?
3. Why have mutual savings banks increased their investments in real estate loans even though they are not legally required to do so?
4. Discuss the reasons insurance companies are looking more for ownership interests in real estate rather than making direct mortgage loans.
5. Why do insurance companies have such a wide variation in their lending practices?
6. How does the Farm Credit System raise funds for making loans?
7. Explain the basic lending policies of the Farmers Home Administration for home loans.
8. What efforts are being made to attract pension and trust fund money into the real estate mortgage market?
9. Describe the type of loans preferred by commercial banks.
10. Are there any good sources of mortgage money available in your locality outside of the regulated lending institutions?
11. What new mortgage lending authority has been given to credit unions?
12. Discuss the purpose of the Community Reinvestment Act.

4

Mortgage Money:
The Secondary Market

KEY WORDS AND PHRASES

Secondary market

Price

Yield

Discount

Points

Basis points

Federal National Mortgage
  Association (FNMA)

Open window commitment method

Debenture bonds

Federal Home Loan Mortgage
  Corp. (FHLMC)

Steadfast rate

Participation loans

Net basis

Mortgage Participation Certificates
  (PCs)

Tax-exempt bonds

Mortgage-backed securities

Trustee

Passthrough security

Collateralized Mortgage Obligations
  (CMOs)

Government National Mortgage
  Association (GNMA)

Real Estate Mortgage Investment
  Conduits (REMIC)

Federal Agricultural Mortgage
  Corporation

Introduction

In the last chapter the focus was on the primary market—the loan origination market. Prior to the mid-1970s, the loan origination market was dominated by regulated depository institutions. This group of lenders held the major source of deposit assets that could be used to fund long-term loans. Unless a lender had money on deposit to fund loans, there was little opportunity to enter the business except in a loan brokerage capacity. Mortgage companies handled the brokerage function.

Using deposits to fund mortgage loans worked fairly well for about four decades following the Depression of the 1930s. There was a federal limit on interest rates that never exceeded 5½ percent paid to depositors (Federal Reserve's Regulation Q). This allowed long-term mortgage loans to be made at not more than 7 to 8 percent with reasonable protection to the lender of a stable cost of funds. Access by home buyers to this huge, low-cost source of funds started to unravel as interest rates began to escalate in the late 1970s.

While the real growth of the secondary market began in the early 1970s, its participants throughout that decade were generally limited to loan purchasers who were familiar with mortgage loans. These included large savings associations and savings banks, plus Fannie Mae and Freddie Mac. This was because the purchase of a mortgage loan by a secondary market investor generally included certain responsibilities for managing the loan itself. It was not until the development of the mortgage-backed security concept, which converted mortgage loans into a more acceptable type of security, that the secondary market was opened to all investors in the international financial markets.

Expansion of the Secondary Market

Besides the earlier constraints of interest rates, there were other problems limiting the mortgage market prior to the 1970s. It was difficult to sell mortgage loans for two important reasons: First, the documents used for conventional loans were not uniform; and second, there was no acceptable insurance protection against loan default. Only the FHA and VA had been able to overcome these problems. Both offered uniform documentation that enabled an investor anywhere in the country to know in advance exactly how a note and mortgage instrument would be worded, and both offered a very acceptable underwriting guarantee (the VA terminology) or an insured commitment (the FHA term).

It was not until 1972 that steps were taken to create a class of conventional loans offering similar advantages to the FHA/VA loans. The move was undertaken by the Federal National Mortgage Association (FNMA, or better known as Fannie Mae), in an effort to increase its market. Prior to that time, only FHA and VA loans could be purchased by FNMA, and they amounted to about 20 percent of the total mortgage market.

Introduction of Uniform Documentation. In 1968, Fannie Mae was partitioned by Congress and part became the Government National Mortgage Association (Ginnie Mae), and part remained as Fannie Mae but converted to a private corporation, no longer a government entity. Obviously, conventional loans with 80 percent of the market offered a big opportunity for expansion as a private corporation. Thus, Fannie Mae, joined by Freddie Mac (the Federal Home Loan

Mortgage Corporation that was created in 1970), began a several-year process of devising uniform documents acceptable for conventional loans. The result has been the "conforming loan," a loan written with uniform documents that is readily marketable throughout the country.

Private Mortgage Insurance. The other problem of needing some form of default insurance was solved at about the same time (1972) when the Federal Home Loan Bank Board approved the writing of 95 percent loans (formerly the limit was 90 percent loan to value) by federally chartered savings associations. The requirement for writing the higher ratio (95 percent) loan was that anything over 90 percent must be insured against default. Prior to that time, there had been no default insurance requirement. Thus, within a matter of a few months, the private mortgage insurance industry that had been rather dormant suddenly came alive. Within two years of the FHLB approval, one insurance company, Mortgage Guaranty Insurance Co. (MGIC) of Milwaukee, was writing more default insurance than the entire FHA!

In essence, that was how the secondary market was able to expand beyond the limited range of trading in FHA and VA loans.

Selling Mortgage Loans

So what is the secondary market? The foregoing information has described its expansion as a market for buying and selling mortgage loans. Basically, it is the market wherein loan originators are able to sell loans, thus recovering their cash for originating more loans. But the secondary market uses a different terminology as its function differs from loan origination. The secondary market investors do not "lend" money, they "purchase" mortgage notes as investments to earn a return. The return is also called "yield" and it represents the money earned on an investment. In the mortgage market, yield is the combination of interest earned over the life of the loan, plus the discount taken at loan origination. This is more fully explained next.

Procedures Used in Secondary Markets

Now note the difference in terminology at this point. The originator of a loan speaks to customers, who are *borrowers*, in terms of *loaning money*, and expresses the cost of the borrowed money as interest plus *points* of discount and fees. Once the originator closes the loan to the borrower, the note and mortgage instrument become marketable paper that can be assigned—and the terminology changes.

The mortgage note is now a salable commodity and is negotiated as such. The originator of the loan becomes a *seller*, and the large investing institutions that deal in the secondary market for mortgage loans are called *purchasers*. When a mortgage loan is thus offered for sale, the potential purchaser is interested in only one factor for loans of similar type, size, and quality, and that is the *net yield*.

Pricing Loans to Adjust Yields

Since the interest rate on the loan or loans held by the originator has already been established, the only way a seller can change the yield to a purchaser is to adjust the *price* of the loan. For example, if the mortgage note is for $10,000 at 7 percent interest, the yield would be 7 percent. If the seller must offer a higher yield than 7 percent to attract a purchaser, the loan must be sold for less than $10,000; that is, discount the face value to increase the yield. By selling the $10,000 loan for, say, $9,500, the purchaser is putting up less cash but still collects the originally agreed interest and principal payment applicable to the $10,000 loan at 7 percent. Hence, a greater return or yield for the $9,500.

The principal balance due on an existing mortgage loan normally changes each month, making it difficult to quote a price in dollars as is commonly done in the bond market. Therefore the price is quoted as a percentage figure. The price is that percentage of the loan balance for which the loan is sold. One hundred is, of course, par. If we were quoting the $10,000 loan mentioned to sell for $9,500, the price would simply be "95." This indicates a 5 percent reduction in whatever the principal balance due on the mortgage note may be, or a *five-point discount*. (One point is 1 percent of the loan amount.)

In times of falling interest rates, a loan calling for a higher than current market interest can sell for a premium*—at, say, 102 percent or even 104 percent of its face value. Examples of prices and yields are shown in Table 4–1 to illustrate their relationship.

A simple reading of the table shows that the length of time a loan is outstanding has a direct effect on the yield for that loan. Since loans vary considerably in the time for payoff, it is necessary to use some standard payoff time for the loan. The reason is that the discount is a lump-sum amount paid at closing, and must be spread over the life of the loan to calculate an expected annual yield.

*Paying a premium for higher than market interest loans is a common practice in the bond market. Many investors in mortgage loans refuse to pay any premium because of the ease with which mortgage loans can be refinanced at lower rates when the market declines.

TABLE 4–1
Price/Yield Table Calculated at 7 Percent Interest for Term of 30 Years

Price	Discount	Yield if Prepaid 8 Years	Yield if Prepaid 10 Years	Yield if Prepaid 12 Years	To Maturity
102	+2 (premium)	6.66	6.71	6.74	6.81
100	0	7.00	7.00	7.00	7.00
96	4	7.70	7.61	7.54	7.41
92	8	8.44	8.24	8.12	7.85

Yield and Discount

For this purpose, *yield* can be defined as the return to the investor expressed in percent of the price paid for the note. *Discount* is the difference between the face value of the note and the price the investor paid for the note. Yield includes both the interest earned and the discount taken. So to express the discount as a part of the yield, it must be converted to an annual percentage rate. The discount is a one-time charge; a lump sum taken at the time the loan is funded. To determine how much this adds to each year's earnings, or yield, the discount must be spread over the life of the loan. But what is the life of the mortgage loan? While most residential loans, including FHA- and VA-supported loans, are granted for a term of 30 years, the realistic life of the loan is approximately 10 to 12 years; that is, within 10 to 12 years the average loan is paid off, usually by resale and refinancing. So FNMA and FHLMC use a time span of 12 years to determine the yield value of a discount.

The purchase requirements for FNMA to buy a loan are expressed in terms of a yield, usually carried to two decimal places. The accepted yield can be converted to a discount mathematically, or more easily, by means of a standard conversion table. Table 4–2 shows several typical yield figures, and the sequence of steps shows the fixed interest rate for the note, the price that is used to achieve the yield, and the discount needed to achieve the price.

The mortgage banking industry is able to use the FNMA negotiated yields as solid criteria from which to base its own handling of individual mortgage loans. For example, a mortgage company is making mortgage loans at 9½ percent, which is competitive in its current market, and must meet a yield of 9.80 percent to sell the loans. Using Table 4–2, we determine that the price must be 97.45, which requires a discount of 2.55 points to achieve. The mortgage company would probably ask a discount of 2¾ points as a rounded-out figure if the market is strong. Added to the quoted discount is the brokerage fee and the charge for

TABLE 4–2
Example—Conversion of Yield to Price

For a Yield Amount	At Interest Rate	Price Must Be	Points to Achieve
9.500	9.500	100	0
9.800	9.500	97.45	2.55
10.600	9.500	91.12	8.88

mortgage insurance. Further, the originator would add .250 to .375 percent to the interest rate to cover a loan servicing fee. Loan originators using the FNMA yields as a guide to trends would be watching for an upward or downward movement to further influence their decision as to what discount they might need to be making loans at a price, or yield, at which they could be sold.

Points

In the jargon of mortgage lending, discounts are sometimes identified as "points." It is accurate insofar as discounts are usually *measured* in points. A point is 1 percent of the loan amount. But the two words, point and discount, are not synonymous. A point as a unit of measure is frequently used to identify other costs such as mortgage insurance premiums, an origination fee, and various other charges. Yet it is not uncommon to lump all the costs of financing, even attorney's fees and title insurance, into one lump sum and call it "points." This practice can be confusing to the borrower-consumer.

From a practical standpoint, the borrower should demand that each cost be identified. It may help to uncover an error, or possibly an overcharge. Further, for a home buyer, the discount is tax deductible in full in the year paid—the same as interest on a home loan.* (Commercial borrowers must amortize the discount over the life of the loan.) But the cost of services, such as an origination fee, or private mortgage insurance, is not tax deductible to the home buyer.

Basis Points. To identify fractions of a point, the financial markets use a finer measure. A "basis point" is one-hundredth of 1 percent. It has long been used to report the small daily fluctuations in Treasury bill rates and is now moving into the mortgage language. For example, to identify a servicing fee of, say, one quarter percent, it can also be called "25 basis points."

*In a May 1986 ruling, the IRS disallowed the discount as a deduction in the year paid if the purpose is *refinancing* a personal residence. It may be deducted over the life of the loan.

Loan Purchasers

As defined earlier in this chapter, the secondary market is where loan originators can sell their loans, where they can convert their loans back into cash in order to originate more loans. Loan purchasers operate in two different ways:

1. *Purchase for portfolio.* Purchasers of loans may acquire them as a sound investment. This would include some savings institutions, insurance companies, pension funds, housing agencies, Fannie Mae, and, to a lesser degree, Freddie Mac.

2. *Acquisition for underwriting.* Some loan purchasers do so with the intention of creating mortgage pools that can be used as collateral for issuance of mortgage-backed securities. These purchasers, as well as some loan originators, use their own funds to create the mortgage pools, then recover their cash through the sale of securities. Among those active in this field are large investment bankers such as Salomon Brothers, Inc., large commercial banks such as Citicorp and Chase Manhattan, plus Fannie Mae and Freddie Mac.

Purchase for Portfolio

The secondary market originated with the idea of purchasing mortgage loans to be held in portfolio. It began when Congress created the Federal National Mortgage Association (Fannie Mae) as part of the act that also created the Federal Housing Administration in 1934. The original purpose was a simple one: provide a market for FHA loans. As an agency of the federal government, Fannie Mae was able to sell debenture bonds (unsecured promises to pay) that paid a fairly low rate of interest, such as 4½ to 5 percent. The money derived from the sale of bonds was then used to buy FHA mortgage loans that paid 6 to 6½ percent interest. That gave Fannie Mae a margin of 1 to 2 percent over its cost of funds. In 1968 Fannie Mae held $7 billion of such loans.

The risk to Fannie Mae was to maintain that margin. If its cost of funds increased, there was no way it could increase the interest earned on its investment in fixed-interest, long-term loans. Fannie Mae sold debenture bonds that offered short terms because the interest paid to short-term investors is less than that for long-term money. For many years the system worked very well. In industry jargon, Fannie Mae was borrowing money on the short term and lending on the long term. It was not until market interest rates began to escalate between 1979 and 1981 that cost of funds exceeded the interest earned. Losses ensued for all holders of mortgage loans, not just Fannie Mae.

During this same time period, the largest group of institutions holding mortgage loans was the savings institutions. Their cost of funds had been protected by the federal limitation on interest rates paid to their savings account depositors. While the federal limit was not removed until March of 1986, it was substantially undermined in the late 1970s by the introduction of a variety of savings certificates that paid higher interest rates. The result was substantial losses for savings institutions and a general dissatisfaction with the "portfolio approach" to mortgage loans.

Nevertheless, there remains a substantial market for mortgage loans purchased by those who hold them as investments. Some of the risk of fluctuating interest rates has been reduced by the introduction of adjustable rate mortgage designs. Also, mortgage rates that were once held low by an artificial restraint on lenders' cost of funds have now increased to compare favorably with other kinds of investments.

Purchase for Underwriting

"Purchase for underwriting" is an overly abbreviated title for this section. What is meant is to explain those who purchase, or otherwise acquire, mortgage loans for the express purpose of creating mortgage pools. A mortgage pool is a block of loans—it can be a particular kind of mortgage loan distinguished by its collateral, such as all condominium loans. It can be a geographically diversified block as is most commonly found in the Freddie Mac offerings. It can be exclusively FHA/VA as is required for a GNMA type pool. Or it can be a block of commercial loans. However, today, almost all pools comprise residential loans.

Participants in this type of secondary market activity are mostly investment bankers, commercial banks, Fannie Mae and Freddie Mac. These companies have the cash to acquire huge blocks of loans, establish the specific mortgage pool with identification of the individual mortgages assigned to it, then issue a series of securities that are backed by the mortgage pool. The securities are then sold to various investors.

All pools are organized in a manner that collects and accounts for the payments received on the individual loans, then passes this "cash flow" on through to the investors who have bought the securities. Just how the cash flow is handled as it passes through to the security holders differs in a number of ways. It is these differences that distinguish one kind of mortgage pool security from another, as will be explained later in this chapter.

How do the participants in the creation of mortgage pools make money? It is easier to understand if you think of the process as selling the cash flows rather than the mortgages. In fact, the mortgages themselve remain locked up in the care of a trustee. The trustee may be a bank's trust department, or it could be the issuer of the securities backed by the mortgages, if properly authorized to do so.

The point is that the mortgages themselves are not "delivered" to the security purchaser, just the cash flows that are generated by those mortgages are.

There has to be a margin between what the mortgages deliver in cash flows and what is passed on to the holders of the securities. That margin is generated by three factors:

1. Investors in high-grade securities accept lower interest rates for the low-risk investments. In spite of some adverse publicity, home loans are classed as a low-risk investment, and in the form of a security can command lesser interest rates than more risky investments.
2. Larger investments are usually made at lesser rates than are small ones, so long as the risk justifies it.
3. By segmenting the cash flows to the security holders, the issuers can attract the even lower cost money from the short-term money market. This is the purpose of the "collateralized mortgage obligation."

While the handling of cash flows differs, and the margins between what mortgages pay and what is delivered to the security holders vary slightly with almost every issue, the following example illustrates a hypothetical profit margin for an issuer of a mortgage-backed security.

Example

Assume a mortgage pool of $1 million with each of the mortgages in the pool paying 10 percent interest. This amounts to a cash flow of $100,000 in interest plus whatever is repaid on principal each year. Say the issuer of the security backed by this block of mortgages offers to deliver a 9 percent interest rate—the security is free of mortgage loan management headaches and represents a sound investment. A logical purchaser of this security would be a pension fund; the fund pays $1 million for the security and accepts $90,000 a year in interest. The $10,000 difference in interest between what is paid in and what is paid to the security holder must be divided: the loan servicer (usually the loan originator) will earn between 1/4 and 3/8 of that 1 percent differential; if a trustee is involved, they would earn maybe 20 basis points (1/5 of 1 percent), and the rest belongs to the security issuer.

The above example is deliberately reduced in size for easier understanding, and in practice is much too small to attract any issuer of securities. They deal in pools that range from $100 million to perhaps $800 million. With those kinds of numbers, the margins are far more interesting! To attract investors, the huge pools are offered in a series of securities with smaller denominations such as $100,000 units, and even lesser amounts.

A key point in this kind of transaction is that the risk of interest rate fluctuation passes to the holder of the mortgage-backed security. In the past, those who held mortgages in portfolio were exposed to the risk of rising interest rates. This meant their cost of funds might increase to an amount greater than the earnings on their portfolio of loans. While this fact has not changed—those who hold mortgage loans in portfolio are still exposed—there is now another option. By converting mortgage loans to securities, the risk is also passed on to the security holder.

To explain the meaning of this "passing of the risk" let's take another look at the example of the $1 million block of loans converted to a $1 million security. Say that security was sold to a pension fund. What the pension fund holds as an asset is a $1 million security (call it a mortgage-backed bond) that pays 9 percent each year on the principal balance. What happens if the market interest rate now moves from 9 to 11 percent? This would reduce the pension fund's $1 million asset by about a 12-point discount, to an asset value of approximately $880,000. If the pension fund has to sell that mortgage-backed bond for some reason, it would take a $120,000 loss. However, pension funds, and other investors of their kind, do not face depositors who can withdraw their cash whenever they want, so it is very unlikely that such an investor would be forced to accept such a loss. If held to maturity, the underlying mortgage pool would eventually repay the full $1 million in principal plus interest, and all parties would recover precisely what they expected when the investment was made.

In fact, the attraction of mortgage-backed securities has encouraged savings institutions to exchange their portfolios of mortgages for securities. This was the cause of the massive "swaps" that boosted pool underwriting from 1982 to 1984. A swap is where an institution exchanges its own block of mortgages to, say, Freddie Mac, in return for a whole series of mortgage-backed securities. This may appear to be an unrealistic exchange. After all, doesn't the savings institution still carry the risk of interest-rate fluctuation if it holds a security tied to the mortgages? And the answer has to be "yes." But there are two differences that account for its attraction. First, a security is more easily sold than a mortgage loan, thus providing greater liquidity should cash be needed, and second, the security carries an additional protection against loss that was not available for the individual mortgage loan. The additional protection is an underwriting guarantee of the mortgage pool by a federal agency. This kind of underwriting is the subject of the next section.

Federal Underwriting of Mortgage Pools

The concept of a block of loans serving as collateral for the issuance of a security is not new. And it is not limited to only mortgage loans. It is used in other areas of supplying credit, such as car loans. Those who issue securities backed by blocks of loans can range from banks to home builders; from investment bankers to finance companies; from retail merchants to real estate brokers.

But what has substantially enhanced the wide acceptance of mortgage-backed securities has been the rapid growth of federal agency underwriting. To expand upon the idea presented in the previous section: remember the issuers of mortgage-backed securities earn a margin between what the individual mortgages pay each month and what the issuers have to pay the holders of the securities. The larger the margin, the greater the profit. Add to that, the lower the risk, the lower the rate that has to be paid security investors. What federal underwriting has added is an element of reduction in the risk for the holders of mortgage-backed securities.

Since reducing the risk for the investor encourages lower interest rates, the long-range results are not only slightly higher margins for the issuers, but also lower interest rates for home buyers. In fact, the reduction in risk was quantified by the Federal Reserve Bank Board with a ruling effective in 1989. An increase in banks' capital requirements from 6 to 8 percent was tied to the risk level of their assets (meaning loans outstanding). For most kinds of loans, the capital requirement is $8.00 for every $100.00 of loans outstanding, reduced to 50 percent or $4.00 for every $100.00 of approved mortgage loans, to 20 percent for federal agency insured mortgage-backed securities, and to zero for government guaranteed loans (the last category includes Ginnie Mae mortgage-backed securities).

So who are the federal underwriters offering these benefits? There are four: the Government National Mortgage Association (Ginnie Mae); the Federal Home Loan Mortgage Corporation (Freddie Mac); the Federal National Mortgage Association (Fannie Mae); and the newest entrant in the field in July of 1989, the Federal Agricultural Mortgage Corporation (Farmer Mac). Except for the latter, none of the agencies is limited in its activities to only underwriting mortgage loan pools. Each will be described next as to origin, ownership, underwriting requirements, and other functions.

Government National Mortgage Association

The Government National Mortgage Association, better known as "Ginnie Mae," was created by partitioning the Federal National Mortgage Association in 1968. As a result, Fannie Mae became a private corporation and Ginnie Mae was assigned to the Department of Housing and Urban Development (HUD). Of the four federal underwriting agencies, Ginnie Mae is the only one that belongs to the government. It is actually part of the federal government and thus carries unique powers.

Ginnie Mae was assigned two of the three functions formerly handled by Fannie Mae. These were to implement special assistance for housing as may be required by Congress or the president, and to manage the portfolio of loans assigned to it by the partition from Fannie Mae. Ginnie Mae is responsible for these same functions today. To minimize duplication of facilities, some of Ginnie Mae's operations are handled by agreement through the offices of Fannie Mae.

What has overwhelmed the original intent for creating Ginnie Mae is the success it has had with "managing" its loan portfolio. To liquidate some of its early loans, Ginnie Mae created pools of these loans and issued a guarantee certificate backed by the pools as a type of security. The pool guaranty concept became the mechanism by which mortgage loans are converted into more salable securities.

However, Ginnie Mae does not purchase mortgage loans to create its pools. It approves "loan poolers," usually investment bankers who purchase mortgage loans from loan originators across the country. These loans must comply with Ginnie Mae requirements. Then, Ginnie Mae issues its guaranty certificates, which are backed by specific loan pools, and as the individual mortgage loans are paid, the cash passes through the servicing agent, to the loan pooler, and on to the holders of the Ginnie Mae certificates. Ginnie Mae guarantees the payment to holders of the certificates but *not* the individual mortgage loans. Farmer Mac functions in this same way; it approves loan poolers but does not purchase the loans themselves. Fannie Mae and Freddie Mac are different in this regard. They have programs for purchasing mortgage loans that meet their requirements and form their own pools.

Of the four underwriting agencies, Ginnie Mae is the only one authorized to issue a "government guarantee," a commitment backed by the full faith and credit of the United States. For this commitment, Ginnie Mae charges a fee amounting to 6 basis points (six one hundredths of 1 percent of the commitment amount).

A Ginnie Mae certificate can be collateralized by only the FHA, VA, or certain Farmers Home Administration loans, and offers a powerful incentive for an investor. It carries the risk equivalent of a government bond and offers up to 1 percentage point higher return than bonds! In 1988, "Ginnie Maes" outstanding amounted to $330 billion, or a little over 10 percent of the $3,056 billion of mortgage debt in this country. Ginnie Mae held a little less than $45 million in its own portfolio, which is the only government money actually invested at this time in mortgage loans among the four agencies.

Federal Home Loan Mortgage Corporation

With a bit of imagination added, the acronym applied to FHLMC becomes "Freddie Mac." It has become the second largest underwriter of mortgage loans in the country, and operates under the Federal Home Loan Bank Board. However, Freddie Mac is not owned by the government, but is a federally chartered corporation owned primarily by the savings association industry. Its 15 million shares of participating preferred stock are owned by some 3,000 savings associations, and 100,000 shares of common stock are owned by the Federal Home Loan Bank. Ownership of its preferred shares was opened to the general public in 1988, in part to improve the value of the stock held by savings associations. Since it is under the control of the Federal Home Loan Bank, Freddie Mac is classed as a government agency.

From its creation in 1970 for the purpose of purchasing mortgage loans (primarily from its member savings associations), Freddie Mac has favored securitizing loans. Rather than purchasing loans for its portfolio, a practice initially followed by Fannie Mae, Freddie Mac elected to raise its money through the sale of mortgage participation certificates. These certificates, called "PCs" in the financial market, are backed by multimillion dollar blocks of geographically diversified single-family (one- to four-family) loans that serve as collateral. The certificates are unconditionally guaranteed by Freddie Mac. While this is an "agency" guarantee, it falls short of a federal government guarantee. What is meant by an agency guarantee is that, while the agency is not part of the government, its ties are close enough that investors assume the government will not allow it to default on an obligation. But there is no legal obligation to do so.

Freddie Mac acquires its loans through purchases from its approved sellers/servicers. Its sellers/servicers are loan originators—mostly savings associations, but the right to do business with Freddie Mac is open to any company that meets its qualifications. While not limited in its loan purchases to savings associations, Freddie Mac's policies are more suitable for loan originators who hold deposit assets. Most of its purchases are conventional loans that must carry private mortgage insurance, but it may also acquire FHA and VA loans.

Even though Freddie Mac earns most of its money through the fees it charges for underwriting blocks of mortgage loans, it still holds a relatively small amount of mortgage loans in its own portfolio. In 1988, its loan portfolio amounted to a little over $16 billion, while its mortgage-backed securities programs amounted to $216 billion.

Federal National Mortgage Association

The oldest participant in the secondary mortgage loan market is Fannie Mae. Fannie Mae began its life in 1938 as a government agency responsible for purchasing FHA loans. Congress had anticipated a rejection of the FHA-insured loan program by regulated lenders, and so created another method of funding loans through the sale of these loans to secondary market investors. In those early days, the loan originators willing to work with FHA loans were mortgage companies. They were able to fund their loans through sale to Fannie Mae. Ever since, Fannie Mae has worked closely with mortgage companies in providing forward loan commitments that give some assurance of funding.

Since 1968, Fannie Mae has been a private corporation with its stock publicly listed on the New York Stock Exchange. However, by its federal charter, it holds close ties to the United States government. For example, five of its 18 directors are appointed by the President of the United States, and it can borrow up to $2.25 billion from the U.S. Treasury. Because of these and other ties it is classed as a "government agency" in the financial markets. After becoming a private corporation, Fannie Mae expanded its portfolio purchases to include conventional loans.

Fannie Mae has long followed the policy of selling short-term securities, mostly debenture bonds, and using the proceeds to buy loans for its own portfolio. Its profits have been the difference between what it paid its bondholders and what it could earn on its mortgage loan portfolio. When this margin dried up in the early 1980s, Fannie Mae shifted to selling services for fees. In 1982, one service it undertook was to guarantee mortgage-backed securities for its sellers/servicers. The guarantee is by Fannie Mae, classed as a government agency, but it is not a federal government guarantee. In addition, Fannie Mae began assembling its own blocks of mortgage loans to use as collateral for other mortgage-backed securities (MBS).

In a very few years, Fannie Mae's MBS programs exceeded its portfolio of loans! In 1988, Fannie Mae held $102 billion in portfolio while its mortgage-backed securities exceeded $157 billion. Fannie Mae's combined activities, amounting to $259 billion, represent 8 percent of total mortgage debt, about equal to that of Freddie Mac.

Federal Agricultural Mortgage Corporation

To expand the source of funds for farm lenders, Congress established the Federal Agricultural Mortgage Corporation by the Agricultural Credit Act of 1987. Its initial capitalization was through $20 million subscription sale of common stock. Farmer Mac, as it has become known, is patterned after Ginnie Mae as an underwriting agency for pools of farm loans. It is under the supervision of the Farm Credit Administration.

Farmer Mac has a $1.5 billion line of credit with the U.S. Treasury and provides a 90 percent guarantee for the timely repayment of principal and interest on securities backed by pools of qualified agricultural and rural housing loans.

The guaranty fee initially was 50 basis points plus an annual fee of one-half of 1 percent of the outstanding balance of the pool.

Companies that pool loans for underwriting by Farmer Mac issue mortgage-backed securities that are a little different from those issued for guarantee by the other three underwriters. The Farmer Mac securities must comply with Securities and Exchange Commission registration requirements. In addition, poolers (those assembling the loan pools that are underwritten by Farmer Mac) are required to establish a 10 percent reserve for each pool.

The program was implemented in July 1989, and as of this writing, all the eligibility standards are still not fully determined. A qualified agricultural real estate loan is defined as one secured by land or structures that are used for the production of one or more agricultural commodities. In general, individual loans may not exceed $2.5 million, a measure intended to preserve the concept of the smaller, family-run farm. Loan pools may also consist of rural housing loans. Such loans are defined as those made to finance single-family residential dwellings in rural areas with not more than a 2,500 population and a purchase price of not more than $100,000. Loans may not exceed an 80 percent loan-to-value ratio.

Loan Pools

Assembling a block of loans into a "loan pool" can be arranged by a number of different types of companies: investment bankers, commercial banks, finance companies, large real estate brokerages, and even home builders. Loan pools serve as the collateral for a class of securities generally identified as "mortgage-backed" securities. Federal underwriters, as previously described, issue guarantee certificates of various kinds that enable those who pool loans to sell the securities more readily and at slightly lower interest rates. The guarantees, of course, reduce the risk of the security. Loan poolers now generate about half the money used to fund mortgage loans.

A pool can be assembled by two different methods. One is to acquire the loans for the pool first; that is, the block of loans is put together through purchase or by origination of the loans. For example, an investment banker, such as Salomon Brothers, purchases huge blocks of loans from loan originators throughout the country. A commercial bank, such as Citicorp, generates its own blocks of loans through a computerized loan origination network. Once the blocks are assembled in the kind of loan that meets a particular federal underwriter's requirements, a guaranty is obtained and the fee paid to the underwriter. With the underwritten loan pool serving as collateral, a series of securities can be issued and sold to investors throughout the world.

The other method of assembling a loan pool is to first sell the securities, then use the proceeds of the sale to purchase those mortgage loans that meet the requirements of the issuer of the securities. This method is most commonly used by states and municipalities to fund various housing agency programs. Following is a more detailed explanation of the two methods: first, the tax exempt bond procedure that raises the money *before* the loans are acquired, then the alternative method of assembling the block of loans first, then issuing the mortgage-backed securities.

Tax-Exempt Bonds

The most effective way of bringing lower-cost money into the mortgage market has been through the sale of tax-exempt bonds. A tax-exempt bond is a type of security sold by states and municipalities paying interest that is not subject to federal income taxes. The federal government does not tax states or municipalities. Whether or not this freedom from taxation should extend to funds used to assist an individual purchasing a house, or for entrepreneurial industrial development, has been a debatable question for many years. However, the procedure has proven beneficial to home buyers and other community development projects. So it carries substantial political support.

The reason "bond money" is lower cost is that the tax savings are generally passed on to the borrower. The attraction to invest in tax-exempt bonds comes from people in upper tax brackets: They can benefit from a lower interest rate not subject to income taxes. For example, a corporate bond paying a 10 percent rate subject to tax would yield only a 5 percent return to a taxpayer in the 50 percent bracket. A municipal or state bond offering just 5 percent, and not subject to tax, would produce an identical net return for the taxpayer. Thus a reduction in the top income tax bracket reduces the advantage of tax-exempt bonds. A person subject to a 28 percent tax bracket would equate the 5 percent tax-exempt rate with a 7 percent taxable rate rather than a 10 percent taxable rate for a 50 percent bracket.*

Almost all states and many municipalities have entered this market to raise the lower-cost money through the sale of various kinds of securities. In most cases, the money raised from the sale is used to buy mortgage loans from approved lenders within the state or community. Thus, tax-exempt bond money becomes another source of secondary market funding. In some cases, however, housing authorities use this money to make direct loans to qualified borrowers. Almost

---

*A simple formula to determine comparative yields for investors: Divide the municipal bond rate offered by the result of 100 percent less the taxpayer's tax bracket. The result is the yield equivalent for an investment subject to tax.

always, there is an upper-income limitation for home buyers so as to direct the money primarily to middle- and lower-income families.

Another use of tax-exempt bonds is to finance industrial development projects. Sometimes a single developer may be the beneficiary of the low-cost money, or it can be used to finance a project open to any qualified commercial development. The basic purpose of these bond issues is to attract business to a community or state, and thus increase available jobs.

Since any claim of tax exemption falls under the scrutiny of the Internal Revenue Service, some qualifying requirements have been issued. Further, the loss of tax revenue resulting from the proliferation of tax-exempt issues became a concern of the U.S. Treasury Department. Each year, changes have been made in what states and municipalities may do in qualifying tax-exempt issues when the proceeds are used to make mortgage loans. At this writing, a compromise is in effect that limits the total of such issues by an allocation of dollar amounts to each state. Also as of this writing, tax-exempt bonds issued to fund mortgage loans were phased out after 1989. However, Congress tends to extend this kind of assistance.

Mortgage-Backed Securities (MBS)

The growth of the secondary market indicates the success lenders and investors have had with developing practical procedures and uniform instruments for mortgage loans. Yet mortgage loans carry certain problems as investments, such as a need for long-term supervision of each individual loan, and an uncertain return caused by unpredictable prepayments. Further, most major investors are more comfortable dealing in securities-investments that can be bought and sold with greater ease than mortgage loans. By packaging a block of mortgage loans to be held as collateral for an issue of securities, mortgage loans are in effect converted to securities and become more acceptable to investors.

While the Federal Home Loan Mortgage Corporation and the Government National Mortgage Association have offered mortgage-backed securities for many years, it has only been since the early 1980s that other lending institutions and companies began entering this field. One reason for the surge of activity in mortgage-backed securities was the losses sustained by traditional mortgage lenders, beginning in the late 1970s as interest rates climbed. Holding long-term, fixed-rate investments inevitably lost some of its appeal. Another reason was the climb in mortgage interest rates to levels at, or above, other long-term investments, particularly government bonds. The higher rates proved attractive to investors and allowed those packaging the blocks of mortgages a profitable margin for their work. And the big New York investment bankers moving into this field represent huge pools of investment cash primarily devoted to various kinds of securities.

So the shift to the securities market to raise mortgage money offers lenders a more than adequate replacement for the loss of passbook savings money, but at a higher cost.

There are two basic kinds of mortgage loan pools available: (1) those underwritten by a government entity, which is by far the largest to date; and (2) those offered by private lenders such as banks, savings associations, and some of the "nonbank" banking institutions. Private issuers of securities seldom offer a guarantee other than default insurance covering the mortgage loans held as collateral.

MORTGAGE PASSTHROUGHS

The original concept of a mortgage-backed security was to assemble a diversified block of mortgage loans, generally identified as a "pool" of loans, then issue a security collateralized by that block of loans. The issuer of the security may, or may not, guarantee the security. If the security is issued by a private institution or company it is seldom guaranteed, and these prove more difficult to sell. As the popularity of a government agency underwriter dominated the market, the guarantees became the security that is sold.

At first, the purpose was to simply pass on the risk of a fluctuating interest rate to other investors more familiar with the risks involved. And the handling of the payments was to pass the income derived from the underlying block of loans in *pro rata* shares on to the security holders. If a loan paid off prematurely, the additional principal was passed through to the security holder, thus repaying a portion of the security itself. If interest rates increased, the payments on the underlying block of loans remained unaffected. In such an instance, the security holder would suffer a loss of value in the security, but that was a risk they understood. The passthrough type of payment created some uncertainty in its cash flows, and thus in the true yield on the investment itself. To overcome this inherent problem, the financial market issuers of these securities developed an alternative method of handling cash flows to investors. This is the collateralized mortgage obligation more fully described next.

COLLATERALIZED MORTGAGE OBLIGATIONS

Another method of offering a variation on the mortgage-backed security is the Collateralized Mortgage Obligation (CMO). The first CMO was issued by the Federal Home Loan Mortgage Corporation in June 1983. It has several advantages over the mortgage passthroughs that are attractive to traditional investors in corporate-type bonds. By early 1986, securities dealers (investment bankers), home builders, mortgage bankers, thrift institutions, commercial banks, and insurance companies had also issued CMOs reaching a total issuance exceeding $30 billion.

DIFFERENCES BETWEEN CMOS AND MORTGAGE PASSTHROUGHS

The innovation of the CMO structure is in the segmentation of the mortgage cash flows. The older passthrough type of mortgage-backed security offers its holders an irregular cash flow since it includes the repayment of principal whenever a home buyer prepays a loan or refinances to achieve a lower interest rate. This happens because holders of mortgage passthroughs own undivided interests in a pool of mortgages. Whatever the particular pool of mortgages produces in principal payments and interest is then passed directly through to the security holders. In contrast to this procedure, the CMO investor owns bonds that are collateralized by a pool of mortgages or by a portfolio of mortgage-backed securities. The variability and unpredictability of the underlying cash flows remain, but since the CMO substitutes a sequential distribution process instead of the passthrough's *pro rata* distribution of these cash flows, the stream of payments received by the CMO bondholder differs dramatically from that of the holder of a passthrough security.

STRUCTURE OF A CMO

The CMO structure creates a series of bonds with varying maturities that appeal to a wider range of investors than do mortgage passthroughs. While all CMOs follow the same basic structure, wide variations have developed in how the segmentation is set up. Following is the basic pattern:

1. Several classes of bonds are issued against a pool of mortgage collateral. The most common CMO structure contains four classes of bonds: the first three pay interest at their stated rates from date of issue; the final one is usually an accrual class bond.

2. The cash flows from the underlying mortgages are applied first to pay interest and then to retire bonds.

3. The classes of bonds are retired sequentially. All principal payments are directed first to the shortest-maturity class A bonds. When these bonds are completely retired, all principal payments are then directed to the next shortest-maturity bonds—the B class. This process continues until all the classes of bonds have been paid off.

One of the attractions for investors in CMOs is that some of the bonds offer shorter maturities. The first-priority class A bonds may offer maturities as short as two years. Class B and C bonds may offer maturities from four to 10 years. The interest rate offered on these bonds is usually measured against U.S. Treasury securities of similar maturities, only at a slightly higher rate to attract investors. Following is a general description of the basic bond classes:*

Class A. The shortest maturity class of bonds receives all prepayments from the entire pool of mortgage collateral until the entire Class A issue is paid off. Holders of A bonds begin to receive significant principal payments from the first payment date.

Class B and C. The intermediate classes receive only interest payments until each of the prior bond classes has been retired. The interest payment is a known, fixed amount, but the principal repayment will depend on how quickly the mortgage collateral pays down.

Class Z bonds. Class Z bondholders receive no principal or interest payments until all earlier classes have been retired. However, the interest earned by the Z bond is added to the principal balance (compounded), accruing additional interest. During this accrual period, the cash that would otherwise be used to pay interest on the Z bonds is used to accelerate the retirement of the shorter-maturity classes. When all the earlier classes are retired, the accrual period ends, and principal and interest payments to Z bondholders commence.

The purpose of CMOs is to broaden the market for mortgage-backed securities and thus assure a sufficient flow of capital into the mortgage market. They attracts investors by offering higher returns than Treasury Securities of similar maturities, albeit with a slightly greater risk. This kind of financing, that is, mortgage-backed securities sold in the financial markets, became practical when interest rates on mortgage loans increased to a level that exceeded other high-quality securities. The higher rates offered a margin that made it profitable for the issuers of securities to pool blocks of mortgage loans as collateral for their various securities. It is this process that effectively converts a mortgage loan into a security that is attractive to more investors.

---

*In the financial community, these bond classes are also identified as *tranches*, such as first tranche, second tranche, and so on. Tranche is a french word for "slice."

Real Estate Mortgage Investment Conduits (REMIC)

Tax liabilities of the various handlers and holders of mortgage-backed securities created some confusion. For instance, does the issuer of a mortgage-backed security owe income taxes on the interest income that is passed through to a security holder? To clarify the situation and avoid double taxation that might diminish the availability of mortgage money, Congress approved the Real Estate Mortgage Investment Conduit concept in 1986. A REMIC is a tax device that allows cash flows from an underlying block of mortgages to be passed through to security holders without being subject to income taxes at that level. Thus the interest income is taxed only to the security holder, not to the trustee or agent handling the passthrough of the cash. Various requirements must be met to establish a REMIC and reports on its activities must be made to the IRS, and are handled by the issuer of the security involved.

Questions for Discussion

1. Without a national mortgage exchange, how are mortgages traded in the United States?
2. Explain the relationship between the price and the yield on a mortgage loan.
3. Define the word "point" and how it is used, and list the different charges that can be quoted in points.
4. Explain the role of FNMA in the secondary market and the system it uses to purchase mortgage loans.
5. What market does the Federal Home Loan Mortgage Corporation serve and how does it raise its money for the purchase of mortgage loans?
6. How can tax-exempt bonds offer lower-cost mortgage money and how is the money generally used?
7. Explain the two basic kinds of mortgage pools used to back securities and the two different methods used to generate the securities.
8. What roles does a trustee play in the standard mortgage-backed security transaction?
9. Explain the differences between a CMO and a mortgage passthrough type of security.
10. What is the purpose of a REMIC?
11. Define a mortgage purchase "for portfolio."
12. Discuss the purpose and operation of Farmer Mac.

$\boxed{5}$

The Mortgage Documents

KEY WORDS AND PHRASES

Mortgage instrument	Deed of Trust
Promissory note	Open-end mortgage
Redemption	Construction mortgage
Title theory	Release clauses
Lien theory	Junior mortgage
State law controls	Purchase money mortgage
Principal amount	Package mortgage
Prepayment of loan	Blanket mortgage
Acceleration	Contract for Deed
Right to sell	Equitable title
Due on sale	Recording
Assumption	First mortgage
Alienation clause	Second mortgage
Hazard insurance	Subordination
Ad valorem taxes	Conforming loans

Loans made with real estate as the collateral security can be traced back as far as the ancient Pharaohs of Egypt and the Romans of the pre-Christian era. Even then, some form of pledge or assigment of the property was used to ensure repayment of an obligation to the lender. The development over many centuries of this type of property assignment illustrates the interplay of individual rights, more specifically, the rights of a borrower as against the rights of a lender.

History and Development

The Mortgage as a Grant of Title to Property

In its earliest forms, a property pledge to secure a debt was an actual assignment of that property to the lender. During the term of the loan, the lender might even have the physical use of that land and was entitled to any rents or other revenues derived from the land pledged. Thus, the earliest form of land as security for a loan was the actual granting of title to the lender for the term of the loan.

Due to the primitive conditions of communication and transportation then in existence, the practice of granting title to property for a loan tended to foster a number of abuses by lenders. For example, a slight delay in payments, which might even be encouraged by the lender, easily created a default and forfeited the borrower's rights for any recovery of the land. Sometimes borrowers who felt they had been unjustly deprived of their property appealed to the king, or perhaps to an appointed minister, to seek a hearing for their grievances and to petition for just redress. And if it was subsequently determined that a wrong had been committed, the borrower might be given a chance to redeem his land with a late payment of the obligation. Thus the *right of redemption* came into being.

However, lenders were not happy with this redemption privilege and initiated a countermove by inserting a clause in future loan agreements that specifically waived the right of redemption. The borrower had to accept this clause or be denied the loan. As our civilization progressed from the unchallenged rule of an absolute monarch into written codes of law, the granting or refusal of redemption became a matter of law or of statute often referred to as *statutory redemption*. Variations in such laws among the states are substantial, going all the way from a total lack of redemption rights upon default up to two full years after default to pay off the loan and recover the property.

The Mortgage as a Lien

Another way in which land can be pledged as security for a loan is by means of granting a lien. A *lien* constitutes an encumbrance on property. It is a declaration of a claim to a parcel of land for some purpose that is recorded in the public record. In states where the lien form is prevalent, a pledge of land as security for a loan grants no title except under default of the obligation. So when a default does occur, the lender must convert lien rights into an actual title to the property through court action, as the particular state may require.

While there is some variation in the precise usage of the lien as a form of pledge, and the limited assignment of title as another form of pledge, all property laws concerning mortgages can be classified into one form or the other. The advantages and disadvantages of each can be weighed as legal arguments, but for purposes of finance, it is important mainly to be aware of the existing differences and to know under what laws a particular property can be mortgaged.

Lenders have learned to live with various requirements and can obtain adequate security for their loans by adapting their pledges to the many different laws. For example, they have adjusted even to the unique law spelled out in the original constitution of the state of Texas protecting a family homestead from all creditors with just three exceptions: (1) a loan for purchase of the property, (2) mechanics' and material suppliers' liens, and (3) property taxes.

State Laws Control Property Rights

Property rights in the United States are spelled out primarily under state laws, not by the federal government. Each state has written into its code of law specific rights that must be adhered to with regard to land ownership in that state. The local variations and shadings in these laws reflect the background and origins of the particular region. In the East, for example, the great body of English parliamentary law and common law guided the New England and mid-Atlantic states in setting up their constitutions and subsequent statutes. In the South, on the other hand, the French legal codes were reflected in the Louisiana Territory and were especially evident in the growing city of New Orleans. In still another section of the country, the Southwest, Spanish heritage determined the laws, and these laws recognized Catholic religious ties in marriage as well as patriarchal protection of wife, children, and family relationships. As a result, community property statutes were enacted, and for many years special protections, as well as special limitations regarding women's property rights, were in force in this region of the country.

An attempt to cover such a broad field of law as real property rights on a national basis would be out of place in this text since it is a subject more properly handled by qualified attorneys, skilled in interpreting these rights according to the laws of each state. It can be pointed out, however, that most states have laws specifically limiting any conveyance of property rights solely to written agreements, and all states require certain procedures to record conveyances of land in the public records. The result has been an increasingly accurate record of land titles, with a corresponding increase of protection for property owners' rights and those of any other interest parties.

The Mortgage and Promissory Note

There are certain basic instruments used in real estate loans that have essentially the same purpose throughout the country. The collateral pledge that has given its name to the entire field of real estate finance is the *mortgage*. A mortgage is simply a pledge of property to secure a loan. It is not a promise to pay anything. As a matter of fact, without a debt to secure, the mortgage itself becomes null and void by its own terms, or, as the French derivative of the word *mortgage* indicates, a "dead pledge." Due to the differences in state laws, the precise definition varies somewhat, but for our purposes a mortgage can best be defined as a conditional conveyance of property as security for the debt recited therein, which can only be activated by failure to comply with its terms.

The promissory note is the debt instrument. It is the promise to pay, and is usually a separate instrument. The Uniform Commercial Code sets the standards for drafting an enforceable and negotiable promissory note. A negotiable note can be assigned. If the collateral securing the note (as pledged by the mortgage instrument) proves insufficient to cover the indebtedness, the holder of the note can obtain a deficiency judgment against the debtor for the balance due. If the note is labeled "nonrecourse," the borrower cannot be held personally liable on the note.

Both promissory notes and mortgage instruments must contain certain standard words and phrases to assure the accomplishment of their purposes. Nevertheless, the balance of the terms and conditions can be worded however the individual attorney preparing the documents deems proper. Obviously, the variations could be substantial and, in years past, this made the selling of conventional mortgage loans very difficult. HUD/FHA and VA have always required their standardized forms to be used if the loan is underwritten by the agencies, but there was no such requirement for conventional loans, meaning those not underwritten by the government.

By 1970, the Federal National Mortgage Association (newly authorized as a private corporation) decided to add residential *conventional* loans to its purchases of mortgages. Prior to that time, they were allowed to purchase only HUD/FHA and VA loans. To buy conventional loans, standards were needed. In cooperation with the Federal Home Loan Mortgage Corporation, public hearings were held to help decide what should, and should not, be included in these important documents.

No single form could be used throughout the country because of variations in state property laws. So the result of this work has been a series of standardized mortgage instruments designed specifically to meet each state's requirements, plus an accompanying series of promissory notes to match the mortgage instruments. Because notes are unilateral promises to pay and convey no property rights, there are fewer differences between the states' laws. So FNMA/FHLMC have been able to combine a number of their promissory note instruments into "multistate" documents. Examples of several notes and mortgage instruments are reproduced in the Appendix of this text.

The work begun in 1970 to create uniform mortgage documents has formed the basis for a standardized conventional loan known as a "conforming" loan. The industry trend is toward further standardization of residential loan procedures.

While the preparation of mortgage instruments is a legal matter, there are a number of points that are important for the layman to understand. The following discussion is generalized. Specific questions should be asked of qualified attorneys.

Promissory Note

A promissory note is a written promise by a person, or persons, to pay a sum of money to another. The use of the wording "or order" or "or bearer" is important as it is these words that make it possible for the note to be endorsed and transferred, thus becoming *negotiable*. If the note is negotiable, only one copy should be executed. If other copies are made, the note maker could initial them, but should not sign them.

Mortgage Instrument

PARTIES INVOLVED

The mortgage instrument must identify the names of the parties involved. They may not be the same as those on the promissory note. Since the mortgage is a conveyance-type instrument, it is necessary to have all of the owners indicate agreement by signature. The rules of contract law apply to mortgages, so they must be in writing, and the parties must be legally competent to contract. Whether or not the marital status of the parties involved needs to be stated depends upon state law. If the parties are married, both signatures may be required, as marital rights, homestead rights, and/or community property rights may be involved.

IDENTIFICATION OF PROPERTY

Identification of the property offered as collateral to secure the promissory note must be accurately described so as to distinguish it from any other property in the world. A street address is never acceptable, nor are boundary lines based on physical features, such as the "big live oak by the river bend." Accurate legal descriptions are normally used either by "metes and bounds" (a surveyor's description of boundary lines from a fixed starting point, thence proceeding in specific compass directions and distances around the property back to the starting point), or, more commonly in urban areas, by lot and block taken from a subdivision plat registered and approved by a local government authority. An erroneous description of the property, even a typographical error, can render the mortgage instrument void but does not necessarily invalidate the promissory note.

PRINCIPAL AMOUNT DUE

Most mortgage notes are paid on an installment plan, wherein each payment includes the interest due to that payment date, plus a portion of the principal due. Thus, with each payment, the balance is reduced. When mortgage notes are transferred, only the principal balance then due can be conveyed. Business practice places confidence in the seller of a note to deliver accurate information on the precise balance due at the time of transfer.

Estoppel. The term "estoppel" is sometimes applied to a mortgagee's information letter. This letter is a statement from the mortgage lender to the borrower giving information on the current status of that mortgage loan, including the amount of principal balance then due. Such information is normally obtained as part of the property listing process. An older practice, and one still used sometimes with large commercial loans, is to require an estoppel agreement when a note is transferred. The purpose of the agreement is an acknowledgement by both borrower and lender of the loan amount due at that time. In effect, it "stops" a subsequent purchaser of the note from claiming any greater amount. The legal doctrine of estoppel has a broader application in that it prevents a person from asserting rights that are inconsistent with a previous position.

PREPAYMENT PENALTY

If all or part of the principal balance of a loan is paid before it becomes due, there is a possible additional charge involved. The purpose of the prepayment penalty is to allow the lender to recoup a portion of the interest that the lender had expected to earn when the loan was made. To explain the lender's viewpoint with an example:

A loan of $90,000 for 30 years at 12 percent interest is expected to earn the lender $243,273.60 in interest over the life of the loan. (Monthly payment 925.76 × 360 payments = 333,273.60. The principal is 90,000, the balance is interest).

The lender has a contractual right to this interest and some claim to compensation for a forfeiture of this right.

On the other hand, the borrower views the repayment as placing cash in the hands of the borrower that can easily be loaned to another to earn interest plus additional origination fees. So there is no compensable loss to the lender.

There is a variety of compromises on these conflicting views. First, there are no prepayment charges permitted on HUD/FHA, VA or conforming loans. On other residential loans the prepayment penalty (sometimes called a "premium" by the lender), might be from 1 to 3 percent of the loan amount that is prepaid.

For instance, if the charge is 3 percent and the amount prepaid is $20,000, the borrower would owe an additional $600 at time of prepayment. Another fairly common solution to the prepayment question is to allow up to 20 percent of the original loan amount to be prepaid in any one year with no additional charge. Under this option, the borrower could repay the loan in full within five years at no extra cost. Whatever the prepayment requirements may be, they should be clearly indicated in the loan documents.

Lock-In Provisions. Another kind of prepayment requirement found in some commercial loans is the "lock-in." Commercial loans usually do not offer borrowers the same kind of regulatory protection that can be found in residential loans, so the lock-in is a more restrictive provision than would be found in a residential loan. What it does is lock in the interest charge for a certain minimum number of years. For example, a loan for an apartment project might require all interest to be paid for the first eight years of the loan term. Prepayment during the first eight years would cost all interest otherwise due for that time period, and most likely would make any prepayment too costly.

ACCELERATION

A clause in the mortgage instrument or promissory note that gives a lender the right to call the entire balance due, in full, in advance of due date upon the occurrence of a specified event is called an *acceleration clause.* The event is most likely to be default on an installment payment. But there are other kinds of defaults that could trigger an acceleration clause including destruction of the premises, placing an encumbrance on the property, or its sale or assignment. It is a very important clause in an installment obligation, as without it the alternative could be to foreclose each month as the payments actually come due.

RIGHT TO SELL—DUE-ON-SALE CLAUSE—ASSUMPTION

As a general rule, mortgaged property can be freely sold by the owner or mortgagor, either with an assumption of the existing debt by the new buyer or, if that is not permitted, by paying off the balance due on the existing mortgage. In the past decade, as loan assumptions became more important in the successful sale of a house, serious questions developed over what rights a borrower might have versus those of a lender in loan assumptions. The borrower (mostly homeowners in this question), took the position that any restriction on a loan assumption by the lender amounted to an unreasonable restraint on the right of the owner to sell the property. In legal terminology, this restraint on a sale is called a *restraint on alienation*. Thus, a right-to-sell clause in a mortgage is sometimes referred to as the *alienation clause*. Most states prohibit any *unreasonable* restraint on alienation—a limitation that has been mostly concerned with discrimination. For example, a restrictive covenant in a property deed that forbids any sale to a female would most likely be classed as an unreasonable restraint on the owner's right to sell. The question of whether or not a lender's right to increase an interest rate on an assumption, or otherwise deny the right to sell, amounts to an unreasonable restraint has been the subject of much controversy. A review of this situation and the present resolution follows.

When interest remained at lower and more stable rates, lenders were more cooperative in allowing sales and assumptions of their loans. But as interest rates moved upward in the late 1960s, more lenders eyed the loss of value in their older loans, which had been made at much lower rates. And many began to insert clauses in their mortgage instruments that required specific approval by the lender before the borrower could make any sale of the property that included an assumption of the loan. The price of that approval often proved to be an adjustment of the interest rate upward on the balance of the loan to a percentage rate closer to the then-existing market rate. This interest adjustment is sometimes demanded without releasing the original borrower from the obligation.

Since the late 1970s a number of legal challenges have been made and legislation passed that affected the right of a lender to increase the interest rate on an existing loan in the event the property is transferred and the loan assumed. These questions have been lumped under the name of *due-on-sale* clauses. (The FNMA-FHLMC uniform mortgage documents, Covenant 17, identify the items as "Transfer of the Property: Assumption.") The conflict stems from a lender's right, or obligation, to protect the loan collateral through periodic inspections and to make sure that the usage of the property and its occupancy is not detrimental to the property's value. As this right to approve a new occupant; that is, a new buyer, was extended to include the right to increase an interest rate upon the loan being assumed, homeowners found it more difficult to sell their property. And challenges in the court began.

By 1982, about one-third of the states had passed legislation or applied court decisions that severely restricted, or prohibited, lenders from increasing interest rates in the event of a loan assumption. In the same year, the United States Supreme Court ruled on a homeowner's challenge to a lender's right to increase an interest rate on a fixed-rate mortgage agreement. The court decided that a federally chartered institution does have the right to adjust an interest rate upon assumption, regardless of state law, provided the right to adjust is clearly stated in the mortgage agreement.

The U.S. Supreme court ruling did not affect state-chartered lenders that remained subject to state restrictions until passage of the Garn/St Germain Depository Institutions Act in October 1982. This act allowed enforcement of due-on-sale clauses for new originations by all lenders. There was an exception in the act for 11 states with restrictions on due-on-sale enforcement allowing existing loans to be assumed during a "window period" ending October 15, 1985. The Garn Act further allowed states to extend restrictions beyond 1985 on due-on-sale enforcement and five elected to do so: Arizona, Minnesota, Michigan, New Mexico, and Utah.

The right to adjust an interest rate on an assumed loan is a moot point in periods of declining interest rates; assuming an older high interest rate loan has little attraction for the home buyer. If an adjustment of rate is not possible, the loan might be refinanced at the lower market rate.

One further point: The foregoing information does not mean that due-on-sale clauses are unacceptable. There is no obligation on the part of any lender to allow a loan assumption if that fact is clearly stated in the loan agreement. This condition is most commonly found in mortgage loans that are made by home sellers as a way to help sell the house. Home sellers are not normally in the business of making loans and can include a clause forbidding any loan assumption; that is, if the buyer subsequently resells the house, the existing loan must be paid in full.

INSURANCE

Mortgages require property insurance coverage for the lender's protection. This is also termed *hazard insurance*. Principally, it includes fire and extended coverage and is required by the lender where any buildings are involved in an amount at least equal to that of the loan. To make certain that insurance payments are made, the lender generally requires a full year's paid-up insurance policy before releasing the loan proceeds, plus two months of the annual premium paid into an escrow account. Then, with each monthly payment, one-twelfth of the annual premium must be paid. The original policy is held by the lender, and it is part of the lender's responsibility to maintain the coverage with timely payments made from the borrower's escrow account.

Insurance companies in most states have another requirement controlling the minimum amount of coverage that can be carried to establish full coverage in case of a loss. Since most fire losses are partial in extent, it is not unusual for a property owner to carry only partial insurance hoping that any fire would be brought under control before the damage exceeds the amount of insurance coverage. To distribute the cost of insurance more equitably over all policyholders, many insurance companies require that the insured maintain insurance of not less than a given percentage of the actual cash value of the building at the time of the loss. These clauses are known variously as *coinsurance clauses, average clauses,* or *reduced rate contribution clauses.* A common minimum amount of insurance to provide full coverage is 80 percent of the actual cash value of the building at the time of the loss. By carrying less than the agreed percentage of insurance, the property owner cannot collect in full for a loss but will have to bear a part of the loss personally. The insurance company will be liable only for such percentage of the loss as the amount of insurance carried bears to 80 percent of the actual cash value of the property at the time of the loss. The insurance company's liability may be expressed by the formula

$$\frac{C}{R} \times L = A$$

where
   C = the amount of insurance carried
   R = the amount of insurance required
   L = the amount of the loss
   A = the amount for which the insurance company is liable

In periods of rapidly rising property values, any failure to maintain proper insurance coverage can expose the lender as well as the property owner to uninsured losses.

   Another insurance problem to be considered in a mortgage involves determining just how the proceeds should be paid in case of an actual loss. Earlier mortgages required payment of the insurance money to the lender, who in turn decided how to apply the funds; that is, whether to permit the funds to be used for restoration of the property, the usual procedure on smaller losses, or to apply the insurance proceeds to the payoff of the loan. As time has passed, recent mortgages have given the borrower a stronger position in the distribution of insurance proceeds, as is apparent in the FNMA/FHLMC standard conventional mortgage covenants.

PROPERTY TAXES

Property tax, also known as *ad valorem tax*, becomes a *specific lien* on real property from the time the tax is assessed. Tax records are normally filed in each county as a separate section of information. Property subject to tax (some land is exempt) must stand good for its payment. If the tax is not paid, the property is subject to foreclosure by the state. In some states an assessment by a properly authorized neighborhood maintenance association carries the same status as a property tax. It is a high priority claim in a foreclosure action, preceded only by the administrative costs of the sale. Thus, property taxes hold a higher priority of claim than other secured claimants regardless of the date other claims are recorded.

   Because property taxes take precedence over a first mortgage loan, lenders normally require the protection of handling the tax payment as a part of their escrow requirements. To do this, a cushion of two months of taxes is usually deposited with the lender at loan closing, and one month (one-twelfth of the annual payment) of taxes is added to each monthly payment of the mortgage loan. Then the lender is responsible for making the tax payment directly to the tax authority as part of their loan servicing function.

Federal Tax Claims. A tax claim by the federal government is considered a *general lien,** but only when it is filed of record. Such a lien may be assessed against any taxpayer's property, real or personal and, under the federal claim of supremacy would carry a higher priority than a property tax in a foreclosure proceeding. However, the property tax would not necessarily be satisfied in such a foreclosure action—it simply remains with the land as a continuing claim unless title passes to the federal government.

Mortgage Variations

The underlying purpose of the mortgage instrument is to provide a pledge of property as collateral to secure a promissory note. To properly serve the various needs of borrowers, some variations in the mortgage conditions create differences in the instruments used. This is not the same as the special differences that derive from how a mortgage is repaid. Following is information on major differences as they are structured to serve specialized purposes.

Regular Mortgage

A *regular mortgage* is a two-party legal document used to secure performance of an obligation. The borrower is the "mortgagor" who grants certain rights to the lender (the "mortgagee") that pledge property as collateral. The rights granted may be in the nature of a lien or a conditional grant of title. The mortgage creates rights in real property and should be recorded.

Deed of Trust

A *deed of trust*, sometimes called a trust deed, is a mortgage in which title to property is conditionally conveyed to a third-party trustee as security for an obligation owed to the lender, who is called the beneficiary. The trustee can be an individual or a corporate trustee as selected by the lender. In the event of a

---

*A *general lien* is a claim against all assets of the target of the lien; a *specific lien* is a claim against one specific asset, such as a tract of land.

default, the lender notifies the trustee requesting that action be taken to protect the lender's interest. The trustee then notifies the debtor in accordance with the state law that foreclosure is pending. On the date of foreclosure, the trustee offers the property to the highest bidder, and has the authority to deliver title to the property in a nonjudicial action. In those states that allow it, the procedure is much faster and at a lower cost than judicial procedure, which requires court action in order to foreclose.

Open-End Mortgage

The *open-end mortgage* sets a limit to the amount that may be borrowed and allows incremental advances to be made secured by the same mortgage. This type of mortgage is often used in farm loans to meet seasonal needs, much like a line of credit. By maintaining some balance due on the mortgage obligation, the priority of the mortgage lien can be retained. Even so, it is a good idea for the lender to require a title search when an incremental advance is made, as certain claims, such as property taxes, can create a higher priority.

Construction Loan

A *construction loan* is a short-term loan to cover the costs of building. It is sometimes called an "interim" loan although that term describes a broader range of loans. A construction loan differs from other mortgage loans in that the funding is handled through periodic advances as the construction progresses. The loan may be funded after certain stages are completed, or after certain time periods, such as each month, for work completed up to that point. It takes a construction-wise loan officer to ensure that funds are released as the building progresses. In this way, the value of the building as collateral increases at approximately the same rate as the amount of the loan. Nevertheless, the risk of a construction loan lies in the ability of the borrower/builder to complete the project within the total amount of money available to do so. (For additional information, see Chapter 11.)

Interim Loan

The term "interim" is often used synonymously with a construction loan. While jargon varies somewhat, an *interim loan* has a broader meaning. It is any loan that is expected to be repaid from the proceeds of another loan. To further illustrate the meaning, compare this with other kinds of loans. For instance, a home loan is expected to be repaid from the borrower's personal income; an income property loan is expected to be repaid from income derived from the property itself. So an interim loan is expected to be repaid from other borrowed money. An interim loan is sometimes used for short-term financing until regular financing has been completed. When used for this purpose, the financing is also called a *gap loan* or a *bridge loan*. Since it is true that most construction loans are made with the expectation of repayment from a permanent loan when the building is completed, they easily qualify as an interim type of financing.

Mortgage with Release Clauses

When money is borrowed for the purpose of land development, it is necessary to have specific release procedures to enable the developer to sell lots, or a portion of the land, and deliver good title to the portion. This is the purpose of a *release clause*. The conditions are stated so that the developer can repay a portion of the loan and obtain a release of a portion of the land from the original mortgage. In a subdivision of building lots, the developer would be required to pay a percentage of the sales price of the lot or a minimum dollar amount against the loan for each lot released. The lender would calculate the payoff so that the loan would be fully repaid when around 60 to 80 percent of the lots were sold.

Under regular mortgages, there is no provision to allow a partial sale of the property. So a development loan requires considerable negotiation to work out all the details necessary for success. The lender will want some control over the direction of the development; that is, lots must be developed and sold in an orderly manner that will not undermine the value of any remaining land. A time pattern must be negotiated to allow realistic limits on how fast the lots must be sold. The clause that permits the release of a portion of the mortgaged land is also called a *partial release*, since the remainder of the land continues to be held as security for the loan.

Junior Mortgage

The term *junior mortgage* applies to those mortgages that carry a lower priority than the prime or first mortgage. These are *second* and even *third* mortgages. The lower priority makes this kind of mortgage higher risk and of greater cost.

The mortgage instrument carries no designation in its text describing its lien position. The order of priority, which determines the exact order of claims against a piece of property, is established by the time of the recording of that instrument. This becomes of extreme importance in a foreclosure proceeding.

Example

If a property considered to be worth $50,000 carries a first mortgage for $30,000, and a second mortgage for $8,000, and that property is forced into a foreclosure sale that results in a recovery of $35,000 in cash after payment of legal fees—how, then, should the money be distributed? The priority of the liens exercises control and, assuming that no other liens, taxes, or otherwise, have shown priority, then the first-mortgage holder is in a position to recover the full $30,000 from the $35,000 proceeds, and the remaining $5,000 is awarded to the second-mortgage holder, leaving the payment $3,000 short of recovering the $8,000 loan. Due to the promissory note; the second-mortgage holder may have a right to seek a deficiency judgment against the borrower to recover that $3,000. However, it becomes evident that the security of the land has been wiped out in the foreclosure sale and resulting settlement.

Later in this chapter, the subject of recording, as related to the question of establishing the priority of mortgage liens, will be discussed in more detail.

Purchase Money Mortgage

A *purchase money mortgage* is one taken by the seller of a property as all or part of the consideration. Such a mortgage carries certain priorities over other claims. This is possible because the delivery of a deed occurs simultaneously with the taking back of the purchase money mortgage, allowing no time for any other lien to intervene. A purchase money mortgage of this kind carries the special status of a *vendor's lien*. Also, depending on state law, a deficiency judgment may or may not be permitted upon default of a purchase money mortgage.

A second definition of a purchase money mortgage is one where the loan proceeds are used to buy the property secured by the mortgage. For instance, in Texas, only a purchase money mortgage can sustain a valid mortgage claim against a person's homestead.

Chattel Mortgage

Chattel is tangible personal property and it can be mortgaged to secure a debt; thus, *chattel mortgage*. This procedure is more likely to be used when additional security is needed for a loan or as part of a loan on real property when it is important to identify certain personal property assets. In the acquisition of personal property, chattel mortgages have been replaced by the bill of sale with a security agreement that is regulated by the Uniform Commercial Code.

Package Mortgage

A *package mortgage* pledges both real and personal property to secure a loan. It is most likely to be found in the acquisition of a new house. The buyer/borrower includes in the package a number of essential furnishings needed for the house, and is thus able to pay for them over an extended period of time. Most package mortgages also require the borrower to sign and file a financing statement in accordance with the provisions of the Uniform Commercial Code.

Blanket Mortgage

A mortgage is not limited to pledging a single parcel of land. Sometimes the security pledged for a loan may include several tracts of land. When more than one tract of land is pledged in the mortgage instrument, it is called a *blanket mortgage.*

Wraparound Mortgage

A *wraparound mortgage* is a new mortgage that encompasses, or "wraps around," any existing mortgages and is subordinate to them. The purpose is to acquire additional funding on a loan while retaining the priority of lien of the existing mortgage plus any differential in interest retained with the older mortgage.

In periods of escalating interest rates, the design proved popular as a method of capturing an older, lower-interest rate loan which served to benefit both buyer and seller.

Example

A property worth $150,000 has a mortgage with a $40,000 balance at 9 percent interest. In today's market, say new financing costs 12 percent.

To acquire the property, the buyer is willing to pay $20,000 down and is seeking $130,000 in financing.

The buyer has three possibilities:

1. All new financing of $130,000 first-mortgage loan at an interest rate of 12 percent.
2. Assume the existing loan of $40,000 and borrow the additional $90,000 (difference between 40,000 and 130,000) needed on a second-mortgage loan that would carry a higher interest rate of, say, 14 percent.
3. Arrange a wraparound loan for $130,000 at, say, 11 percent that includes the existing $40,000 loan—net new cash is $90,000.

Further examination of the wrap procedure shows that it could be advantageous for both the buyer and seller to agree on such a loan, providing *the existing loan is assumable*. The advantage to the buyer, obviously, is lower-cost (11 percent) financing than otherwise would be possible. For the seller accepting a wraparound mortgage, the advantage is 11 percent on the new funding of $90,000 *plus* a 2 percent additional earned interest on the existing loan that requires no new cash. In effect, the buyer makes the payment to the seller on a $130,000 loan at 11 percent interest, while the seller passes on the payment to the existing mortgage holder of $40,000 at 9 percent interest.

Two reasons have brought a decline in the application of the wraparound mortgage design. One is that fewer mortgages are now assumable with new regulations and requirements. Also, interest rates have been declining in the period from 1981 to 1988. There is little interest in capturing an older, higher-interest loan in a wrap procedure! However, if that decline reverses into an increase in rate, there could be renewed interest in this procedure.

"Subject To" Mortgage

In the conveyance of property, it is possible for title to be delivered *subject to* an existing mortgage. The phrase has a legal intent and means that the buyer is not personally liable to the lender for payment of that mortgage note. It in no way changes the claim of the lender holding the mortgage; it simply means that the new buyer does not accept the liability. In the event of a default, the lender holds whatever rights were granted by the mortgage but has no right to pursue the new buyer for any deficiency. Such liability remains with the original debtor.

While the procedure is used in several different circumstances, it is most commonly found when a wraparound mortgage is used (see previous section). Another use of the subject to procedure is when property is acquired for the purpose of rehabilitation and resale.

It should be pointed out that transferring property with a subject to procedure is definitely a transfer of interest and could trigger a due-on-sale clause. This is true even though the loan itself is not assumed.

Contract for Deed

A *contract for deed* is a sale and financing agreement. It is not a mortgage although it is often misunderstood as one. Under a contract for deed, the buyer receives only the rights of possession and enjoyment, much the same as with a lease. After a part, or all, of the payments have been made as agreed, the seller is then obligated to deliver legal title to the property. That is what distinguishes a contract for deed from a lease with option to buy: the buyer holds an equitable title during the payment period and the seller is obligated to deliver legal title when payments are completed.

State law varies as to how it treats the buyer/borrower under a contract for deed. Some states grant the buyer certain rights to the property as payments are made. Others recognize only the ownership rights retained by the seller to the extent that such contracts may not even be recordable. What the buyer's "equitable title" means is that there is a right for the buyer to achieve title by meeting the contract terms and there is no way the seller can deny that right unilaterally. But there are some pitfalls.

These are the risks that concern a buyer:

1. The greatest risk for the buyer is that title is not delivered until after payment has been made. During the payment period, it is possible that the seller will become unable to perform. While legal title remains in the seller's name, it is subject to any adverse claim that may accrue against the seller. Or the seller may be a corporation with only limited liability for the directors and shareholders.
2. Delivery of title when it becomes due may be difficult if the seller suffers a legal disability, becomes bankrupt, or dies.
3. If there is an underlying mortgage on the property, a payment escrow account should be used to assure the buyer that payments are properly made to the mortgage holder.

Next, the risks that concern a seller:

1. If a buyer defaults, or becomes bankrupt, there is a problem of clearing title, which may be costly.
2. A contract for deed is subject to contract law that offers differing interpretations.

Although there are special problems with a contract for deed transaction, the procedure serves some valid purposes. One use is to allow possession of a home to someone who has difficulty qualifying for a mortgage loan. The difficulty might be a laid off employee with a new job unable to meet a lender's length of time on the job requirement. Another possibility is when a property has a known title defect that is curable but will take time. The present condition of its title disqualifies the property as collateral. A contract for deed could convey possession, while allowing time for the title to be cleared, so that a mortgage loan can be obtained to pay off the seller.

Contracts for deed are often used in the sale of lots in resort areas. And they can be found when the purpose is to achieve a fast sale under high pressure tactics. With legal title to the property held by the seller, there is less need to fully qualify the buyer. It is easier to push for a quick closing. And because title is not conveyed at closing, there appears to be less need to assure good title with a search of the abstract or title insurance. This can be dangerous for an unwary buyer as title defects can just as easily interfere with a later delivery of title as with an immediate delivery. Contracts for deed can be found under an assortment of names that cause some confusion for buyers. Among names that may be used are land contract, installment contract, agreement of sale, conditional sales contract, or even just real estate contract.

Mortgage Procedures

Several important procedures are associated with mortgage instruments that merit further discussion. While legal practices do differ between the states, the purpose or reason for certain practices is generally the same.

Recording

Modern society protects land ownership with the help of its public records, which are open to anyone with an acceptable instrument to file. Recording is the act of entering into the public record a written instrument that affects title to property. There are other sets of public records separate from that for real estate that have a bearing on the quality of title to real estate. These include the records regarding taxes, probate, marriage and judgments.

Individual state laws define what is necessary for an instrument to be recorded; generally, it must be in writing and properly acknowledged. The instrument must be recorded in the county in which the land is located.

To record a document gives constructive notice to the world of the existence of the document and its contents.

Failure to record a document does not invalidate the agreement between the parties thereto. Nor does such failure to record invalidate the agreement for any other parties who have notice of its existence. What recording laws advise is that if a document is not recorded it generally is *void* as against any subsequent purchaser, lessee, or mortgagee acting in good faith who does not have knowledge of the unrecorded document. What this means, for example, is that if a deed transferring property ownership is not recorded, the record title remains with the seller insofar as innocent third parties are concerned. In such an instance, a subsequent judgment against the seller could result in a valid claim against the property that had already been sold. Where does that leave the purchaser who did not bother to record the deed? Most likely with a difficult lawsuit and possible loss of the property to the judgment claimant.

One more point on the nature of recording: If a recorded document is, for some reason, void, recording does not make it valid.

Priority. From a practical point of view, recording gives priority to documents based on the time they are recorded; thus, a mortgage filed before another has a higher priority. However, there is a separate class of liens whose priority is not based on time of filing. This includes tax liens, mechanics liens, and special assessment liens that are considered to be a matter of public record. Tax liens for income taxes and payroll taxes *must be recorded* to take a priority position against subsequent claims. One other way to alter the priority of a claim is a subordination agreement, which will be discussed shortly.

Releases. Recording is so often thought of in terms of conveying property, or asserting a claim, that the reverse procedure is sometimes overlooked. It is also important to record a *release* of any claim if available. And if a claim is based on a written document, so should a release be a written document when the claim is satisfied. This is most important when dealing with a mortgage. It is true that a payoff of a mortgage note voids the mortgage that secured it. Nevertheless, the mortgage document remains a matter of record for any subsequent review of the chain of title. Depending on state law, *two* releases may be needed. If there is a vendor's lien (a claim that derives from a purchase-money debt), a release is needed when that is paid off. And if there is another mortgage claim against the property it, too, requires a release. The releases must be in a recordable form. Sometimes the return of the lien instruments, or the note marked "paid in full," are thought to satisfy release requirements. But it takes recorded releases to actually clear the title to property.

Subordination

Subordination is a method of altering the priority of claims to property by a written agreement. It is commonly used in development projects when the land is seller-financed, or even when the land is leased. The land seller would hold a purchase-money mortgage if the land is sold, and would agree to subordinate the mortgage in favor of the construction lender. This allows the developer/ purchaser to obtain a first-mortgage loan to build the intended improvement. Thus, the subordination agreement alters the normal rule of giving priority to the mortgage that is recorded first.

If land is leased to a developer for a project, rather than sold, the landowner could subordinate the fee in favor of a construction loan (or other mortgage claim). Technically, the fee cannot be subordinated to a leasehold mortgage—it is more properly called "encumbering" the fee. But the end result is the same: The lender holds a prior claim on the property for repayment of the loan.

A subordination clause can be included in a mortgage instrument permitting a subsequent mortgage to take a higher priority. This is a fairly standard type of clause found in a junior mortgage when an existing prior mortgage is recognized in the junior instrument.

Conforming Loans

A major step toward standardization of conventional loans within the mortgage industry is the growing use of uniform documents, cited shortly. In addition, many primary market lenders are operating within limitations established by the major secondary market participants: the Federal National Mortgage Association and the Federal Home Loan Mortgage Corporation. It is not uncommon to find their standards explained to a borrower as "government limits." And, in a sense, they are, in that both agencies, the FNMA and FHLMC, are quasi-government agencies. But the limitations are not in the same class as a government regulation. The standards apply only if the loan originator intends to sell the loan later to either FNMA or FHLMC. And whether or not an originator intends to sell the loan, a conforming loan is more easily sold than is a nonconforming conventional loan should the need to do so arise later on.

A conforming loan is a conventional loan since it is not underwritten by any government agency. Neither FNMA or FHLMC provide default insurance for individual loans. There are conforming loans written on nonuniform documents. These comply with FNMA/FHLMC loan parameters but do not use their documentation. Examples of uniform documents are reprinted in the Appendix, and include the following:

Residential Loan Application

Uniform Residential Appraisal Report

Request for Verification of Deposit

Request for Verification of Employment

Deed of Trust—North Carolina

Fixed Rate Note

Adjustable Rate Note

Adjustable Rate Rider

One further point: *No lender is required to make any kind of loan.* All the parameters specified by the various underwriting agencies (FHA and VA), as well as the secondary market limitations, and the rules spelled out by the regulatory agencies on permissible types of mortgages, are applicable only if a lender chooses to write that particular kind of mortgage. Further, any lender may set limitations *lower than the rules may permit.*

Questions for Discussion

1. What procedure is used in your state to handle a pledge of security for a mortgage loan?
2. What is the purpose of a promissory note? Of a mortgage instrument?
3. Distinguish between an acceleration clause and an escalation clause in a mortgage.
4. What is the underlying purpose of requiring a borrower to escrow money each month for the annual payment of property taxes?
5. Distinguish between a general lien and a specific lien.
6. Describe what is meant by an open-end mortgage; also, a deed of trust.
7. What is the principal risk for the buyer-borrower in a contract for deed?
8. Describe a wraparound mortgage procedure.
9. What is meant by the legal phrase "subject to"?
10. What is the purpose of recording?

6

Mortgage Repayment Plans

KEY WORDS AND PHRASES

Alternative mortgage repayment
Adjustable rate mortgage
Graduated payment mortgage
Index
Application of an index
Index plus margin
Caps
Negative amortization

Pledged account mortgage
Buy-down mortgage
Shorter-term loans
GEM mortgages
Home equity revolving loans
Shared appreciation mortgages
Shared equity mortgages
Reverse annuity mortgage

For the past half century there has been one dominant mortgage design used in this country: the fixed interest rate, constant-level payment, fully amortized plan. This orderly system began to change in the mid-1970s when lenders and regulators became concerned for the future of mortgage lending and one of its principal purposes: the acquisition of houses. Rising housing costs and increasing interest rates could overwhelm the market. Two major problems were involved: first, lenders with fluctuating and rising costs of money needed a method to match their income more closely to their cost of funds; second, home buyers needed a method to enter the housing market at a lower initial cost than was permitted with the high-interest constant-payment mortgage.

To assist the lender, regulators approved a series of mortgage repayment plans that allow the lender to make periodic adjustments in the rate of interest charged for a long-term loan. These interest adjustment plans, generally known as *adjustable rate mortgages*, have proliferated. There are well over 250 different plans now in use throughout the country. However, a few plans began to dominate the market in 1985, and the trend toward simplification of the various plans is continuing.

To assist the home buyer, another series of mortgage repayment plans has been developed that are known as *graduated payment mortgages.* The key element in the graduated payment plans is that the monthly payment amount is arbitrarily reduced during the early years of repayment with annual increases in the payment amount until the loan becomes fully amortized. The advantage is that the borrower is qualified as to payment amount versus income level based on the lesser payment amount for the first year.

The first major move toward greater flexibility in loan repayments began with the variable rate mortgage, which found wide acceptance in California through state-chartered savings associations. Then, in 1974, the Federal Housing Administration started an experimental program with graduated payment mortgages that resulted in congressional approval to implement the program nationally as of November 1, 1976. In the meantime, the Federal Home Loan Bank Board (FHLBB) had begun its own research into new designs for residential mortgage instruments—the Alternative Mortgage Instruments Research Study. As a result of this study, the FHLBB approved the writing of four new mortgage designs for federally chartered savings associations effective January 1, 1979. The four new mortgages were (1) variable rate mortgage (VRM), (2) graduated payment mortgage (GPM), (3) pledged-account mortgage (PAM), and (4) reverse annuity mortgage (RAM). For the first time, national approval had been given for the writing of conventional loans with other than constant-level amortization payments. Later, on March 27, 1981, the Comptroller of the Currency gave approval for adjustable rate mortgages to be written by national banks. As both lenders and regulators saw the need for greater flexibility in mortgage repayment plans to meet buyer capabilities and to soften the impact of higher-cost loans, new ideas proliferated.

By the early 1980s, it seems that everybody making mortgage loans wanted to design their own specialized plan. Too many minor variations in repayment plans caused some confusion. However, the need for more standardized mortgage designs by secondary market purchasers reduced the number to a few dominant plans.

Repayment plans can be classed in three categories: (1) fixed-interest, constant-level plans, (2) adjustable rate mortgages, and (3) graduated payment mortgages. A discussion of each category follows.

Fixed-Interest, Constant-Level Plan

The repayment schedule for a fixed-rate loan involves a constant payment for the life of the loan. Each payment is calculated so that all interest due to payment date is included, plus a portion of the principal. The periodic reduction of the principal balance is called *amortization.* For over half a century now, this has been the most widely used plan for home loans. It gave assurance to the home buyer that the loan payment would not increase during the life of the loan. It was not until the late 1970s that fluctuating interest rates and higher construction costs brought some changes in how loans could be repaid.

The new repayment plans, first called "alternative mortgage designs," gave both lenders and borrowers much greater flexibility in how to best meet changing requirements. Nevertheless, the fixed-rate loan has remained a very popular design. This is true even though it is usually offered at interest rates about 2 percentage points higher than adjustable rate mortgages. While the usage varies from time to time, fixed-rate loans generally account for about one-half of all loan originations. There are several reasons for its continuing popularity:

1. In periods of relatively low interest rates, borrowers are reluctant to commit to an adjustable rate mortgage that might suddenly increase in cost. So the fixed rate offers a sense of protection.

2. The growing use of mortgage pools to raise lendable funds in the financial markets tends to encourage fixed-rate loans. One of the problems for an investor in a mortgage-backed security is the uncertainty of cash flows: How frequently will borrowers prepay the principal? When you add to that the uncertainty of an adjustable rate pool of mortgages, the projection of an accurate return to the investor becomes even more difficult.

Adjustable Rate Mortgages (ARM)

An adjustable rate design is one that allows a lender to make a change in the rate of interest at periodic intervals without altering other conditions of the loan agreement. The term "adjustable rate mortgage," or ARM, is not always used in a precise manner. In media reports, the term has been used to indicate *any mortgage* wherein the payment amount changes. Another repayment plan, the graduated payment mortgage, offers changes in payment amounts but it is calculated on a very different basis and should not be confused with an ARM.

Adjustable rate mortgages are not new. Other free-world countries have wondered how the United States has been able to stick with fixed rates for so long. British mortgage lenders, called Building Societies, have offered only variable rate mortgages since 1932. Canada developed a pattern of short-term mortgage loans, like five years, that allows a lender to *renew* the note when it comes due and to make an adjustment in the interest rate. The renewal type of note has become known as the *Canadian Rollover*.

The early designs of adjustable rate mortgages contained limitations on the frequency and amount of each adjustment plus a "cap" on the total increase in interest rate permitted over the life of the loan. The first such design approved by the FHLB for federally chartered savings associations was called a *Variable Rate Mortgage* (VRM). It was not very widely accepted by lenders primarily because the limitations rapidly proved too restrictive in an escalating interest market. Remember, no lender is required to make any kind of a loan. An "approved" mortgage plan only means that it is legal for a regulated lender to offer such a mortgage—the lender does not have to offer the plan, and many have not. The initial VRM design limited interest rate changes to a maximum of .5 percent per year and to not more than 2.5 percent of the life of the loan. Such caps have generally been increased or eliminated.

Borrower Protection

The right to change an interest rate *during the term* of a mortgage loan can cause hardship for a borrower. Because both lenders and regulators are concerned over the problems that may be created for a home buyer, a number of protective measures have been written into residential ARM requirements. To clarify these measures, the Federal Reserve Bank Board amended its Regulation Z (the Truth-in-Lending regulation), effective as of October 1, 1988. It requires lenders to provide more extensive information to consumers/borrowers on the characteristics of adjustable rate mortgages. The rules have been adopted by federal agencies and other lending authorities and provide more uniform requirements. More specifically, the requirements fall into two categories as follows.

UP-FRONT INFORMATION REQUIRED

Certain information must be provided to the consumer at the time an application form is provided, or before a nonrefundable fee is paid, whichever comes first. The information required follows.

1. An educational brochure about ARMs must be given to the applicant. This can be either the *Consumer Handbook on Adjustable Rate Mortgages* published jointly by the Federal Reserve Bank Board and the Federal Home Loan Bank Board, or a suitable substitute.
2. Applicant must be shown by historical example how payments on a $10,000 loan would have changed in response to actual historical data on the index to be applied.
3. A statement must be given the applicant showing the payment amount on a $10,000 loan at the initial interest rate (the most recent rate shown on the historical example), and the maximum possible interest rate that could apply to the loan during its term.

SUBSEQUENT DISCLOSURE REQUIREMENTS

Notices must be given to the borrower during the term of the loan showing any adjusted payment amount, interest rate applied, index rate, and the loan balance at the time of adjustment. This notification must be made once each year during which there is a rate adjustment whether or not there is a payment change. The notice must be mailed not less than 25 days, nor more than 120 days, before the new payment is due. Further, the disclosure must indicate the extent to which any increase in the interest rate has *not* been fully implemented (meaning how much the index rate plus margin would exceed the rate cap). The notice must also state the payment required to *fully* amortize the loan if that payment is different.

Following is a more detailed explanation of the meaning of these requirements.

Use of an Index

One of the major protections offered to borrowers who accept an ARM loan is that any change in the rate of interest must be tied to the change in an index. The rule applies to regulated lenders making residential loans. An index is a published rate or yield approved by the lender's regulatory authority. Unlike the well-known banker's prime rate of interest, an index is not controlled by the lender. While a number of indexes have been approved by authorities across the country, four have achieved greater popularity. These are:

National Median Cost of Funds. Each month, insured savings institutions report to the FSLIC their cost of funds. This figure would be the average cost of all interest *paid* to their depositors on passbook savings accounts, savings certificates, and certificates of deposit.

Average Contract Interest Rate. Each month, insured savings institutions report through the FSLIC the interest rate *charged* for mortgage loans made the previous month. The rate reported is on new home loans and also on existing home loans.

One-Year Treasury Security Rate. The constant maturity yield on U.S. Treasury securities is reported daily, weekly, and monthly by the Federal Reserve Bank. While it is a more volatile rate than the others, it has become the most widely used index rate because FNMA/FHLMC apply it to their one-year ARM purchases.

Three-Year Treasury Security Rate. The U.S. Treasury security rate for 3-year notes is applied to ARMs that offer an adjustment period of three years; that is, the adjustment is made only once every three years.

HISTORICAL RECORD OF INDEXES

To illustrate the differences that can be found in the most popular indexes, Table 6–1 gives a comparison.

TABLE 6–1
Historical Record of Indexes

Year*	Cost of Funds	Contract Rate	One-Year Treasury	Three-Year Treasury
1977	n/a	8.84	5.29	6.22
1978	n/a	8.95	7.28	7.61
1979	n/a	10.08	10.41	9.50
1980	8.09	11.78	12.06	10.88
1981	9.50	13.24	14.08	13.01
1982	11.44	15.37	14.32	14.64
1983	10.14	13.04	8.62	9.64
1984	9.89	11.70	9.90	10.93
1985	9.75	12.09	9.02	10.43
1986	8.50	10.40	7.73	8.41
1987	7.22	9.19	5.78	6.41
1988	7.12	8.92	6.99	7.87

*Percentages as of January each year.

APPLICATION OF AN INDEX

Indexes are applied differently. Of the four indexes described in the previous section, only the "Contract Rate" index would normally be applied directly as the rate charged to the borrower. That is, if the contract rate indicated 10.40 percent in January 1986 (as shown in Table 6–1) at the time of loan origination, that would become the rate charged to the borrower. Assuming a one-year adjustment period, the rate shown in the index for January 1987 as 9.19 percent would apply for the second year. Then, for the third year, the rate would become 8.92 percent as shown in the table for January 1988. Lenders normally adjust these rates to the nearest quarter percent; thus, the 8.92 percent as applied would become 9 percent.

Rate Based on Index Plus Margin. Indexes other than the contract rate as illustrated in the previous section require the addition of a *margin*. The margin is determined by the lender and it is not a regulated amount. Normally it amounts to 2 to 2½ percentage points and is added to the index amount. The margin remains constant for the life of the loan; it is the index that changes. The most widely used index today is the one-year Treasury security rate illustrated in the following example.

Example

Using a one-year Treasury security rate as shown in Table 6–1, plus a 2½ percent margin, and applying it to a $10,000, 30-year loan, we get:

Loan Year	Index Rate	+	Margin	=	Rounded Rate	Remaining Term	Monthly Payment $10,000 Loan
1986 First	7.73%		2.5%		10.25%	30 yrs	$89.61
1987 Second	5.78%		2.5%		8.25%	29 yrs	$75.70
1988 Third	6.99%		2.5%		9.50%	28 yrs	$85.20

Rate Based on Index Movement. Another way to apply an index is to originate the loan with an agreed rate, then add or deduct the *movement* of an index. *Note*: the initial rate charged is not a regulated or controlled rate. This allows the lender greater flexibility in setting an initial interest rate while still complying with the requirement to tie any change to a regulator-approved index. The following example applies the same index as used in the previous example. The difference is that an origination rate of 11 percent is applied, then the *change* in the index each year is added or deducted from the previous year's rate.

Example

Using a one-year Treasury security rate as shown in Table 6–1 and applying the *movement* of that index to a $10,000, 30-year loan originated at an 11 percent rate.

Loan Year	Rate Last Year	Movement of Index Previous Rate	Present Rate	Percent Change	Rate Next Year	Remaining Term	Monthly Payment $10,000 Loan
1986 First					11%	30 yrs	$95.20
1987 Second	11%	7.73%	5.78%	−1.95%	9%	29 yrs	$81.00
1988 Third	9%	5.78%	6.99%	+1.21%	10.25%	28 yrs	$90.60

Obviously, there can be a difference in the rate paid by a borrower even though the identical index is applied. Regulations require that a rate be reduced if the index declines. However, an increase in accordance with an index is optional with the lender. The decline in all indexes between 1982 and 1988 meant that those homeowners with adjustable rate mortgages paid lower payments each successive year. So adjustables are not the cause of payment hardships during that period, as often reported in the various media.

Caveat. While a surge in foreclosures in the early 1980s discouraged lenders from offering low initial payments based on less than market interest rates (sometimes called "tease" rates), the practice still exists. The idea is to qualify a borrower's income for a lesser payment amount during the first year and then adjust the payment to a market rate the next year. In one instance, a home builder offered buyers first-year payments based on a 6.875 percent rate, moving the second year to an adjustable rate based on a Treasury security plus a 2.5 percent margin. If rates had remained unchanged, the second year's payments would be based on a 13 percent interest rate. It is this kind of potential increase in a payment amount that inspired the expression "payment shock," and rightfully so. Because sharp increases in payment amounts can cause a default, many lenders now limit the initial payment level. For example, the requirement might be "the effective interest rate for initial payments cannot be lower than 3 percent less than the nominal or actual interest rate for the loan." Because wording of the repayment clause in a mortgage can be difficult, it is important that the borrower (or the broker adviser) read the mortgage agreement carefully and ask questions of the lender until a complete understanding has been reached. There have been so many changes in how repayment clauses are handled that even some loan officers have found it difficult to stay abreast of the situation!

LIMITATIONS ON CHANGES (CAPS)

When regulatory authorities began approving adjustable rate designs in the late 1970s, there was concern for the potential of catastrophic increases in mortgage payments hurting home buyers and lenders alike. Initial limitations were tight, such as the FHLBB's variable rate design in 1979 that limited interest rate changes to not more than ½ percent per year and 2½ percent over the life of the loan. These introductory years for ARMS, 1979 through 1981, happened to span the greatest increase in mortgage interest rates of all times, averaging 2 percent each year for the three years. The result was little interest from lenders to offer the new designs. In the next year or two, regulators backed off the tight limitations in an effort to encourage the use of adjustable plans. And since the design is basically a lender-benefit plan, lenders began to show more support and ARMS became competitive: initial interest rates on ARMs were lowered to 1½ percent to 3 percent less than rates on fixed interest loans. Adjustable plans reached over half of the mortgage origination market by 1983. However, burgeoning foreclosures in 1983 and 1984 brought renewed interest in limitations on changes, this time by lenders who were hurt by foreclosures.

While regulations vary, and lenders' self-imposed limitations vary, the caps center on the following four aspects of adjustable rate plans:

1. *Interest rate change*   One of the more popular limits is the change permitted in the interest rate at the adjustment period. A 1 percent cap is commonly used, but some plans permit 2 percent.

2. *Interest rate change over the life of loan*   Sometimes called a limit on "rate swings," a popular cap is 5 percent. This means that over the life of the loan, regardless of index fluctuation, the payment cannot be increased, and in some loans decreased, more than 5 percent.

3. *Frequency of rate change*   This is a limit on how often a rate can be changed. It is a distinguishing feature of residential mortgage lending that does not permit a rate change every time the lender may want to do so. Federal regulations permit a change at least once a year, and up to once every five years. Some states permit changes as often as every six months. By far the most popular adjustment period is once a year.

4. *Mortgage payment amount*   A more recent popular limitation has to do with the payment amount itself. This kind of cap limits any increase in the payment amount to a percentage of the payment. The most popular limit has become 7½ percent. Thus, a $1,000 per month payment could not be increased to more than $1,075 in the second year, regardless of what the index might show on the interest rate.

Caveat.   A very important point in regard to all limitations: The cap may apply to the amount the borrower pays during the year, *but may not limit the amount owed*. There is no real standard on how the limits may be applied. Thus, an average rate change, or a payment amount, may offer a specific limit on what the borrower pays, but if the index shows a greater amount is actually due, the lender may add the unpaid amount to the principal balance. If this procedure is limited, it can be called a limit on *negative amortization*. Like all other repayment conditions this, too, must be disclosed and agreed to in the mortgage terms. Careful reading of these clauses becomes most important!

Another condition, of perhaps lesser concern, is the fact that some limitations apply to both increases and decreases in the application of an index. Thus, a 5 percent life-of-loan limit could stop a 13 percent loan from ever falling to less than 8 percent.

Graduated Payment Mortgage (GPM)

The graduated payment mortgage concept was first tested by the FHA as a method of allowing home buyers to pay lower initial monthly payments in the earlier years of a mortgage term, with payments rising in successive years to a level sufficient to amortize the loan within a 30-year term. With a lower initial monthly payment, the buyer might qualify for a loan with a lower income or, conversely, be able to buy a larger house with the same income. An added requirement is that the buyer must show reasonable expectation of an increase in annual income so as to meet the annual increase in monthly payments.

An inherent problem with the GPM is that even a constant-level payment, long-term mortgage loan allows very little payment on principal in the early years. So, with only a modest reduction in the payment amount, any allocation to principal may easily be eliminated along with a portion of the interest payment due.

Example

The constant-level payment on a $50,000 loan at 10 percent with a term of 30 years amounts to $438.79. The amount of this monthly payment allocated to pay off principal is about $25.00 during the first year. Thus, a reduction of the monthly payment below $413.00 per month would not allow for any reduction of principal, and would result in a probable accumulation of unpaid interest. When the graduated payment plan allows for payments so low that not all the interest is paid, each year's unpaid interest is added to the principal balance for repayment in later years.

For most of the plans currently in use, there is an accumulation of unpaid interest in the early years of the mortgage term; thus, the borrower ends the year with larger principal balances owing than when the loan was first undertaken. As mentioned previously, this is called *negative amortization*—the loan balance *increases* with each payment, rather than decreases. To avoid the possibility that the increasing amount of the loan balance could exceed the initial value of the property collateral, GPMs generally call for higher down payments than are necessary for constant-level payment plans. Down payments for this type of loan are calculated so the loan balance will not exceed the limits permitted, which are 95 percent of the initial property value for conventional loans, and 97 percent of the initial value for FHA-type loans.

A legal qualification is necessary in some states for this type of loan. The act authorizing the FHA program specifically pre-empts any state law that prohibits the addition of interest to the principal of a mortgage loan as it pertains to the manner in which the loan is repaid. This preemption is also claimed by federally chartered institutions that come under federal banking rules, not state rules.

The popularity of the FHA Section 245 GPM program has made the term *graduated payment mortgage* almost synonymous with FHA. (See Chapter 7 for more details on the FHA Section 245 program.) What the FHLBB approved in 1979 was a *conventional* loan to be written with graduated payment terms. However, the FHLBB leaned heavily on the experience developed under the FHA program and has used FHA procedures to set maximum limits for the conventional plans. Federally chartered savings associations are not required to offer a GPM but, if they elect to do so, whatever plan they offer cannot exceed authorized limits. As set by the FHLBB, these limits include a maximum annual increase in monthly payments for a five-year period of 7½ percent and a maximum annual increase for a 10-year period of 3 percent. The loan-to-value ratio cannot exceed 95 percent during the term of the loan. Under the FHLBB rules borrowers have the right to convert a GPM to a standard mortgage form at the borrower's option. To convert the mortgage, a borrower must be able to meet the association's normal underwriting standards. In most cases, this would mean that the borrower's income must be sufficient to allow a constant-level payment. Also, no fees or penalties are permitted for the conversion, providing all other terms remain the same.

Approval to write a conventional mortgage permitting graduated payments was granted during a period of considerable market uncertainty. Savings associations at that time were not seeking new ways in which to loan their limited funds. Under more competitive market conditions, there would be greater interest in this mortgage form as it fulfills a need. Young families buying their first home do not have the benefit of an escalating equity interest in an existing house to trade with. So, permitting lower initial monthly payments enables more family incomes to qualify for loans.

Initial concern with the GPM concept centered on the requirement for larger down payments to qualify. Would families with limited incomes and in need of lower monthly payments be those capable of making larger down payments? In practice, many families have taken advantage of the FHA program and have been able to handle the down payment—some with savings, some with parental help.

Pledged-Account Mortgage

For a number of years, some state-chartered savings associations have been making mortgage loans using a pledged savings account to provide additional collateral. Funds are withdrawn from the pledged account each month to supplement the mortgage payments. Normally, no additional cash is required to establish the pledged account since it comes from the money the buyer would otherwise have used as a down payment. The purpose of the procedure is the same as that of the GPM: to establish a lower initial monthly payment that can be used to qualify a lesser income for a larger house.

As of January 1, 1979, federally chartered savings associations have been permitted to write pledged-account mortgages. No change has been made in the maximum permissible loan-to-value ratio at 95 percent, and loans over 90 percent LTVR must carry mortgage default insurance. The calculations used to administer the pledged-account payments must contain the net risk within the 95 percent limit. The balance held in the pledged account is considered a part of the loan collateral and thus reduces the net mortgage risk.

A pledged-account plan conceived by Allan Smith of Newtown, PA, using the name *Flexible Loan Insurance Plan, FLIP mortgage,* and marketed as a computer program, provides a practical example of the calculations needed to implement the program. An example is used to illustrate the repayment plan.

Example

Consider a house costing $70,000 and a cash requirement of the buyer for $20,000. Instead of paying all the cash to the seller, a portion is deposited in a pledged account with the lender and becomes a part of the collateral securing the loan. For this example,

To pledged account	$12,100
Paid to seller	7,900
Total requirement	$20,000

The $7,900 paid to the seller gives the following mortgage requirement:

Cost of house	$70,000
Cash paid to seller	7,900
Remainder borrowed	$62,100

The mortgage loan in the amount of $62,100 is paid with an initial combination of the buyer's monthly payments plus a monthly supplement withdrawn from the pledged account. The sum of the two each month equals the $735.81 payment needed to amortize the $62,100 loan fully at 14 percent in 30 years. Each month the lender withdraws a portion of the pledged account principal, adds the earned interest on the account, and applies the sum of the two to the mortgage payment. Each year the supplement is reduced and the buyer's portion increased until the buyer is making the full payment. For this example, the buyer's payment and the supplement each month are calculated for a five-year supplemental period as shown in Table 6–2.

The lender initially holds as security for the loan a house worth $70,000 *plus* control of the pledged account, which adds to the collateral in the amount

TABLE 6–2
Pledged Account Mortgage—Sequence of Payment Changes

Beginning of Year	Buyer's Monthly Payment for Year	Plus	Pledged-Account Principal	Plus	Interest on Pledged Account	Equals	Total Monthly Payment
1	$380.05		$308.64		$47.12		$735.81
2	441.29		263.12		31.40		735.81
3	507.14		210.29		18.38		735.81
4	577.92		149.40		8.49		735.81
5	654.01		79.61		2.19		735.81
6	735.81		–0–		–0–		735.81

of $12,132.73.* Thus, the initial risk exposure of the lender is reduced to a loan-to-value ratio of only 71.38 percent. As the pledged account is reduced during the five years of withdrawals, the risk exposure climbs to a high (for this example) of 87.32 percent, well within the lender's risk limits. Table 6–3 is the annual change in mortgage balance and loan-to-value ratio.

Why pledge a portion of the $20,000 cash requirement in a pledged account? Wouldn't it be better to use the entire $20,000 to reduce the mortgage loan to $50,000 (the $70,000 price of the house less $20,000 equals $50,000)? The answer is clear: a $50,000 loan at 14 percent interest for 30 years requires a monthly payment of $592.44. Using the FLIP calculation for a pledged-account mortgage, the initial monthly payment drops to $380.05.† Obviously, more borrowers could qualify at the lower monthly payment amount.

TABLE 6–3
Pledged-Account Mortgage—Cumulative Effect of Payments

Beginning of Year	Mortgage Balance	Pledged-Account Balance	Net Mortgage Balance	Cost of House	Loan-to-Value Ratio
1	$62,100	$12,133	$49,967	$70,000	.7138
2	61,955	8,429	53,526	70,000	.7647
3	61,788	5,272	56,517	70,000	.8074
4	61,598	2,748	58,849	70,000	.8407
5	61,378	955	60,422	70,000	.8632
6	61,125	–0–	61,125	70,000	.8732

*The sum of $32.73 must be added to the pledged account to make the five-year supplemental payments exactly balance.

†Figures in this example used with permission of FLIP Mortgage Corporation, Newtown, PA 18940.

Buy-Down Mortgage

One of the more popular methods to arrange an alternative financing plan is for the seller, usually a home builder, to "buy down" the initial payment amounts. This is simply a variation on the normal discount procedure. The major difference is that a buy-down is a prepayment of interest costs for only a few years, whereas the discount is normally considered as prepayment of interest costs over the life of the loan.

Buy-downs can span any period, but generally are offered for periods of one to five years. The average buy-down, and the one acceptable for purchase by FNMA, is a three-year buy-down amounting to a 3 percent less-than-market rate in the first year, 2 percent for the second, and 1 percent the third. The procedure is sometimes called "3-2-1." The purpose is the same as that achieved by graduated payment plans—to reduce the monthly payments for the buyer in the early years of loan repayment. This helps a larger market of qualified buyers to be reached.

What the seller is actually doing is paying a portion of the interest cost in the early years. The following figures illustrate the cost reduction of interest on a $50,000 loan at a nominal interest rate of 16 percent with a three-year buy-down. The *nominal rate* means that named on the note and is the only interest rate shown.

Example

First, consider the round figure cost of a buy-down: To reduce the interest cost from 16 percent to 13 percent for the first year, the seller must pay 3 percent of the cost:

$.03 \times \$50,000 =$ $1,500

For the second year, the cost is 2 percent—

$.02 \times \$50,000 =$ 1,000

For the third year, the cost is 1 percent—

$.01 \times \$50,000 =$ 500
Total cost
   of buy-down $3,000

With a portion of the interest paid in advance, the buyer makes reduced monthly payments on a 30-year loan in the following amounts:

Year 1—$50,000 @ 13% = $553.10
Year 2—$50,000 @ 14% = $592.49

Year 3—$50,000 @ 15% = $632.22
Year 4—$50,000 @ 16% = $672.38

The precise calculation of the cost of a buy-down is not always uniform as lenders vary somewhat in allowing for the time value of money; that is, money paid in advance earns the lender additional interest, which can be used to reduce the cost of the initial buy-down payment.

While buy-down mortgages are an attractive inducement for buyers, they have lost favor with secondary market purchasers. Buy-downs have caused more than their share of home foreclosures in recent years and some limitations have developed. One limitation is to qualify the buyer at the note rate, not the first year's payment amount. Another similar limit is to require borrower income qualification based on the payment amount that will amortize the loan within its term.

Balloon Payment Note

An installment note that is only partially amortized over its term reaches maturity with a balance due (the periodic installments are insufficient to fully repay the loan during its term). So a final payment larger than the previous installment payments comes due. The final payment is often called a "balloon payment" because of its greater size.

The purpose of a balloon note is to keep the periodic installment payment at a lower level than otherwise required. One fairly common way of handling this kind of note is to set a term of, say, 10 years for repayment. Then the periodic payments are calculated as if the term were 30 years.

Example

A $100,000 loan is made at an interest rate of 10 percent for a term of 10 years. To fully amortize the loan over 10 years requires a monthly payment of $1,321.57. To allow a lesser payment, the amount is calculated as if the term is 30 years, thus offering a monthly payment of $877.58. At the end of 10 years, the balance due amounts to a balloon payment of $90,900.

If the federal Truth-in-Lending provisions apply to the loan, the amount of the balloon payment must be clearly stated in the contract.

Interest Only Note

An "interest only" note is one that calls for payment of the interest due at periodic intervals and the principal balance due in full at maturity. It is also known as a *term loan* and as a *straight mortgage note*.

A straight note is a nonamortized note usually made for a short term, such as three to five years. Prior to the 1930s, straight loans were very common in residential mortgage lending but have generally been replaced with fully amortized notes.

Shorter-Term Loans

As interest costs have remained relatively high and equity growth due to inflation has diminished, borrowers are looking more favorably at paying off mortgage loans in shorter terms. A good example of this trend is the following: In 1984, the Federal National Mortgage Association bought less than 1 percent of its loans with 15-year terms; in 1985 the percentage had increased to 15 percent for the shorter terms.

The 30-year term for a residential mortgage loan has become so widely accepted that many consider it an optimum time period. In an earlier era, there was greater concern for keeping a low equity in a house to make it more salable. For this purpose, the long-term mortgage had an advantage as very little is paid in the early years toward reduction of principal. Enthusiasm for minimal down payments and smaller monthly payments reached a peak in the 1970s when government housing experts began pushing the 40-year mortgage term. The longer term does reduce a payment amount but by very little. For example, in the accompanying payment chart (Table 6–4), the difference between a 30- and

TABLE 6–4
Cost Comparison Table for a $100,000 Mortgage Loan
at 13 Percent Interest

Term	Monthly Payment	Months Paid	Total Cost	Interest Cost
40-year	$1,089.17	480	$522,802	$422,802
30-year	1,106.21	360	398,236	298,236
20-year	1,171.59	240	281,182	181,182
15-year	1,265.27	180	227,748	127,748
10-year	1,493.16	120	179,179	79,179

a 40-year term payment amounts to $17.04 per month! The $1,106.21 monthly payment for a $100,000, 30-year, 13-percent loan is reduced to $1,089.17 on the 40-year schedule, but requires the payment for 10 years longer!

As construction costs and interest costs escalated in the 1970s, so did the value of houses. Indeed, a house became one of the better investments a person could make. With a profit almost assured from resale, little thought was given to interest costs over a longer period of time. But the 1980s produced a shocker as housing prices flattened and actually began to decline in some areas of the country. As the value of equity lost part of its allure, home buyers began looking for other ways to reduce housing costs.

What had been overlooked is the beneficial effect of reducing, rather than increasing, the loan term. The results in total savings on interest costs can be spectacular as shown in the payment chart.

The idea that shortening the term of a loan substantially increases the monthly payment seems to frighten many borrowers. For instance, doesn't cutting a 30-year term loan to 15 years just about double the monthly payment? Not at all! Take a closer look at the table and compare the monthly payment amounts. The difference between payments on a 30- and 15-year loan amounts to $159.06, or an increase of only 14 percent. And the loan is paid off in 15 years with a savings of $170,488 in total interest costs!

Biweekly Payment Plan.   Another method of accelerating the payment of principal to reduce total interest costs is the biweekly plan. For borrowers who are paid every other week, this method might be easier to budget. The calculation for such a payment amount is normally just one-half of a monthly payment, paid biweekly. For example, if the monthly payment for a 30-year loan amounts to $1,000, the borrower would pay $500 every other week. This amounts to 26 biweekly payments over the span of one year, amounting to $13,000. Compare this to the 12 monthly payments, which would total $12,000. The additional payments applied to principal reduction in the biweekly plan will pay off the loan in about 20 years depending, of course, on the rate of interest.

An important encouragement for this type of loan is that it recently became an approved loan for purchase by Fannie Mae. Loan originators can now offer this kind of loan and be assured of funding.

Growing Equity Mortgage.   Still another method that is used to shorten a loan term, and thus reduce interest costs, is called a growing equity mortgage, or possibly a *graduated equity mortgage*, both having the acronym of GEM. Many variations may be found, but the basic pattern is to make certain increases in the payment amount each year. Then, the entire amount of the increase is applied to repayment of the principal. Depending on the interest rate, of course, an increase of, say, 4 percent in the payment amount each year can reduce the term of a 30-year loan to 13 or 14 years. And the impressive reduction in total interest costs is similar to that described under the 15-year term.

Both the FHA and VA have approved this concept for early payment of a loan. For the FHA, acceptance comes under its Section 245(a) program (the graduated payment program), because it authorizes insurance on mortgages with varying rates of amortization.

Critics of the 15-year loan, the biweekly loan plan, and GEM mortgages suggest that a comparative analysis of the impact of loss of interest expense deductions and opportunity costs of not investing the 14 percent payment increase be considered on an individual taxpayer-borrower basis. There is no question these factors reduce possible savings but vary with each taxpayer.

Home Equity Revolving Loans

Pledging the equity in a home, or other property, to borrow money on a second mortgage has been a common procedure for many years. What is new is pledging the property to secure a *revolving line of credit*. Unlike a traditional second mortgage, which provides a single lump-sum payment, a home equity credit line stays in place for years. It gives the borrower more flexibility to finance everything from a child's education to a trip around the world. Interest is paid only on the portion of the credit that is used, just like a credit card account. Generally, the interest rate on the loan is adjusted periodically and floats without a maximum ceiling other than usury limits.

Equity credit lines have grown since the concept was first tried in California in the 1970s. By 1986, home equity revolving loans accounted for 23 percent of all outstanding second mortgages, which then totaled about $150 billion. What increases interest in this type of credit are the tax consequences. Since the collateral is a home, it is eligible for the same tax treatment for interest deductions as a home loan, but with certain limitations.

Only a few financial institutions, including some commercial banks and savings associations, offer home equity revolving credit lines. The concept presents some risks in that collateral may be adequate, but the borrower's income may become too easily overextended. It is this kind of credit line that gives some justification to the comment: "I bought the house on my credit card!"

Other Alternative Plans

Three other basic concepts need to be considered in the many variations now available in mortgage repayment plans. Two are shared financing methods, and the other is borrowing against home equity with a reverse annuity mortgage.

Shared Appreciation Mortgage (SAM)

When home values show a prolonged appreciation in value, lenders may find it profitable to take a portion of the expected return of their money from the appreciation. In the late 1970s, the Federal Home Loan Bank explored the idea and considered allowing its regulated institutions to write such a mortgage and accept a portion of the appreciation as "contingent interest."

For example, if market rates are at a 15 percent level, the lender could offer to make a loan at 10 percent and take one-third of any appreciation in property value over, say, the next 10 years. If the property is sold sooner, the lender is entitled to one-third of the appreciation at the time of sale. If the owner does not sell, the loan agreement could call for an appraisal at the end of 10 years. Based on the appraised value, the lender could then claim one-third of any net increase (additions to property not included). Payment to the lender could be made in a lump-sum cash payment, or it could be added to the loan balance and a new note written.

Obviously, in areas with declining property values, this concept would not be acceptable.

Shared Equity Mortgage

Shared equity is sometimes confused with shared appreciation. They are quite different. In the shared appreciation mortgage, the lender holds a claim, a lien, on that portion of property value representing an increase from the time of loan origination. But it falls short of title to the property. With a shared equity mortgage, two or more parties hold an ownership interest in the property.

The shared equity might be used in a family wherein a parent wants to help a son or daughter purchase a house. Or the concept is sometimes used by an employer, such as Stanford University, wishing to attract a new employee. Starting salaries may be insufficient to purchase houses in a high-cost area. In such a case, the employer shares ownership and mortgage liability with the employee. Or it might be used as an added inducement to encourage an employee to move to a remote or less desirable area. Normally, the employee in such cases is given an option to buy out the employer's share within a limited number of years. Or, in case of a transfer, the employer would be obligated to purchase the entire property at a fair price.

Reverse Annuity Mortgage (RAM)

The reverse annuity is another of the mortgage forms approved by the FHLBB as of January 1, 1979. However, it does not finance the acquisition of real estate as the other forms do. Rather, the reverse annuity utilizes the collateral value of a home as a means of financing living expenses for the owner. The basic purpose is to assist older homeowners who are pressed to meet rising living costs on fixed retirement or pension forms of income. With the use of a reverse annuity, the increased value of the home may be utilized without the owner being forced to sell it.

Where state laws permit (the owner's homestead rights may preclude this form of mortgage), a lender can advance monthly installment payments to the homeowner, using a mortgage on the home as security. The FHLBB rules governing the writing of RAMs require extensive disclosures to reduce the possibility of misunderstandings by the homeowner. Among the requirements is that a seven-day rescission period be allowed the borrower should a change of mind occur. Another is that a statement must be signed by the borrower acknowledging all contractual contingencies that might force a sale of the home. Repayment of the loan must be allowed without penalties and, if the mortgage has a fixed term, refinancing must be arranged at market rates if requested at maturity of the loan.

Interest on this type of loan is added to the principal amount along with each monthly payment made to the borrower. For a savings institution, the monthly payout of loan proceeds with interest added to the principal presents an altogether different cash flow problem.

In 1989, HUD/FHA introduced an experimental program to ensure a limited number of "reverse mortgages," and both Fannie Mae and Freddie Mac agreed to purchase them for their own portfolio investments. The amount of the loan is based on the equity value of the home but, for HUD/FHA approval, it cannot exceed a range of $67,500 to $101,250 depending on the geographic area. The monthly advances, plus accrued interest added each month, are designed to reach the maximum loan amount in terms of three to 12 years. Several different repayment plans are offered, including a sale of the house at time of death. To qualify, borrowers must be 62 years or older and live in the home, with little or no mortgage debt. A loan origination fee of one point may be charged, plus an up-front HUD/FHA mortgage insurance premium of two points. The annual insurance premium for the loan is one-half of one percent of the loan balance each year.

Questions for Discussion

1. How does a graduated payment mortgage help a home buyer?

2. Explain why an increase in interest rate without a change in the payment amount alters the term of a loan.

3. What is the major constraint on lenders in setting new interest rates on an adjustable rate mortgage?

4. Discuss the quality of the major indexes cited in the text.

5. Describe how a lender uses the "movement of an index" in setting a new interest rate at the adjustment period.

6. What is negative amortization and why is it associated with graduated payment mortgages?

7. How does a pledged-account mortgage function and why is it beneficial to the home buyer?

8. Describe a buy-down mortgage.

9. What is a growing equity mortgage?

10. Discuss the advantages and disadvantages found in shorter-term mortgage loans.

11. What is a "home equity revolving loan"?

12. Describe a reverse mortgage and its purpose.

7

Federal Government Underwriting Programs

KEY WORDS AND PHRASES

Federal Housing Administration
  (HUD/FHA)
Veterans Administration (VA)
Value for mortgage insurance
  purposes
Closing costs
Prepaid items
Mortgage insurance premium (MIP)
One-time MIP
Simple assumption
Formal assumption
Section 203(b)
Insured commitment
Section 203(b) Vet
Section 203(k) Rehabilitation
Section 234(c) Condominium
Section 245 (GPM)

Title 1 Home Improvement
Direct Endorsement Program
Property value
Loan guaranty
Veteran eligibility
Veteran entitlement
Restoration of entitlement
VA loan assumption
Veteran release of liability
Supervised and nonsupervised lender
Maximum interest rate
Funding fee
Maximum loan amount
Manufactured home attached to
  land
Certificate of Reasonable Value

There are many federal programs that provide assistance to people buying homes, or rehabilitating homes, or in need of housing following a natural disaster. However, this chapter is limited to the two major underwriting agencies that have assisted many people buying and/or rehabilitating their homes. Several of the government agencies that make direct loans to borrowers were discussed in Chapter 3 as a part of the primary market lenders. Neither of the agencies considered in this chapter makes direct loans, although both acquire properties in the course of their underwriting activities. And to facilitate the disposal of repossessed properties, they are in a position to help finance the resale.

The oldest, and probably the best known, of all government housing agencies is the Federal Housing Administration, now part of the Department of Housing and Urban Development. Its major programs will be outlined in this chapter. The Veterans Administration was granted authority during World War II to offer housing assistance to qualified veterans in the form of a partial guaranty of a home loan.

Both agencies have one feature in common: their underwriting activities are not paid for from tax revenues. They are all paid for by fees charged to those who use the programs. Occasionally, Congress approves subsidy programs that may be handled through HUD/FHA, but these are a separate category from the underwriting programs discussed in this chapter.

Department of Housing and Urban Development/ Federal Housing Administration (HUD/FHA)

The Federal Housing Administration was one of several score of agencies spawned during the Depression of the 1930s to help resolve economic problems that plagued the nation. It is one of the very few that has survived, and it has proven its value over nearly six decades of operation.

The reasons for which the FHA was formed in 1934 are still valid today, although the area of operations has expanded tremendously from the initial assistance program for home buyers. The purposes of the FHA are (1) to encourage wider homeownership, (2) to improve housing standards, and (3) to create a better method of financing mortgage loans. All these aims have been realized, even beyond original hopes. This was done without making a single loan, simply by sound use of government credit to insure mortgage loans. From its initial widespread rejection by many private lenders, a government-insured commitment now is readily salable to a large number of investors. Even in the tightest money markets, there has always been funding available for a government-insured loan.

Early History

When the FHA stepped into the housing picture in 1934, houses had been financed for 50 to 60 percent of their sales price on a first mortgage of three to five years, with a second mortgage and even a third mortgage at increasingly higher interest rates. By offering to insure a single large loan up to 80 percent of value (an extremely high ratio in those days), the FHA was able to insist that the down payment be made in cash, permit no secondary financing, and command a moderate interest rate. The loans were for long terms—up to 20 years at first —and were fully amortized over the life of the loan. Equal monthly payments were charged for principal and interest. Escrow accounts were established for hazard insurance and for taxes, to collect one-twelfth of the yearly cost each month. Each of these monthly payments also included a fee of one-half percent of the unpaid mortgage balance annually to cover the cost of mortgage default insurance. Most of these features were later incorporated into the loan guarantee program of the Veterans Administration, and have now become normal procedure for conventional loans as well. While none of these ideas actually originated with the FHA, this agency gave them wide usage for the first time and therefore brought about a sweeping reform in the field of residential financing.

As the FHA gained strength in its housing assistance, more titles and sections were added to its program. While the FHA has over 50 different programs to offer in its portfolio of assistance to borrowers for home loans, improvement loans, and multifamily project loans, our concern is primarily with loans for single-family residences. Under the assistance programs for home loans, the FHA has special help for members of the armed services, civilian employees of the armed services, and disaster victims, as well as programs in experimental housing, urban renewal, and condominium housing.

Implementation of the Insurance Commitment

All programs are implemented by the issuance of a Certificate of Insurance, which protects the lender against default. The differences between the programs are based on the kind of property and the qualifications of the individual who needs the help. There may be lower cash requirements and, in certain programs, an actual subsidy of interest costs. Also, the property must meet certain standards to qualify for an insured commitment.

Until several years ago, the FHA had been required to analyze each loan on the basis of its economic feasibility, and to limit its insured commitments solely to those families who presented a reasonable credit risk. The care with which the FHA has exercised its authority over the years is indicated by the fact that it has, in the past, returned over two-thirds of its insurance fees to the federal Treasury.

In the last 15 years, Congress has seen fit to recognize a growing social need for housing and has introduced a number of new programs through HUD/FHA, which are based not only on economic feasibility but also on a family's need for housing. This country has long supported various types of public housing built by government agencies and rented to lower-income families for well-below-market rents. Public housing of this sort has not worked out very successfully, and in 1965 Congress altered the direction of the program to place the problem in the hands of private business. Money previously allocated to support public housing was now to be used to subsidize private developers with the expectation that they could do a more effective and efficient job. The programs to activate these social objectives have been channeled through the FHA with the first funding for such a project as far back as 1966.

In January 1973, the Secretary of HUD announced a suspension of all government-subsidized housing programs pending a re-evaluation. Abuses and profiteering had been uncovered in some areas, and the Nixon administration felt a better method of giving assistance might be found. Meanwhile, reduction in spending would be more helpful. By January 1976, housing shortages and high costs continued to plague the home buyer, and President Ford ordered the release of the remaining assistance money that had been impounded three years earlier. Public policy has fluctuated in regard to subsidized housing programs since that time, but some assistance continues. Housing for the elderly, the handicapped and lower-income families still has subsidy assistance programs, but at a much lower level of funding than previously. In 1989, the Bush administration announced plans to improve housing programs.

HUD/FHA Terminology and Basic Procedures

To handle qualification of borrowers and the property offered as collateral, HUD/FHA follows certain procedures as detailed in its *Underwriter's Guide*. There are some words and phrases with special meaning in the world of HUD/FHA loan qualification. For example, a conventional lender measures the loan amount against the property value. With an FHA loan, the closing costs are added to the property value resulting in a sum called *value for mortgage insurance purposes*. The conventional lender focuses its cash requirement on a *down payment*; the FHA looks at the *cash required to close*. The purpose of qualification procedures is the same, whether FHA, VA, or conventional, and that is to qualify the borrower and the property. Nevertheless, to understand FHA procedures, it is necessary to understand the language.

Value for Mortgage Insurance Purposes

The amount of mortgage insurance available under any HUD/FHA insurance program is limited to a percentage of the *value for mortgage insurance purposes*. This value is a unique feature of the FHA-type loan and amounts to the sum of the property value plus permissible closing costs. In some of its literature, the FHA identifies this sum as "total acquisition cost." The amount used for property value is the *lesser* of the purchase price or the appraised value. To this value, HUD/FHA allows the buyer to add permitted closing costs and thus borrow additional money. Closing costs permitted are defined by the regional FHA insuring offices, in accord with local practices, and thus are not uniform. These costs include the HUD/FHA application fee, a lender's origination fee, costs of the title search, legal fees to prepare necessary closing instruments, and miscellaneous costs such as notary fees, recording costs, and a credit report charge.

Prepaid Items

HUD/FHA distinguishes between closing costs and prepaid items. In most FHA programs, prepaid items must be paid in cash at closing; that is, prepays are not included in the loan amount. Prepaid items are the costs of insurance premiums and property taxes, most of which are placed in an escrow account with the lender.

Hazard Insurance Premiums. A full year's premium for property insurance must be paid in advance of closing plus one month of premium placed in escrow. (HUD/FHA requires one month of all annual prepays to be held by the lender but allows two months to be held as a cushion.) The same requirement applies to flood insurance if applicable.

Mortgage Insurance Premium. While most of the popular FHA programs now require mortgage insurance to be paid in a one-time premium amount at closing (see next section for details), some of the programs still use the older one-half percent of the anniversary loan balance method annually (payable at one-twelfth of the annual amount each month). If the older monthly payment plan is applicable, an escrow deposit is required for it also.

Property Taxes. The borrower must pay whatever pro-rata share of property taxes may fall due for the first year plus one month in escrow at closing. (Lender is allowed to hold two months in escrow as a cushion rather than the one month that is required.)

To Apply for a HUD/FHA Loan

The application for an FHA-insured commitment must be made to an approved FHA mortgagee. The Veterans Administration requires the same procedure; the applicant must first apply to a VA-approved mortgagee. The mortgagee, to obtain "approved mortgagee" status, must be well acquainted with all agency procedures and stay abreast of changes that might occur.

The applicant works with the mortgagee to prepare the necessary loan documentation that may be required. The initial loan application made by the borrower (mortgagor) to the mortgagee is the standard Residential Loan Application form (see reprint in Appendix). The mortgagee handles the necessary verifications and assembles the loan package as will be needed for submission to the FHA underwriter. The HUD application for mortgage insurance is actually prepared by the mortgagee, not the borrower, for delivery to the FHA with the completed loan package.

As the loan package is assembled, the mortgagee must make sure certain documents are examined by the loan applicant, who must sign certifications of acceptance. This requirement applies to both the appraisal of the property and to the HUD-1 Settlement Statement used at closing. (See Chapter 12 for more details.)

Mortgage Insurance Premium (MIP)

Since its beginning, the FHA has charged the buyer/borrower a mortgage insurance premium of one-half percent on the loan balance per year. The "loan balance" is figured each year on the anniversary date of the loan origination. The one-half percent is divided into 12 monthly installments and is added to the monthly mortgage payment.

In 1983, a new payment procedure was adopted, then simplified in 1984, requiring payment of the full premium covering the life of the loan in cash at closing; or, as an alternative, the full amount of the premium could be added to the loan amount and becomes a part of the monthly mortgage payments. The new procedure is identified as "one-time MIP" and applies to certain programs as follows: 203(b), home mortgage insurance; 203(n), unit in co-op housing; 203(i), outlying properties; and 245, graduated payment mortgage (except that a 245 loan on a condominium unit is not subject to one-time MIP). The calculation is made with Table 7–1, which varies the premium with the term of the loan.

When the one-time MIP amount is added to the loan it can result in a loan in excess of the property value. This is acceptable to the FHA inasmuch as the one-time MIP payment is earned over the life of the loan and would be subject to substantial refund to the borrower in the event of a sale in the early years of ownership. To avoid confusion in processing loans, the actual loan-to-value ratio

TABLE 7–1
One-Time MIP Factor Table

Portion of MIP Financed	Repayment Term in Years			
	Less than 18	18–22	23–25	More than 25
100%	.02400	.03000	.03600	.03800
0%	.02344	.02913	.03475	.03661

is determined on the basis of the mortgage amount *without the MIP* divided by the appraised value of the property.

Under the newer rules, the buyer must either finance 100 percent of the MIP or pay the entire amount in cash. This applies to *all* the aforementioned programs, whether owner/occupants, nonowner/occupants, low-ratio loans, or Section 245.

To apply Table 7–1, the factor is multiplied times the loan amount.

Example

If the borrower opts to finance 100 percent of the premium, as most do, and the loan is $80,000 for 30 years, the premium would be

.03800 × 80,000 = 3,040.00 (total premium)

In this example, the premium amount of $3,040.00 would be added to the loan amount (see Section on 203(b) program later in this text for further example). Or, if the borrower opted to pay cash at closing, the amount would be .03661 × 80,000 = 2,928.80.

The calculation of one-time MIP is based on the discounted value of the older one-half percent annual premium. The one-time charge is approximately the present worth of the income stream generated by the one-half percent premium. By adding the one-time premium to the loan balance, a buyer pays about the same each month as under the older procedure. However, for government accounting purposes, the new procedure allows the premium to be reported as income at the time a loan is closed.

Premium Refund. While the FHA has always offered a refund of any unearned insurance premium when an FHA loan is paid off, it now has greater meaning. Under the older monthly payment method, unearned premium accumulated in the later years of the mortgage term and was seldom considered as being worthwhile. With one-time MIP, an early payoff of the loan can produce a substantial refund. The FHA uses factors depending on the number of years the loan is outstanding to determine the refund.* This should be considered in any FHA loan payoff or refinancing transaction.

*To satisfy the demand for information on potential refunds, HUD/FHA installed separate phone lines in their Washington office. For loans insured by monthly premium payments, call (202) 755-5645. For one-time MIP accounts, call:

For Mortgagee Case Numbers	Call
01001 to 22699	(202) 755-5250
22700 to 51799	(202) 755-5181
51800 and above	(202) 755-8156

Assumption of an FHA Loan

For many years, an FHA loan classed as "freely assumable." This meant that a borrower holding an FHA mortgage loan had the right to sell the property and assign repayment of the loan to a new buyer, without FHA or mortgagee's approval. While this right did exist, what was overlooked was the fact that an assignment by the mortgagee of the mortgage to someone without good credit-rating approval resulted in *no release of liability for the seller*. Thus, the seller remained fully liable for repayment of the loan for its life. So long as house prices escalated as they did in the 1970s through the early 1980s, there was not much of a problem. The few foreclosures that occurred generally resulted in repossession of a house of greater value than the mortgage obligation.

This situation began to change in the mid-1980s when repossessions increased as house values declined in some depressed areas of the country. What the FHA encountered was houses occupied by persons unknown to them, and the effort to notify the original obligor who remained liable was difficult since he or she most likely had moved away. Further trouble resulted when the original obligors contended they were no longer liable as the house had been conveyed along with the mortgage in accordance with what they believed to be an acceptable procedure.

To correct the situation, HUD/FHA changed the rules for loans underwritten after December 1986. Under the new rules, the "simple" assumption procedure was modified, while the "formal" assumption method remained intact. Further explanation follows.

Simple Assumption. For mortgages originated pursuant to an application signed by borrowers on or after December 1, 1986, HUD/FHA rules require a review of the creditworthiness of each person who seeks to assume an FHA-insured mortgage during the first 12 months after execution if the seller is an owner-occupant, and during the first 24 months if the seller is an investor (i.e., a rental house). Failure to comply with this requirement can result in acceleration of the loan balance through foreclosure action. After the one- or two-year period, HUD/FHA loans may be assumed without prior approval. However, should such an assumption occur, both buyer and seller remain fully liable on the loan balance for five years after the mortgage is executed. If the loan is not in default after five years, the seller is automatically released from liability.

The rule does apply to subsequent sale transactions consummated with a contract for deed, a lease purchase agreement, or a wraparound note. An exception applies if properties are transferred through devise, descent, or other operation of the law.

The automatic release after five years provision does limit the liability of the seller to a fixed term somewhat less than the former "remaining life of the loan." However, it clearly requires an approval for an early sale of mortgaged property under an assumption and points out the continuing liability of a seller in any assumption wherein the seller does not seek a release of liability as provided with a "formal assumption."

Formal Assumption.   HUD/FHA has always allowed, and encourages, home sellers to insist that any loan assumption be made only after the new buyer has been qualified. The procedure is called a formal assumption and allows a release of any further obligation on the part of the seller providing the new buyer meets FHA credit standards and formally agrees in writing to assume the loan obligations.

The additional time necessary to meet qualification standards for the new buyer can be irritating to both buyer and seller, but it is a safer course to follow. This is particularly true now that the FHA policy is to pursue collection of defaulted loans to the original obligors if they remain liable for same.

Loan Default and Foreclosure

The insured commitment on a HUD/FHA loan covers 100 percent of the loan amount since lenders normally loan exactly the insured amount. In the event of a default and foreclosure action, the usual practice has been for the FHA to pay off the loan balance with interest in exchange for an assignment of the mortgagee's claim to the foreclosed property. The property becomes federally owned and subject to resale as permitted under FHA rules.

With the substantial escalation of foreclosures beginning in the mid-1980s, HUD/FHA undertook a new policy. When a foreclosure becomes necessary, HUD/FHA appraises the property to determine its fair market value. If this value proves to be less than the amount due on the loan, the FHA will pay the difference between the fair market value and the loan balance to the lender. The lender is then allowed to make its claim for that difference without a conveyance of the property. The practice is known within the industry as a "claim without conveyance."

Its purpose, of course, is to limit the number of properties returned for the FHA to manage, rehabilitate, and resell. So long as the determination of fair market value by HUD/FHA is accurate, losses to the lender could be minimized. Nevertheless, lenders have been skeptical of the practice as it allows the FHA to set its own price on the amount of the insured commitment. Further, lenders feel much better served if they never have to undertake repossession of a foreclosed property.

Reporting Defaults and Foreclosures. Another change in practices since late 1986 is that the FHA, having been faced with some massive foreclosure problems, requires mortgagees to notify credit bureaus of defaults and foreclosures. This includes the names of original obligors who remain liable for the five-year time period in a simple assumption, should they fail to make good on the obligation.

Interest Rate

In August 1982, HUD/FHA offered the "Negotiated Interest Rate Program," which abandoned the long-standing mandatory limit on permissable interest rates. For the first time a borrower was permitted to pay a discount under certain popular FHA programs. By 1984, the FHA no longer issued interest rate ceiling quotations. However, the VA continued interest rate limitations for its own loan guarantees. Probably because of the long relationship between the FHA and the VA, the marketplace continued to categorize FHA loans in the same interest-rate-limited class as VA loans.

The purpose for setting out limitations to begin with was to protect a government underwritten loan from being abused by private lenders. Clearly, the borrower should not be forced to pay extra fees to a private lender for the government assistance. In practice, however, the marketplace has long balanced the mandatory fixed interest rate limits against current market yield requirements through an adjustment of the discount. The discount had to be paid by the seller and often was added to the price of the house. As the market for mortgage loans enlarged, and all mortgage loans competed with other credit demands, the true purpose of a discount prevailed—to adjust an interest rate so as to meet a market yield requirement. No lender is interested in earning less money simply to accommodate a government program. They can easily invest their funds in other kinds of loans. So in recognition of this market procedure, HUD/FHA now permits the applicable interest rate to float with current market conditions.

Secondary Financing with HUD/FHA-Insured Commitments

If the mortgagor uses any funds that require a lien to be placed on the property, it is considered as secondary financing and must be taken into consideration when determining the maximum insurable amount. This is true whether or not the note may be forgiven at some future date depending on the borrower's continued employment. HUD/FHA will insure first mortgages on property with secondary financing under the following conditions:

1. The first and second mortgages cannot exceed the applicable loan-to-value ratio or maximum mortgage limit for that area.

2. The payments under the insured first mortgage and the second mortgage do not exceed the mortgagor's reasonable ability to pay.

3. Any periodic payments on the second mortgage are collected monthly and are substantially in the same amount.

4. The repayment terms of the second mortgage (a) do not provide for a balloon payment before ten years or such other terms not acceptable to HUD/FHA, and (b) permit prepayment by the mortgagor without penalty.

HUD/FHA Program Details

There are now over 50 different programs offered by HUD/FHA. Their utilization varies somewhat across the country according to local situations. Some programs have become inactive due to loan limitations or qualification standards that no longer fit the changing housing market. This section examines the qualifications needed and the restrictions placed on several of the more popular programs.

1. Section 203(b)—Home Mortgage Insurance (including the special assistance offered veterans).

2. Section 203(k)—Rehabilitation Home Mortgage Insurance.

3. Section 234(c)—Mortgage Insurance for Condominiums.

4. Section 245—Graduated Payment Mortgages.

5. Title 1—Home Improvement Loan Insurance.

Section 203(b)—Home Mortgage Insurance

The basic 203(b) program authorized in the initial act of 1934 is still the most widely used home mortgage insurance program. Experience gained from this program has been used extensively in the development of many succeeding plans. As with all HUD/FHA programs, the property to be acquired and used as collateral for the loan must meet applicable standards. While there are no special requirements for the individual borrower, he or she must have a good credit rating and demonstrate an ability to make the required investment as well as handle the monthly mortgage payments.

Mortgage Limits. HUD/FHA no longer applies a standard limit on loan amount for the entire country. The Housing Act approved in April 1980 set the maximum loan amount at 95 percent of the median price of all new housing in the local area with a national limit of $67,500 for one living unit. Since that time, limits have been increased in specific areas of the country where costs have risen. Thus the limit is no longer uniform but varies in different sections of the country. In

1988, the maximum permissible limit was raised to $101,250. Higher limits are set for two- to four-living units.

Maximum Insured Commitment. As described, the insured commitment is a percentage of the value for mortgage insurance purposes (which is the value of the property plus closing costs). The various programs offered differ in which percentages are used and how they are applied. Following are limits currently in effect for the Section 203(b) program:

1. *For property approved prior to construction or completed more than one year,* 97 percent of the first $25,000 plus 95 percent of the value in excess of $25,000.

2. *For a nonoccupant mortgagor,* the maximum insured commitment shall be the lesser of (a) the statutory mortgage limit in the subject area, or (b) 75 percent of the value plus closing costs, or (c) 75 percent of the acquisition cost.

3. *For property not FHA approved prior to construction and less than one year old,* 90 percent of the value including closing costs unless covered by an acceptable insurance-backed protection plan. (This limit also applies to veteran applicants.)

Example

203(b) Insured Commitment Calculation

Value of property and closing costs =		$63,400.00
.97 × 25,000 = 24,250.00		
.95 × 38,400 = 36,480.00		
60,730.00		
Amount rounded down to nearest $50		60,700.00
Cash required to close		$ 2,700.00
One-time MIP for 30-year loan 100% financed:		
60,700 × .038 =	2,306.60	
Plus: Property commitment	60,700.00	
Total insured commitment	$63,006.60	

Section 203(b) (Veteran). Under 203(b), HUD/FHA has a special concession for qualified veterans—it allows an insured commitment of 100 percent of the first $25,000 instead of the insured commitment of 97 percent it allows for nonveterans. The program is valuable because it has a broader application than the one available under the Veterans Administration. The basic differences are

1. The FHA qualification requires 90 days of active duty and a discharge other than dishonorable. The VA has longer time spans of required service at different periods of time such as hot war, cold war distinctions. (See VA requirements later in this chapter.)

2. The FHA does not require owner occupancy for veterans to qualify, while the VA does. VA limits its benefit to one house at a time, to be occupied by the veteran.

3. The FHA does not take into consideration any prior commitment of the veteran's entitlement, while the VA must deduct any previous usage of the entitlement if the loan has not been paid off or assumed by another veteran acceptable to the VA.

HIGHER COMMITMENT FOR SMALLER LOANS

On June 24, 1985, the insured commitment amount was increased for loans under certain sections of the Act for property with a value for mortgage insurance purposes of $50,000 or less. The insured commitment is a flat 97 percent of the value (which includes closing costs). There is no 95 percent calculation. Application is for Sections 203(b), 203(k), 223(e), 234(c), 245(a), and 251 only.

Example

Property value for mortgage insurance	$50,000
Insured commitment:	
.97 × 50,000 =	48,500
MIP: .038 × 48,500 =	1,843
Total insured commitment	$50,343

In the above example, the insured commitment exceeds the value of the property. It is an acceptable amount because the mortgage insurance premium is earned over the life of the loan. Default of the loan in the early years would cause a release of the unearned portion of the premium.

Section 203(k)—Rehabilitation Home Mortgage Insurance

To help restore and preserve the nation's existing housing stock, a major revision of the old 203(k) program was implemented in June 1980. Unlike any other HUD-insured program, 203(k) combines a purchase money mortgage with a construction loan. The new revision offers an insured commitment [same limits as 203(b)] that allows the purchase of an existing house over one year old, plus sufficient additional money to rehabilitate the property. The program is limited to one- to four-family dwellings and can be utilized as follows:

1. To purchase and rehabilitate a dwelling and the real property on which it is located.
2. To refinance existing indebtedness and rehabilitate such a dwelling.

A single insurance commitment combines the funds needed to purchase the property or refinance existing indebtedness, the costs incidental to closing, and the money needed to complete the proposed rehabilitation. The money allocated to rehabilitation must be escrowed at closing in a Rehabilitation Escrow Account. This fund includes any money allocated to the contingency reserve as determined by the HUD Construction Analyst, but the contingency cannot exceed 10 percent of the cost of rehabilitation. This account must be kept separate and cannot be used to pay taxes or insurance. Further, the account must pay interest each month to the borrower at not less than 5 percent per annum.

If the 203(k)-insured commitment involves insurance of advances, which would be normal when rehabilitation is required, then a Rehabilitation Loan Agreement must be executed by the lender and the borrower. As a part of this agreement, there must be an Inspection and Release schedule that details the amount of escrowed money that can be released at each stage of completion.

Before any release of funds can be made by the lender holding the escrow account, an inspection must be made to determine satisfactory completion of the work to that stage. Inspection is made by HUD-approved fee inspectors from a list provided by the HUD field office. The number of inspections required will vary with the complexity of the rehabilitation but cannot exceed four plus the final one.

While the program does not specifically list it, Section 203(k) can be used to convert existing single-family homes into multiple-unit dwellings for up to four families. Because this program is fairly complex and requires additional supervision by the mortgage lender, it has not been widely offered.

Section 234(c)—Mortgage Insurance for Condominium Housing

HUD/FHA insures mortgages for the purchase of individual family units in multifamily housing projects [234(c)]. They also insure loans for the construction or rehabilitation of housing projects intended for sale as individual condominium units [234(d)]. A condominium is defined as joint ownership of common areas and facilities by the separate owners of single-family dwelling units in the project. To be acceptable for FHA insurance, the project must include at least four dwelling units, and it must be approved by FHA. At least one other unit in each project must be acquired under the government-underwritten program. One person may own as many as four units financed with HUD/FHA-insured mortgages, provided he or she lives in one of them. However, the FHA will only process one nonowner-occupant for every owner-occupant.

Before a loan can be insured for a single condominium, the entire project must meet HUD/FHA minimum standards just as a new subdivision must meet compliance standards. The agreement under which a homeowners association may function comes under scrutiny, as do the rights of the developer. A question such as "When does the developer vacate the premises?" becomes more important with a condominium as it affects control of the common areas. Under FHA requirements, the developer may not claim a right of first refusal to offer condominiums for resale.

Mortgage Limits and the Insured Commitment. Both the maximum amount of mortgage loan permitted and the calculation of the maximum insured commitment are determined on the same basis as that of the 203(b) program described earlier in this section.

Section 245—Graduated Payment Mortgage

Several years of experimental testing provided the groundwork for HUD/FHA to offer an insurance program for graduated payment mortgages approved nationally in November 1976. The purpose of the program is to reduce monthly payments in the early years of the mortgage term so that families with lower income and reasonable expectation of future increases can qualify for suitable housing in a higher-cost market. Acceptance of the program has been very favorable and has enabled many young families to purchase their first home. The key benefit for the applicant is that income qualification is based on the monthly payment required for the first year.

Section 245 is limited to owner-occupant applicants—there are no other special qualifications. As in other programs, the applicant must have a good credit record, demonstrate ability to make the required down payment, and be able to handle the monthly mortgage payments. There is one additional requirement—the applicant must have a reasonable expectation of an increased annual income in future years. Initially, the program was targeted for first-home buyer families but was not so limited.

The lower monthly payments in the early years under most of the HUD/FHA Section 245 plans are insufficient to pay anything on principal and not all of the interest due each month. Consequently, each year the unpaid interest is added to the principal balance due. Since the loan balance is increased, rather than reduced or amortized, the result is called *negative amortization*. To prevent an increase in the loan balance from exceeding the value of the property, higher down payments may be required.

Section 245—Repayment Plans. HUD/FHA insures graduated payment mortgages with five different repayment plans. These are differentiated by the rate of payment increases each year and the duration of the escalation period. Three plans offer 2½, 5 and 7½ percent annual increases for the first five years; two plans offer 2 percent and 3 percent increases for the first 10 years. Stated another way, the initial monthly payment amount is so calculated that it can be increased each year at a fixed, or predetermined, rate so as to reach a constant-level payment amount by the sixth year for the five-year plans and by the eleventh year for the 10-year plans. The amount of the monthly payment, the mortgage insurance premium, and the down payment required depend on the interest rate and the term of the loan. To simplify the calculation of these amounts, the FHA has published a series of tables that give factors to be used in the calculation of payment requirements. The calculation method and an example are given later in this section.

Mortgage Limits. The maximum amount of the insured commitment (equals the loan amount) for Section 245 is the same as that applied to Section 203(b) commitments. Section 245 plans make it possible for the loan amount (that is, the principal balance due on the loan) to increase due to the negative amortization feature (adding unpaid interest to the principal balance each year). Thus the loan balance can increase to an amount greater than the initial authorized maximum loan amount. This possibility is recognized and does not constitute a violation of the National Housing Act, so long as the down payment computations are made in accordance with Section 245 instructions.

Calculating the 245 Insured Commitment. To comply with the requirements, it is necessary to make two separate calculations to establish the correct maximum insured commitment. Since the insured commitment almost always becomes the amount of the loan, the difference between the commitment and the contract price is the required down payment. The first calculation that determines the insured commitment, called Criterion I in the example that follows, is the same as that required for Section 203(b) qualification. The second calculation, Criterion II, is in accordance with the Section 245 formulas. The *lesser* of the two calculations is the amount of the insured commitment. Under Criterion II for the nonveteran applicant, the procedure is to take 97 percent of the property value (including closing costs) and divide the result by the highest outstanding balance factor for the applicable plan and interest rate. Different procedures apply for veterans and for property constructed without FHA prior approval, or less than one year old.

Example

To calculate the down payment amount and the monthly mortgage payments applicable to a HUD 245 mortgage loan the applicant must refer to a HUD/FHA Graduated Payment Factor Table.* The table provides factors listed in accordance with differing interest rates and the HUD payment plan that applies. An example of the factors is shown in Table 7–2 on a very limited basis as applied to only three plans and two different interest rates.

For this example, assume a property value of $60,000 and closing costs of $1,000, for a total value for mortgage insurance purposes of $61,000. Say that the loan requested is for a 30-year term, at an interest rate of 13 percent, using Plan III. (Plan III offers payment amounts increasing at 7½ percent each year for the first five years.) Remember, the calculation must be made by two separate criteria to determine which offers the *lesser* loan amount.

Criterion I [same as 203(b)]
.97 × $25,000	= $24,250
.95 × $36,000	= $34,200
Loan amount	= $58,450

Criterion II (245 calculation)
.97 × $61,000	= $59,170
$59,170 ÷ 1,089.8422	= 54.2922
54.2922 × $1,000	= $54,292

TABLE 7–2
HUD/FHA Section 245 GPM Factors

	Principal Balance Factor	Monthly Principal and Interest (P & I) Factors (per $1,000 of original loan balance)					
		Year 1	*Year 2*	*Year 3*	*Year 4*	*Year 5*	*Year 6+*
		RATE: 13.00%					
Plan I	1020.7547	10.1560	10.4099	10.6701	10.9369	11.2103	11.4906
Plan II	1055.1576	9.3243	9.7905	10.2800	10.7940	11.3338	11.9004
Plan III	1089.8422	8.5618	9.2040	9.8943	10.6363	11.4341	12.2916
		RATE: 14.00%					
Plan I	1025.4470	10.9008	11.1734	11.4527	11.7390	12.0325	12.3333
Plan II	1063.2066	10.0279	10.5293	11.0558	11.6086	12.1890	12.7985
Plan III	1100.2169	9.2252	9.9171	10.6609	11.4604	12.3200	13.2440

*Available from any HUD/FHA office.

By the calculations, Criterion II offers the *lesser* loan amount and, therefore, is the applicable number, rounded down to $54,250. The difference between the loan amount and the purchase cost is the down payment; thus, $61,000 minus $54,250 equals $6,750.

Now the cost of the mortgage insurance premium must be added as a one-time charge at closing. For this example, consider that 100 percent of the MIP will be financed (added to the loan amount at closing). To calculate:

54,250 × .03800	2,061.50
Add: Property loan	54,250.00
Total insured commitment	$56,311.50

The next step is to figure the monthly payment amounts. Again, refer to the abbreviated Table 7–2. At a 13 percent interest rate for Plan III, the table shows a monthly P & I factor of 8.5618 for the first year's payments. To calculate, change the loan amount to $1,000 units as follows:

56.31150 × 8.5618 = 482.13 (first year's P & I payment)

And for the second year,

56.31150 × 9.2040 = 518.29

Then continue the calculation for each successive year, always applying the P & I factor to the initial loan amount. The amount of the sixth-year payment in this example remains constant for the life of the loan.

Title 1—Home Improvement Loan Insurance

One of the popular programs offered by HUD/FHA is insurance on loans to finance home improvements. The money may be used for major or minor improvements, alterations, or repairs of individual homes and nonresidential structures, whether owned or rented. Lenders determine the eligibility for these loans and handle the processing themselves. The smaller loans in this category are usually handled as unsecured personal loans (recording of a mortgage instrument is not required).

Any creditworthy property owner is eligible for a Title I loan. Loans may also be made to tenants for improvement of leased apartment units, providing the lease term is at least six months longer than the term of the loan. In addition, Title I covers the insurance of loans on mobile homes (manufactured housing) that do not qualify as real estate. Whether or not a mobile home qualifies as real estate depends on state laws and how it is taxed. States generally base the tax on whether or not the unit is permanently attached to the ground.

HUD/FHA Qualification Procedures

Since its beginning, HUD/FHA has trained its own valuation and mortgage credit groups to handle the qualification of loan applicants so as to assure compliance with the special requirements of the various programs. Guidelines are furnished in a comprehensive "Underwriter's Guide," supplemented with an almost continuous flow of updated information to stay abreast of changing needs and new laws. Even so, the process has never fitted a computerized program and still requires personal decisions by the underwriter to determine qualification accurately. No two applications are alike, and judgment calls are necessary to determine proper approval or disapproval. The system has always permitted sufficient flexibility to allow a review of the decision if the applicant or mortgagee feels an error has been made.

Direct Endorsement Program

In 1983, HUD established the Direct Endorsement Program in an effort to both reduce its costs and simplify the process for mortgagees (the mortgage lenders) to secure insurance endorsements. Under this program, the mortgagee underwrites and closes the mortgage loan without prior HUD review or approval. The authority to participate in this program is a privilege granted to mortgagees on the basis of demonstrated qualifications, experience, and expertise. Key elements of the program include the following:

Underwriter. The focal point of the program is the underwriter who must be a full-time employee of the mortgagee with authority to bind the company on the origination of a mortgage loan. The underwriter must meet special HUD/ FHA qualifications for knowledge and experience and carries direct responsibility for compliance with HUD/FHA rules and instructions.

Mortgagee Staff Technicians. Mortgagees may use their own staff to perform appraisals (with certain exceptions), inspections, and mortgage credit analyses. The individuals involved in this work must meet HUD/FHA qualifications for the various disciplines.

Offices. Each office of a mortgagee (main office and branches) must be approved by the HUD field office to which it submits mortgages for insurance.

Under the Direct Endorsement, the mortgagee qualifies both the property and the borrower in accordance with the appropriate HUD requirements. Under "post endorsement status" (meaning after conclusion of the learning stage called "pre-endorsement status"), the designated underwriter for the mortgagee reviews the loan package for full compliance with HUD standards, authorizes the loan to be closed with funds disbursed, and executes an "Underwriter Certification" for submission to the HUD field office. HUD then reviews the documentation to determine (1) eligibility of the mortgagee for Direct Endorsement, (2) whether or not there are any unauthorized variations in loan term or maximum dollar amount, and (3) that required forms and certifications are included. If these provisions have been met, the mortgage is endorsed for insurance and the executed Mortgage Insurance Certificate is sent to the mortgagee.

The program has been designed to give the mortgagee sufficient certainty of HUD approval to justify undertaking the responsibility. Essentially what HUD requires is compliance with its rules and does not "second-guess" the underwriters' qualifications decisions. HUD does make a post-endorsement review, and if underwriting deficiencies are discovered in the loan documents an underwriting report is sent to the mortgagee. However, the insurance contract is incontestable except in cases of fraud and misrepresentation. If the mortgagee continues to submit marginal-type loans under this program, its authority under Direct Endorsement may be withdrawn.

Analyzing the Loan Application

In the past few years, the various government agencies involved with underwriting home loans have made a concerted effort to simplify the procedures with standard forms used by all agencies and the acceptance of each others' appraisals and general procedures. A big step was taken in January 1982, when a new application form was released combining HUD Form 92900, VA Form 26-1802a, and the FMHA Home Loan Guaranty form. This is the application form that a mortgage company submits to HUD/FHA for mortgage insurance based on information obtained from the borrower's loan application and subsequent verifications.

The property and the borrower are processed separately in determining qualification. Procedures that are followed for approval of the property are outlined in the paragraphs that follow. Qualifying the borrower is explained in Chapter 8, Borrower Qualification, which includes both the VA and conventional methods so that an easier comparison of the processes can be made.

QUALIFYING THE PROPERTY

The FHA requires an appraisal of the property offered as collateral to be made by one of its staff appraisers or by an FHA-approved fee appraiser. Here are the distinctions made for four basic categories of property:

1. *Proposed construction*   To qualify, plans and specifications are submitted to HUD/FHA *prior* to the start of construction. If found acceptable, the approved plans and specifications are certified and returned to the mortgagee.

2. *Low-ratio properties*   For loans of 90 percent of the value, not approved by HUD or VA prior to construction, not covered by an acceptable warranty plan, and the property is less than one year old at date of application, HUD requires an appraisal by its own staff or a HUD-assigned fee appraiser to determine the value.

3. *Existing construction*   Property completed at least one year prior to date of application must be appraised by a staff appraiser or a fee appraiser assigned by HUD/FHA.

4. *Warranty plan*   If a property is covered by a warranty plan approved by HUD, a conditional commitment by HUD/FHA or a VA CRV (Certificate of Reasonable Value) may be used to qualify the property.

Property Value.   HUD/FHA defines property value; that is, the value of the house and land, as the *lesser* of the FHA-appraised value or the acquisition cost. Since it is normal for an earnest money contract to be signed *prior* to making an appraisal, it is possible for an appraisal to reflect a lower value than the agreed-upon price. Should this occur, FHA rules permit the buyer to withdraw from the earnest money contract (unilaterally rescind it) and recover the earnest money in full. Or, should the buyer prefer, the purchase can be made, but any amount paid over the appraised value must be made in cash. The amount of the loan is calculated as a percentage of the appraised value in such a case. Another frequently used option is to renegotiate the contract to reflect the appraised value.

Determining Value.   HUD/FHA appraisals are made in the same manner as other appraisals with one slight difference: because of the volume of FHA activity, they retain substantial records of previous transactions that can be used for making good comparisons with other sales. However, the FHA has the same problem as VA and conventional loan underwriters with the impact of seller buy-downs of loans on the price of a house that may be used as a comparable. Over a period of time, it is quite possible for a home builder to offer an attractive buy-down for a loan, add its costs to the price of the house, and develop an inflated "market value" that could be used as a sales comparable. HUD/FHA addresses this problem in two steps: (1) all appraisals must now include as additional information the amount of loan discount when the house was acquired, and (2) excessive buy-downs must be deducted from the value of any house used as a comparable.

Example

Say that a $70,000 loan was made to the homeowner with an 8-point discount and buy-down tied in. Say that in the region involved, the FHA considers anything over 5 points to be "excessive." This would mean that 3 points amounting to $2,100 of the $70,000 loan amount is considered a reduction in the sales price for that property. Thus, if the listed sale price had been $76,000, its true price for use as a comparable would be $73,900 ($76,000 minus $2,100 equals $73,900).

Scope of Appraisal. The HUD/FHA appraisal contains other important information. The appraiser also determines what repairs may be needed to restore the property to acceptable FHA standards. Special inspections may be called for to examine the roofing, plumbing, electrical system, the heating/air conditioning system and the water heater. If deficiencies are found, the property must be brought up to standard before the loan can be funded. The seller may make the repairs or, in some cases, the buyer may do the work as part of the buyer's cash contribution—a "sweat equity" contribution.

Veterans Administration

The popularly called GI Bill of Rights was passed by Congress in 1944. It was designed to give returning World War II veterans a better chance upon resuming civilian life than their fathers had after World War I. While the initial bill, and subsequent additions, provided numerous other benefits such as hospitalization, education, employment training, and unemployment benefits, our interest here will be confined to the home loan section.

Section 501 of the act provides for a first-mortgage real estate loan that is *partially* guaranteed by the Veterans Administration and is subject to strict rules covering all phases of the loan: the borrower, the lender, the property, the interest, the term and loan amount, plus collections and foreclosures. The primary interest of the VA is to aid the veteran, and to this end the rules are directed.

While the HUD/FHA *insures* 100 percent of its approved loans, the Veterans Administration *guarantees* only a portion of the loan amount. Since the guarantee reduces the risk exposure for a lender, it is a very acceptable loan. The VA does not have a cash requirement for a borrower to qualify. No down payment is required, payment of closing costs is not required, and the borrower is prohibited from paying any loan discount unless the new loan is refinancing to pay off existing loans. Even the 1 percent VA funding fee can be added to the loan amount. However, the "no cash" rules describe what is acceptable to the VA for its loan approval. This does not prohibit a lender from requiring a down payment and an origination fee paid by the veteran, so long as the requirements are applied in a nondiscriminatory manner. Nevertheless, the lender cannot require the veteran to pay any portion of a loan discount; that must be paid by the seller. Thus, even though a VA loan may be found with no cash required of the veteran, many lenders believe some investment on the part of a borrower makes a more acceptable loan.

Not all veterans are eligible for a home loan guarantee. They must meet certain minimum requirements of time served on active duty. The differences between what is meant by *eligibility* and *entitlement* are more fully described next.

Eligibility of a Veteran

To be eligible for a home loan guarantee, the veteran must have served on active duty a minimum amount of time that varies during different periods—lesser time during periods of "hot wars" and longer for others. Table 7–3 lists the time periods and duration of active duty required for eligibility. Certain surviving spouses of persons who died as a result of service-connected disabilities or while on active duty in the armed services may also be eligible.

Eligibility is no longer subject to an "expiration" date. The former limits that would deny veterans of previous wars their eligibility at certain points in time have been eliminated.

For any veteran considering the purchase of a home, it is a good idea to ask the Veterans Administration Regional office to confirm eligibility. This is done by submitting VA Form 26-1880, Request for Determination of Eligibility and Available Loan Guaranty Entitlement. The VA response answers both questions: Is the veteran eligible? and if so, How much is available in the entitlement?

TABLE 7–3
Eligibility Qualification

Period of Time	Days of Active Duty
September 16, 1940 to July 25, 1947	90
July 26, 1947 to June 26, 1950	181
June 27, 1950 to January 31, 1955	90
February 1, 1955 to August 4, 1964	181
August 5, 1964 to May 7, 1975	90
May 8, 1975 to September 7, 1980	181
September 8, 1980 to present	24 months*

*Persons on active duty are required to serve 181 days with certain exceptions permitted.

The Loan Guaranty Entitlement

The amount of money that the VA will guarantee for a veteran is called an *entitlement*. At its origin in 1944 the entitlement amounted to $2,000, increasing in later years, as shown in Table 7–4, to the limits set in 1988 on a sliding scale up to $36,000. Always there has been an additional limitation that is a "not-to-exceed" percentage of the loan amount. That limit was 60 percent until February, 1988, when the percentage limit was reduced to 50 percent on loans up to $45,000 and 40 percent for larger loans.

If both husband and wife are eligible veterans, the guarantee may be twice the dollar amount, but cannot exceed the applicable percentage limitations.

ENTITLEMENT HISTORY

As housing prices increased over the years, Congress increased the amount of entitlement available to veterans. Table 7–4 lists the changes.

TABLE 7–4
Entitlement Increments

Original act, 1944	$ 2,000
December 28, 1945	4,000
July 12, 1950	7,500
May 7, 1968	12,500
December 31, 1974	17,500
October 1, 1978	25,000
October 7, 1980	27,500
February 1, 1988	36,000

PARTIAL ENTITLEMENTS

If a veteran sells a house with an assumption of a VA loan, the Veterans Administration remains liable to the holder of that note (the lender) until it is paid off. This is true whether or not the selling veteran has obtained a release of liability from the note. So when this occurs, the veteran's entitlement for that particular loan remains committed insofar as the VA is concerned. This means that the amount of entitlement committed cannot be used to acquire another property. However, when the entitlement amount itself is increased, the additional amount becomes available for further use. Thus, under such circumstances, a veteran may be eligible for *partial entitlement*.

Example

Consider a veteran who purchased a home in 1975 on a VA guaranty that amounted to $17,500 at that time (refer to Table 7–4). The home is sold in 1988 with an assumption of the old loan by the new buyer. If the veteran seller did not obtain a restoration of full entitlement at the time, there is still a new entitlement amounting to the difference between the $17,500 that remains committed and the 1988 entitlement of up to $36,000, or a possible $18,500 available.

RESTORATION OF ENTITLEMENT

Referring again to the above example, had the veteran taken the necessary steps at the time the old house was sold, it would have been possible to restore a full entitlement for further use. There are two ways that the veteran can regain the use of the guaranty privilege, or to use the VA's terminology, "restore the entitlement." These are:

1. Pay off the loan through sale of the property. Restoration of the entitlement can be obtained by disposition of the property and paying off the loan in full. Under a VA guaranty, a veteran can own only one house, which must be his or her principal residence.

2. Under a provision of the Veterans Housing Act of 1974, a new procedure was added that is Substitution of Entitlement. To qualify under this provision, the veteran can sell his or her home on an assumption basis, but only to another qualified veteran. The purchasing veteran must (a) have the same amount or more of entitlement as the selling veteran, (b) meet the normal income and credit requirements, and (c) agree to permit the entitlement to be substituted.

For many years the VA also required that there be a compelling personal reason for the sale, such as a job transfer, to restore a veteran's entitlement. *This is no longer necessary.*

SLIDING SCALE ENTITLEMENT

Effective February 1, 1988, Public Law 100-198 introduced a new concept into the calculation of a veteran's entitlement amount. Under the old formula, the entitlement was the *lesser of* the dollar amount (prior fixed amount was $27,500) or 60 percent of the loan amount. The new concept is a sliding scale of entitlement amounts derived through a merging of dollar limits and percentage limits as follows:

Loan Amount	Entitlement
Up to $45,000	50% Guaranty
$45,000 to $56,250	$22,500 Guaranty
Above $56,250	Lesser of $36,000 or a 40% Guaranty

Example

The following list uses the sliding scale entitlement formula as it applies to examples of specific loan amounts:

Loan Amount	Amount of Guaranty
	(50% on loans to $45,000)
$30,000	$15,000
35,000	17,500
40,000	20,000
45,000	22,500
	(40% on loans above $45,000. Capped at $36,000. Minimum guaranty is $22,500)
$50,000	$22,500
55,000	22,500
60,000	24,000
65,000	26,000
68,750*	27,500
70,000	28,000
75,000	30,000
80,000	32,000
85,000	34,000
90,000	36,000
$90,000+	36,000

*The 1988 formula provides less protection than the previous formula on loans of less than $68,750, and added coverage for loans in excess of $68,750.

Assumption of a VA Loan

Prior rules allowed the assumption of a VA loan by any purchaser, veteran or nonveteran, without approval by the VA. What became lost in the long upswing in the housing market from the 1970s into the early 1980s was the fact that the seller remained primarily liable for repayment of that assumed loan—the loan could be transferred, but not the responsibility for its repayment. Unless the selling veteran took the available steps to obtain a release of liability from the loan, the obligation remained. When the economy in certain areas of the country began to decline in the mid-1980s, defaults and foreclosures became far more prevalent. Many problems resulted when the private mortgage lender was forced to foreclose on properties that had been conveyed to buyers unknown to the VA. Such a debt is a liability owed to the federal government (as is an FHA claim) and subject to collection from the debtor(s) through the U.S. Government's right of indemnification and/or subrogation (dependent upon state law). To prevent a recurrence of this kind of problem, the VA changed the assumption rules for all VA guaranteed loans underwritten *after* March 1, 1988.

NEW ASSUMPTION RULES

For loans underwritten after March 1, 1988, loan assumptions are not permitted without underwriting approval by the lender or VA. This rule does not apply to loans underwritten prior to that date.

The new rules (Public Law 100-198) exact a harsh penalty for failure to comply. A selling veteran with a loan underwritten after March 1, 1988 must notify the mortgagee *before the property is transferred.* The mortgagee must then determine if the prospective buyer meets credit standards. If the selling veteran fails to notify the mortgagee before transferring the property, or if the property is transferred to a buyer who has failed the credit worthiness test, the *lender has the right to accelerate the loan.*

There is a right of appeal for the selling veteran. Should the lender determine that the prospective buyer is not credit worthy, the seller has 30 days to appeal the decision. If the VA overrides the lender's determination, the lender must then approve the assumption.

To protect the veteran and to make sure the new rules are fully disclosed, mortgage instruments underwritten after March 1, 1988 must show in large type on the first page the following sentence: "THIS LOAN IS NOT ASSUMABLE WITHOUT THE APPROVAL OF THE DEPARTMENT OF VETERANS AFFAIRS OR ITS AGENT."

A *transfer fee* of one-half of 1 percent of the balance due on the loan shall be payable at the time of transfer to the loan holder, or its authorized agent, as trustee for the Secretary for Department of Veterans Affairs. In the event the fee is not paid, it shall be added to the debt secured by this instrument.

RELEASE OF LIABILITY

The above-stated rules underline the importance of selling a house to someone who is capable of making payments on the loan if it is to be assumed. While it will take many years for the older and more easily assumed loans to work their way out of existence, selling veterans continue to have the right to obtain a release of liability in a sale with a loan assumption.* A selling veteran is entitled to a release of liability if the following conditions are met:

1. The loan must be paid currently.
2. The purchaser/assumptor must qualify from the standpoint of income and be an acceptable credit risk.
3. The purchaser must agree to assume the veteran's obligations on the loan.

The veteran need not sell the house to another veteran in order to obtain a release of liability for a loan assumption. The purchaser need only meet the above-listed requirements. Release of liability is a separate form and should be completed at the time the transaction is closed.

Other VA Requirements and Procedures

To assure the veteran that the home loan will be properly handled and that the government guaranty will not be abused, the VA has a number of specific requirements relating to the loan and how it is handled. Essential areas of VA concern are:

The Lender. To protect against an unscrupulous lender, the VA distinguishes between *supervised* and *nonsupervised* lenders. A supervised lender is one who is subject to periodic examination and regulation by a federal or state agency. Savings and loan associations, commercial banks, and insurance companies would all qualify as supervised lenders. As such, they can process loans on an *automatic* basis. In this procedure, the supervised lender takes all the necessary steps to qualify a borrower, asks for a VA appraisal, and then makes its own underwriting decision. If favorable, the information is submitted to the VA in a Loan Report that the VA is obliged to honor with the issuance of a guaranty certificate.

A nonsupervised lender is anyone who does not qualify as a supervised lender. Mortgage companies, fraternal associations, and individuals would be some examples of nonsupervised lenders. To obtain a certificate of guaranty from

---

*A *release of liability* is sometimes confused with a *restoration of entitlement*. They are quite different: release of liability applies to an old loan; restoration of entitlement applies to obtaining a new loan. To secure one or the other requires meeting different requirements and filling out separate forms.

the VA, the nonsupervised lender would first have to obtain approval from the VA to make a loan to the veteran applicant, and would have to submit all required information to the VA office for their underwriting approval.

A third category of lender, which was established by the Veterans Housing Act of 1974, is a nonsupervised lender who qualifies for automatic loan processing. Mortgage companies that are wholly owned subsidiaries of a supervised lender subject to the same periodic examination as their parent firm are listed in this category. If the VA qualifications are met, the nonsupervised lenders may submit their own approved applications for guaranty in the form of a Loan Report, and receive the same automatic issuance of a VA guaranty certificate as a supervised lender.

Owner-Occupied. The VA guaranty can be used *only* by a veteran to buy a house to live in as the principal residence. It cannot be used to purchase rental property, except an approved one-to-four-family dwelling that is also occupied by the veteran buyer. The definition of an owner-occupant has been expanded to include the qualified veteran's spouse during the time the veteran may be on active duty out of the country.

Interest Rates. In 1975, Congress gave the Administrator of Veterans Affairs the authority to set the maximum rate of interest that would be permitted to a lender under a VA guaranty commitment. Adjustment of the interest rate follows the conventional market rather than leads it. While there is no fixed rule, in practice, the VA rate moves within a range of about one-half to 1½ percent below the current conventional market rates. Any rate change triggers an adjustment in the discount points to match market yield requirements.

Funding Fee. Since its origin, the VA home loan program has been handled as part of the VA's ongoing commitment of service to the veteran. There has been no charge for processing the loan application or for issuing the guaranty certificate. Effective in October 1982, the VA assessed a one-half percent funding fee to the borrower, later raised to the present 1 percent charge. It is payable at closing and may be included in the amount of the loan. There are a few exceptions. For example, the fee is not paid by veterans receiving compensation for service-connected disabilities or surviving spouses of veterans who died in service or as a result of service-connected disabilities. The fee applies to all types of VA-guaranteed loans, including interest-rate reduction refinancing loans, home improvement loans, graduated payment mortgages, growing equity mortgages, and loans with buy-down plans. The VA accepts the possibility that the addition of this fee may make the loan in excess of the property value.

Amount of the Loan. The maximum loan that can be approved by the VA for issuance of its guaranty is the amount of the Certificate of Reasonable Value— the VA-appraised value. If the price exceeds the appraised value, the additional amount must be paid in cash by the borrower. Regardless of the amount paid for a house, the VA guaranty on the loan is limited to the amount of the guaranty. There is another limit set by Ginnie Mae on the amount of a VA loan. Since Ginnie Mae provides funding for almost all VA loans through its underwriting of mortgage loan pools, it can set requirements for the kind of loan allowed into the mortgage pool. The Ginnie Mae requirement is that the amount of the guaranty, plus cash paid by the borrower, must equal at least 25 percent of the loan amount. Within the industry, a common interpretion of the rule is that the maximum amount of a VA loan is "four times the guarantee." So a guaranty of, say $30,000, would permit a loan of $120,000 to be delivered into a Ginnie Mae guaranteed pool.

Term of the Loan. A VA home loan can be obtained for up to 30 years. Shorter terms are approved by the VA if required by the lender and accepted by the veteran. The veteran has the right to repay all or any part of the principal balance due on the loan at any time with no additional interest charges or penalties.

Loan Servicing. The administration of a VA loan is not prescribed by the VA. The approved lenders are expected to follow the normal standards and practices of prudent lenders. The VA expects the veteran-obligor to meet the obligations fully and on time; however, it does encourage reasonable forbearance on the part of the lender with the enforcement of its collections. The lender is required to notify the VA of a default within 60 days after nonpayment of an installment. Failure to file the default notice within the prescribed time limits can result in a reduction of the guaranty allowed for the lender.

Default and Foreclosure. Once the notification of default has been filed with the VA, there is no time limit on when the lender must take action to foreclose the property. If foreclosure does become necessary, the VA must first appraise the property and set a "specified value." This value becomes the minimum amount for which the property can be sold, and serves as a protection for all parties involved.

In years past, the VA has followed the practice of paying a lender in full on a foreclosed loan and taking title to the repossessed property. It was not legally obligated to do this but believed the assurance to a lender of full recovery of its loan balance with interest provided greater credibility for the VA guaranty. And certainly it did so.

More recently, as foreclosure problems escalated, the VA altered its policies into what is commonly called a "no-bid" action in foreclosure proceedings. What this means is the VA now estimates the property's net value to the VA prior to a lender foreclosure action. If the cost to the VA would be less to pay off the amount of the guaranty to the lender (rather than the balance due on the loan) it simply chooses to not bid at the foreclosure auction (no-bid) and forfeits any further claim to the property. This possibility has lessened the value of a VA guaranty for many lenders.

Manufactured Home Loans

The Veterans Housing Act of 1970 (updated 1974) authorized the VA to guarantee loans made by private lenders to veterans for the purchase of new and used mobile homes now identified as "manufactured houses." The same rule applies with a manufactured home as with a house—it must be occupied by the veteran as the principal residence. The unit so acquired may be a single-wide or a double-wide, and the authorization to guarantee also covers a suitable lot for a manufactured home.

Because the status of a manufactured home as real versus personal property is not always clear, the VA now offers two categories under which lenders may request guarantees. The older procedure, identified as Section 1819 (of Title 38), offers a guaranty at the lesser of 50 percent of the loan amount to a maximum of $20,000. Effective on March 2, 1984, a new provision was added to Section 1810 increasing the maximum guaranty for manufactured homes permanently affixed to a lot if the manufactured home is considered real property under the laws of the state where the lot is located. A Section 1810 loan allows longer repayment terms and may be guaranteed as the sliding scale permits. Section 1810 permits a veteran to purchase a manufactured home already permanently affixed to a lot, a home and a lot to which the home will be permanently affixed, or to refinance an existing loan secured by a manufactured home permanently affixed to a lot. The veteran is allowed to pay a reasonable discount on the refinancing portion of the loan. The term of these loans can be for as long as 30 years and 32 days. Manufactured home loans are not an additional entitlement for the veteran as the privilege is reduced by the amount of entitlement already committed, similar to a regular home loan.

The maximum interest permitted on a manufactured home loan is adjusted periodically as may be needed to meet market conditions. The rate for a permanently affixed home and lot loan is limited to a simple interest rate the same as for a VA house loan.

The same rules that apply to regular VA house loans regarding a veteran's entitlement and liability for repayment also apply to the manufactured home loan.

Analyzing the Loan Application

Both the property to be pledged as collateral and the veteran applicant must meet VA qualification standards. Because both HUD/FHA and the VA have similar underwriting goals (that is, a sound building as collateral and a creditworthy borrower), their qualification standards are similar. And both agencies now accept the other's qualifications of applicants with a few exceptions.

Property qualification is considered next. The process of qualifying the veteran applicant is examined later in the next chapter with comparisons to the other procedures.

QUALIFYING THE PROPERTY

The VA uses both its own staff and approved independent fee appraisers to inspect and evaluate property that may serve as loan collateral. While the appraisal form has been standardized (see Appendix for an illustration), the VA refers to its appraisal as a Certificate of Reasonable Value, or a CRV. A CRV represents the maximum amount a lender may loan and still obtain an underwriting guarantee from the VA. A veteran may purchase a house at a price exceeding the CRV, but any amount in excess of the CRV must be paid in cash. Or, if the CRV comes in at less than the agreed price, the veteran has the right to withdraw from the contract and recover the earnest money in full.

The requirements mentioned are for VA qualification. Lenders are *not required* to make a loan at the VA-permissible limits. Simply, they cannot exceed those limits and still obtain a VA guaranty. But if the lender's policy is more limited than that allowed by the VA, they are free to apply their own limitations. For example, many lenders will not accept 100 percent loan-to-value loans regardless of VA permission. So long as the loan does not exceed VA limits, the guaranty can be issued. The same applies to all other underwriting programs—FHA, GNMA, and all conforming loans—the lender is free to offer a loan at lower than the designated limits and may still qualify the loan for whatever underwriting program is sought. The point is that loan applicants should not expect government agency maximum limitations to be uniformly accepted by all private lenders.

Scope of the Appraisal. Like the HUD/FHA appraisal procedure discussed earlier in this chapter, there are other pieces of information needed beyond the property evaluation. And like the FHA, VA appraisers are expected to make the necessary adjustments in valuation that will more closely reflect the property's real value rather than an inflated value caused by excessive financial inducements.

The appraiser's responsibility extends to inspecting the property to make sure that it meets VA minimum property standards. If not, repairs may be required to upgrade the property before the loan can be funded.

Questions for Discussion

1. How has the FHA achieved the goals for which it was established?
2. What are the present limits on a HUD/FHA-insured commitment for a single-family residence under Section 203(b)?
3. In the HUD/FHA settlement requirements, what rules apply to the handling of the down payment? The closing costs?
4. Explain the difference between loan commitments made by the VA and HUD/FHA.
5. Distinguish between the release of liability for a veteran and the restoration of entitlement.
6. Explain how a veteran may be entitled to a partial entitlement.
7. What are the requirements for a VA loan assumption?

8

Borrower Qualification

For the purpose of analysis, mortgage loans may be divided into two categories: those made to individuals and families to buy homes and those made to individuals and companies to buy commercial properties. Because the source of loan repayment is different, the analysis differs in emphasis. For a home loan, the analysis focuses first on the applicant's income. It is the buyer's personal income, essentially income unrelated to the property itself, that will be used to pay the loan. For a commercial property loan, the lender normally expects repayment from the income produced by the property, and that source takes priority in the analysis.

This chapter examines, first, the individual as borrower for the purposes of buying a home. Home loans comprise over two-thirds of the mortgage loan market and may be classed in four major categories: (1) HUD/FHA, (2) VA, (3)

156

conventional/conforming, and (4) other conventional. (A conventional loan is one without government underwriting.) Of the four, both HUD/FHA and VA offer fairly clear standards and guidelines for the industry and the consumer. The third category mentioned, conventional/conforming, covers loans made with the expectation of selling them to either FNMA or FHLMC. Both these secondary market purchasers have the same uniform documents and some common limitations (but not always the same standards) on the loans they can accept. The fourth category, other conventional, offers few uniform procedures with many minor variations. Summing up, the field of loan qualification offers no same standards used by everyone! (Some of the variations can be found in Table 8–2 later in the chapter.)

To enable the student to better understand the similarities and the differences among the four major categories of borrower qualification, all are presented in this chapter. Examples are given for each using the same basic applicant's income and loan amount. Generally, the analyses arrive at similar conclusions but use slightly different methods to reach that point.

A requirement for all borrowers is to furnish a credit report. The information found in these reports is explained in this chapter. Also, some information is given on qualification of corporate borrowers. Finally, because private mortgage insurance has become an essential part of mortgage lending practices, this kind of underwriting is reviewed.

Loan analysis begins with the loan application. Lenders no longer have the freedom to ask whatever questions they wish of an applicant. This practice in the past has led to some discrimination in lending practices. The Equal Credit Opportunity Act is a step toward reducing discrimination in all kinds of credit transactions. How this act has affected mortgage lending procedures is discussed next, followed by a review of some of the many kinds of income that might be presented by a loan applicant.

Equal Credit Opportunity Act

The basis for an analysis of the borrower starts with the loan application. In 1974, Congress passed the Equal Credit Opportunity Act (ECOA), which prescribed limits on the information that may be asked by a lender in the application for a loan. The act was implemented under the direction of the Federal Reserve Board and is administered by the Consumer Affairs Office of the Federal Reserve. Initially, the act prohibited discrimination in the granting of credit on the basis of sex or marital status. On March 23, 1976 the ECOA was amended to expand the prohibition against discrimination in credit transactions to include race, color, religion, national origin, sex, marital status, age, receipt of public assistance income, and the exercise of rights under the Consumer Credit Protection Act, of which the ECOA is a part.

The restrictions covering information on sources of an applicant's income do not apply if the applicant expects to use that income as a means of repaying the loan. For example, no questions may be asked regarding alimony, child support, or separate maintenance payments unless the borrower plans to use this money to make the loan payments. No discounting of income is allowed because of sex or marital status or because income is derived from part-time employment. In regard to a credit history, an applicant must be permitted to show evidence that facts in a joint report do not accurately reflect his or her individual ability or inclination to repay the loan. If credit is denied, the lender must provide the reasons for denial upon request of applicant.

The act pre-empts only those applicable state laws that are inconsistent with the federal requirements. Lenders in states that may impose additional requirements, such as additional prohibitions as to what may be on a loan application, must also comply with the state laws. It should be noted that the requirement of the act for separate liability for separate accounts (married persons can demand that separate credit records be maintained in either a married name or a maiden name) cannot be changed by state laws. However, any action taken by a creditor in accordance with *state property laws* directly or indirectly affecting credit worth will not constitute discrimination.

In general, the new laws do not specify how or to whom loans should be made, but do call for lenders to be much more specific with reasons for rejection of a loan applicant. Generalizations and categories of persons not eligible for credit are no longer permissible. For example, a married person who is separated can no longer be categorized as not acceptable for credit, but must be considered as an individual and judged by the same standards as any other person. There will continue to be a difference in the standards that a lender may use for long-term mortgage credit as opposed to a short-term installment type of credit, but the standards must be applied uniformly to all applicants.

The Loan Application

A mortgage loan application offers information for qualification of both the borrower and the property. If the loan is residential, the information requested in the application must conform with the requirements of ECOA. For this purpose, the Federal Reserve has prepared model application forms for five different types of credit, one of which is residential real estate. Although use of the Federal Reserve model forms are not required, most lenders have followed the design closely so as to conform with applicable laws.

On the basis of the Federal Reserve model, Fannie Mae and Freddie Mac designed their own standard forms (FNMA 1003 and FHLMC 65). Then, effective October 1, 1986, all federally chartered banks were required to use a revised FNMA/FHLMC Form 1003 (see Appendix) for all residential loan applications. After November 15, 1986, the new form was required for all lenders. It is one more step toward simplification of the mortgage lending process.

The information required in the residential loan application may be summarized as follows:

1. Identification of borrower (and co-borrower).
2. Employment and income data.
3. Anticipated monthly housing expenses.
4. Cost of house, down payment, financing requested.
5. List of assets and liabilities.
6. Credit references.
7. Applicant's certification as to accuracy of information.

If the loan is for commercial property, the lender is more likely to use its own form because considerably more information is needed. Since most commercial loans are expected to be repaid from the property income rather than from the borrower's personal income, specific information is needed on that income. Either a record of past profitability or a reasonable projection (a pro forma statement) on the anticipated income and expenses is required.

Financial Evaluation of the Borrower

The high loan-to-value ratio (LTVR) of the loan negotiated for house purchases today places a premium on the borrower's repayment ability. The conventional lender or the private mortgage insurance company selected would be hard pressed to make a full recovery of the loan amount based on the collateral in case of an early foreclosure. Proper analysis of the borrower to determine total available income, any claims against that income, as well as the credit record is important for a home loan. A borrower's other assets are helpful as additional security for a loan and can result in a lower rate of interest, but other assets cannot always be counted on for use in repayment. The lender knows that in many cases of actual default in payments the borrower has met with financial problems that were beyond his or her control, such as accidents, job layoffs, or serious illness in the family, and that such problems can deplete most of the family's financial assets, leaving the lender with few means of recourse beyond the house that has been pledged.

No two borrowers ever present the same credit picture. Analysis of a borrower still defies any attempt to impersonalize the procedure to the point of computerization. But there are some guidelines and general rules, mainly based on common sense, that are helpful in determining whether or not a borrower can make a loan repayment. To make a sound prediction, the underwriter of the loan considers two basic questions: (1) What is the applicant's ability to pay? (2) What is the applicant's willingness to pay?

Ability to Pay

More than any other type of loan, the home loan looks to a family's income as the basic resource for repayment. Assets are important, but are used in part to determine the spending or saving patterns practiced in the use of that income. Therefore, a careful review of the employment record, present income, and future potential is important. The following are some of the income elements considered by a lender, with a commentary on each.

Types of Income. Lenders make a broad distinction between *production-related* income and *assured* income. Production-related income means commissions, bonuses and, in some cases, piecework pay. It does not have the certainty of assured income such as wages or a salary and normally requires a longer record of earnings to qualify. Following are major types of income and comments on their acceptability.

1. *Salary.* The salary is the easiest form of income to determine and generally a more secure type of income.
2. *Bonus.* A bonus should not be counted on unless a regular pattern can be established for several successive years.
3. *Commission.* A straight commission job can be very lucrative, or it can be a complete bust. Only a past record of income culled from several years of tax returns can be accepted as factual.
4. *Hourly wages.* The hourly wage is a solid basis for continuing income and one that can usually be confirmed by an employer.
5. *Overtime wages.* This is an uncertain basis for making a larger loan as most employers try to avoid overtime and use it only as an emergency or temporary practice. Again, a consistent pattern of overtime payments for several years would make this an acceptable addition to the gross income.

6. *Second job.* Many persons today hold more than one job on a full- or part-time basis. Teachers, police officers, skilled hourly workers, all can have other capabilities and may spend extra hours augmenting their income. If the second job has been held over a period of several years on a regular basis, it provides a substantial lift to the regular income.

7. *Unreported income.* A few people accept extra work, or even become involved full-time, in jobs that pay in cash and on which income is not reported for tax purposes. Such income, if not reported, is illegal and cannot be used under any condition to justify a loan. This "borrower" could reach an abrupt end to his income via the prison route.

8. *Co-borrower's income.* Prior to the enactment of the Federal Equal Credit Opportunity Act, it was a fairly common practice to reduce the effective income that could be accepted from a working wife. The reasoning then was that young married couples who dominate the home buying market were also interested in rearing families. And earlier customs generally assigned more of the problems concerned with family emergencies, sickness, pregnancies, and child care to the wife. The new laws recognize changing customs, and a lender is now required to apply the same qualification standards to each borrower without questioning marital status or gender.

9. *Income from children.* While many young men and women living with their parents earn substantial money at full- or part-time jobs, these earnings are not generally a recognized addition to the family income for loan purposes. The obligation on the part of the children to contribute to the family finances for support of the home is not a continuing one, since normally they will leave the homestead and set up their own household within a few years. Thus, temporary income supplied by grown children lends no real weight to the loan request. There is another qualification pattern affected by children's income. Many state and local housing authorities offer lower-cost "bond money" with income restrictions. Generally, "family income" is the combined income of all persons who will live in the house to be financed.

10. *Pensions and trusts.* Few home buyers in the past have enjoyed pensions, retirement funds, or other work benefits at a sufficiently early age to apply them toward a home purchase. However, the pattern is changing. For instance, many veterans of military and other government services have now completed 20 or 30 years of employment before the age of 50. These benefits are, of course, one of the most reliable forms of income.

11. *Child support and alimony.* Some states do not permit alimony but provide child support as a matter of court decree. Other states permit both alimony

and child support. Such payments can be considered as regular income for a divorcee or remarried person, depending on the court ruling. However, the record of payment must show dependability over a period of time before it would constitute an acceptable addition to total income in full amount. No information need be given on this source if it is not to be counted as income for repayment of the loan.

12. *Self-employed.* Many persons operate their own businesses or work as individuals in professional capacities. Since there is no employer to verify actual income, the only acceptable method of validating this income is by referral to previous income tax reports. Certified copies of these returns can be obtained from the Internal Revenue Service for a small fee upon application by the taxpayer only. Some small business owners are able to pay certain living expenses from their business (car expenses, entertainment, travel, etc.), but weight can only be given to the actual income reported as taxable.

13. *Interest and dividends.* These funds normally represent a stable income but must be considered from the angle of a possible sale of the asset for another purpose. Again, the past record would indicate the probable future pattern in any given case.

14. *Part-time employment.* Income derived from part-time work has in the past not been accepted at full value toward a person's income applicable to repayment of a mortgage loan. The new ECOA requirements now permit no discounting of this source of income. However, the lender may still require that such income show evidence of stability and reasonable assurance that it will continue.

15. *Welfare assistance.* In the past few years, the concept of welfare as an assist for a disadvantaged person has given way to the idea that this is a right of an individual. Consequently, Congress has determined under the new ECOA requirements that welfare payments must be considered without discount by a lender if the applicant expects to use welfare assistance as a part of his or her income for repayment of the loan.

Stability of Income. Along with the size of an applicant's income, the assurance that it will be continued must be investigated. Two factors are involved: (1) time on the job and (2) type of work performed.

1. *Length of time.* Some lenders hold to a policy of rejecting all applicants with less than three years' tenure at their present job. There is a basis for this restriction in that any new job may or may not work out, either due to personality factors or to lack of accomplishment. But with the more rapid

changes in jobs today, the job tenure can be more fairly judged from the individual's job history. Has the applicant made a record of "job hopping" without noticeable improvement in his income? Is the present job one of greater responsibility and growth potential than the previous job? Has the applicant maintained a record of employment in a chosen field of work and qualifications, or is the present job an entirely new type of work?

The question of job tenure does not lend itself to easily defined limits due to the variables mentioned. But most leaders hold to some minimum term of employment, generally from one to three years.

2. *Type of work.* While a person with a long record of employment provides the soundest answer to the question of income stability, not everyone seeking loans can provide such a record. The type of work engaged in does give good clues as to future stability.

Persons with salaried jobs with larger companies and professional people with tenure are considered the most secure. Hourly workers with the protection of union contracts are far more stable (and often more highly paid) than lower-level management and clerical staff workers. Government employees carry good security as do teachers, police officers, and other service workers. On the lower side of the scale, new sales representatives enticed by stories of high commissions, entertainers, and seasonal workers give poor evidence of continued stable income. To some lenders, socially unacceptable types of work carry unduly low ratings. Self-employed persons should have a record of successful operations to assure stability as more small businesses fail than ever succeed.

For women, only recently has the spectrum of jobs available broadened to include almost every type of work. Rated among the highest for stability are teaching, nursing, and the growing executive group. Secretarial work as a class rates rather poorly, mainly from lack of continued interest, but the top legal, professional, and executive secretaries not only command good salaries but are virtually assured of continuous work today. A few of the less stable categories are clerical workers, models, actresses and waitresses. A growing number of young and older women as well are going into commission sales work with about the same mixed success as men.

Liabilities. All charges or obligations against an applicant's income must be considered in determining the amount available to meet the mortgage obligation. The liability connected with the normal costs of supporting a family and maintaining a house is taken into consideration by limiting the mortgage payment to about 25 percent of the applicant's income.

Both the FHA and VA have developed some standard patterns and ratios to guide the underwriting of their loan commitments insofar as the monthly obligations compare with the applicant's monthly income. With conventional loans, there is considerable flexibility in these limitations. Conventional lenders seldom include housing costs such as utilities and maintenance in their monthly charge ratios. Rather, the basic obligation considered is the mortgage payment, which includes principal, interest, taxes, and insurance (PITI). A very common ratio used to screen a loan applicant, insofar as liabilities are concerned, is that the mortgage payment cannot exceed 25 percent of the monthly income and the total of all fixed obligations cannot exceed 33 percent. As housing costs have escalated a greater portion of family income has been required to meet this expense. Over the past few years, lenders have increased the acceptable ratios. A more liberal measure of liability today is that the mortgage cannot exceed 33 percent of the borrower's gross income, and the mortgage payment plus long-term installment obligations cannot exceed 38 percent of income.

What is meant by *long-term obligations?* The answer is not very specific as lenders differ in what is included. A general definition is any regular payment obligation that extends for longer than 12 months. The obvious payments are for cars, furniture, or other personal goods. Less obvious are such payments as life insurance—some lenders consider this a liability, others class it as a savings and an asset. Revolving charge accounts and credit card obligations are not always easy to classify. Indeed, the growth of consumer credit has resulted in some mortgage loan qualification problems. By 1980, many lenders were reporting that the big problem in borrower qualification was not the mortgage payment itself, but the large amount of other obligations that many families were undertaking.

Assets. Most home buyers are younger couples who have not yet accumulated very many assets. The purchase of a house represents one of the largest investments they will make. But the addition of such assets as stocks, bonds, real estate, savings funds, and others does indicate an ability to live prudently and conserve a portion of the income. Life insurance is both an asset in its cash value and protection features and a liability in its cost. Cars and boats represent some trade-in value. Furniture and personal property are often overvalued in an applicant's statement of assets because of the owner's personal attachment. Employee trust and pension funds can represent value if the interest is a vested one; that is, if employees can take the funds with them if they leave the job. An interest in one's own business should be determined by an actual financial statement of that business. Accounts and notes receivable should be detailed for proper valuation.

Willingness to Pay

The element of willingness to pay, sometimes called *credit character,* is the most difficult to analyze and judge. Yet this factor alone can be the cause of a loan rejection. The most tangible information concerning an individual's record of handling obligations comes from the credit bureau report. Information may also be derived from public records regarding litigation, judgments, or criminal actions. Conversations with persons involved in the house sale transaction can sometimes bring to light information on the applicant's manner of living, personal attitudes, and activities that might give cause for a more detailed investigation. The initial loan application often is taken at the lending company's offices, but it can be handled at the residence of the applicant. Some lenders expect a personal call to be made on the applicant by their agents, as a person's manner of living can be most helpful in judging the credit character.

Under the category of "willingness to pay," lenders have always tried to assess an applicant's *motivation* for owning a home. Lenders in the past have felt that the strongest incentive for owning a home came from a family unit committed to the rearing of children. But lifestyles change, and many persons today are not interested in having a family but do want houses. Even prior to the enactment of the Equal Credit Opportunity Act, lenders were enlarging qualification standards and making loans to single persons, both men and women, and nonfamily units where there was a reasonable assurance of continuity of interest in owning a house. ECOA has eliminated sex and marital status as a basis for a loan rejection, but it has not foreclosed the lender's right to exercise judgment as to the continuing need to repay a mortgage loan. This is an area that does not lend itself to clear-cut definitions and presents problems for a responsible loan officer.

Under this category of credit attitude, a formidable barrier must be surmounted: the problem of invasion of privacy. Attitudes are changing among lenders but still range over a broad spectrum. The older, highly personal approach to a loan is still practiced in smaller communities and by many venerable lending institutions. Some savings and loan associations will not approve a loan without personal contact with the applicant by at least one, sometimes two, lending officers.

At the other extreme we find efforts to make the analysis as impersonal as possible. The thought here is to minimize the effects of personalities, of likes and dislikes, or of prejudices that have relatively little bearing on the strength of the applicant. These efforts center on some form of a rating chart with columns such as "good," "fair," and "poor" for judging 10 to 20 basic factors on the applicant's credit record. Each factor carries a different value in points for "good" or "fair" and must total a certain minimum to qualify. More than one rating in the "poor" column can be an automatic rejection.

It is in this area of trying to bridge the gap for the remote lender that the mortgage banker can serve as eyes and interpreter to bring all the facts into focus. The true picture can be just as advantageous for the borrower as for the lender and is mandatory in making proper judgment on any loan. Individuals asking to borrow someone else's money should be willing to provide complete and accurate information about themselves within the requirements of the Equal Credit Opportunity Act.

Credit Reports

Individual Credit

In most metropolitan areas there are a number of agencies that furnish credit information on individuals and companies. Credit bureaus, by definition, act as impartial gathering points of factual information on consumers. Other reporting firms, known as *investigative* reporting companies, collect credit information and also data required by insurance companies on the individual. There are also firms that compile records on businesses, and these are known as *commercial* reporting firms.

The mortgage business, for the most part, has followed the lead of the FHA and VA that make contracts with one of the major agencies for each area. The one selected is usually affiliated with Associated Credit Bureaus, Inc., and has ready access to exchange information from other credit bureaus in other areas of the country.

Credit bureaus are heavily dependent on the cooperation of local banks, merchants, and other financial institutions to relay factual data to them. From the information collected, a credit report is assembled and is available to firms that contract for credit reporting service.

Credit Reporting Standards

In years past, credit reporting has been the responsibility of approved credit bureaus. If a lender granted acceptance to a local source of credit information, their reports were used without particular regard as to how complete the information might be. As the volume of mortgage loans increased it became necessary to assure complete information was available and that local credit bureaus call upon national repositories of credit data for their input. As a result, five major federal agencies combined their requirements to create standards for credit reports. After July 1, 1988, all loans intended for underwriting by Fannie Mae, Freddie Mac, HUD/FHA, VA, or Farmers Home Administration must comply with the new standards. Since these standards affect almost all residential loans, a review of the major points follows:

General Requirements

- The name of the consumer reporting agency (credit bureau) must be clearly identified; who ordered the report, and who is paying for it?
- The format must be clear, but a specific form is not required.
- The form cannot be delivered to the applicant, only to the requestor of the information.
- Credit information must be furnished from at least two national repositories for each area in which the borrower resided in the past two years.
- Six data repositories now meet the definition of a "national repository," and these are:

    Associated Credit Bureau Services

    Associated Credit Services

    Credit Bureau, Inc.

    The Chilton Corporation

    TRW

    Trans Union

- Responses to all questions must be shown, even "unable to verify."
- Employment must be verified for the previous two years or an explanation given if information is not available.

Legal

- Information on what is available in the public record must be shown and its source disclosed.

Credit Data

- All credit data must be furnished, including a credit history.
- Missing information must be verified by the lender.
- Age of information is that not considered obsolete by the Fair Credit Reporting Act (generally, seven years).
- Record must have been checked within 90 days of the report.

Interview

- If information is incomplete, or undisclosed information is discovered, the lender must hold a personal interview with the borrower.

Warranty

- Lenders are required to warrant that the credit report complies with these standards.

The requirements listed above include all of the older accepted standards, such as the name of the reporting agency, and delivery of the report to the party requesting the information, not to the applicant. And it added several new and important requirements.

First, the demand for information from national repositories provides access to a much greater range of data than has otherwise been required. It gives greater assurance that a debtor with problems and defaults in one area of the country will be known to others. Second, lenders are now required to accept some responsibility for the accuracy of data shown in a credit report. For instance, missing information must be verified by the lender, and incomplete information or the discovery of undisclosed information calls for the lender to personally interview the borrower. Third, and perhaps most important, lenders are now required to *warrant* that the credit report complies wwith the new standards.

RECOMMENDED CREDIT REPORT FORMAT

While there are a number of competing credit bureau organizations in the country, one of the largest associations of bureaus is Associated Credit Bureaus, Inc., headquartered in Houston, Texas. They exchange operating information and keep their members abreast of changing requirements. Their recommendation for a credit report format that meets the new federal agency standards is illustrated in Figure 8–1. An explanation of the abbreviations used in credit reports is found in Figure 8–2.

Credit Reporting Problems

Almost all credit information is now maintained in computerized systems. Large creditors send data to their own bureau on computer tapes minimizing the possibility of errors. Nevertheless, there remain the problems of confusion with persons of similar name, changes of married names, and just plain errors in the recording of data.

Confusion over names is not always simplified by the use of Social Security numbers. The reason is that creditors may *not* demand a Social Security number when considering granting credit. The Social Security Act itself classifies an individual's number as private. However, depository institutions must record a depositor's number in order to report any payment of interest to the IRS. But

NAME, ADDRESS AND TEL. NO. OF BUREAU MAKING REPORT	**RESIDENTIAL MORTGAGE CREDIT REPORT**

Reporting firm certifies that the information meets the standards prescribed by Fannie Mae, Freddie Mac, HUD, VA and the Farmers Home Administration.

NATIONAL REPOSITORIES USED		DATE COMPLETED
□ TVS (ACB Services)	□ CBI	
□ ACS	□ TRW	□ INDIVIDUAL
□ CHILTON	□ TU	□ JOINT

Member Associated Credit Bureaus Inc.

REPORT ORDERED BY:

REPORT BILLED TO: (If Different)

REPORT ON	LAST NAME	FIRST NAME	MIDDLE	SOCIAL SECURITY NO.	SPOUSE'S NAME

ADDRESS	CITY	STATE	ZIP CODE	SINCE	SPOUSE'S SOCIAL SECURITY NO.

PRESENT EMPLOYER	POSITION	SINCE	DATE VERIFIED	MONTHLY INCOME

LOCATION OF EMPLOYMENT	VERIFIED? □ YES ... NAME OF EMPLOYER CONTACT / □ NO ... REASON WHY NOT

FORMER EMPLOYER	POSITION	FROM	TO	MONTHLY INCOME

LOCATION OF FORMER EMPLOYMENT	VERIFIED? □ YES ... NAME OF EMPLOYER CONTACT / □ NO ... REASON WHY NOT

DATE OF BIRTH	NO. OF DEPENDENTS INCL. SELF	□ OWNS HOME	□ RENTS	□ OTHER (Explain)

FORMER ADDRESS	CITY	STATE	FROM	TO

SPOUSE'S EMPLOYER	POSITION	SINCE	DATE VERIFIED	MONTHLY INCOME

LOCATION OF SPOUSE'S EMPLOYER	VERIFIED? □ YES ... NAME OF EMPLOYER CONTACT / □ NO ... REASON WHY NOT

SPOUSE'S FORMER EMPLOYER	POSITION	FROM	TO	MONTHLY INCOME

LOCATION OF SPOUSE'S FORMER EMPLOYMENT	VERIFIED? □ YES ... NAME OF EMPLOYER CONTACT / □ NO ... REASON WHY NOT

WHOSE	KIND OF BUSINESS AND NAME OF CREDITOR	DATE REPORTED AND METHOD OF REPORTING	DATE OPENED	DATE OF LAST PAYMENT	HIGHEST CREDIT OR LAST CONTRACT	PRESENT STATUS			HISTORICAL STATUS			TYPE & TERMS (MANNER OF PAYMENT)	REMARKS
						BALANCE OWING	PAST DUE		TIMES PAST DUE				
							AMOUNT	NO. OF PAYMENTS	NO. MONTHS CREDIT HISTORY REVIEWED	30-59 DAYS ONLY	60-89 DAYS ONLY	90 DAYS AND OVER	

PUBLIC RECORD ITEMS ARE FROM SOURCE(S) CHECKED BELOW

□ NO RECORD FOUND OF ANY PUBLIC RECORDS

□ DIRECTLY FROM COURT RECORDS

□ REPOSITORY, IDENTIFIED BY NAME _____

□ SUBSCRIPTION SERVICE, IDENTIFIED BY NAME _____

IF ADDITIONAL SPACE REQUIRED USE CREDIT HISTORY SECTION OF FORM 2000

This information is furnished in response to an inquiry for the purpose of evaluating credit risks. It has been obtained from sources deemed reliable, the accuracy of which this organization does not guarantee. The inquirer has agreed to indemnify the reporting bureau for any damage arising from misuse of this information, and this report is furnished in reliance upon that indemnity.

FORM R-400   6/86

FIGURE 8–1

TERMS OF SALE

Open Account (30 days or 90 days) . . . . O
Revolving or Option (Open-end a/c) . . . . R
Installment (fixed number of payments) I

COMMON LANGUAGE FOR CONSUMER CREDIT

CURRENT MANNER OF PAYMENT (Using Payments Past Due or Age from Due Date)	Type of Account		
	O	R	I
Too new to rate; approved but not used	0	0	0
Pays (or paid) within 30 days of payment due date, or not over one payment past due	1	1	1
Pays (or paid) in more than 30 days from the payment due date, but not more than 60 days, or not more than two payments past due	2	2	2
Pays (or paid) in more than 60 days from payment due date, but not more than 90 days, or three payments past due	3	3	3
Pays (or paid) in more than 90 days from payment due date, but not more than 120 days, or four payments past due	4	4	4
Pays (or paid) in more than 120 days or more than four payments past due	5	5	5
Making regular payments under debtor's plan or similar arrangement	7	7	7
Repossession. (Indicate if it is a voluntary return of merchandise by the consumer)	8	8	8
Bad debt	9	9	9

—Revised 1988

A. Column 1, "Whose Account", provides a means of showing how a credit grantor maintains the account for ECOA purposes. Examples: 0—Undesignated, 1—Individual account for individual use, 2—Joint account contractual liability, 3—Authorized user spouse, 4—Joint, 5—Co-maker, 6—"On behalf of" account, 7—Maker, 8—Indiv. Acct. of spouse, 9—Subject is no longer associated with account.

B. Column 3, "Method of Reporting", indicates how a trade item was placed in file: A—computer tape or TVS, M—Manual.

C. When inserting dates, use month and year only (Example: 12-88)

D. Manner of Payment using Common Language coding (I-$175-1) will be printed in column 14 for in-file trade items which do not contain information for credit history.

E. Remarks codes (Examples)

ACC —Account closed by consumer.
AJP —Adjustment pending.
BKL —Account included in Bankruptcy.
CCA—Consumer counseling account. Consumer
    has retained the services of an organization
    which is directing payment of his accounts.
    —Placed for collection.
    —Dispute following resolution.
CLA —Dispute. Resolution pending.
DIS —Judgment obtained for balance shown.
DRP —Moved. Left no forwarding address.
JUD —Paid P & L Account.

MOV

PPL

PRL —Profit and loss write-off.
RLD —Repossession. Paid by dealer.
RLP —Repossession. Proceeds applied to debt.
    —Repossession.
RPO—Repossession, redeemed.
RRE —Returned voluntarily. Paid by dealer.
RVD —Returned voluntarily.
    —Returned voluntarily, proceeds applied to
RVN debt.
RVP —Returned voluntarily, redeemed.
    —Plate stolen or lost.
RVR —Account included in Chapter 13 Plan for
STL Adjustment of Debts.
WEP

F. Account Numbers, if shown, should appear on second line just below each trade item.

G. Disputes and comments associated with specific trade lines should be printed on second or third line in cases where account numbers are printed.

FIGURE 8–2

the refusal to disclose a Social Security number to a creditor cannot be used as a basis for denial of credit.

The Fair Credit Reporting Act

In 1970, Congress passed the Fair Credit Reporting Act setting standards for how credit bureaus should handle credit information. In addition, the act grants individuals the right to examine information contained in their own credit reports. If erroneous information is discovered in a report, the individual has the right to demand a correction. However, the credit bureau has an obligation to maintain accuracy and would require some proof of an error before a correction could be made. After seven years, information is considered outdated and should be deleted from a person's record. It behooves a person seeking credit to review their own credit file before submitting a loan application.

Credit bureaus normally make a service charge for anyone to examine their own records. Some will even mail a copy of the information on file upon request of an individual for his or her own credit record. If an individual has been denied credit for reason of an unacceptable credit report, that person has the right to examine the credit record at no charge.

However, only persons and companies who are in the business of extending credit, and are members of the credit bureau itself, are authorized to examine the credit records of others, and such examination must be for the purpose of approval or disapproval of a credit applicant.

The agency responsible for administering the Fair Credit Reporting Act is the Federal Trade Commission headquartered in Washington, D.C., with regional offices in major cities.

Qualifying the Applicant

All lenders have the same underwriting goal: a borrower capable of repaying the loan plus a property providing adequate collateral. In considering qualification for a residential loan, the lender analyzes the applicant's personal income since that is where the money will come from to repay the loan. And the obligations against that income must be weighed to determine if an additional burden can be undertaken. It does neither party, the lender nor the borrower, any good to place an overload of debt on a home buyer. There are several different paths used to reach a judgment on qualification, but in the final analysis, the decision has to be a "judgment call," a decision by a human underwriter, not a mathematical calculation.

Following are several different methods used for qualifying an applicant: first, HUD/FHA, then, VA, followed by some conventional/conforming loan standards.

HUD/FHA Borrower Qualification

HUD/FHA uses a percentage guideline method to measure the adequacy of an applicant's income. In 1989 the measures were simplified and are now similar to those used for conventional loans. The applicant's Social Security and with-holding taxes are no longer deducted for calculation of adequacy. Housing expense no longer includes the costs of maintenance and utilities. These items are now considered payable from the residual income—that income remaining after the required expenses have been deducted.

PERCENTAGE GUIDELINE METHOD

The percentage guideline method takes an applicant's monthly liabilities at two separate stages and measures the amounts against the applicant's effective income. The two points for measurement are:

1. *Housing expense* should not exceed 29 percent of the applicant's effective income.

2. Housing expense *plus* other recurring charges is identified as *fixed payment* and should not exceed 41 percent of effective income.

How HUD/FHA defines the measures that are used is important. A brief expla-nation of the major items considered follows:

Effective Income.   This includes gross income from all sources, including bor-rower and co-borrower, that can be expected to continue for the first five years of the mortgage. Even though an applicant's income is properly verified, HUD/ FHA reserves the right to adjust, or disallow, unacceptable income. A bonus or unusually large commission should be supported by a record of equivalent pre-vious earnings. The owner of a business would be allowed the amount he or she withdraws as salary, provided this amount does not exceed actual earnings. Money reimbursed for travel expenses cannot be accepted, nor any repayment of principal on a capital investment.

Housing Expense.   These expenses include the mortgage payment of principal, interest, real estate taxes, and hazard insurance. (In conventional loans, this payment is often identified simply as PITI.) Housing expense also includes any monthly mortgage insurance premiums and homeowners association or condo fees if any are applicable.

---

*At this writing the new procedures had been approved by the Office of Management and Budget, were published in the Federal Register, but were not yet in effect.

Recurring Charges. These include any debt that matures in more than six months or is continuous in nature such as child support and installment and revolving accounts. In addition, any *large* monthly debt that matures in less than six months must be given underwriting consideration.

Fixed Payment. The fixed payment is the sum total of the housing expense and the recurring charges.

Residual Income. This is gross effective income minus fixed payment. Because residual income is affected by tax liabilities, Social Security deductions, and utility and maintenance expenses, HUD/FHA does not establish a required residual income amount as is found in the VA procedures.

RATIOS

The measure of adequacy is determined by ratios. By dividing the housing expense by the applicant's gross effective income, a ratio is determined. At this point, it should not exceed 29 percent of income. The second ratio is for the total fixed payment. By dividing fixed payment by gross effective income, the ratio should not exceed 41 percent.

These ratios are guidelines and subject to an underwriter's judgment. If compensating factors are present, the ratios may be exceeded. Examples of compensating factors are a borrower who:

- Invests 25 percent or more in a down payment.
- Owns substantial reserves for contingencies.
- Is a limited user of credit.
- Has no automobile.

To illustrate the key elements of an applicant's income qualification, a simplified example is offered next.

Example

Percentage Guideline—Monthly Basis

Gross effective income		$3,000
Housing expenses		
Mortgage principal and interest	$660	
Taxes and insurance	165	
Total housing expense		$825

Percentage Guideline—Monthly Basis (cont'd.)

Recurring charges			
Car payment	$240		
Revolving account payment	90		
Total recurring charges		$330	
Total Fixed Payment			$1,155
Ratios			
Housing expense	825/3,000 = 27.5		
Fixed payment	1,155/3,000 = 38.5		

In this example, the housing expense shows 27.5 percent of effective income, which falls within the HUD ceiling of 29 percent. The other measure, fixed payment, shows a 38.5 percent ratio of effective income, which also falls within the HUD 41 percent guideline. If either exceeds the guidelines, the underwriter would look for other compensating factors that might justify the granting of an insurance commitment.

BORROWER RATING

One further judgment must be made by a HUD/FHA underwriter, and that is a "borrower rating." An older method using a five-point gradient scale (from excellent to reject) has been replaced with only two grades—acceptable or rejection. A rejection on any one of the ratings is cause for denial of the loan commitment. The four elements that are rated are:

1. Credit characteristics.
2. Adequacy of effective income.
3. Stability of effective income.
4. Adequacy of available assets.

VA *Borrower Qualification*

How the VA qualifies property offered as collateral was discussed in the previous chapter. This section examines the methods used by the VA to qualify an applicant-veteran. In addition to meeting the requirements stated in Chapter 7 for eligibility and entitlement, the applicant must show an income adequate to repay the loan and have an acceptable credit record with other creditors. To qualify an applicant's income, the VA now requires two separate sets of calculations. One, called the *residual method*, has been used for many years. The other, a newer procedure using *income ratios*, became effective October 1, 1986. Explanations and examples of the two methods, and guidelines for each, follow.

RESIDUAL METHOD OF INCOME QUALIFICATION

The VA's residual method of qualifying an applicant's income might be called a summation procedure. It starts with the applicant's *gross monthly income*, then deducts the applicant's monthly tax liabilities, shelter expenses, and other fixed obligations to see what the applicant has left. What remains after the applicable obligations have been deducted is called *residual income*. How the VA underwriter considers the various items is discussed next.

Gross Income.   The recognized income of both borrower and spouse are added together, and that income should have a *reasonable expectation* of continuing.

Tax Liabilities.   The applicant's tax liabilities include federal and state income taxes, social security tax, and any other tax liabilities that may be due. The amount of tax is based on that shown by tax tables applicable to an applicant's recognized income and may not be the same as what the taxpayer pays. Tax liabilities are deducted from the gross income resulting in the applicant's *net take-home pay*. Take-home pay is not a critical number for the VA as it is *not used* as a basis for qualification.

Shelter Expenses.   For the residual method only, the VA adds certain shelter expenses not found in either FHA or conforming loan qualification calculations. In addition to the standard mortgage payment (principal, interest, taxes, and insurance—PITI), and any special assessments, the VA adds estimated *maintenance* and *utilities*. (These two expenses are not included in the VA's income ratio method.) The costs of maintenance and utilities are established by the VA Regional Office.

Other Monthly Obligations.   Under other monthly obligations, the VA lists installment obligations (such as a car payment) with six or more monthly payments still due, revolving account payments, alimony or child support, and job-related expenses (such as union dues). If the applicant is obligated for other state and local taxes or life insurance premiums, these should also be listed.

Residual Income.   After deducting the taxes, shelter expenses, and other monthly obligations from the applicant's gross monthly income, what remains is called *residual income*. For qualification, the residual income must be sufficient to cover the applicant's required *minimum* residual income. The minimum residual is a cost of living amount that varies by region, by family size, and by loan amount. It is adjusted periodically by the VA to meet changing conditions.

Cost of Living Expense.   Unlike any other underwriting procedure, the VA residual method uses a calculated figure for determining the cost of living. These costs include food, clothing, transportation, personal and medical care, and other consumption items. Since 1986, these costs have been determined by the standards for the four census bureau regions: West, South, Midwest, and Northeast. The actual figures are developed by the VA from Department of Labor data on consumer expenditure surveys.

Table 8–1 gives the cost of living figures for the four regions (effective February 1, 1988) by family size and loan amount. The applicant's residual income (that remaining after total monthly obligations have been deducted), must be sufficient to cover the applicable cost of living amount.

TABLE 8–1
Veterans Administration—Table of Residual Incomes
by Region
(EFFECTIVE FEBRUARY 1, 1988)

LOAN AMOUNTS OF $69,999 AND BELOW

Family Size*	Northeast	Midwest	South	West
1	$348	$340	$340	$379
2	583	570	570	635
3	702	687	687	765
4	791	773	773	861
5	821	803	803	894

*For families with more than five members, add $70 for each additional member up to a family of seven.

LOAN AMOUNTS OF $70,000 AND ABOVE

Family Size*	Northeast	Midwest	South	West
1	$401	$393	$393	$437
2	673	658	658	733
3	810	792	792	882
4	913	893	893	995
5	946	925	925	1,031

*For families with more than five members, add $75 for each additional member up to a family of seven.

Whatever amount remains from the applicant's income after total obligations and cost of living expenses are deducted is called *excess* residual income. The "excess," if any, may be used to help qualify marginal applicants, as will be shown later.

Example

Residual Guideline Method—Monthly Basis

Gross salary or earnings		$3,000
LESS:		
Federal income tax	330	
Social Security tax	205	
Tax liabilities		535
Net take-home pay		2,465
LESS:		
Principal and interest	660	
Realty taxes	105	
Hazard insurance	60	
Maintenance	55	
Utilities	125	
Monthly shelter expense		1,005
LESS:		
Installment obligation	240	
State and local taxes	90	
Total other obligations		330
APPLICANT'S RESIDUAL INCOME		$1,130

If the applicant in the example is a family of two living in the South region and the loan amount is less than $69,999, the minimum required residual (from Table 8–1) amounts to $560. Since the applicant has a residual income of $1,130, it is adequate to meet the requirements.

Excess Residual Income. There is one more piece of information to be derived from this method of calculation, and that is how much the applicant's residual income exceeds the minimum required amount. To continue using the same example above, the *required* residual amounted to $570. Subtracting that amount from the applicant's residual income of $1,130 leaves an "excess residual" of $560 (1,130 − 570 = 560). It is not the amount but the ratio that is significant. To achieve this, divide the applicant's excess residual by the minimum required residual to determine the *excess residual ratio*. In the example above, dividing $560 by $570 gives a ratio of .98, or 98 percent. This ratio fits into the qualification measure if there is a problem with the *income ratio* qualification calculation. If the excess residual ratio is 20 percent or greater, the applicant may still qualify even though the income ratio guidelines are not met. The income ratio method of calculation is explained next.

VA INCOME RATIO METHOD OF QUALIFICATION

As of October 1, 1986, the VA added a new "income ratio" method of qualifying an applicant's income. It is used in conjunction with the residual method: if the income ratio is not met, an applicant may still be approved, providing the excess residual is at least 20 percent of minimum required residual. The income ratio method uses some different measures, one being the applicant's income is gross income; income taxes and social security taxes are *not* a recognized deduction.

Shelter Expenses. The same expenses apply for the income ratio method as for the residual method with the exception of utility and maintenance costs. These are *not included* when calculating the income ratio.

Other Monthly Payments. Recurring monthly obligations include loan repayments, installment obligations, and such other obligations as child support. Federal tax obligations are not included.

Income Ratio. The sum of housing expenses plus other monthly payments (as briefly defined above), is then compared with the applicant's gross income. The limitation is 41 percent. That is, the listed costs should not exceed 41 percent of the gross income.

Example

Income Ratio Method—Monthly Basis

Applicant's total gross income		$3,000
Less: Housing expenses		
Mortgage principal and interest	$660	
Taxes and insurance	165	
Other monthly payments		
Car payment	240	
State and local taxes	90	
Total monthly obligations		$1,155
Ratios:		
Gross income	$3,000	
Total monthly obligations	$1,155/3,000 = 39%	

In this example the total monthly obligations amount to 39 percent of the applicant's gross income. Since this is within the VA 41 percent guideline, the applicant would meet the test for adequate income.

Comparison with Residual Guideline. As a final step in qualifying an applicant's income, the underwriter must review the results of the residual method qualification. This becomes most important if the income ratio method exceeds the 41 percent guideline limit. Should that occur, the underwriter then reviews the amount that the applicant's residual exceeds the minimum residual as required by the VA cost-of-living figures. As explained earlier, if the excess residual ratio is 20 percent or greater, the applicant may still qualify.

OTHER QUALIFICATION CONSIDERATIONS

While the VA considers the income available for family support a significant factor, it is not the sole criterion for approving or rejecting a loan. Other important considerations for qualification are:

1. Applicant's demonstrated ability to accumulate liquid assets such as cash, securities.
2. Applicant's ability to use credit wisely and refrain from incurring excessive debt.
3. Relationship between proposed housing expenses and the amount applicant is accustomed to paying.
4. The number and ages of applicant's dependents.
5. The likelihood of increases or decreases in income.
6. Applicant's work experience and history.
7. Applicant's credit record with other obligations.
8. The amount of any down payment made.

Conventional/Conforming Qualification

While both FNMA and FHLMC use the same basic documents in processing their loan applicants, there are a few key differences in the standards applied and the kinds of repayment plans that are acceptable. Because of substantial increases in loan delinquencies and foreclosures beginning in early 1984, most lenders and private mortgage insurance companies tightened their qualification requirements. Many of these standards are accepted throughout the industry.

Fannie Mae will no longer purchase adjustable rate mortgages that include negative amortization, nor will it consider graduated payment plans combined with ARMs. For application qualification, the minimum down payment for an ARM without negative amortization is 10 percent. For fixed rate mortgages, the new standard has been tightened for borrowers seeking 95 percent loans. For the higher ratio loan (anything over 90 percent), the mortgage payment cannot exceed 28 percent of the applicant's income, and that added to other monthly obligations cannot exceed 33 percent of gross income. For a 90 percent loan, the older standards still apply: mortgage payment not over 28 percent, plus other obligations not over 36 percent. *Note*: For conforming loans, the applicant's gross combined income is used to measure adequacy.

Mortgage Payment. Conforming loans measure only the mortgage payment amount, which includes principal, interest, taxes, and insurance, plus any special assessments that may be included. Unlike the VA, maintenance and utilities are not considered. This does not mean these costs are overlooked. It is simply that they are expected to be paid from the 64 percent of the applicant's income that is not designated for specific payments.

Other Monthly Payments. Recognized obligations include installment obligations that extend for 10 months or longer, revolving account payments, and those payments that represent a fixed claim on the applicant's income.

Example

Conforming Loan Qualification

Applicant's total gross income		$3,000
Mortgage payment (PITI)		
Mortgage principal and interest	$660	
Taxes and insurance	165	
Total mortgage payment		825
Other monthly payments		
Car payment	240	
State and local taxes	90	
Total other payments		330
Total mortgage plus other payments		$1,155
Ratios:		
Total mortgage payment		$ 825/3,000 = 27.5%
Total mortgage and other payments		$1,155/3,000 = 38.5%

These figures would disqualify an applicant from a conforming loan. The total mortgage payment ratio of 27.5 percent is within the 28 percent limit for a 90 percent loan. However, the total of mortgage payment plus other monthly payments at a 38.5 percent ratio exceeds the 36 percent limit for a 90 percent loan. If either ratio exceeds the limit, the applicant's income does not qualify.

Other Conventional Loan Qualification

As mentioned earlier, there are few standards in the matter of conventional loan qualification. When a lender is offering its own deposit assets to fund a loan, it is free to set standards that meet its own requirements. There are some general limitations such as nondiscrimination laws, state usury laws, and perhaps the biggest restraint: the need to attract borrower-customers. Borrowers usually investigate more than one source for loans, and if the qualification standards are unreasonable, there are other sources available.

Table 8–2 indicates the substantial variation that is present in just a few loan qualification standards.

Corporate Credit Analysis

To analyze adequately the creditworthiness of a company, it is necessary for the underwriter to become acquainted and fully cognizant of every phase of the business under scrutiny: management, sales, production, purchasing, research and planning, personnel policies, and the physical plant and equipment, as well as to make a careful study of the financial statements. There is wide latitude in the quantity and quality of detail needed to answer the fundamental question of whether or not it would be advisable to make a loan to the corporate applicant.

The underwriter expects to have a current, preferably audited, financial statement presented along with the loan application. An *audited* statement is one in which all the pertinent data is verified by the certified public accountant preparing the report. The figures are presented in a form and according to rules determined by the accountants, and in which the final conclusions are certified as correct and accurate by the accredited accountants. The principal factors a lender will look for are the record of profitable use of existing assets, the accumulation of cash and property versus outstanding obligations, and the very important working ratio of current assets to current liabilities. The latter indicates both the manner of operation and the immediate cushion of assets available to protect the company against a temporary reversal.

Personal interviews with company officers are utilized to fill in more detail of what the company's plans are and how it intends to carry them out. Where larger loans are involved, it is routine procedure to verify the company's market

TABLE 8–2
A Comparison of Industry Standards[1]

Requirement	Fannie Mae	Freddie Mac	FHA	VA
Investor loans allowed?	Yes, limited to five units including own (whether or not FNMA holds loans).	Yes.	Yes, requires 25% down. Limit: seven contiguous rental units.	N/A.
Minimum down fixed rate.	10% (tougher income standard if less than 10% down).	5%.	3% to 5% down depending on program used.	No down payment.
Minimum down ARMs without negative amortization.	10%.	5%.	5%, cap of 1% per year increase, 5% over life of loan.	N/A.
ARMs with negative amortization.	Not acceptable.	Allowed, but requires 10% down.	Allowed.	N/A.
Graduated payment ARM.	Not acceptable.	10% down.	Allowed.	Allows GPM but negative amortization cannot increase LTVR above 100%.

Contributions (builder buydowns, favorable financing, etc.).	Fixed rate, less than 10% down: limit to 3%. Fixed rate, 10% down: limit to 6%. ARM: no contributions.	No limits but full disclosure.	2% limit. Full disclosure and show cash-equivalent value.	Allows buy-downs if 3/2/1; full disclosure required in appraisal.
Gifts.	Buyer must have 5% down in addition to gift.	Disclose.	Allow valid gift letters with money on deposit.	Gift letters for closing costs are allowed if valid.
Co-borrowers.	Less than 10% down: co-borrowers must occupy and take title. More than 10%: co-borrowers take title and be immediate family.	Disclose and sign note.	If closely related, they need not occupy. Shared equity agreement required for investors.	If two veterans, both must take title and occupy. If an investor is co-borrower, only half the loan will be insured.

N/A = not available.
[1]As of September 1988.

and its ability to sell its product. Comparative balance sheets and profit and loss statements covering the previous 10 years of operation give excellent indications of how the company has handled its business and what the general trend will be. Also, a report by Dun & Bradstreet (one of the largest national credit reporting services) can give something of the history on the company, which helps to project future capabilities. It is the long-range ability of the company to operate profitably that is the real key to the trouble-free recovery of a loan.

To evaluate the results of the loan on the company's finances, it is customary to prepare a pro forma statement—both the balance sheet and the profit and loss statement. These statements are a *projection* of what the loan will do, such as increase the investment in productivity, add a new product line, provide an additional service, or broaden a market, as well as the expected effects of that loan on the profitability of the company.

To assure the lender that the proceeds of the loan are used as projected, a loan agreement is drawn up that spells out the purpose of the loan and can provide penalties for nonconformance. In addition, certain restrictive covenants are often added to the loan agreement that will place limits on such things as loans or advances to officers or employees until the loan is paid off, control the payment of salaries and dividends, limit any other borrowing, and require approval of the lender before any major assets, patents, or leasehold interests can be sold. All terms of the loan agreement are negotiable and are designed primarily to assure the lender's interest in the company over a period of time during which the ownership and management can change drastically but the loan obligation continues on.

Private Mortgage Insurance

Many years ago, in the jargon of the mortgage industry, an "insured loan" was simply another name for either an FHA or VA loan. The government-backed insurance programs created a standardization of loan practices and a mortgage package that could be readily sold to investors throughout the country. Conventional loans, those not covered by government insurance, remained localized in their procedures and documentation for many years. Prior to the 1980s, the major funding for conventional loans was found in savings associations and a few banks. As this source of funds declined, the need for a national market in conventional mortgage loans helped fuel the growth in private mortgage insurance. As sources of funds became further removed from the geographic location of a mortgage loan, the need for protection against loan default increased.

The idea of writing an insurance policy to protect a lender against loss in the event of a loan default began with the creation of the Federal Housing

Administration in 1934. It was not until the 1950s that several entrepreneurs began testing the market for default insurance coverage for conventional loans. Progress was slow at first as few lenders required the coverage; after all, if an insured loan was needed, just contact the FHA or VA! It was not until 1971 that private mortgage insurance became a requirement for higher ratio conventional loans. In that year the regulatory authorities expanded lending limits for conventional residential loans and required the use of default insurance coverage. Federally chartered savings and loan associations were permitted to make loans up to 95 percent of appraised value, compared with 90 percent previously, provided that the higher-ratio loans were insured. The result was a tremendous growth in private mortgage insurance.

One major insuring company, Mortgage Guaranty Insurance Corporation (MGIC, picking up the acronym Magic) based in Milwaukee, increased its loan coverage volume to $2.8 billion in 1971 and then to $7.5 billion in 1972 with about 40 percent of the coverage in 95 percent loans. The private sector topped the FHA coverage in that year and has retained its lead in the field.

By the end of the decade of the 1970s, private mortgage insurance companies had become popular growth companies on the nation's stock markets. More growth meant higher stock values, and many companies overlooked loan quality in the competitive surge for more premium income. The fall-out came in 1982 and 1983 when loss ratios increased dramatically due to more foreclosures. A few companies withdrew from the mortgage insurance market, but most tightened their loan qualification requirements and raised premium rates to rebuild their resources.

Company Qualifications. As a specialized type of insurance, only about 15 companies offer the PMI coverage. They all work through loan originators who serve as agents for the insuring company. The loan originator must first qualify with the insurance company as an approved agent. Then, each loan must undergo an evaluation by the insurance company's own underwriting people before a certificate of insurance coverage is issued.

Qualifying Information Required. Qualification for private mortgage insurance is normally handled by the submission of certain documentation to the insurance company for approval. In addition, the insurance company relies on the loan originator to submit complete and accurate information on the applicant. A request for coverage includes submitting: (1) a property appraisal made by a professional appraiser approved by the insurance company; (2) a copy of the loan application; (3) a credit report on the borrower; (4) several verifications; and (5) any other data helpful in analyzing the loan. Once the necessary documents and information have been submitted, processing of the application tends to move quickly and is usually completed within 24 hours.

Coverage Offered. While private mortgage insurers, the HUD/FHA and VA offer protection against the same risk, the coverage differs somewhat. HUD/FHA insures 100 percent of the loan amount, VA guarantees a portion of the loan, and private mortgage insurance carriers issue a variety of policies for residential loans that range from a low of 12 percent of the loan amount insured to a high of 35 percent.

Further, there is a difference in the term of insurance coverage. While HUD/FHA and VA offer their commitments for the life of the loan, private mortgage insurers limit their coverage to a shorter term of years. The range varies from three to 15 years. An example of the coverage range available is illustrated in a price list shown in Figure 8–3.

Private mortgage insurance can be found on a greater variety of property than is available with the government programs. Residential loans that can be insured include primary residences, second or leisure homes, multifamily properties, mobile homes (if permanently secured and classed as real estate by state law), and modular housing. Commercial loan coverage is available for hotels, motels, shopping centers, office buildings, warehouses, and others. The loans may be participation loans, loans secured by junior liens, and seller-financed mortgages. Each insurance company may set its own standards for the loans it will cover as there are no national requirements.

Nevertheless, it is the lenders and loan underwriters (such as Fannie Mae and Freddie Mac) who set their own minimum insurance requirements for coverage, and this is what governs the kinds of insurance policies that are issued. In practice, the borrower has little voice in the selection of coverage or the insurance carrier, as that decision is made by the loan originator. The reason is that it is the lender who is protected by the coverage, not the borrower. What the borrower gains is an easier qualification for perhaps a larger loan and a lower down payment than might otherwise be available.

In a March 1989 announcement, Freddie Mac reduced the time period after which PMI could be canceled from seven to five years provided the homeowners's equity has increased to 20 percent and timely payments have been made. If the homeowner achieves the 20 percent equity point by adding improvements to the home or prepayment of principal, the PMI can be dropped after only two years. Proof of the increase in value of the property would require a new appraisal. It could be worth that cost as PMI adds $200 to $300 a year to payments. The rule applied by Fannie Mae is that borrowers can drop PMI after only one year if they can prove 20 percent or more in equity. It is important to note that the holder of the mortgage is not required to comply with this rule and may elect to continue PMI coverage as a prudent measure. Since there is no automatic notification to the borrower of a lender's policy on PMI, it is a good idea to ask whoever holds the mortgage note what their policy is.

30 Year Mortgages* Annual Premium Plans

Fixed-Payment[1]

MGIC Coverage	LTV	Reduces Exposure To[7]	1st-Year Premiums[6]	Renewal Premiums		
				Declining[3]	Constant[4]	
					Yrs. 2-10	Yrs. 11-Term
25%	90.01-95%	72%	1.10%	.50%	.49%	.25%
	85.01-90%	68	.65	.35	.34	.25
	85% & under	64	.50	.35	.34	.25
22%	90.01-95%	75	1.00	.50	.49	.25
	85.01-90%	71	.55	.35	.34	.25
	85% & under	67	.45	.35	.34	.25
20%	90.01-95%	76	.90	.50	.49	.25
	85.01-90%	72	.50	.35	.34	.25
	85% & under	68	.40	.35	.34	.25
17%	85.01-90%	75	.40	.35	.34	.25
	85% & under	71	.35	.35	.34	.25
12%	85.01-90%	80	.35	.35	.34	.25
	85% & under	75	.30	.30	.29	.25

Nonfixed-Payment[2]

MGIC Coverage	LTV	Reduces Exposure To[7]	1st-Year Premiums[6][8]	Renewal Premiums		
				Declining[3]	Constant[4][5]	
					Yrs. 2-10	Yrs. 11-Term
25%	90.01-95%	72%	1.35%	.55%	.54%	.25%
	85.01-90%	68	.75	.45	.44	.25
	85% & under	64	.60	.45	.44	.25
22%	90.01-95%	75	1.20	.55	.54	.25
	85.01-90%	71	.65	.45	.44	.25
	85% & under	67	.55	.45	.44	.25
20%	90.01-95%	76	1.10	.55	.54	.25
	85.01-90%	72	.60	.45	.44	.25
	85% & under	68	.50	.45	.44	.25
17%	85.01-90%	75	.50	.45	.44	.25
	85% & under	71	.40	.40	.39	.25
12%	85.01-90%	80	.40	.40	.39	.25
	85% & under	75	.35	.35	.34	.25

NOTES

(1) Fixed-payment mortgages feature level payments for the first five years of the mortgage and must (a) fully amortize the loan over a maximum of forty (40) years; (b) have the initial payment rate equal to or greater than the initial accrual rate; and (c) have no temporary buydowns, potential negative amortization, rate concessions, or GPM features.

(2) Nonfixed-payment mortgages feature payment changes, or the potential for payment changes, during the first five years of the mortgage.

(3) Declining renewal premium is an annual rate that is applied to the outstanding loan balance.

(4) Constant renewal premium is an annual rate that is applied to the original insured loan balance.

(5) On nonfixed-payment loans that feature the potential for negative amortization, add .035% to the renewal premium for years 2 through 10, and .02% for years 11 through term.

(6) On loans with a base LTV of 90% or less, the first-year premium can be included in the insured loan balance.

The premium rate, LTV category, and dollar premiums are computed using the base loan amount. The renewal is calculated on the total loan amount.

(7) This column assumes that the first-year premium is paid at closing. If the first-year premium is financed, the exposure threshold will increase and more MGIC coverage may be necessary. Refer to MGIC PLUS Annual Premium Selector for details.

(8) **Loans featuring the potential for negative amortization are not eligible for premium financing.**

Mortgages with terms greater than 15 years.

Premium rates may vary from state to state and must be selected based upon the location of the property. To select the appropriate rate card, see your MGIC rate card matrix.

FIGURE 8-3 (*Source*: Mortgage Guaranty Insurance Corporation, Milwaukee, Wisconsin. Reprinted with permission of the Mortgage Guaranty Insurance Corporation, Milwaukee, Wisc. 53201)

Premiums Charged.   Since private mortgage insurance usually covers less than the full amount of a loan for a shorter term, the premiums are less than those found with a HUD/FHA loan. As a type of insurance, PMI comes under the regulation of state insurance commissions in those states with that kind of authority.

Premiums on PMI may be paid as a single premium at time of closing, or in installments as an annual premium plan. The premium amount is expressed as a percentage of the original loan amount, measured in "points."

PMI Obligations in the Event of Foreclosure.   Even though PMI coverage is limited to a percentage of the loan amount, insurance companies have generally followed a practice of reimbursing the lender in full on their mortgage loan should a foreclosure become necessary. By then taking title to the foreclosed property, the insurance company relieves the lender of any further problems. The purpose, of course, is to make the insurance coverage more competitive in a market that places a high value on service.

As foreclosure problems escalated in some parts of the country, many insurers were forced to limit their exposure to the legal obligation contained in the insurance contract; that is, reimburse the lender for the amount of the loan actually covered.

Questions for Discussion

1. How does the Equal Credit Opportunity Act reduce discrimination?
2. List the essential information that a prospective borrower must provide in a loan application.
3. Discuss "ability to repay" a loan as may be indicated by type of income and stability of income.
4. How is the income of self-employed persons verified?
5. Define "willingness to pay" and how it can be evaluated.
6. What information is normally obtained from a credit report?
7. In analyzing corporate credit, what further investigation would an underwriter employ beyond a careful study of the company's financial statements?
8. What is the risk insured by private mortgage insurance?
9. Explain the basic differences between private mortgage insurance and that offered by the Federal Housing Administration.
10. Who selects the mortgage insurance coverage?

11. Discuss the guidelines used by HUD/FHA and VA in determining the effective income of a loan applicant.

12. In the HUD/FHA settlement requirements, what rules apply to the handling of the down payment? Closing costs?

9

Property Analysis

Underwriter
Property appraisal
Designations
Appraisal principles
Cost approach
Depreciation
Obsolescence
Market approach
Comparable property
Income approach
Capitalization
Discount analysis
Physical characteristics
Hazardous waste areas

Property location
Disaster-prone areas
Neighborhood red-lining
Apparent age of property
Remaining useful life
Owner-occupied housing
Condominiums
Common areas
Homeowners associations
Cooperative apartments
Land survey
Lot and block
Metes and bounds
Geodetic survey

General Analysis of Loans

The process of analyzing and approving a loan is called *underwriting*. The individual who assembles and analyzes the necessary data and is authorized to give a company's consent to a specific loan is referred to as the *underwriter*. Properly underwriting any loan requires a complete analysis of all pertinent factors, including: (1) the borrower's ability and willingness to pay; (2) the property, its condition, location, and usage; (3) all relevant economic influences; (4) laws controlling foreclosure procedures and assignments of rent; and (5) any unusual conditions that may exist.

An underwriter must examine the future, estimate the continued stability of the borrower, and try to judge the continuing value in a specific property. The underwriter must look beyond a normal appraisal, which provides an estimate of past or present value, and weigh the forces that affect the future based on his or her experience in this field.

A loan analysis covers a wide assortment of information and, from these diverse elements, an underwriter must determine the degree of risk involved. There is no such thing as a risk-free mortgage loan. It is the underwriter's prime responsibility to determine the magnitude of the risk and to compensate for it in the terms and conditions of the loan. The degree of risk determines the ratio of loan to value, the length of time for repayment, and the interest required by the lender.

As one of the essential elements in underwriting any mortgage loan, the property to be pledged must be examined for suitability. As discussed in the previous chapter, for a residential loan, it is the personal income of the borrower that is expected to repay the loan. For commercial loans, it is the income from the property that becomes more important. So the analysis of property that will be pledged as collateral for a loan differs somewhat between residential and commercial types of loans. For a residential loan, the property serves as a backup, a pledge of something of value that better assures repayment of the loan. But it is not something the lender expects to use for repayment of the loan. So the thrust of a property analysis for a residential loan is simply to determine the market value—what can the property bring on a resale?

For a commercial loan, the property analysis must look further. Generally, the loan is expected to be repaid from income generated by the property. While the property does serve as collateral—a backup in case of loan default—it is more important for the underwriter to make sure the property income can sustain loan repayment. While the two approaches, residential versus commercial, are somewhat different, they both rely on professional appraisals as a starting point.

Property Appraisals

A property appraisal is used as one important measure of loan amount. Lenders limit loan amounts to a percentage of property value for residential loans. For commercial loans, the loan amount may be limited to a percentage of the property's income, which also is a direct reflection of the property's value. In addition, an appraisal serves as a support document for institutional lenders when they undergo regulatory examinations.

Determination of "appraised value" is made by persons specially qualified in the field. In the not-too-distant past, a lending institution's loan officer might have estimated the property value based on personal knowledge and experience in the area. However, as mortgage lending has grown in volume and increased in complexity, almost all appraisals are made by professionals. Some work as employees of a lending institution, and some as independent fee appraisers.

Today, there are many professional organizations offering appraisal designations to those who qualify under the organization's standards. These are "peer groups" made up of appraisers who are interested in maintaining and improving the quality of their profession. Each organization offers certain "designations" indicating qualification in a particular area of appraisal work. The requirements differ somewhat but all are based on a minimum prescribed level of education and experience plus passing some rather difficult tests. Following is a brief listing of some of the better-known organizations and the designations granted by each:

American Institute of Real Estate Appraisers (AIREA)
RM—Residential Member
MAI—Member, Appraisal Institute (highest designation)

American Society of Appraisers (ASA)
ASA—American Society of Appraisers

Society of Real Estate Appraisers (SREA)
SRA—Senior Residential Appraiser
SRPA—Senior Real Property Appraiser
SREA—Senior Real Estate Analyst (highest designation)

Appraisal Institute of Canada
AACI—Accredited Appraiser Canadian Institute

National Association of Independent Fee Appraisers
IFA—Independent Fee Appraiser Member
IFAS—Independent Fee Appraiser, Senior Member
IFAC—Independent Fee Appraiser, Counselor

National Association of Review Appraisers
CRA—Certified Review Appraiser, Senior Member

Of the listed organizations, two are older and better known within the industry. One is the American Institute of Real Estate Appraisers, which was organized under, and requires an applicant to be a member of, the National Association of Realtors. The other is the Society of Real Estate Appraisers, which developed primarily from the savings and loan group of staff appraisers.

Licensing of Appraisers

Peer designations are important to lenders as many base their minimum standards for acceptance of an appraisal on them. Nevertheless, appraisers and their qualifications came into question as a result of substantial property foreclosures during the mid-1980s.

In certain areas of the country, defaulted real estate loans were one of the principal causes of failure in some lending institutions. Whether or not faulty appraisals were involved, many states began examining the need for better practices. As a result, a growing number of states are establishing licensing boards to set standards for the qualification of appraisers. In addition, the federal government is considering legislation to correct appraisal abuses and inconsistencies.

In an effort to correct any deficiencies among themselves and to help set guidelines for legislation, eight appraisal organizations joined together to set their own standards. In the fall of 1987 this group established the Appraisal Foundation. Its purpose is twofold: (1) to promote uniform standards for the preparation of appraisals; and (2) to establish qualification criteria for professional certification.

Definition of an Appraisal

An appraisal may be defined as an estimate of the value of an adequately described property as of a specific date, which is supported by an analysis of relevant data. An appraisal is an evaluation of ownership or leasehold rights. Appraisals can be delivered in three forms: (1) a letter form that describes the main points; (2) a standard form such as the combined FHLMC–FNMA appraisal report illustrated in the Appendix; or (3) a narrative report that goes into considerable analytical detail to substantiate the findings.

Principles of Appraising

How do appraisers approach their problems? What are they looking for in determining values? What analytical details should lenders or borrowers expect to find in written appraisals?

Principles of Appraiser's Analysis.　First, let us look at the broad theory behind a professional appraiser's analysis. There are certain principles that guide their thinking in evaluating property. Most important among these are the following:

1. *Supply and demand*　The same theory underlying all economic practice is that scarcity influences supply and that what people want controls the demand.

2. *Substitution*   The value of replaceable property will tend to coincide with the value of an equally desirable substitute property.

3. *Highest and best use*   It is the use of the land at the time of the appraisal that will provide the greatest net return. This requires the proper balance of the four agents of production (labor, coordination, capital, and land) to provide the maximum return for the land used.

4. *Contribution*   This principle applies to the amount of value added by an improvement, such as an elevator in a three-story building, or the value added to a building lot by increasing the depth of that lot.

5. *Conformity*   To achieve maximum value, the land use must conform to the surrounding area. An overimprovement, such as a $200,000 house built in a neighborhood of $60,000 homes, will lower the value of the larger house.

6. *Anticipation*   Since value is considered to be the worth of all present and future benefits resulting from property ownership, the anticipation of future benefits has to be evaluated.

With the theory of the appraisal principles as a background to guide that analysis, the appraiser presents information in a logical sequence. The narrative report, which is the most comprehensive form of appraisal, uses the following pattern and guidelines.

Description of Property.   The property should be defined in accurate legal wording, and the precise rights of ownership must be described. The rights may be a leasehold interest, mineral rights, surface rights, or the full value of all the land and buildings thereon.

The Date and Purpose of the Appraisal.   Appraisals can be made for times other than the present, such as when needed to settle an earlier legal dispute. The date of the appraised value must be clearly shown. Also, the purpose of the appraisal should be stated as it will influence the dominant approach to value. In professional appraisals there is no such thing as the buyer's or seller's value—this is not a "purpose" as identified here. An example of purpose would be to estimate value for an insurance settlement, which would involve a cost approach to value as claims are adjusted on the basis of cost. If the purpose is a condemnation action, the most relevant approach would be the market value.

The Background Data.   While the standard form and simple letter report will not provide any economic background data, the narrative report discloses the economic information as clues to value. An overall study of the market region, which may be as large as an entire state, is made. The focus is then narrowed down to the local area—the town or the portion of a city where the property is located. From there the analysis narrows even further to the specific neighborhood and then to the actual site under appraisal.

The Approaches to Value.   Appraisers use three common approaches to estimate value: (1) cost, (2) market, and (3) income. All approaches should be used wherever possible, and all should reach approximately similar values, although these values are seldom the same. In certain appraisals, only one approach may be practical, such as valuing a city hall building for insurance purposes. In this analysis only a cost approach would be practical as there is not much buying or selling of city halls to provide market data, nor is there a true income from the building itself to provide figures for an income approach. A single-family residence may appear to lack any income for analysis, but certain neighborhoods have sufficient houses being rented to provide enough data to reach an income approach conclusion. The three approaches to value are discussed in greater detail later in this chapter.

Qualifying Conditions.   If, in the analysis of the property, the appraiser discovers any material factors that will affect the property's value, these can be reported as further substantiation of the conclusion.

Estimate of Value.   This is the real conclusion of the study, the figure most people turn to first when handed a finished appraisal. Each of the approaches to value will result in a firm dollar valuation for that approach. Then, it is the purpose of this estimate to explain why one of the approaches to value is favored over the others. For example, with an income property such as a motel, the value judgment would rest most heavily on the income analysis. The final conclusion is a single value for the property and represents the considered knowledge and experience of the appraiser making the report.

Certification of the Appraiser and His or Her Qualifications.   The professional appraiser certifies to his or her opinion by signature, and disclaims any financial interest in the property being appraised that could influence a truly objective conclusion. A recitation of the appraiser's educational background, standing within the profession as indicated by professional ratings, and previous experience such as appraisals previously made and for whom, serves to substantiate the quality of the appraisal for the underwriting officer.

Addendum.   Depending on the need for clarification, the appraisal will include maps of the area under consideration with the site pointed out, plus the location of comparable properties referred to in the analysis. Charts may be used to indicate such things as the variables in a market analysis. Photos of the actual property are usually mandatory.

Three Approaches to Property Values

To understand more clearly the use of the three approaches to value, which is the essence of an appraisal, each is discussed in the sections that follow.

Property Value as Estimated by Cost Approach

The cost approach is developed as the sum of the building reproduction costs, less depreciation, plus land value. The reproduction costs can be developed the same as a builder would prepare a bid proposal by listing every item of material, labor, field burden, and administrative overhead. Reproduction cost estimates have been simplified in active urban areas through compilation of many cost experiences converted to a cost-per-square-foot figure. The offices of active appraisers collect such data in-depth for reference.

Depreciation, by definition, detracts from the value and must be deducted from the reproduction costs. Depreciation consists of three separate types:

1. *Physical deterioration.* The wear and tear of the actual building—this is the type most commonly associated with the word *depreciation.* Examples would be the need for repainting, a worn-out roof needing new shingles, and rotting window casements. These are *curable* items and under the breakdown method should be deducted from value as a rehabilitation cost. All other items of physical deterioration are *incurable*, meaning not economically feasible to repair. An illustration would be the aging of the foundations or of the walls, and this kind of deterioration should be charged off as a certain portion of the usable life of the building. Another method of handling physical deterioration, in contrast to the breakdown method, is the engineering or observed method wherein each major component of the building is listed and a percentage of its full life is charged off. This method recognizes that each major component of a building may have a different life and the percentage of depreciation would vary at any point in time.

2. *Functional obsolescence.* Equally as important as physical deterioration is that category of loss in value resulting from poor basic design, inadequate facilities, or outdated equipment. These elements, too, can be curable or incurable. An example of incurable functional obsolescence would be a

two-bedroom, one-bath house, which was very popular at the end of World War II, but now is a hard item to sell in today's more demanding market. There could be an excess of walls or partitions in an office building, which would cost money to remove and modernize, but would be curable. Lack of air conditioning in a hotel or office building is another example of curable functional obsolescence.

3. *Economic obsolescence.* The third type of depreciation has a more elusive quality and really is not in the building at all. Economic obsolescence is that set of factors outside and surrounding the property that affect the value, requiring the determination of the plus or minus effect of these forces. Some are very obvious influences—a new freeway bypassing an existing service station, the construction of an undesirable industry in an area adjacent to residential property, or the bridging of a stream to open new land for development. The more difficult problem is ascertaining economic impact of the long-term rise or fall of a specific neighborhood. While landowners are able to exercise some voice in protest or encouragement of these outside forces, for the most part what is done with neighboring properties is not controllable and is not curable. And it will always be a force that will affect the value of an individual property.

The third factor to be considered under the cost approach is the value of the land. Lately, almost all land has been marked by a steady appreciation in value. But economic factors can adversely affect land value as well as favorably influence it. Normally, land value can be determined through an examination of recent sales of similarly located properties—the same basic method as used under a market approach to value. However, there are sometimes specific reasons for changes in the appraised value of land. Buildings can and do deteriorate, while the land itself can continue to increase in value due to the same outside factors noted in economic obsolescence. For example, as urban areas expand, certain intersections become more and more valuable, new throughways and freeways concentrate greater flows of traffic, and huge shopping centers add to the value of all surrounding land. As the suburban sprawl moves outward, former farmland increases in value when it is converted into residential subdivisions; or, as another example, in some older sections of a city, the land can become more valuable than the building. The building itself may represent such poor usage of the land that it becomes a liability to the property value, and its removal costs can be deducted from the stated value of the land. By ascertaining these fluctuations in land value, the appraiser can bring a cost analysis into step with a changing market value.

Property Value as Estimated by Market Approach

Also known as a sales-comparison approach, the estimated value by market approach is determined by prices paid for similar properties. Since no two properties are ever precisely comparable, much of the analysis under this method concerns itself with the detailing of major characteristics and whether these add to or subtract from the value of the property. These details of comparison cover items such as date of sale, location of property, size of lot, type of materials used in construction, and many other factors that the appraiser considers relevant.

The market approach represents one of the most important analyses, as the true worth of any property is the actual amount for which it can be sold. And to this end, accurate information on the present market is essential.

Some confusion does exist in the use of sales prices and asking prices. The appraiser is primarily concerned with completed sales and with sales uncomplicated by extraneous pressures such as forced sales, estate disposals, or transfers within a family. The asking or offering price is considered by most to represent a ceiling or maximum value for the property. Appraisers usually recognize the inherent inaccuracy of an asking price, especially one set by homeowners. This figure is often arrived at by adding the original purchase price, plus the full cost of all improvements that have been made, plus the selling commission, plus the owner's amateur notion of general market appreciation. But every so often an owner actually receives such a sales price from a willing buyer, and this makes the professional feel a bit foolish!

Property Value as Estimated by Income Approach

Because the income approach looks at the actual return per dollar invested, it is the most important method for any investment property.

When people buy investment property, they normally expect to recover, or *recapture* in appraisal terminology, their money with a profit. They do this from two sources: (1) the annual earnings (excess income over all costs) and (2) the proceeds from a resale at the end of the term of ownership, called the *residual value*.

There are several acceptable methods used to estimate value with an income approach. However, any method based on the value of future income suffers from the same problem: Real estate does not offer the certainty of future income that other kinds of investment may provide. Nevertheless, once an income stream has been developed for analysis purposes, two methods are more widely used to convert the income stream into a value of the income-producing asset—the *capitalization* method and the *discount analysis* method, described following.

Capitalization Method.   Probably the oldest, and simplest, method of converting an income stream into an asset value is capitalization of the income. This is done by using the following formula:

$$\frac{\text{income stream}}{\text{rate of return}} = \text{value}$$

In the formula, the income stream is the expected profit derived from the property for the year. The rate of return is that return, expressed as a percentage, that the investor expects to receive from the property. The return is determined by the investor, or the analyst, as one commensurate with current market conditions and the degree of risk involved.

Say, for example, the subject property shows an income stream of $20,000.* A fair rate of return for the present market, including comparable risks involved, is, say, 9 percent. Using the formula,

$$\frac{\$20,000}{.09} = \$222,222$$

So, if you are offered a property showing the foregoing returns, you can place a value of $222,222 on the cash flow. Add to that amount the residual value of the property at the end of a holding period, and it will give the property value by one income approach. Thus,

Value of income stream	$222,222
Value of residual (estimated)	85,000
Total value	$307,222

Discount Analysis Method.   Another analysis method, this one derived from the financial markets, is discount analysis. This procedure takes each year's future cash flow and reduces it to its present worth. The investor receives a return on the investment delivered at intervals in the future. Yet payment for the income-producing asset is expected at time of purchase, either in cash or by borrowing the money to deliver the cash at closing. So the question is: How much are the future cash flows worth in dollars today? By referring to a "Present Worth of a Dollar" table, the discount can be easily calculated. Using the same numbers as in the previous example gives the result shown in Table 9–1.

---

*The term "income stream" is not precise: it can mean different things to different analysts. However, when comparisons between properties are made, the same measure must be applied to each.

TABLE 9–1
Present Worth of Cash Flow Plus Residual

At End of Year	Annual Cash Flow		Present Worth of a Dollar Factor* at 9% Rate		Present Worth of Cash Flow
1	$20,000	×	.91743	=	$18,349
2	20,000	×	.84168	=	16,834
3	20,000	×	.77218	=	15,444
		Sum of annual cash flows		=	50,627
At the end of year 3, the property is sold for $250,000, discounted to its present worth equals $250,000 × .77218				=	193,045
	Total present worth of cash flows plus residual			=	$243,672

*Present Worth Factors are obtained from financial tables such as "Ellwood Tables for Real Estate Appraising and Financing," L. W. Ellwood, Ballinger Publishing Co., Cambridge, Mass.

The figures in Table 9–1 are hypothetical and are intended only to illustrate the discount calculation. In practice, the holding period would most likely be much longer. And the annual cash flows would be projected with such variations as might be anticipated in occupancy and rental rate adjustments. This kind of calculation can be made easily with a computer using any of several software programs that are available.

Property Characteristics

Property analysis extends beyond an appraisal and includes some of the conditions discussed in the following sections. Most of this information refers to residential loans. When dealing with this type of loan, there is often a similarity in neighborhoods that precludes a detailed study of each house. But with commercial loans, the property is almost always considered on a "case-by-case" basis. Because of its greater emphasis on property analysis, commercial lending is considered in more detail in Chapter 11.

Physical Characteristics

There are several considerations concerning the property's physical characteristics that may be used as "go, no-go" determinants in the approval of a mortgage loan.

Dwelling Units.   Statistical references class one- to four-family housing as *residential.* However, many lenders in the conventional loan market separate this group into single-family housing, which qualifies for prime loan rates, and commercial property, which is rated for higher-risk loans. Both the FHA and VA issue commitments for two-, three-, and four-family housing, but the limits are not as favorable as those for single-family units.

Townhouses and Condos.   Townhouses attached to the ground are treated in the same manner as single-family housing. And in all states, condominiums are classed as real estate by enabling legislation that permits first-mortgage loans to be made on them.

Number of Bedrooms.   Conventional lenders no longer consider the number of bedrooms a major consideration. Years ago it was not unusual to restrict loans to housing that had more than one bedroom. But the market has changed so that a number of buyers prefer limited bedroom space. As long as the lender believes a reasonable market exists for the property should foreclosure become necessary, the collateral is acceptable. (The FHA does base some of its loan limits in certain programs on the number of available bedrooms.)

Square Footage.   Minimum house size based on square footage is no longer used as a loan determinant. As builders have endeavored to reduce housing costs, the size of houses has been reduced. The old standard of "not less than 1,000 square feet of living area" is simply not applicable in today's markets. Actually, the importance of square footage is more relevant to the value of the house in an appraisal.

Paved Streets.   While most cities have managed to pave their streets, there are some smaller communities that have not. Lenders have used the lack of paving as a "no-go" situation for a loan if it can result in a lessening of the collateral value. For example, the cost of paving is often handled in the form of an additional assessment on the property fronting the new pavement. If the assessment's amount is unknown, it is difficult to make adequate provision for the charge.

Utilities.   A loan application may be rejected if the property offered as collateral does not have adequate sewer and water facilities. Top preference is given to a municipally operated or a regulated private operation furnishing both sewer and water services. The use of septic tanks or private water wells may be a cause for rejection. Some lenders will permit a septic tank if the percolation tests of the soil surrounding it meet certain minimum requirements. Also classed as utilities are the services of electricity, natural gas, and telephone. The lack of any of these services, however, is not detrimental for a loan. Also, there are no requirements for electricity or phones to be furnished through underground systems at the present time.

Building Materials.   As important as building materials would seem to be, they are not used as a determinant in underwriting a loan. Whether the building is sheathed in aluminum, asbestos, wood, brick, or stone is important to an appraiser in evaluating the building, but not to a lender in determining a "go, no-go" situation. The quality of the building materials is expressed in terms of the value of the building and in its estimated life or apparent age.

Amenities.   The extra niceties that exist in some buildings are reflected in the value of the property but are not considered critical for the underwriter. A swimming pool, fine landscaping, exterior lighting, a neighborhood club, or recreational area are all added features that increase property value but are never considered a requirement for loan approval.

Hazardous Waste Areas

A more recent concern in the evaluation of real property as collateral for a loan is whether or not the land is on, or near, a hazardous waste area. While the problem is more likely to be found in a commercial area, residential developments may also be involved. Amendments to the Superfund Act and the Reauthorization Act of 1986 established more uniform rules of responsibility for environmental hazard clean-up costs. One result is that it can turn an asset into a tremendous liability overnight!

If a hazardous waste area is detected, the responsibility for its clean-up applies to *all parties who may be involved*. The liability is retroactive, strict, joint, and several for all parties involved. What this means is that the party with the "deepest pockets" is most likely to be held responsible. The potentially responsible parties are as follows:

- owners or operators at the time the waste was disposed of,
- parties who disposed of the wastes,
- persons who transported the wastes,
- current owners or operators of a site with hazardous substance problems.

The concern of lenders, of course, is twofold:

1. A loan with collateral that is determined to harbor hazardous waste material could quickly bankrupt the borrower.
2. Foreclosure on any property loan could place the lender in the position of "current owner" of a hazardous waste site, and immediately subject to total costs of clean-up.

Thus, environmental risk has become an added factor in all real estate transactions. Ignorance of the problem does not relieve an owner of responsibility. Cases have multiplied of owners encountering unexpected environmental risks from conditions that they were unaware of when the property was purchased. The potential risk can be minimized by a professional investigation of the environmental risk prior to purchasing a property.

Construction lenders have been among the first to add an environmental risk study to their loan processing procedures. The consideration of any loan on an existing building should include an inspection for asbestos that may have been used. And foreclosure of older loans made before the new clean-up rules were enacted should now include an environmental risk examination. In some instances, lenders have forfeited foreclosure action to avoid becoming the current owner of a hazardous waste site.

Location of Property

Lines are drawn by most conventional lenders among urban, suburban, and rural housing. The differences are not always clearly delineated, but they do provide a broad classification that is useful in describing packages of loans.

Due to the sprawl of our great metropolitan areas, the term *suburban* now means almost any location in a recorded subdivision of land in the general area surrounding cities—the region of greatest growth in our country. *Urban* means the downtown and near-downtown areas of our cities. *Rural* identifies farm housing and, to many lenders, houses existing in the smaller towns. Rural is also occasionally used to identify housing without access to a central water and sewer system.

Neighborhoods.   Lenders no longer specify areas or neighborhoods within a city as acceptable or unacceptable for making loans. Obviously, a neighborhood that is allowed to deteriorate does not make an attractive location for a 30-year loan. However, recent federal regulations prohibit lenders from drawing lines on a geographic basis that could constitute discrimination. The practice is known more commonly as "red-lining," from the lines drawn on city maps to guide loan officers. The prohibition is aimed at the elimination of racial discrimination that could result from arbitrary lines drawn around certain neighborhoods. Lenders are asked to qualify houses on their individual merit rather than on the neighborhood in which they are located. Further, federally regulated lenders are required to disclose the geographic areas in which they have made their loans by census tract or by postal ZIP code number.

Flood-Prone Areas.   The federal government has defined certain areas of the country over the past decade as flood plain zones. These are areas that have been flooded in the past 100 years, or that, if records do not exist, are calculated to have a 1 percent chance of being flooded. Houses built in a designated flood plain may not be financed by any lender subject to any federal regulatory body unless minimum elevation requirements are met. The government will assist a homeowner by subsidizing flood insurance in cooperation with selected private insurance companies in approved areas.

Other Disaster-Prone Areas.   As new real estate developments increase in areas that are subject to certain kinds of natural disasters, many lenders are refusing to consider taking on loans for such properties. The potential for disasters includes earthquakes, volcanic eruptions, flooding, swelling soils, subsidence of the land, landslides, and geographic faulting. Where adequate hazard insurance is available, however, most lenders will generally make the loans. One problem emerging now is an increasing concern for the continuation of lending in areas where growth has been unintentionally encouraged by government-subsidized hurricane and flood insurance.

Age of Property

The age of a house is a simple, frequently used criterion for determining acceptable and unacceptable loans. The range varies from an insistence by the lender on exclusively new houses, which is unusual, to no fixed limit. Many lenders couple the age of the property with the location of the house. Some neighborhoods maintain their desirability over the years, and 30- to 40-year-old homes may qualify for prime loans. Older houses that are not in the prime neighborhoods may still qualify for mortgage loans but at higher interest rates and for shorter terms. The originator of a loan must always keep in mind what the specific requirements of various sources of money are in regard to age.

Conventional loans are handled in two ways regarding the question of age. Standard loans are most often based on the actual age of the property. A "no-go" limit is set at a maximum age, such as not to exceed 15 years, for example. A lender may commit to take loans on new houses only, or perhaps on houses not over 3 years old, or not over 20 years old. It is the responsibility of the appraiser to determine the age of the house, and some flexibility is allowed in his or her professional opinion. It is not necessary, in most cases, to report the date of a building permit or the exact day of commencement of construction. Rather, the appraiser can make a judgment on the *apparent* age of the house. Obviously, a well-kept house and yard would indicate a lower age than would one that had been allowed to deteriorate.

The second method used to determine the age of a property for purposes of a conventional loan is the appraiser's judgment of its remaining useful life. In this connection, both FNMA and FHLMC use the same standard as the FHA to qualify loans that they will purchase: the term of the loan cannot exceed 100 percent of the remaining useful life of the property. Prior to 1986 the limitation was 75 percent of remaining useful life.

Usage of Property

Residential properties can be said to fall into four categories of usage insofar as mortgage loans are concerned. These are:

1. *Owner occupied* This property is considered to show prime security usage and accounts for most residential loans. Only owner-occupied units can command the highest-ratio loans.

2. *Tenant occupied* Such property falls more into the commercial category of loan analysis, though it is still considered a residential loan for savings association tax purposes and so far as banking regulations are concerned. Since a rental house would not command first call on the owner's income, a lender could downgrade the collateral and make a smaller loan of, perhaps, 75 to 80 percent of the value.

3. *Resort housing* Until recently, resort houses could be described as cottages, sometimes poorly built of nonpermanent materials, and generally not acceptable as security for loans. The locations often lacked proper fire and police protection, were subject to vandalism and excessive storm damage, and were often not connected to municipal utility systems. In recent years the growth of new, higher-class subdivisions in lakefront or mountainous areas has greatly improved the quality and thus the acceptability of these homes as collateral. Lenders do, in fact, make many resort home loans, but they adjust the amount downward from, perhaps, 65 to as high as 90 percent loan-to-value ratio.

    In resort-type developments, it is not unusual for a developer to buy a loan commitment, paying the discount fee necessary to provide potential customers with a dependable, economical source of mortgage money.

4. *Second homes* Second homes are a close corollary to the resort home, though they differ in several ways. The more affluent society has produced a growing number of families financially able to live in two different houses. On occasion, the house in the city might be less lived in and less occupied, on the whole, than the so-called second home in the country. With regard to financing, a lender usually makes a careful determination as to which house might be considered the primary housing entitled to preferential treatment and which one should be downgraded as a second home, receiving

an 80 percent or lower loan. A decision such as this would be required where the borrower was interested in making a purchase that is primarily based on a substantial annual income and not enough other assets. The lender must then consider the loan from the viewpoint of a sudden decrease in income due to job loss or working disablement. Which house, then, would most likely have to be forfeited under adverse circumstances?

Condominiums

Changes in lifestyles have supported the growth in demand for condominiums in place of free-standing houses. The advantages include less maintenance responsibility, access to more amenities, and the same tax advantages that go with all homeownership. Those most interested in this type of dwelling are singles, the young marrieds, and senior citizens, together comprising over half the adult population.

It has required state-passed enabling legislation to make a condominium unit, separated from any direct attachment to the land, eligible for a mortgage loan. All states presently have such laws. Generally, these laws state how condominiums can be described as real property, and thus acceptable as collateral by regulated lending institutions. From a lender's viewpoint, a condominium loan involves more questions than does a free-standing house because of the common areas usually owned jointly by all unit owners and the homeowners association, or management agreement, handling the operations of the property.

A major concern is the way maintenance costs are managed and how they are allocated to the unit owners. With new properties, a developer may hold maintenance costs to a minimum during the sell-out period, but this may leave an overload of maintenance costs for unit owners later on. While a lender has little voice in the continuing operations of a condominium project, a careful screening of the management agreement may point out troublesome provisions. Maintenance costs present two problems for a lender: one is an overburden on the borrower with an increased potential of default, and the other is the rights associated with collecting a maintenance assessment. In some states, these rights may be similar to those of property taxes, that is, they can take priority over a mortgage lien. So fair and reasonable maintenance assessments are important to the lender as well as the unit owner.

Lenders generally require a copy of the management agreement, or the homeowners association operating contract, for the condominium as part of the loan documentation. A review of this agreement takes time, and lenders usually require more than one unit loan in a project before granting approval.

Several pitfalls that occurred in some of the earlier projects have been fairly well overcome by now. These involved problems with apartment conversions and new developments with developers who held onto a management control for too long. Some of these problems are a retention of the exclusive right to all future sales of condos, controlling the distribution and resale of utilities to the individual units, and holding an unlimited right to expand the project that could overburden existing amenities.

While property qualification for a condominium differs as outlined, the qualifications for a borrower buying a condo are the same as for any other residential loan.

Cooperative Apartments

A cooperative apartment is one in which the ownership of the entire project is vested in a tenant-owned corporation or trust. To purchase an apartment, it is first necessary to buy shares of stock in the owning corporation or trust. Then the apartment is leased from the corporate owner. The requirement to buy stock allows the other tenant-owners to restrict who may purchase stock and, in so doing, who may occupy the premises. The difficulty of freely marketing a co-op unit has made this type of ownership less desirable than that of a condominium.

Nevertheless, cooperative apartments may offer an owner similar tax advantages as those available to the owner of a condominium. There are some differences in tax questions, though, as the common areas of a co-op are owned by the corporate owner rather than jointly by the unit owners.

Financing the construction of a cooperative apartment (or a condominium project) has the disadvantage of requiring a number of units to be built with the initial commitment of money. Unlike a single-family housing development, which allows houses to be built at about the same rate as they are sold, the cooperative apartment must be built as a complete project. One method that is sometimes used to assure a construction lender of loan repayment is to presell a certain number of the units. Release of the construction funding can be made contingent on the presale of a specified number of units.

Mobile Homes

Unless permanently attached to the ground as may be defined by a state's property laws, a mobile home is considered personal property, not realty. As such, its use as collateral for loans follows different procedures. Financing of these homes will be considered briefly here, since they represent about 20 percent of the housing units built for sale or rental in this country each year.

Partly because they are an outgrowth of the much smaller house trailer, the mobile home is often financed in a similar manner to an automobile. Many states license and tax them as a highway vehicle, causing some dissension and controversy within communities where mobile homes locate and utilize local schools and police and fire protection facilities.

Underwriting programs by both the FHA and VA have provided some impetus to the growth of mobile home sales. And conventional procedures have kept pace. All these loans follow the pattern of a consumer loan, not a mortgage loan, and are secured by an assignment or a lien on the title registered with the state agency for vehicles.

The term for mobile home loans is longer than for a car, generally running for 10 to 12 years. But the interest is the same add-on type used in car loans. According to this method, for example, a 7.5 percent add-on interest produces a 12.41 percent annual rate for a 10-year loan and a 12.10 percent annual rate for a 12-year loan.

The majority of conventional lenders handling mobile home loans employ the services of one of several companies specializing in the insuring and processing of vehicle loans. For a small fee, usually a percentage of the monthly payment, the service company sells a default insurance policy similar to that handled by private mortgage insurance for homes. In case of a default on the payments, the service company itself pays off the lender and undertakes the repossession of the mobile home. Some lenders prefer to make their loans through the service company. In this procedure, the service company handles the collections and accounting for the outstanding loans and performs in a similar capacity as that of a mortgage banker for home loans.

Surveys

One of the recurring problems in passing land titles and in making sure that a lender is actually receiving a mortgage on the proper land is the identification of that land. Improper identification of the property to be mortgaged, through field error or typographical error, will invalidate the mortgage instrument (but not the obligation to repay the loan). It is to identify physically a parcel of land that a survey is made. A survey is an accurate measurement of the property, not a legal description of it.

An example of an error in property description occurred in a motel loan several years ago. In this case, the property described in the mortgage was identified by the perimeter of the building rather than by the boundaries of the land on which the building stood. The parking areas surrounding the building, which provided the only access to the premises, were not included in the mortgage indenture. When it became necessary to foreclose, the mortgagee learned that he did not have access to the property!

A survey for our purposes is the physical measurement of a specific piece of property certified by a professionally registered surveyor. In processing a mortgage loan, no lender will accept any measurements other than a professional's. It is a precise business, and the loan package requires an accurate description of the land being mortgaged.

When a licensed surveyor defines a piece of property, it is customary to drive stakes or iron rods into the ground at the corners and to "flag" them with colored ribbons. It is not unusual for a lending officer physically to walk the land, checking the corner markers, thus making sure of the shape of the parcel, and whether or not there might be any encroachments that would infringe on the mortgage lien. However, the prime responsibility in locating encroachments belongs to the surveyor, which is one of the reasons why a survey is necessary.

Legal Descriptions

A completed survey is a map showing each boundary line of the property with its precise length and direction. A survey should not be confused with the legal description of a piece of land. A legal description describes property in words, while a survey describes by illustration. Legal descriptions are most commonly found in the following three forms.

Lot and Block

The best-known type of legal description is that found in incorporated areas that have established procedures for land development. A subdivider, in obtaining city approval to build streets and connect utilities, submits a master survey of the entire block of land, showing how the subdivision is broken into *lots*, which are then numbered and grouped into *blocks* for easier identification. Once the subdivision plat is accepted, it is recorded in the county offices and becomes a readily available legal reference to any lot in the plan.

For lending purposes, where the need is to identify a specific property over a period of 30 or even 40 years, the recorded subdivision plat is a much better method than a street address. Street names change and numbers can be altered, but the lot and block numbers remain secure because they are recorded. It may be argued that a street address gives a much better picture of where a property lies in discussing various houses or properties, but such identification is not sufficiently accurate to be acceptable to a lender. The common method of clearly identifying property in real estate transactions is, first, to give the legal description, followed by a phrase such as "also known as," and then to provide the street address. To illustrate, a property identification might be spelled out as, "Lot 6, Block 9, Nottingham Addition, Harris County, Texas, also known as 1234 Ashford Lane, Houston, Harris County, Texas."

Metes and Bounds

When recorded plats are not available for identification of land (and sometimes when plats *are* available), it becomes necessary to use an exact survey of the boundary lines for complete identification. This might be true of a recorded lot that has a stream or river as one boundary—the precise boundary being subject to change through erosion or realignment.

The method used is to define a starting corner with proper references to other marking lines, then note the direction in degrees and the distance to the next marking corner, and so on around the perimeter of the property back to the starting point. These descriptions can be quite lengthy and involved. An example of the wording used to describe several boundary lines might be " . . . and thence along said Smith Street south 61 degrees 32 minutes 18 seconds west 948 and 25/100 feet; thence continuing along said Smith Street south 64 degrees 45 minutes 51 seconds west 162 and 80/100 feet to the point of beginning."

It is obvious that considerable accuracy is required to figure the necessary directions down to a second of a degree and to measure the distances over highly variable and often rough terrain in order to close the boundaries properly. Such a description is acceptable only if certified by a registered surveyor.

In some rural areas, land is identified in the form of metes and bounds by the use of monuments. A *monument* may be something tangible, such as a river, a tree, rocks, fences, or streets, or intangible, such as a survey line from an adjoining property. Physical monuments such as these are subject to destruction, removal, or shifting, and do not provide lasting identifications for long-term loans.

Geodetic or Government Survey

As long ago as 1785, the federal government adopted a measurement system for land based on survey lines running north and south, called *meridians*, and those running east and west, called *base lines*. The system eventually applied to 30 western states with the exception of Texas. A number of prime meridians and base lines were established. Then the surveyors divided the areas between the intersections into squares called *checks*, which are 24 miles on each side. These checks are further divided into 16 squares, each measuring 6 miles by 6 miles, called *townships*. The townships are then divided into square-mile units (36 to a township), called *sections*, which amount to 640 acres each. These sections are then divided into halves, quarters, or such portions as are needed to describe individual land holdings. An example is shown in Figure 9–1.

During the growth years of our country, much of the western land was laid out in this fashion by contract survey crews. Marking stakes were duly placed to identify the corners, and these stakes are frequently used today. The fact that many of the surveys accumulated errors, including the failure to close lines, has created some confusion that concerns principally the oil and mining companies today who are attempting to identify leases, and ranchers claiming property lines against a neighbor.

However, these faulty descriptions have not constituted a serious problem for lending institutions. Land described, for example, as "Section 16, Township 31 north, Range 16 east, New Mexico Prime Meridian," could effectively handle a farm or ranch loan, and a minor inaccuracy in describing such a tract would not undermine the basic security of the collateral.

In pledging property where there is the possibility or probability that some slight inaccuracy has occurred as to the exact amount of land involved, it is customary to use a qualifying term such as "comprising 640 acres, more or less." Any variation in property size should be considered in the light of what might be termed "reasonable." A few acres out of line among 640 acres would not matter a great deal, but a few feet in a downtown city property could well be of critical importance.

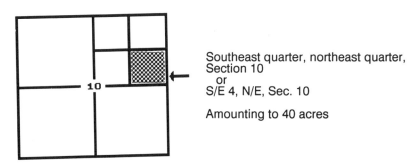

Southeast quarter, northeast quarter, Section 10
or
S/E 4, N/E, Sec. 10

Amounting to 40 acres

FIGURE 9–1 Section of a Township Divided into Quarters

Questions for Discussion

1. Define an appraisal.

2. What qualifications does a mortgage lender require for an appraiser? Identify the leading professional designations for appraisers.

3. What is meant by the "highest and best use" of land?

4. Describe each of the three approaches to value, and give examples of the property type for which each would be most applicable.

5. Name the three categories of depreciation associated with real property. What is the function of each?

6. How would you capitalize an income stream so as to show a property value? What is the advantage of a discounted or present worth analysis?

7. Name a physical characteristic of a residential property that might cause a rejection as collateral.

8. What is meant by red-lining?

9. Define apparent age of a property.

10. Why is a loan for a condominium more difficult to analyze than one for a free-standing house?

11. Distinguish between a survey and a legal description.

12. Give an example of a typical legal description made by lot and block numbers.

10

Other Financing Practices

KEY WORDS AND PHRASES

Home builder commitments	Supplier financing
Loan-to-value ratio	Seller-financed mortgages
Dollar limits	Refinancing
Land leases	Title protection
Unsubordinated ground lease	Abstract of title
Subordinated ground lease	Title insurance
Build to lease	Torrens System
Sale and leaseback	Foreclosure
Syndication	Deficiency judgment
Realty fund	Default insurance obligations
SEC regulations	Indemnity

While practices in the real estate business do vary across the country, there are a number of conditions, terms and procedures that are commonly used. It is the purpose of this chapter to explain many of these practices.

Home Builder Commitments

When a new home is purchased directly from a builder, the builder may already hold a commitment for mortgage money that can be used by the home buyer. Some of the ways these commitments are handled are discussed in the sections that follow.

Competitive Method. The small- to medium-sized builders may have their construction money secured without any commitment for the permanent loans. For example, a commercial bank carrying the construction financing would have little interest in making a permanent loan. If there is no commitment, the purchaser is free to seek whatever source of mortgage money that may be found.

Commitment Method—Construction. When a builder, and this would cover all sizes of builders, obtains construction money, the lender may request a first-refusal right to all permanent loans on the project. The construction lender thus ties up a good source of loans for the future, which is one of the incentives to make the construction loan in the first place. To enforce this right, the lender can add a penalty provision in the construction loan agreement that provides for an extra one-half or 1 percent of the construction loan to be paid for a release of the construction mortgage if the loan is not handled through the same lender. A purchaser cannot be required to borrow money from a particular lender, but it can be a bit more costly to go elsewhere.

Commitment Method—Purchase. Some of the larger builders who can qualify for the lowest rates on their construction money, or use their own funds for this purpose, may purchase a future commitment for money direct from a savings association or other major source to protect future customers needing loans. The builder will pay at least 1 percent of the total commitment amount to hold the money or may pay additional fees to ensure the future home buyers a lower, more competitive interest rate. This expense, which in effect is a prepayment of interest by the builder for the benefit of the buyer, is charged back into the cost of the house. It is in this manner that some builders can advertise lower than market interest rates and obtain a competitive advantage in the housing market.

Associated Companies. A few of the larger builders who are basically national in scope are organized with their own affiliated mortgage companies or money sources to provide permanent loans. The tie-in is generally competitive with the market rates for money and is intended as a convenience for the buyer. These companies seldom press their full range of services upon a customer, but they carry a competitive edge by being available at the proper time.

Loan-to-Value Ratio (LTVR)

The loan-to-value ratio is the amount of a loan as a percentage of the property's value. For this purpose, the property value is the lesser of the appraised value or the sales price. An exception is VA's valuation that accepts only their own appraised value for property offered as collateral. Of course, if a sale is not involved, the appraised value would be the proper measure.

The LTV ratio is an important standard for mortgage lenders. It is used by the industry in the following ways.

1. *As a standard for pricing a loan.* The higher the ratio, the greater the risk requiring a higher price. A borrower offering 5 percent down has a lesser stake in the property than one offering 20 percent down. Lender experience indicates that those with greater equities are less likely to allow a default to occur. Thus, a 95 percent LTVR loan would require the highest interest rate and the greater number of discount points. Generally, the price distinction levels out at an 80 percent LTVR. A buyer offering more than 20 percent down achieves only marginally better pricing.

2. *As a standard for default mortgage insurance.* Federal rules require that residential loans greater than 90 percent LTVR must be insured against default. Most lenders apply their own rules that require such insurance down to 80 percent LTVR loans. Buyers making down payments of 20 percent or more can usually obtain loans with no default insurance required. Also, the price of mortgage insurance varies with the LTVR.

3. *As a standard for quality of loan.* Federal rules set standards for conventional residential loans at a maximum permissible ratio of 95 percent. (HUD/FHA and VA apply their own measures.) When a regulated lender undergoes an examination of its loan portfolio, one important measure is the LTVR of each loan. If a loan exceeds the approved ratio for that type of loan, it can be disallowed as an asset of the lending institution. Whether or not an excessive LTVR loan was caused by the initial loan amount, or an unrealistic appraisal, has created some regulatory problems.

Dollar Amount of Loan

There are some limitations on the dollar amount of residential loans. HUD/FHA and VA set their own limits as described in Chapter 7. For conventional loans, the various regulatory agencies can set limits. Most of these involve a limitation on the amount of any single loan as a percentage of the lender's total assets and limits on the amount that can be loaned to any individual. In years past, states have set limits on dollar amounts for single-family residential loans, but most of these have since been eliminated.

Fannie Mae/Freddie Mac Limits. A widely used standard for loan limits is that applied by Fannie Mae and Freddie Mac. Each January, the two federal underwriting agencies adjust the limit on the dollar amount of a loan that they can purchase (or allow into a mortgage pool). The limit can be increased each year by the rate of change in the average purchase price reported by the Federal Home Loan Bank Board between October and the October of the previous year. The loan limit itself began at a higher level than earlier purchase price averages and remains somewhat higher now. For example, the average purchase price in October 1988 amounted to $136,900. The average purchase price for the prior October (1987) was $123,100. The increase for the 12-month period amounted to $13,800 or an 11.2 percent increase. Since the 1988 FNMA/FHLMC loan limit amounted to $168,700, the limit for 1989 must be increased by 11.2 percent. Thus the new limit for 1989 becomes $187,600 (168,700 × 1.112 = 187,594, rounded to 187,600).

The limit increases for the number of dwelling units and for higher cost areas as follows:

FNMA/FHLMC 1989 Loan Limits

Number of Units	Loan Limit	For Alaska, Hawaii and Guam
1	$187,600	$281,400
2	239,950	339,925
3	290,000	435,000
4	360,450	540,675

Minimum Loan Limits. There are no regulatory minimums for mortgage loans but there are some practical limits. Smaller loans are those most likely to be needed by lower income families, and to set limits could cause discrimination. Nevertheless, the smaller the loan amount the smaller the related servicing fees. A three-eighths of 1 percent servicing fee on a $20,000 loan amounts to $75.00 per year or $6.25 per month. This may be less than it costs to handle the work involved. The result is that smaller loans are more difficult to sell and usually require much larger discounts to offset the cost. As an asset for the holder of the loan, it has a greater loss in value than the larger, more profitable loans.

Large Residential Loans. As the average cost of homes increases in certain areas above the $200,000 level, the need for larger loans becomes more important. Loans that exceed the conforming loan limit (just described) are more difficult to sell and are more likely to be held in portfolio by the lender. Even so, the amounts may exceed the lender's own limits for a single loan. To overcome this problem, two or more lenders may combine to fund the loan. This is called a *participation* loan. One lender services the loan and accounts to the other participants as their percentage of the loan may require.

Land Leases

While most developments are built on land owned by the developer or builder, there is a growing use of land leases for development purposes. There are several reasons for leasing land rather than buying outright.

Land Not for Sale. In some areas of the country such as Hawaii, Orange County, California, and certain high density downtown areas, land is simply not available for purchase. The owners see greater value in leasing than converting the land asset into cash subject to tax.

Leasing May Be Lower Cost. It is quite possible to negotiate a lease on land that allows its use for many years at a cost less than the purchase price could be financed. Lease payments are tax deductible (if used for business purposes) while land is nondepreciable as an asset.

Separating Ownership. Another purpose for a land lease is to separate the ownership of improvements from the land ownership. The separation allows either one to be sold without capital gains tax assessed on the other. And a sale of either one, rather than both, could reduce the financing requirements.

Financing Development on Leased Land

When a lease on land is consummated between a landowner and a builder/ developer, the contract is generally known and referred to as a *ground lease*. The landowner's interest is termed the *underlying fee*, and the lessee's (builder's) interest is known as the *leasehold*. Ground leases are usually net leases that create a tenancy for years, typically with terms of 55, 75, or 99 years. The 99-year limit derives from some early state laws that held that leases of 100 years or longer were transfers of title rather than leases.

Financing construction on land that is leased has some limitations as the builder can pledge only the lease-hold interest, not the underlying fee, as collateral. This can cause a problem for lenders accustomed to working with mortgages that include a pledge of the land itself. While the legal terminology varies a bit, there are two basic ways to handle loans involving property where the land is leased: an unsubordinated ground lease and a subordinated agreement lease.

UNSUBORDINATED GROUND LEASE

Under this procedure, the landowner does not subordinate the ownership (fee title) to the leasehold interest. This means that if the ground rent is not paid, the landowner can foreclose and terminate the leasehold rights. In such a case any improvements could be claimed by the landowner, thus defeating any claim by a lender holding only a pledge of the leasehold interest. To minimize such a consequence, with this kind of lease the lender would normally require that the borrower pay the ground rent to the lender as a part of the mortgage payment. The lender would then pass the ground rent on to the landowner, or even advance the ground rent, if necessary, to protect the lender's collateral position. The procedure is fairly common with smaller properties. The handling of the ground rent as part of the mortgage payment may be likened to the handling of property taxes.

SUBORDINATED AGREEMENT LEASE

With a subordinated ground lease, the landowner grants the lease and then encumbers the fee title with a subordination agreement. What this means is that the landowner subordinates the ownership of the land in favor of the mortgage holder. With this kind of lease the developer, in effect, with only a leasehold interest, can pledge the land itself as part of the collateral to secure a development loan.

The concept is often used in the development of motel properties and some fast food operations. It is true that the landowner places valuable property at risk with a subordination agreement, but would do so if a greater return can be realized than simply holding unimproved land. If the mortgage loan for the development is not paid, the mortgagee has the right to take both the land and improvements in a foreclosure action. To protect the landowner against such a consequence, the subordination agreement would normally require timely notification of any act in default on the mortgage loan. If such should occur, the landowner would then have the right to step into the position of tenant/borrower with rights to the property's cash flow and the obligation to pay the balance due on the mortgage note.

Build-To-Lease

A popular investment with lesser risk for the investor is for the lessor to agree to construct a building to certain specifications in return for a lease commitment from the prospective tenant. The procedure is also called "build-to-suit" or "build-to-let." The builder/investor has an assured tenant immediately upon completion of the building and an immediate cash flow. The tenant obtains a specially designed building that meets its needs more precisely. Examples of how this procedure is used would be free-standing store buildings for a tenant such as Safeway Corporation (grocers) and service stations built for major oil companies. This method is also used by the U.S. Post Office for outlying facilities. The post office leases buildings built to their specifications based on open bidding of projected rental rates.

Sale and Leaseback

Another financing technique that involves lease procedures is for an owner to sell his or her property to an investor, and simultaneously lease it back for continued occupancy. For the owner/seller, the advantage is the cash realized from the sale that can be used for further expansion of a company. The continued occupancy of the facilities allows an uninterrupted operation. And the lease payments are deductible as they would be for a business purpose. The investor/ buyer obtains a sound real estate property with an immediate cash flow presumably calculated to yield a fair return.

While the procedure is most commonly used with commercial properties, it also has an application for a homeowner. A homeowner, perhaps a parent, sells a house to a son or daughter and leases the premises for continued occupancy. While the lease payments are not tax deductible for the tenant (it classifies as property used for personal purposes), the son or daughter now owns the property as an income-producing asset subject to all deductions available for rental property, including depreciation. (*Caution*: Any transaction between family members must be at fair market values else the tax treatment may be disallowed.)

The sale-and-leaseback technique is also used in certain instances of company acquisition. To reduce the up-front cash needed to acquire a company, a buyer may arrange a sale and leaseback of property owned by the company to be acquired. Simultaneously, with the closing of the acquisition, the buildings are sold to an investor and the cash applied toward the purchase of the company. At the same time, the buildings are leased back to the acquired company with no interruption in its operation.

Sale of Equity Interests

Two types of equity investment have become popular as methods for financing real estate: syndications and realty funds.

Syndication

The *syndication of land* is a term that describes land or property acquisition and ownership by a group of participants. The participants may be individuals, partnerships, or corporations. A syndicate is not a type of business organization;

rather, it is a name applied to any group set up to pursue a limited objective in business. While there are a number of forms that may be used in the organization of a syndicate, the most popular is the *limited partnership*. As a business form, the limited partnership is recognized in all states. Essentially, it provides for one or more general partners who are responsible for the management and personally liable for the partnership's obligations. Another class of partner is also recognized—the limited partners, who are not permitted to participate in management decisions, and whose liability is limited to the amount of their invested capital. A limited partnership must file its chartering agreement with the state in accordance with the applicable laws.

Two basic types of syndicates are:

1. *Sale of interests in existing properties* Under this method, the property is identified for the participants. For example, a builder or developer (usually called a *syndicator*) owns or controls (by option or contract of sale) a suitable investment property. The syndicator then sells participating interests to raise the money to develop the land, or possibly to complete the acquisition of an existing building.

2. *Sale of interests in property to be acquired* A syndicator sells interests to raise money for the acquisition of property as determined later by the syndicator. This procedure is also referred to, quite accurately, as a *blind pool*. Because it allows so much freedom to the syndicator in the use of other people's money, many states forbid its use.

Since a participating interest in a syndicate can be classed as a type of security investment, most states place limits on the number of participants that can be *offered* without a complete registration under the state's security law. If the sales are made across state lines, or the number to whom participations are offered exceeds 35, then a registration must be made with the federal Securities and Exchange Commission. Failure to comply with the law can result in felony action against the syndicator for the sale of unregistered securities.

Realty Funds

Whenever a larger group is formed to participate in a real estate venture, registration with federal and state regulatory agencies is necessary. The participation can be in the form of "units" purchased in a realty fund, usually formed as a limited partnership.

Realty funds are organized by persons or companies wishing to raise equity money for real estate projects, such as the purchase of raw land, a construction development, or the purchase of existing income properties. The interests are sold in the form of participating certificates at a fixed price per unit. A unit generally costs anywhere from $100 to $5,000, depending on the plan of organization, and represents a certain percentage of interest in the total fund. Federal and most state laws classify the sale of such participating interests as a sale of securities that must be registered and approved before any sale can be made.

The participant is actually a limited partner and may share in the tax losses and depreciation as well as the profits generated through the fund's investments. The organizer of the fund is usually the general partner, or a company controlled by the general partner is so designated, and also serves as managing agent for the fund's properties.

SEC Regulations for Real Estate Transactions

As mentioned briefly in the introductory chapter of this text, the Securities and Exchange Commission (SEC) is one of the agencies created during the Depression years to correct possible abuses in the sale of securities to the general public. There are several ways that real estate transactions can become involved with SEC requirements.

Sale of Mortgage Bonds.   Large, well-known corporations have an alternative method of raising money not generally available to the individual. This consists of borrowing in the financial markets through the sale of bonds. If the purpose for the money is to build a commercial or industrial building, the builder might sell mortgage bonds. Such an issue of bonds would be secured by a pledge of the real estate being developed. If such an issue is sold to the general public, it would be subject to approval by the SEC. SEC examination of any proposed security issue is directed toward ensuring accuracy of the information distributed for the protection of the general public. It does not, however, assess the risk of any issue.

Advance Payments on Real Estate.   There are many ways of offering real estate for sale. Only a few present any possible problems with the SEC. In general, the SEC considers a transaction designed to raise money from the general public through the sale of "paper," rather than delivery of a title to property, to be suspect. Under certain circumstances, the paper could be construed to be a security and consequently subject to the SEC registration requirements. The sale of securities in violation of SEC regulations is a felony offense.

The kinds of real estate transactions that may be subject to SEC registration are those such as the sale of predevelopment certificates for lots, the sale of condominium units yet to be constructed, and the sale of limited partnership interests, if offered publicly. In those instances, where the line between selling real estate and selling a security is difficult to draw, it is best to consult with competent legal counsel.

Supplier Financing

Under certain conditions it might be possible for a builder/developer to obtain financing assistance from a supplier. It is a tool sometimes used to gain an advantage in a competitive market. The assistance may be obtained two ways: (1) extended terms that allow later payment; or (2) a direct loan by the supplier. Both are discussed next.

Extended Terms

Most companies selling a service or product need their accounts receivable paid promptly and often offer cash discounts for such payments. A few companies utilize credit terms as an incentive to do business with them and, in so doing, provide additional financing for the customer.

In building an apartment, an office building, or even a house, a major supplier such as a lumber dealer, cement company, or electrical or plumbing contractor may agree to extend payment terms for 60 or 90 days or, in some cases, until the project is finished and sold. This method does conserve cash for the builder/developer, but usually comes at a higher price—an increase in the product or service price plus interest. And the supplier may be exposed to a payment delay that usually means a forfeiture of lien rights if it exceeds 120 days.

This *extended terms* method of auxiliary finance is not to be confused with slow payment or nonpayment of material suppliers' bills; both are very poor procedures. Building supply companies are fully aware of the 90- to 120-day time limits within which to file liens for nonpayment, and normally make sure that their interests are protected.

Supplier Loans

In recent years some of the major appliance companies and, in a few cases, utility companies, have given larger builders/developers financial assistance with outright loans secured by second mortgages. The ulterior motive in such cases is always to ensure the use of the lender's products. This could be heating and air conditioning equipment, or a full range of kitchen equipment, or it could be a utility company seeking a competitive advantage.

Seller-Financed Home Mortgages

In the early 1980s, interest rates were increasing at a substantial rate. The resulting high costs made it very difficult to sell almost any building or resale property without some financing assistance by the seller. Indeed, in 1982, the National Association of Realtors reported that over 60 percent of the homes sold that year involved some form of seller financing. As a result, a whole new category of loans developed under the umbrella name of "creative financing." The thrust of creative financing schemes was to soften the blow of high costs to the buyer but limit the length of time for the seller financing. Generally, the lower cost to the buyer was accomplished by reducing the payment amounts for the first one to three years. The reduction took the form of "interest-only" payments, buy-down types of payments, wrap-around mortgages or, perhaps, lease payments. Then after a limited term of a year or so, the entire principal balance came due. The buyer was expected to refinance at much lower rates, but this did not actually come to pass until about 1986. In the meantime, many seller-financed deals had to be restructured, or in some cases simply fell into default.

One positive result of the seller-financing period is that two programs were developed to assist sellers willing to accept mortgage notes for the sale of their homes. While both programs have become fairly dormant due to the sharp decline in seller financing, they are worth pointing out as the market can always change. These are (1) default mortgage insurance, and (2) access to the secondary market for the sale of seller-financed mortgages.

Default Insurance. While private mortgage insurance companies have undergone considerable restructuring and some changes in how they do business, some of the insurers do write default insurance for seller-financed transactions. Qualification of the buyer must be handled through an agent of the insurer, generally a mortgage company that represents the insurer. The standards are no different from those applied for any other lender, but the cost is generally a bit higher.

Secondary Market Sale. While there has always been a market for seller-financed mortgages, the cost has been high. A number of finance companies buy first- and second-mortgage loans from individuals, but always at a substantial discount. In 1982, FNMA introduced its own procedures for the purchase of seller-financed mortgage loans, but the program found few takers. It is still available but only through FNMA-approved sellers/servicers. The advantage for a home seller is that the mortgage can be sold at any time to FNMA at whatever discount the market may require at the time of sale. For example, if the mortgage loan is made by the seller at a 10 percent rate, and a year later the home seller elects to sell the mortgage with the market rate still holding at 10 percent, FNMA will pay for the loan in full; i.e., no discount. (Most loan purchasers will not pay a premium on any mortgage loan should the note's face rate exceed the market rate at the time it is sold—maximum is 100 cents on the dollar of loan amount.)

The disadvantage for the seller is that the loan must be originated by an approved FNMA seller/servicer, written on uniform documents with payments serviced solely by the seller/servicer. This raises the question: If the buyer must qualify the same way as for any other lender, why should the seller undertake the loan at all? The reasons differ according to individual needs: It could be for the investment benefit to the seller, or because it gives the seller greater flexibility and some control over the terms, or it might save valuable time in closing the transaction. As of this writing, however, there is adequate money available in the mortgage market at relatively low interest rates, and few sellers are undertaking such financing.

Refinancing

The decline in interest rates between 1983 and 1988 brought many property owners back into the mortgage market, this time to refinance loans at lower rates. The benefits of refinancing differ for each borrower. It involves the amount of rate reduction, the costs of renegotiating the loan (new closing costs and discount), the effect of tax laws on the borrower, and possible new lender requirements such as an adjustable rate instead of a fixed rate loan.

Rate Reduction. While the benefits are difficult to compare, most borrowers have used a margin requirement of at least a two-percentage-point rate savings to justify refinancing. If a 13 percent rate can be refinanced at 11 percent, it might be worthwhile, as indicated in the example below.

Example

At 13% rate, $120,000, 30 years: Annual payment $15,929.40

At 11% rate, $120,000, 30 years: Annual payment   13,713.72

Annual savings from reduced rate = $ 2,215.68

Savings over 3 years = $6,647.04

If the cost of refinancing is less than $6,647.04 and the homeowner intends to remain in the house for three years or longer, refinancing is obviously a wise move.

Where to Refinance.   The best place to start a refinance search is with the holder of the existing mortgage note. Most lenders (but not all!) are aware that mortgage notes can be refinanced when rates drop, and prefer to accept a lesser rate than lose the customer. The market is very competitive and most borrowers have access to more than one source. If the loan holder will not reopen a loan for refinancing in a lower-interest market, there could be other lenders willing to consider such an application.

Refinancing Costs.   No specific regulations apply to the charges that may be assessed in a refinancing transaction; so in a competitive market, the best solution for the borrower would be to try several lenders. Most lenders consider refinancing in the same category (cost-wise) as a new loan. They require a new application fee and a new appraisal, and most require some discount that may be a cash requirement. Even though a discount may be paid in cash, the IRS ruled in May 1986 that a discount for refinancing a home loan must be amortized over the life of the loan. This differs from a discount paid by the buyer at the time of purchase of the house, which may be deducted in the year paid, the same as interest.

Effect of Tax Laws.   Interest paid on a home loan is tax deductible, with the benefit determined by the taxpayer's tax bracket. Thus, a taxpayer in a higher bracket would have greater possible deductions and would need a lower refinance rate to achieve the same benefit as would a person in a lower bracket.

Restructuring the Loan.   Refinancing is a negotiable situation. If a lender agrees to an interest rate concession, it is possible that one bargaining chip would be a change to an adjustable rate repayment plan. The lender is accepting a lower rate and may insist that the rate should be adjustable, should the market rise in the years ahead.

One major problem that some homeowners have encountered in attempting refinancing is that the market value of the house has declined to an amount something less than the balance due on the loan. Or, in the case of some graduated payment designs, the balance due on the loan, which increased in the early years, has exceeded the market value of the property. Except for certain refinancing rules applicable to HUD/FHA and VA loans, generally, a regulated lender will not undertake refinancing of a loan where the collateral value is less than the loan amount. In areas where property values have fallen, it is sometimes necessary for the borrower to pay down a portion of the loan before it can be refinanced at a lesser rate.

However, unlike some other kinds of loans, a mortgage loan is not subject to a call for repayment if the value of the collateral declines to less than the loan amount.

Title Protection

A normal requirement for approval of a mortgage loan is that the title be valid; that is, the lender wants some assurance that the title to the property pledged as collateral is a good one and the parties granting the mortgage are the true owners. Many problems can occur in a chain of title that may impair present ownership rights. These include the possibility of forged documents, undisclosed heirs, mistaken legal interpretation of wills, misfiled documents, confusion resulting from similarity of names, and incorrectly stated marital status.

Three methods are commonly used to protect both the purchaser and the lender from future title problems. One is the opinion of a qualified attorney based on the research of an abstract, one is the purchase of title insurance, and the third is a land registration system, used in a few areas of the country, called the Torrens system. It is most important that a purchaser of real property take the necessary steps to assure good title whether or not a mortgage loan is involved.

Attorney's Opinion Based on Abstract

The older method, and still the only one available for assuring valid title in oil and gas lease transactions, is a research of the abstract by a qualified attorney.

Abstract of Title. The chronological collection of all recorded documents that affect land title is called an *abstract*. It is prepared by an abstracter who specializes in researching county land records. The record includes conveyances, wills, judicial proceedings, liens and encumbrances that affect a particular tract of land. It is simply a history of the instruments that affect title to the land and, by itself, does not assure the validity of title.

Attorney's Opinion. After researching an abstract, a qualified attorney can issue an opinion as to the validity of title. By examining the chain of events that affect title, the attorney can reach a conclusion as to who the present owners are, and report any instruments that have an adverse effect on the ownership rights. Further, the attorney may state what curative steps must be taken to clear the title if there is an adverse claim or a break in the chain of ownership. An attorney's favorable opinion may be accepted by a lender as adequate proof of title.

In large transactions, an attorney's opinion may be a lower cost procedure. However, there are some disadvantages. This method provides no insurance against an adverse claim leaving the purchaser with only the seller as recourse against future loss. Further, it can take more time than the issuance of a title policy, since title insurance companies usually maintain continuous records of all recorded documents.

Title Insurance

The most popular method used to assure valid title in real estate transactions is the purchase of title insurance. It is a specialized type of insurance that protects a policyholder against loss from something that has already happened, such as a forged deed somewhere in the chain of title. Title companies investigate the chain of title to make sure the title is insurable (that there are no defects that could cause a subsequent claim). This is important because the title company also agrees to defend the policyholder's title in court shouuld any lawsuits arise with adverse claims.

Title insurance policies normally list certain exclusions that are not covered by the insurance protection. These exclusions include such things as the rights of parties in possession, unrecorded easements, encroachments, zoning laws, and other governmental restrictions. What is insured is sometimes called a *marketable title* meaning the ownership rights unencumbered by any claim that could create a loss covered by the insurance policy.

There are two different kinds of title insurance—one indemnifies an *owner* against loss, the other indemnifies a *lender* against loss.

Owner's Policy.   An owner's policy protects the owner as long as the insured has an interest in the property. This protection can extend beyond the period of actual possession. When an insured owner sells the property, it is often conveyed with a general warranty deed. The warranty clause in that kind of deed makes the seller liable to "forever defend" against possible defects in the title at the time of conveyance, even though the claim may not arise until long after the property has been conveyed. State limitation statutes normally limit this exposure to a period of 20 to 30 years, after which time the insurance policy itself lapses. The important point is that owner's title insurance does not "run with the land"—it does not transfer to a new owner and is not assignable. The reason is that the previous owner remains liable and holds the protection of that policy.

The owner's policy is issued in the amount of the property value at the time of the transaction. In certain instances it is possible to increase the coverage, should substantial improvements be made or appreciation occur in the property value.

Lender's Policy.   At the same time that an owner's policy is issued, the same property can be insured against the same defects for the benefit of the lender. It is a different policy, however. The lender's policy or mortgagee's policy is issued in the amount of the mortgage loan and declines with each reduction in the principal balance. When the loan is paid off, the lender's policy becomes void. Also, unlike the owner's policy, a lender's policy automatically transfers to whoever holds the mortgage note. If the property is foreclosed and purchased by the mortgagee, the policy automatically becomes an owner's policy.

Who Pays for Title Insurance?   Practice varies throughout the country in regard to payment. A fairly common procedure is for the owner selling the property to pay for the title insurance. The reasoning is that it proves the seller is delivering valid title, even though the coverage protects the buyer. The other side of the question would be that since the buyer is the one protected, then the buyer should pay for the insurance. It is the lender's policy that is most consistently paid for by the buyer as a cost of the loan.

Torrens System

In those states* that permit the use of the Torrens system, it provides a method of registering the ownership of land and encumbrances, except for tax liens. It might be compared with the registration system used for automobiles.

To initiate a Torrens system registration, the landowner petitions a state court to register the subject property. Necessary title information must be filed with the court and notice given to all interested parties. The court's determination is made in the form of a decree somewhat similar to that used in a quiet title suit.

Once registered, title does not pass, nor are encumbrances or conveyances effective, until they are registered on the certificate of title. In some states, Torrens registered property is not subject to a general judgment lien, nor can title be lost through adverse possession.

One of the problems with the use of the Torrens system is that the cost of court action to register a title may easily exceed the cost of title insurance.

Foreclosure

Foreclosure is a legal procedure by means of which property pledged as collateral is sold to satisfy the secured debt. A mortgage grants a lender the right to foreclose in the event of default. While default most often occurs because of nonpayment, there are other reasons that can trigger such action. For instance, the debtor must maintain the property in good condition, keep it free of liens, and comply with all local laws that affect the property. If an act in default occurs, the lender may take such action as is authorized by applicable state laws. In the foreclosure

---

*The Torrens system coexists with regular recording procedures in Colorado, Georgia, Hawaii, Illinois, Massachusetts, Minnesota, New York, North Carolina, Ohio, Virginia, and Washington.

process, title passes to the holder of the mortgage note (the lender), or to a third party who may purchase it at the foreclosure auction sale.

Foreclosure is a step that lenders want to avoid, if at all possible. There are no winners in this action. For the *lender*, it is costly, time consuming, and may require additional funds to be advanced for payment of various foreclosure costs. If the property is vacated, there is danger of vandalism. Also, it brings up the additional problem of future disposition of the property. Foreclosure for the *borrower* results in the loss of property, possibly the homestead. It is a traumatic experience, and can result in a negative report on one's credit record.

For a borrower facing default, the first step should be to discuss the problem with the lender. Most lenders recognize the fact that various personal and business problems, beyond the control of a borrower, can cause default. While the lender is not always able to modify a repayment agreement, it is possible that a moratorium on payments could be granted for a limited period of time. Or possibly the release of some tax escrow funds could provide temporary assistance to the debtor. Lenders do not normally seek out borrowers to offer assistance, as their responsibility is to pursue timely repayment of the loan, so it falls to the borrower to initiate any move to delay or rework the mortgage obligation.

Types of Foreclosure

Foreclosure practices are determined by state laws. They fall into two categories: *judicial* or *nonjudicial*.

A judicial foreclosure is normally used when a regular mortgage is the security instrument. A default is handled by filing the required notices to the debtor followed by a suit in court to foreclose the mortgage claim. If the court agrees with the claim, it can order that the property be sold to satisfy the debt. The sale is handled through a public auction, usually called a "sheriff's sale."

A nonjudicial action is the method by which foreclosure is accomplished when a deed of trust, or a trust deed, is the mortgage instrument. No court action is required as the instrument contains a power of sale within its own terms. Depending on the applicable state laws, proper notification must be given to the debtor prior to the property being offered for sale. Then, the trustee, who is the "third party" in a deed of trust, may sell the property at public auction on behalf of the lender (who is referred to as the beneficiary).

Deficiency Judgments

The sale of property at a foreclosure auction may, or may not, produce sufficient recovery to satisfy all claimants. The lender is entitled only to the defaulted debt (principal balance plus interest) and costs incurred. If, for example, the debt at foreclosure amounts to $42,000 and the property is sold for $35,000, there remains $7,000 due to the lender. Since the borrower is obligated to the lender for the balance due on the note, the lender may have the right to claim a deficiency judgment for the remaining $7,000. However, some states limit the lender's right to a deficiency claim if the property is a person's homestead. In such a case, the lender could only recover the amount realized in the foreclosure sale.

Should a foreclosure sale result in proceeds that exceed the cost of sale and payment of claims, any surplus belongs to the debtor/borrower.

Relief of Debt

There can be an unpleasant tax consequence for the borrower after foreclosure. This can occur if a borrower is granted relief from payment of an unsatisfied obligation. Income tax law treats relief of debt as income to the person granted the relief. If a lender grants such relief, a Form 1099 must be filed with the IRS reporting the amount that the debtor is no longer obligated to pay. To a homeowner who has suffered the loss of a home, an additional tax obligation seems particularly unfair. Nevertheless, present IRS rules consider borrowed money that is not repaid as simply another source of income for the relieved debtor.

Obligations Involved with Default Insurance—Indemnity

When a foreclosure occurs and losses are sustained, who bears the cost? The party holding the note undertakes foreclosure action if there is a default and bears the initial cost. But if the loan is insured against default, the note holder can claim reimbursement for the loss. Exactly how the claim is handled depends on the type of default coverage. This can be private mortgage insurance, a HUD/FHA insured commitment, or a VA guaranty.

Regardless of the type of default coverage, all kinds insure the *lender against loss*, not the borrower. This is true even though it is the borrower who pays the insurance premiums. It is often misunderstood since, unlike other kinds of insurance, the party paying for the coverage is not the one insured. What the borrower is paying for is an assurance to the lender that the loan will be paid should the borrower suffer a default.

There is another major difference between this coverage and other kinds of insurance: As a qualification requirement for coverage, the borrower must *indemnify* the insurance company against loss. This means that if the insurance company must reimburse a lender for a loss, then the insuring company (or federal agency) has a right to demand reimbursement from the defaulted borrower.

This right applies to all three major types of coverage—private mortgage insurance, HUD/FHA, and VA.

Until late 1986, there was little action taken against borrowers who might owe a deficiency claim after foreclosure had been taken. There were two practical reasons for this seeming leniency. First, during most of the 1970s and the early 1980s, property generally increased in value thus limiting the potential loss for a lender; second, in that time period, people tried to hold onto their mortgaged property as it increased in value. If a default did occur, the debtor seldom had sufficient other assets to allow collection of such a claim.

This situation began to change in the mid-1980s. Substantial loss in real property values in certain areas of the country caused some debtors to "walk away" from both their property and the obligation to pay the remaining debt. With property value substantially less than the balance due on a mortgage note, continued payments seemed to be a bad deal to some. As losses mounted, lenders began to take steps to enforce their claims. In October 1986, all federal agencies involved with underwriting home loans required that mortgagees report defaults and foreclosure action to credit bureaus. A further stipulation was that deficiency judgments must be pursued if the debtor holds other assets that may be subject to attachment.

If the claim against a defaulted borrower is made by a private mortgage insurance company, a deficiency judgment must be sought against the debtor through the courts. This judgment, when filed of record, operates as a general lien on the debtor's assets and is collectible in the same manner as any judgment at law. There is a different procedure if the loss is sustained by either HUD/FHA or VA. Since both are federal agencies, an obligation to them becomes an obligation to the government, subject to a federal lien against the debtor. Settlement of a federal lien depends on the debtor's circumstances and is handled on a case-by-case basis. Generally, the obligation can be mitigated only in cases of proven hardship.

Questions for Discussion

1. Discuss methods a builder might use to assist with a home buyer's permanent financing.
2. Discuss dollar limits on loan amount.
3. When is refinancing a mortgage loan practical? Why?
4. Describe two of the three ways that title to property is protected against adverse claims.
5. How is loan-to-value ratio used in lending practices?

6. What kind of real estate transaction might fall under the jurisdiction of the SEC?

7. Who benefits from a sale-and-leaseback deal, and how?

8. What is the risk involved in an unsubordinated leasehold mortgage and how might protection be obtained?

9. What is a syndication? A realty fund?

10. Why would a seller consider offering seller financing in the sale of a house?

11. Describe a judicial foreclosure proceeding. A non-judicial foreclosure.

12. What is meant by a borrower indemnifying an insurance company against loss?

11

Commercial Loans

KEY WORDS AND PHRASES

Commercial loan
Balance sheet
Profit and loss statement
Operating statement
Stabilized statement
Pro forma statement
Certified public accountant
Audited statement
Feasibility report
Present worth of $1.00 table
Amortization tables
Loan constant
Land loans
Land development loans
Release clauses
Office of Interstate Land Sales
   Construction loans
Contract-basis construction loan
Speculative-basis construction
   loan

Standby commitment
Mobile home park loans
Mobile home loans
Special-purpose building loans
Apartment loans
Occupancy
Retail store building
Shopping center loans
Preleased space
Tenant screening
Term leases
Percentage leases
Net leases
Office building loans
Speculative building
Warehouse building loans
Miniwarehouses
Farm and ranch loans

Introduction

In mortgage financing, the term "commercial loan" has a broad and ill-defined meaning. One major discrepancy in the standard, accepted definition is that an apartment loan is considered a commercial type of loan. Yet, for tax purposes such as calculating depreciation, an apartment is classed as residential property.

Perhaps the best definition of a commercial loan would be a very generalized "those loans that are not classed as residential." It is a broad category with considerable variety in the handling of each major class of property. A practical distinction between residential and commercial loans can be drawn from the anticipated source of loan repayment. A residential loan is expected to be repaid from the personal income of the borrower—income unrelated to the property offered as collateral. The commercial loan is a business loan and in most instances expects repayment to derive from the property pledged as collateral. The individual involved with seeking a commercial loan is certainly important, but not crucially so as with a residential loan. Indeed, in many large commercial loans there may not be any personal liability for the principals as individuals. For it is the property that provides both the loan collateral and the anticipated source of loan repayment.

Consequently, commercial loan evaluation focuses first on the property, then on the business applicant who expects to own the property. The following section will discuss the type of information most commonly used and the way it is presented. Beginning with the loan application, it includes financial statements, feasibility studies, and a few of the tools used to determine repayment amounts.

Information Sources

The underwriter of a commercial loan has greater sources of information than are normally found in home loans. The home loan evaluation is based primarily on the applicant's personal income and a market appraisal of the property offered as collateral. Proper underwriting of a commercial loan usually involves a business operation and property expected to produce sufficient income to repay the loan. So, to evaluate a commercial loan, the underwriter would examine the financial statements offered by the business (or individual) applicant, study the income-producing capability of the property offered as collateral, and conduct an examination of the local market for that property's particular product or services. In addition, analysis of a commercial loan application includes extensive interviews with the principals involved in the business operation, and a thorough inspection of the property itself.

The Loan Application

All loans commence with an application. However, unlike residential loans, a commercial loan application is not a standardized form. Further, the application is not subject to requirements of the Real Estate Settlement Procedures Act that mandates limitations on what can be asked of a residential loan applicant. Commercial loan applications are designed by lenders to suit their own specific requirements. Often, the application has specialty sections that focus on different classes of properties, such as the distinctive information needed for a hotel loan that differs from that needed to evaluate an apartment loan application.

Generally, the application information identifies the applicant and the individuals involved, the amount and purpose of the loan, and the source of loan repayment. The detailed information is furnished in separate exhibits that would include complete financial statements, a property evaluation, a projection of how the loan is expected to be repaid, and any supplemental information such as building plans and specifications if construction is involved.

It is normal for the lender to charge a reasonable nonrefundable application fee, for several reasons. One is to deter frivolous requests and another is to defray the cost of studying the extensive, and usually "one of its kind," body of information that supports sound applications.

Financial Statements

How financial information is presented has a few standards and little regulation. What is close to standard is the design of the principal kinds of statements, but the information can vary considerably. Regulations that apply to this type of information are directed to those companies that offer securities to the general public. The statements most likely to be found in a real estate loan application are further described next, followed by information on the professionals who prepare such information.

Balance Sheet. A balance sheet is the most standardized of all the financial statements. It is a listing of a company's (or individual's) assets in a column at the left of the page, plus a listing of the liabilities and the net worth in a column at the right of the page. The difference between the assets (what is owned), and the liabilities (what is owed), amounts to the net worth of the company. By adding the liabilities and the net worth on one side, there must be an equal amount to the assets listed on the other side—thus, a "balance" sheet.

Figures that are of concern to an analyst of the balance sheet are the valuation of assets. This is particularly important when major assets consist of real estate.

A distortion in value can easily present an erroneous picture of the true worth. The careful underwriter will need to know how values are derived: Is it a book value representing the original cost of the property? Is it based on a professional appraisal? Could the value be an owner's concept of market value?

Other figures found in a balance sheet are more easily verifiable with simple auditing procedures.

Profit and Loss Statement.   The P & L is a statement of income and expense —it has nothing to do with assets and liabilities. The figures may be presented in excruciating detail, or can be reduced to three lines: one for gross income, one for expenses, and the third representing the difference between the two, which is the profit (or loss). Normally, the P & L statement gives some detail as to what items comprise the operation's income, followed by a listing of the major items of operating expenses. Subtracting the operating expenses from income results in what is commonly called the "net operating income."

While the net operating income is the best measure of operating profitability, other costs are normally deducted for analysis reasons. These "other costs" include the cost of financing (debt service), and the reserve for payment of income taxes. The reason for distinguishing net operating income as a sound measure of operating profitability is that the cost of financing has little to do with the efficiency of the day-to-day management of operations.

Operating Statement.   An operating statement is often confused with a profit and loss statement and, in fact, there is great similarity. The difference lies in the kind of detail offered and how it is used first, for comparing one investment with another, and second, in ferreting out inefficiency and excessive costs in the property operations.

An operating statement is the kind of information most commonly found in real estate transactions. It gives some detail on the income that can be made (the potential gross income), reduced by vacancy and credit losses. Operating expenses are then listed as a deduction from income. The expenses are given in considerable detail and often shown along with a percentage figure that gives the ratio to the property's gross operating income. For example, to use round figures for simplicity, if a property shows a gross operating income of $100,000 and the cost of electricity is $8,000, that would represent an 8 percent (8,000 divided by 100,000 = .08) measure. Comparing operating costs with gross operating income in this manner gives a better comparison than varying dollar amounts. In other words, it shows whether or not expenses may be increasing because of increased revenue or for some other reason.

Another difference between an operating statement and a P & L statement is that it does not need to show such costs as interest on mortgage debt, depreciation, or income tax liabilities. These are not critical items in analyzing property operations. One other point: In an operating statement, the cost of property taxes and property insurance is shown as an operating expense. This differs from residential loan practice where both taxes and insurance are combined with the principal and interest payment on a mortgage loan and are called the "mortgage payment." In a commercial loan, the mortgage payment is more likely to be called "debt service," and includes only principal and interest.

Stabilized Statements. The identification of "stabilized" is sometimes used to indicate figures that have been adjusted to represent a more accurate, truer picture. For instance, expense items that are paid for during the tax year, such as painting expenses for a building, should be correctly spread over a period of several years. Or an accumulation of tax payments might be more accurately indicated as an expense spanning several years. Stabilized information sometimes is confused with distorted information, although it should not be.

Pro Forma Statement. A pro forma statement is a projection of both income and expenses. It is not a record of what has happened, but what might be expected. Pro forma statements are the only way a new development can be presented. In the hands of a professional analyst, the pro forma provides very helpful information on a proposed investment project. In the hands of a sales enthusiast, however, it can be misleading.

Preparation of Financial Statements

The most important assurance of receiving complete and accurate information on a financial statement is the caliber of the person preparing the statement. The highest professional designation in this field is the Certified Public Accountant (CPA) award granted by each state. Some states offer lesser designations such as "Public Accountant" for those meeting certain requirements, usually preparatory to reaching the CPA level. The requirements vary somewhat among the states, but all demand completion of certain educational courses, some experience in the field, and the passing of exhaustive qualification tests.

In practice, only a CPA may prepare a statement under audit. This means that the information contained in an audited statement is prepared in accordance with accepted accounting practices and that the numbers used have been verified by the preparer and accurately represent the financial condition of the subject. CPAs can also prepare statements without audit that do not offer the substantiation of data given with an audit. For larger commercial loans lenders may insist on audited statements.

The initial presentation of most commercial property investments usually offers financial information compiled by whoever is making the presentation. If this person is an owner, or a sales broker, the information given may be suspect because of the vested interest of the preparer. Nevertheless, such information can be verified to some degree by an interested investor. And such information should be restated on the investor's standard form of financial statement. By using a standard financial form, an investor, or analyst, can make a better comparison of the various investment opportunities that are available.

Property Evaluation

In a commercial loan analysis, the value of the property offered as collateral involves more than determining its present value. In most instances, it is the income produced by that property that is expected to repay the loan, so the study involves its potential for producing sufficient income to handle timely repayment. Each kind of property presents a different set of circumstances that affects its cash flows. Because of this, many lenders simply limit their participation in commercial lending to the types of properties they know best. Experience is a valuable teacher.

The specialized problems of the major classes of income properties are discussed in later sections of this chapter. More generalized information can be obtained from an appraisal and a feasibility study, as explained next.

APPRAISAL

Unlike residential loans, there are no standardized forms and few regulations that apply to how an appraisal must be prepared for a commercial loan. The most common practice is for a lender to require a narrative type appraisal prepared by a recognized professional. Lenders sometimes have a list of appraisers that are known to them and have a sound record of performance. Or the lender requirement might be given as a minimum level of appraiser designation, such as "an MAI appraiser or the equivalent."

For a lender, an appraisal represents several things. It is used to confirm an applicant's opinion of value. And it gives the lender some justification for the size of the loan for examination by their regulatory authority. An appraisal should be recognized as an estimate of value at approximately the time of loan origination, and not an assurance that value will remain unchanged over the life of the loan. Nevertheless, the appraisal industry has come under increasing scrutiny by regulatory authorities (see Chapter 9).

FEASIBILITY STUDY

A feasibility study is a variation of the more standardized appraisal techniques in that it places much greater emphasis on a market study of the product offered by the subject property. Further, appraisers are professionally recognized with designations offered by various peer groups, while those who prepare feasibility reports are not. Even so, feasibility studies are usually prepared by various professionals such as appraisers, property managers, real estate brokers, and market analysts.

As its name implies, a feasibility study attempts to determine whether or not a proposed investment is likely to be successful. Lenders do not always request this particular piece of information, but major investors often do.

A feasibility study presents an estimate of the cost of the proposed property investment, and examines in depth the market for its product, such as whether or not there is a need for additional apartment units. Based on the proven experience of similar properties, the analysis will include a pro forma statement of the expected income and expense of the operation. Also, problems associated with environmental questions are examined as they relate to the subject property. In its conclusion (which is often presented at the beginning of the report), the study attempts to answer the practical question of whether or not the project will be successful.

Some Analysis Tools

Collecting information is only a part of loan processing; determining what it means is crucial to the underwriting decision. Whether or not to grant a loan is always a human decision—a judgment call based on all the information that the underwriter can assemble. To sort through the financial data under study, an underwriter may use various financial tables, a few of which are discussed next.

There are many statistical tables available to the real estate underwriter that may be used to calculate and compare returns from income properties.* Tables are offered that give factors to compute the interest portion of a monthly payment, capitalization of income, remaining principal balances, present and future worth of $1.00, constants for computing principal and interest payments, and many others. Even though there are many software programs for computer analysis that already incorporate some of the financial table factors into the calculations, it is helpful for the analyst to know what information is available for the mathematically inclined. However, only three of the more widely used tables are discussed here.

*Financial tables are available from Financial Publishing Co., 82 Brookline Ave., Boston, MA 02215, or Professional Publishing Corp., 122 Paul Dr., San Rafael, CA 94903.

Present Worth of $1.00.   This table tells what a dollar is worth in cents today if delivered at a future time. The present worth depends on the rate of return and the length of time until delivery. It is an important measure because most income properties deliver returns in future years. The question is: What are those future returns worth in dollars today? The key element is that a dollar in hand today can be put to work earning interest, and therefore is worth more than a dollar delivered in the future. It is not a measure of inflation, only the power of money to earn money. It is the *time value* of money.

Payment to Amortize a $1,000 Loan.   The amortization tables more commonly found in commercial loan analysis differ from those found in residential lending. For residential loans, tables are offered as a sequence of interest rates and a sequence of loan amounts. In commercial loans, the most appropriate tables are those used to amortize a $1,000 loan. Such a table offers a payment amount for a given interest rate and loan term on a $1,000 loan amount. This payment amount multiplied times the number of $1,000 units in the subject loan quickly provides the total payment needed. Thus, it is more adaptable to the larger loans found in commercial real estate. Also, the $1,000 tables can be found in monthly, quarterly, semiannual, and annual payment amounts covering almost all possible payment intervals.

Loan Constant.   A loan constant is the annual (or monthly) debt service expressed as a percentage of the loan amount. The constant figure is often used in the negotiation and comparison of commercial loans because it gives the required debt service rather than the interest rate and term, which make comparison difficult. For example, if a loan applicant is offered loans from two different sources—one at 11 percent for a 20-year term and the other at 10 percent for a 15-year term—a quick comparison as to which has the lesser debt service is difficult. But if the first offer mentioned is quoted as a "constant of 12.39" and the second as "12.90," the comparison is simple. The constant times the amount of the loan is the debt service (in this example, principal and interest expressed as the sum of 12 equal monthly payments).

Land Purchase Loans

Considered as a class, land loans are probably the most difficult of all mortgage loans to obtain. Undeveloped, or raw, land offers no income that might be used to repay the loan. And there is a need for additional cash each year to pay property taxes, possibly insurance, and various "standby" charges. As a result, not too many lenders will even entertain an application for a land loan. Lenders who do make this kind of loan are likely to restrict approval to those with (1) a good track record of repayment of land purchase loans, (2) substantial other assets available, or (3) an assurance of a future resale of the land. And the loan itself is usually limited to 50 or 60 percent of the property value. Any mortgage loan that is expected to be repaid through the sale of the collateral carries a higher risk for the lender. A future sale is not always an assured condition.

With respect to a future intended use or sale, the land may be purchased for a housing development, or perhaps a shopping center, and so more time is needed to complete plans and permanent financing. The lender assisting in the immediate purchase of the land is therefore in a prime position to make the construction and permanent loans if the conditions meet the lender's requirements.

Sometimes a land broker or developer will locate a tract of land highly suitable for a particular purchaser. It could be a small tract for a service station or a larger parcel on which to erect a retail store outlet. But at the time the property becomes available, the ultimate user may not be in a position to consummate the land purchase. In such a circumstance, a binding letter of intent issued to a real estate broker or developer of some substance would greatly facilitate a raw land loan to acquire the chosen site. The land broker would be presenting the lender a reasonably sure sale for the land within a specified time period, with the land itself as collateral.

Land Development

The next step after the purchase of raw land is its development. *Land development* for loan purposes means the building of streets and utilities to prepare lots for resale as home sites. The development work associated with the construction of an apartment or office building project is in the category of *site development*, or land preparation, and is an integral part of the project construction costs.

Since the work called for in the land development plans can easily identify the project for residential purposes, such a loan is much more acceptable to a savings association than the land purchase itself.

A development loan can be made for as much as 75 or 80 percent of the appraised value of the finished lots, but is seldom permitted to exceed the costs incurred in the land acquisition and construction costs. This is one of several types of loans that generate what might be called a certain distortion in values, due to the fact that the very development being financed greatly enhances the value of the raw land. Federal regulations for savings associations permit a loan at 75 percent of the appraised value for residential land development. Conceivably, the appraised value of the completed lots based on an existing market would be substantially greater than the development costs. A 75 percent loan would permit the developer to borrow an amount in excess of the actual investment.

In lending terminology, the amount of a loan that exceeds a borrower's actual costs is called *walking money*—money the borrower can walk away with upon completion. The prudent lender is reluctant to permit a borrower to obtain a cash "profit" from a development or construction loan since this has a tendency to lessen the incentive to sell the property as intended.

An integral part of a land development loan agreement is the *release* mechanism. This is the clause that spells out when, how, and at what price any lot or lots may be released. The release terms may call for an order of priorities by which the land can be developed, and will state in what manner the lot will be released. Most important, it will specify the amount of money from each lot sale that must be paid to the lender for the release.

The release itself is a specific release of the mortgage lien on the lot or lots being sold, and is intended to permit the delivery of a clear title to the lot purchaser by the developer. The amount of money required to release a lot may be a percentage of the sales price of the lot, stating a minimum sales price. In this procedure, any increase in sales price over the minimum would increase the payment to the lender and amortize the loan more rapidly. Another method is to set a flat sum on each lot for release and let the developer sell at whatever price he or she can. The flat sum per lot is usually calculated so as to repay the development loan with interest in full when somewhere between 50 and 75 percent of the lots have been sold.

Office of Interstate Land Sales.   Since 1968, the Department of Housing and Urban Development (HUD) has had an Office of Interstate Land Sales charged by Congress with the responsibility of establishing guidelines and procedures for land developers in an effort to minimize deceptive practices and outright frauds. Sales of lots, developed and undeveloped, have grown substantially in this country and have brought out some unscrupulous operators. Basically, the rules require nothing more than a full disclosure of the essential facts for the land buyer, and serve as a protection for both buyer and seller. As one explanation goes, a developer can still sell a lot that is completely under water but must state in writing that it is under water! The rules apply to any development with over 50 lots for sale, of less than five acres each, and on which no construction is required. Failure to comply with HUD regulations can involve a fine and imprisonment for the *lender*, as well as the developer and sales agents.

Construction Loans

The construction industry employs over eight million people in this country and depends heavily on the availability of lendable funds. However, several large segments of the construction business are not so dependent on the capital market. These are government projects such as streets, highways, dams, and public buildings, which can be paid for from tax revenues. Various types of bonds, which are usually based on a pledge of tax revenues, might be sold to finance the construction. Another major factor in the construction market is the large corporation that builds industrial plants and utilities. These corporations often finance expansion out of their own revenues, or perhaps through the sale of bonds.

The type of construction lending discussed in this section concerns a building loan—the money needed to construct a house, an office building, or a shopping center. While these loans vary substantially in size, there is a similarity in the risks involved. All are secured by a first mortgage on the property to be constructed, all are funded only after each stage of construction has been completed, and almost all require a permanent loan commitment or takeout of some kind to assure repayment of the construction loan immediately upon completion of the project. So where is the big risk?

The risk to the construction lender is whether or not the building can be completed with the available money and whether it meets all required specifications. Many factors that are difficult to foresee enter into the successful completion of a building. Some are the weather, labor difficulties and strikes, delays in the delivery of materials, changes in the plans or specifications, and the latest requirement, namely, environmental considerations, that have resulted in time-consuming lawsuits.

Definition

The definition of a construction loan focuses on the special requirements for this type of financing. A construction loan is initially a loan commitment that provides for the money to be disbursed at intervals during construction in a manner that ensures payment of all construction costs and finance charges, and requires completion of the building in accordance with the plans and specifications so as to deliver a valid first mortgage upon completion. Further explanation of each part of the definition follows:

Disbursement During Construction. Unlike other types of loans, a construction loan is not funded when the borrower signs the note. All the borrower has at the beginning is a commitment that funds will be released as construction progresses. There are two basic ways that progress payments are released: one is on a time-interval basis and the other is on a by-work-completed basis. With the time-interval method, usually monthly, the building progress is inspected each month and the amount of work completed is duly noted. The lender then releases that portion of the loan that has been allocated to the work accomplished. Under the by-work-completed plan, the lender and borrower agree at the outset on about five stages of progress which, when reached, will release that amount of the loan proceeds. An example of a first stage might be the completion of all underground work and the pouring of the foundation.

Assurance of Payment of Costs. While it is the borrower's prime responsibility to use the loan proceeds for the payment of charges on the construction, the lender has an important stake in making sure that all labor and materials are paid as the money is released. Every so often, a builder, by design or in error, may mix the records and use the proceeds from one construction loan to pay charges accruing from another project. The result can be labor liens and material suppliers' liens filed on the property while still under construction. There are many ways that lenders can use to minimize the risk of improper disbursement. One is for the lender to handle the payments to contractors and subcontractors. Another is to require proof of payment for costs incurred by the borrower before any funds are released from the loan. Another is to require a waiver of lien form signed by each contractor involved with every progress payment. Perhaps the most important protection for the lender in this regard is to know the borrower's reputation for handling building projects, then make close inspection a standard procedure.

Completion in Accordance with Plans. Again it is the borrower who is primarily concerned that the building is constructed according to the plans and specifications. But the lender also has a real interest in this question, as failure to meet the plans can be a cause for refusal by the permanent lender to release the loan. The problems are mostly technical, such as the size of pipes and wiring, the grade and thickness of concrete, the amount of reinforcing used, the compaction of foundation and parking areas, and many others. A construction lender should employ a knowledgeable construction person on its staff who can check the work as it progresses. On small projects, the lender may rely on its own staff for inspection approvals. On large projects it is more common to employ an independent firm or professional to serve as the inspector. Architects and engineers are both used for this purpose, and the decision of the professional is usually accepted by both the borrower and lender as final determination of the acceptability of the project as it is built.

Delivering a Valid First Mortgage. Insofar as the lender is concerned, the goal of the successful construction loan is to complete the project within the money allocated, all bills paid, and no liens filed. The construction loan can then be repaid through funding of a permanent loan or the sale of the property.

Additional Comments. It is customary in a construction loan for the lender to withhold 10 percent from each progress payment until final completion. The purpose is to provide a reserve against unexpected liens. Some lenders will hold this reserve until the statutory lien period has expired after completion before releasing it to the borrower. If an unexpected cost is encountered that was not allowed for in the loan amount committed, the lender will ask, or demand, that the borrower make such payment. The same procedure is used if the borrower decides to make some changes in the plans after the loan has been committed. Such changes must be approved by the lender, and if they should cause an increase in the anticipated cost, the borrower will be expected to use his or her own funds for payment. The lender does not want to have a building only partially completed with all loan funds exhausted.

The personal endorsement of the borrower-owner is almost always required on a construction loan. The same lender may agree to make a long-term permanent loan with no personal endorsement required, but will refuse to do so on the construction loan for the same project. The reason is not just the added security given by another endorsement but, in addition, it is the borrower-owner who is in a controlling position during construction to insist on changes in the plans or create costly problems that can upset orderly construction work. The lender just wants to make certain that the borrower-owner carries a full share of responsibility.

The principal sources for construction money are commercial banks with specialized construction loan departments, savings associations, and mortgage companies. The commercial banks' interest is in the higher yields and short terms represented in construction lending; savings associations and mortgage companies prefer the higher yields, but also are usually in a position to pick up permanent loans at a minimum of expense to themselves.

There are many variations in the handling of construction loans. Some procedures used in major categories of buildings are outlined in the following discussion.

Construction Loans for Residential Properties

Single-family detached houses and some townhouse projects are financed by builders on both a contract basis and a speculative basis.

Contract Basis. A house built for an owner under contract represents a reduced risk to the construction lender. The normal sales contract is a firm commitment by the purchaser and includes a permanent loan commitment for closing. Often the permanent commitment is made by the same lender handling the construction financing as a sort of package deal, which minimizes paperwork. On such a loan the risk to the construction lender is primarily in the builder's ability to complete the house within the contract terms. The builder's record must be known to the lender.

In smaller communities and rural areas, houses are often constructed under contract by a local builder, who also operates a lumber yard, with the builder providing the construction financing from personal resources. A nearby savings association will have already agreed to make the permanent loan when the house is completed.

Speculative Basis. Many builders, mostly in the growing suburban areas, build houses with the expectation of selling them by the time they are completed. To the risk of being able to complete the house within the projected cost figure is added the risk of selling the house at a profitable price upon completion. A lender must look at the strength and capability of a speculative builder before accepting such a loan. As a builder proves himself to the lender, his construction line of credit can be expanded.

When the housing market fluctuates downward, the speculative builder is the first to be hurt. He can be caught with many unsold houses on which the high interest of the construction loan continues to eat at any profits. More and more, construction lenders are seeking to protect themselves against a soft market by demanding a *takeout commitment* before they will agree to the construction loan.

Takeout Commitment. A takeout commitment, sometimes called a "standby" commitment, is a promise to the home builder by an acceptable mortgage lender to make a permanent home loan directly to the builder in the event the subject house is not sold within a certain time limit, usually one year. The commitment is usually in the form of a simple letter agreement and costs the builder at least one point payable upon delivery of the letter agreement. The amount of the commitment would be the same as the construction loan, normally 80 percent of the sales value of the house. However, the commitment is not really expected to be used. It serves more as an insurance policy to protect the construction lender's loan. To encourage the builder to sell the house, rather than rely on the takeout commitment, the rate of interest is set at one to three percentage points over the going rate, and the term much shorter, probably 10 years, than if the loan had been made to the intended occupant-buyer. The builder still has the problem of selling the house but has a little breather in facing a monthly amortization payment rather than full repayment of the construction loan, while the construction lender is clear with all his money back.

Construction Loans for Income Properties

Apartments, office buildings, shopping centers, and warehouses all use construction financing, sometimes termed *interim financing*, to accomplish the building of the project. As pointed out earlier, only the very strongest builders-developers are capable of commanding construction financing of any income property without a permanent loan commitment to pay off the construction loan at completion. The terms of the permanent loan influence the manner in which the construction money can be handled. Special requirements for funding the permanent loan, such as an 80 percent lease-up before release of the loan proceeds, place the construction lender in a far more risky position. If a permanent lender is currently unavailable, the developer may resort to a standby commitment within the same framework as described for a home builder. The construction lender must have a closing date for the takeout within a reasonable period (one to three years) for proper recovery of the construction loan.

Construction lending calls for highly experienced personnel who can work with builders and who understand construction progress and procedures, so as to make timely releases of the loan proceeds. Most lenders will not release a progress draw without physically inspecting the project or having an independent architect inspector submit an estimate of work accomplished. The trick is to be able to complete the project within the money available and still have 10 percent of the loan amount retained at completion to protect the lender against any unforeseen contingencies. When the lender is satisfied that all bills are paid and that no valid liens can be filed, this 10 percent retainer can be released.

Mobile or Manufactured Home Parks

As a style of living, mobile home parks offer a fairly new concept. The idea of living in a small, closed community, in similar kinds of houses, and with a number of community activities to enjoy as a group has had its greatest appeal in resort and retirement areas of the country. Such states as California, Arizona, and Florida have long offered excellent mobile home park living styles, but only since the late 1960s has the idea developed in other parts of the country.

The development and ownership of a mobile home park offers some special advantages for an investor and some different problems for the lender to resolve. It is the purpose of this section to examine the special nature of a mobile home park.

Mobile home parks as considered in this text are those projects that are built for the leasing of land space to the owners of mobile homes. Some mobile home parks are handled much like ordinary subdivisions in that the land is sold to the mobile home owner. As a subdivision development for the sale of lots, the financing would be much the same as discussed earlier in this chapter under the heading of Land Development. The use of the completed park facility for the *rental* of lots presents the problem of permanent financing for the entire development. This can be done either with a conventional loan similar to an apartment loan or with an FHA-insured commitment.

Design of a Park

The original impetus for mobile home parks, outside of resort areas, was to provide a lower-cost type of housing. The mobile home, no longer just a trailer that could be pulled behind the family car, became a completely furnished living unit 40 to 60 feet in length. The smaller units can be purchased, including furniture, for $8,000 to $15,000, can be parked in a space that provides little more than a parking lot, and can provide adequate living accommodations at considerably less cost than a normal house. The larger units with "double-width" sections can exceed average housing costs.

So again there is considerable variation in the size of investment involved in a mobile home park. The more Spartan projects provide 10 or 20 spaces, often built personally by the owner of the land, and can be very lucrative if kept occupied. One of the major attractions to this form of land use is the low maintenance costs.

The middle-sized mobile home park has shown the greatest growth, and was spurred by a broadening of the Federal Housing Administration insuring requirements in 1969. In an effort to provide more housing for middle- and lower-income families, the FHA increased its insurable limits to 90 percent of the finished park's value and to terms of 30 years. The insurance provided by the FHA brought in many private investors who would otherwise not have been able to finance such an undertaking. And the FHA set some sound standards of quality for its parks to avoid the "parking lot syndrome." Paved streets were required, minimal landscaping was specified, and some storage space for each housing unit was included. The density of units per acre was limited to a maximum of eight, and recreational facilities such as a clubhouse, swimming pool, or tennis courts were encouraged.

Because the FHA procedures called for a final closing of the permanent loan that would include the entire project, it was necessary to complete all spaces, or pads, in one stage. Lease-up of the large parks thus developed was often slow and caused financial drains to the investors.

Conventional lenders for mobile home parks permit the development in stages to allow for lease-up and growth of income before proceeding with the next stage.

In 1970, the Veterans Administration added a new benefit for veterans to permit a mobile home to be financed and a lot to be purchased under its guarantee programs. The interest rate and term allowed initially were not sufficient to provide much enthusiasm among lenders, but further modification has helped promote some growth in mobile homes as a living accommodation.

Analysis of a Park

Like other forms of income property, a mobile home park must be well located and serve a market demand. The "building" consists of site preparation, underground utilities, connecting streets, and concrete or all-weather pads for placement of the housing units. The only structures involved are usually a clubhouse-office building, a laundry building, and such recreational facilities as the developer elects to provide.

Maintenance requirements are minimal as the tenant is primarily leasing a piece of land. Mobile home parks operate on a cost as low as 20 to 25 percent of their gross rental income.

Mobile home living has been most popular where at least one of the following five situations exists: (1) a military base, (2) a construction project, (3) a college or university, (4) a resort area, or (5) a retirement-oriented community.

One of the problems in profitable development has been the longer lease-up period. Unlike apartments, which can be leased to good occupancy over fairly short periods in a strong market, the mobile home park tends to lease-up at a slower rate. Sources within the industry have reported an average rate of rent-up at 10 to 12 spaces per month for a new park. However, it has also been observed that once a mobile home is moved into location, it seldom moves out of the park. One reason, of course, is that mobile homes are not built for travel, but are actually semipermanent dwellings. Also, where moving is contemplated, the cost of moving at $2 to $3 or more per mile serves as a deterrent since the moving costs could easily exceed the value of the equity in the mobile home. Hence, it is far more common for an owner who may be transferred to a new location simply to offer the mobile home for sale on its present location and purchase another at the future destination. The result for the owner of a mobile home park is that a more stable income than in an apartment investment can be counted on. Once the pad is leased, there is a security provided by the mobile home itself that provides good assurance of continuous rental payments.

Special Purpose Buildings

In a sense, all buildings are special purpose as their design generally restricts the use to a specific kind of tenancy. However, in the jargon of real estate, "special purpose" has a more precise meaning. It is that category of building that offers a specific kind of service and is more difficult to convert to any other usage. Examples of special purpose buildings include fast food stores, bowling lanes, service stations, recreational structures, theaters, and automobile dealerships. Because of the close relationship between the building and the specialized services offered, they are often owned by the business operator. But many are built by investors for lease to professional operators.

Another feature of a special purpose building is a much greater dependence on the ability of the operator/manager to achieve profitable operation. While management is important in other kinds of income property, such as apartments and office buildings, it is less critical than with special purpose property. For instance, an office building, once leased up, will continue to show a cash flow even with changes in the management. But an automobile dealership or a fast food franchise is heavily dependent on the particular skills of management for its profitability.

Because of this emphasis on management, lenders must look beyond the building itself and examine the capability of those who will be managing the property. This is never an easy determination, and is particularly difficult if the loan applicant is a newcomer to the business. To overcome some of these obvious problems, several alternative procedures may be used.

Earnings Record of Applicant. If the company requesting the loan has a good record of steady earnings, and is credit worthy, there is little further problem in approval. Examples of building owners that would fall into this category are large oil companies building service stations and fast food franchisers expanding their operations.

Endorsement. A method of credit enhancement sometimes used to expand automobile dealerships or recreational facilities is for a manufacturer to endorse the obligation. This means that the manufacturer agrees to accept a contingent responsibility for repayment of the mortgage obligation. The purpose of under-taking such a risk would be for the manufacturer to increase its sales outlets.

Purchase Contract. Yet another method of credit enhancement that has a broader application than just special purpose buildings is a future purchase contract. Consider a situation where a large grocery chain desires assurance of a special product made by a small local supplier. By offering the supplier a large continuing contract for its product, the supplier would have a proven source of cash flow to induce the lender's favorable decision on a loan to expand. As additional security, the lender might ask that the purchase money be paid through the lender's offices as the product is delivered to the grocery chain. While such a contract, assigned to the lender or not, falls short of an endorsement of the obligation, it does give a lender some assurance as to how the loan will be repaid. And that is the key question of all lenders.

Apartment Buildings

An apartment building, or multifamily housing as the FHA classifies it, represents an investment in residential property. In the past, residential property, particularly low-income housing, has enjoyed certain tax advantages and is subject to some restraints that serve to protect the rights of tenants. While tax advantages for a while tended to distort investment decisions, the principal determinant for sound apartment investment still remains the occupancy of such projects in each market area.

Underlying the achievement and maintenance of good occupancy are several qualifying factors. Experienced apartment operators judge three factors to be of almost equal importance in a successful operation: (1) location; (2) physical facilities; and (3) management. Obviously, a careful underwriting analysis must consider all three factors in determining the risk involved.

Location. *Location* is usually the first limiting requirement of an apartment seeker along with size of the unit and its price. A major consideration of location is easy access to jobs—freeways affect and broaden accessibility. Also important in judging location is proximity to schools and churches. The availability of recreational facilities, such as parks and golf courses, along with restaurants and other entertainment, is also to be considered. Apartment dwellers, as a group, are not as burdened with housework and yard maintenance as single-family residents would be.

Since location is a major determinant of the available market, it is necessary to evaluate the market in that area. For instance, does the proposed rental structure fit the requirements and will it be competitive? Do the size and type of units meet these demands?

Physical Facilities. *The physical plant* must meet the market requirements, not only in size of units but also in architectural style and amenities available. Amenities would include such factors as playground areas, tennis courts, swimming pool, club room, and entertainment facilities. If the market is primarily a family type, the two- or three-bedroom units would be the most popular choice; if intended for young singles, the one-bedroom and studio design would be in greatest demand. The elderly, on the other hand, might prefer one or two bedrooms with a minimum of stairs to climb. Sometimes an assortment of units is used with the hope of covering all phases of the market. This "shotgun" approach is a poor substitute for careful analysis of the market as it may result in one type or style of unit easily rented and maintaining good occupancy while others go begging for tenants. Before building begins on an apartment complex, knowledgeable operators (developers) study the market for particular requirements, and then use their merchandising power to attract suitable occupants.

Management. *Management* is a major factor well known by experienced operators and too often underestimated by newcomers to the field. Together with the location and the physical plant, management, too, can be a "make or break" factor. Large cities throughout the country have companies that specialize in apartment management, offering a complete management service for a fee of 3 to 5 percent of the gross revenues. Maintaining routine cleanliness of the public areas, prompt repairs of equipment or damaged sections of the building, and fair enforcement of rules for the mutual well-being of the tenants are all necessary in order to achieve and maintain a high occupancy rate. Experienced operators learn how to cope with the special requirements of rental properties such as initial screening of tenants, the most effective methods of collecting rents and keeping them current, the special problems created by domestic pets, and the handling of skip-outs and of tenants who create disturbances for other occupants. Consequently, an underwriter will look much more favorably, riskwise, on a property under the management of competent individuals or companies.

As apartment-style living proliferates in the cities, an underwriter must recognize that the better-planned, better-maintained facilities are those that will sustain occupancy in soft or competitive markets. And a continuous high occupancy rate is the key to survival in this business.

Anlaysis of Income and Expenses

On proposed apartment construction, a projected statement can be prepared to show anticipated gross revenues from each unit and all miscellaneous revenues (for example, from laundry rooms), less a vacancy factor and credit losses. This will produce an effective income from which deductions can be made for all expenses. Fixed expenses include such items as taxes and insurance, which do not fluctuate with occupancy rates. Operating expenses comprise the costs of utilities, maintenance, supplies, labor, and management. A special expense that is frequently overlooked or underestimated is the replacement cost—items such as drapes and carpeting, equipment such as ranges or dishwashers, all in continuous use, have a tendency to wear out, and allowances must be set aside for replacements. The cash remaining after these deductions then becomes available for debt service. Any remaining cash, after all expenses and debt service have been covered, serves as a cushion against a loss or a slow period.

It is apparent, then, that there are many variables among these figures that are subject to interpretation. For example, what occupancy rate may be reliably projected? The FHA uses a percentage figure of 93. Conventional lenders generally tend to select an occupancy rate substantiated by actual rates prevailing in a particular area. Most lenders require proof of an occupancy rate near 90 percent before they will entertain a loan application. Rental rates also must be in line with the going market. Expenses can be projected with reasonable accuracy. In general, they range from 36 percent of the gross operating income to 45 percent, depending on the size of the operations and the efficiency of the management.

As previously defined, debt service is the monthly or annual cost of interest and principal payment and should be tailored to ensure timely retirement of the full loan. By careful analysis of the cash available for debt service, the underwriter can determine the most effective loan for the proposed apartment. Adjustable and negotiable factors are the *term*, which ranges from 15 years upward to 30 years, and the *loan-to-value* ratio, which determines the equity cash required. The interest rate may be adjustable or a fixed rate, usually pegged to market rates, and less subject to negotiation.

APARTMENT LEASES

Apartments are usually leased under the conditions of a "term lease"—a short-term lease that may or may not be in writing. While state laws control how leases may be handled, a general rule is that a lease for less than one year need not be in writing. The short-term nature of the lease allows the landlord to make periodic increases (or decreases) as the market may require. Occupancy is more volatile in an apartment property and can create a lack of stability in its continuing income.

Fair Housing Requirements

The Fair Housing Amendments Act of 1988 extended the prohibitions against discrimination of the 1968 Fair Housing Act for all residential real estate transactions. Prior law considers unlawful any discrimination because of race, color, religion, sex, or national origin. The new amendment added *handicap* and *familial (family) status* to the prohibitions. The additional restrictions are of particular importance in the rental of multifamily dwellings.

The new category of handicapped applies to the design and construction of multifamily dwellings (those covered by the act) for first occupancy by March 1991. The building and its facilities must provide accessibility and usability for physically handicapped people. Persons with AIDS are now included in this category. The category of family status means that housing must be open to families with children. "Adults only," or predominantly adult communities, are no longer permissible, with the exception of housing specifically designated for the elderly only.

Tax Deductions

Apartment property has always held some special tax advantages for investors. Under current law (the 1986 Tax Act), as residential property an apartment is eligible for depreciation deductions over 27½ years rather than the 31½ years applicable to nonresidential property. Another advantage is that since the building, not the land, is depreciable, an apartment offers a favorable combination of values. The building portion of the investment is relatively high compared with the nondepreciable land. Also, items classed as personal property such as drapes, appliances, and carpeting necessary for apartment operation are eligible for even greater depreciation deduction rates than the building, and the calculation can be made using accelerated rates.

Revisions in the 1986 Tax Act change certain kinds of property formerly considered as real estate to the class of personal property eligible for faster depreciation deductions. Such land improvements as roads, fences, and landscaping are now placed in the 15-year class and eligible for either straight-line or accelerated type of depreciation deductions. Another possible tax break is that sewer pipe is listed in the 20-year class.

While tax deductions have been diminished since the early 1980s, there are still important benefits available for all real estate investors. Depreciation deductions are based on the total value of the building, not just the equity interest in it. Since this kind of deduction represents a noncash item it protects cash flows, allowing more money for debt service. Nevertheless, it is true that lenders are skeptical of any cash flow that depends on the unstable nature of tax law.

Retail Store Buildings

The free-standing store building, or a strip of stores, is an interesting investment for individuals as well as large companies. The more conservative way to handle such an investment would be to first obtain a lease for the premises; then build to suit the tenant. Nevertheless, many such buildings are constructed on strictly a speculative basis, attracting tenants later.

Analysis of Income and Expenses

A retail store rented to a business tenant for a fairly long term, say 10 or 15 years, offers a stability of income not found in apartment-type properties. A well-drawn lease agreement should allow periodic rental increases, either as a fixed amount every few years, or as an escalation clause. The escalation clause ties an increase in rentals to increases in the landlord's operating expenses.

With this kind of property, the payment of expenses is usually negotiable between the landlord and tenant and is spelled out in the lease agreement. A common division of responsibility for maintenance is that the tenant pays the costs of maintaining the interior of the building while the landlord is responsible for the exterior. And the landlord is responsible for handling the insurance coverage and payment of taxes.

NET LEASE

Free-standing store buildings are often leased to major grocery chains and other retailers on a "net lease" basis. What this means is that the tenant is responsible for maintaining the building, providing the insurance coverage, and paying the property taxes. With the responsibility for paying maintenance, insurance and taxes passed on to the tenant, this kind of lease is often identified as "triple net." It is the kind of investment that is attractive to a person who wants to avoid management of the property—the rental rate is based more on a fair return on the investment without the addition of a management cost. Financing for this kind of investment may be enhanced by the assignment of all or part of the rentals. A major tenant is an attractive source of loan repayment for all lenders.

Shopping Centers

The construction of shopping centers is a specialized business. Some developers have not only built major centers but are retained to manage them. And many large retailers have entered the development business themselves to expand their own market reach. Probably more than any other kind of property investment, shopping centers work with pre-leased space. To attract tenants to a new project, the developer undertakes a careful market analysis of the area to be served. Such a market study includes potential sales volumes for the various commodities that will be offered at the center. With this information in hand, the developer can better prove the value for a merchant to open an outlet in the subject area.

Anchor Tenant.   Crucial to the successful operation of a shopping center is having a major tenant. It is this attraction for shoppers that is needed to bring business to the smaller merchant. Major retailers have learned that the smaller stores can also attract customers on their own, thus benefitting all, with greater convenience for the shopper.

The value of an anchor tenant is such that many major retailers have spearheaded their own projects. Some rely on experienced shopping-center developers to implement their plans and manage the center upon completion. Others, such as Sears, Roebuck & Company, have entered the development business themselves. Sears has built a number of major centers through its Homart Development Company subsidiary.

Income and Expenses

Shopping centers require considerable management expertise along with substantial sales promotion. The goal of attracting shoppers to a center is enhanced by the individual merchant/tenants as well as the shopping center itself. The reason, of course, is that shopping center leases are almost always based on a percentage of the tenant's sales.

A popular way of handling the promotional aspect of a center is through a management/tenant association that meets regularly to plan and arrange financing for various sales events. The larger shopping malls are capable of offering rather lavish seasonal entertainment spectacles.

PERCENTAGE LEASES

Shopping centers lease space to tenants at percentage rates based on the nature of the tenant's business, not a flat percentage for the whole center. The rates vary from a low of 1 to 1½ percent for large volume stores such as supermarkets and discount stores, to a high of 10 to 12 percent for smaller shops and boutiques. The percentage is measured against the gross sales volume each month.

Percentage leases normally require a base, or minimum, payment each month. Otherwise it would be possible for a merchant to achieve a profitable operation on high margin merchandise that may produce too low a gross volume for the landlord to operate. The minimum may be stated as a rental "amounting to 6 percent of gross sales each month but not less than $1,500." Or the base rental could be separated from the percentage such as a rental "amounting to $1,500 each month *plus* 4 percent of gross sales." The minimum rental payment may be subject to an escalation clause based on a landlord's cost experience.

Verification of the tenant's monthly sales volume is usually a requirement in the lease terms. It can be achieved through submittal of a copy of the tenant's state sales tax report to the landlord each month. Or the landlord may require a periodic audit of the tenant's sales records.

OPERATING EXPENSES

The costs of operating and maintaining a shopping center are divided between landlord and tenant. There is no standard procedure. The more costs borne by a tenant, the lower the rental. A common practice is that all exterior maintenance of the building and grounds is the responsibility of the landlord, while interior maintenance is the tenant's.

Utility service is usually separately metered to the tenants. However, a recent trend in larger centers is to install their own electric generating plant, even selling power back to the local utility under a co-generation agreement.

Heating and air conditioning may be either centrally furnished or supplied by each tenant with their own equipment. Shopping center management prefers the tenant furnish equipment for several reasons. One is that maintenance and operating costs are not easily predictable and there is a potential liability for lost sales should such equipment fail.

Janitorial service for the public areas is the responsibility of the landlord, while most tenants provide their own clean-up operations.

A growing practice is to separate the base rent from many of the operating costs. This is done by billing such operating expenses as a separate "service fee" to the tenant. It allows a more stable rental structure yet provides the landlord with some protection against the uncertainty of future operating costs. It is an area that requires careful negotiation to achieve a fair balance of responsibility. The alternative method of allowing for changing costs is to include an escalation clause in the rental agreement that allows a change in the rent subject to cost verification by the landlord.

Classification of Centers

Shopping centers defy easy classification as most major developers try hard to be different. Something unique has an appeal not found in the commonplace and the intent is to attract the general public. Roughly, there are three classes based mostly on size and merchandise offered: neighborhood, community, and regional.

Neighborhood Center. These are the smaller centers often consisting of a large corner area with a strip of two or more stores. Merchandise offered is mostly daily essentials such as food, drugs, hardware, and other everyday services.

Community Center. A community center offers all the services found in the neighborhood center plus an anchor tenant offering general merchandise, apparel stores, furniture outlets, professional services, and some recreational facilities.

Regional Center. The largest category, a regional shopping center offers a full range of merchandise and services. It would contain at least two anchor tenants, scores of lesser shops, a variety of restaurants, theaters, and other recreational facilities. Often there is a large mall that offers various kinds of entertainment to attract the general public. Around these centers are found hotels, office buildings, and apartment complexes. Regional centers have become an attraction for business meetings of all kinds since they offer easy access to "off-duty" activities for those attending the meetings.

Location of a Center

Crucial to a shopping center location is a study of the available market. This involves difficult projections of future growth, road and freeway patterns, and the buying habits of the potential customers.

Anticipating Future Growth. Smaller centers require relatively small tracts of land and sites can easily be selected *after* a population growth pattern is identified. By then, of course, the land value will have increased commensurate with the growth of population in that area. For the larger centers, the requirement for land is such that it must be acquired in advance of population growth. This is more of a gamble, but land surrounding urban areas usually maintains its value as there are a number of potential uses for it. Major developers have an advantage in selecting locations, the reason being that a regional center by itself attracts people to that particular area to add supporting services. Thus, a potential market is partially self-generated.

Road and Freeway Patterns. Ease of access is a critical need for a center to be successful. Smaller centers find the existing road system adequate so long as they stick to major intersections. Larger centers require easy access to a major freeway. With most of the freeway system in place or at least in final planning stages, the preferred locations become fairly obvious.

Potential Market. Market surveys are a fairly continuous project with major retailers. With stores in place, the kinds of merchandise that are most popular with customers gives the store buyers accurate information on what kinds of merchandise to stock. However, anticipating market needs for a new center is more difficult. Nevertheless, specialized market analysts are able to make reasonably accurate projections based on studies of census information. From the data available on income levels and ethnic mix, an experienced analyst can project about how many dollars will be spent on the merchandise and services a new center plans to offer. For example, taking the gross income of the trade area as a base, food may take 12 percent of that income; apparel, general merchandise, and appliances, 8 percent; pharmaceutical drugs, 2 percent; and so on through a list of products and services. This total potential buying power must then be reduced to the market share that can reasonably be attained by the subject center. Market information of this type provides the developer with a valuable selling tool in the leasing of new space.

Financing of Shopping Centers

Three categories of retail store facilities must be considered separately for loan purposes. The differences are based on whether or not a merchant wants to own or lease its premises. It is a top policy decision and major retailers differ on the answer. Some prefer to lease their store space and use that capital for other business purposes, which is fairly common for grocery chains. Others see an advantage in anticipating a market growth area and building their own facilities so as to maintain a better control of operating costs. Consider the differences under the categories of owner-occupied buildings, pre-leased space, and speculative projects.

Owner-Occupied.   An owner-occupant merchant seeking financing to buy or build a new facility has several options to work with. The company may use its own cash flow as a source of funds, or, if the company is large enough and well recognized, it may obtain funding through the sale of mortgage bonds in the financial markets. If the decision is to seek financing from a mortgage lender, the financial record of the company itself becomes as important as the building to be acquired. While the building would be pledged as collateral, the success of the company's operations would be a key factor in loan approval.

Pre-Leased Space.   The method used by most shopping center developers is to pre-lease as much space as possible, and certainly this would include the major tenants. With leases in hand, the developer can show a lender exactly what kind of stores will be operating in the center and, more importantly, that there will be a commitment of rental income. It is not unusual for a lender to base the loan amount on the value of the leases rather than the value of the buildings as collateral. Thus, the better the quality of leases, the greater the loan commitment which reduces the equity cash required up front. Few centers are able to fully pre-lease their space and usually include some additional, speculative space. This is easier to lease if the smaller merchants know who the other tenants will be and what kind of competition will be encountered.

Speculative Projects.   Only the financially strong builders/developers are able to construct speculative store space, either as free-standing buildings or neighborhood centers. The risk of leasing is substantial and the quality of the tenant is unknown. Nevertheless, a number of developers are quite capable of erecting such projects and have proven successful. One key is to maintain close touch with the growth in market areas and select appropriate building sites. Another key is to maintain a sound list of prospective clients—merchants who have proven records of success and are aggressively expanding their operations. A track record of successful development is an essential for any loan approval in this field.

Office Buildings

The owners of all types of office buildings, ranging from the largest to the smallest, acquire or construct them for one of two purposes: (1) for their own occupancy, or (2) for lease to others.

Owner-Occupied Buildings

Many owner-occupied office buildings are held by companies or persons with a financial history that makes the decisions on underwriting such a property somewhat easier for the lender. This is due to the fact that the credit reputation of the owner is the major qualifying factor under consideration, whereas the real estate that is to be pledged is of secondary importance. Ultimately, the source of loan repayment is closely tied to the owner-occupant's record of profitability and the manner in which previous financial obligations have been met.

In financing large owner-occupied buildings, an alternative choice to straight mortgage financing would be the sale of first-mortgage bonds through an investment banker or a mortgage banker. Acquisition of large office buildings by investing institutions, such as banks or insurance companies, is a common practice. In this way, the owners simply finance large buildings from their own investment funds.

Various local, state, and federal governments and their agencies build office buildings for their own use with legislative appropriations. But some government buildings, such as post offices, are built by private investors under long-term lease contracts and are financed through private sources.

Office Buildings for Lease to Others

The underwriting of buildings intended for lease to others calls for some specialized techniques of real estate mortgage financing and requires extensive analysis of the property involved. In this category there are three main groups: (1) a builder-investor with pre-leased office space to build, (2) the speculative builder-

investor hoping to attract tenants before the building is completed or soon thereafter, and (3) the owner-occupied building with extra space for lease.

Pre-leased Office Space.   The pre-leased building is the more conservative method
and provides the underwriter with a lease to analyze, a tenant to examine for
credit worthiness, and a building and location to study. If the building is specialized to meet the tenant's unusual requirements (such as heavy electrical gear,
raised or lowered floors, or special wall patterns), the term of the lease should
be sufficient to recover the extra investment. Most underwriters will limit a loan
to a percentage of the total lease payments as this is the main source of the loan
recovery. Similar to a shopping center, a pre-leased office building faces an
inflexible situation in regard to an overrun on construction costs. The building
must be designed and located in such a manner that it meets the projected costs,
and the contractor must have the ability to complete the project within the contract
terms. Bonding of the contractor is a normal requirement. Escalation clauses
should be provided in any long-term lease agreement to cover rising taxes, insurance costs and, more recently, maintenance and operating costs. As mentioned
previously, pre-leased office buildings for single tenants are usually "bare-wall"
leases; that is, the tenant finishes the interior and provides the maintenance.

Speculative Office Buildings.   The speculative builder presents a greater risk to
an underwriter and only the more experienced and credit worthy builders can
command this type of loan. In addition to the usual analysis of the building and
its location, consideration must be given to the market and the regional economic
pattern. What are the chances of the speculative building becoming fully leased?
The underwriter, however, is not in the business of chance by choice, so a
protective restriction can be established that would require the building to have
a 75, 80, or perhaps 85 percent occupancy with bona fide tenants before the
permanent loan will be released. Of course, this throws a real burden on the
construction financing and usually means that the builder of a speculative building
must have the credit strength or cash reserves to build and lease the building
without an assured permanent commitment. It is not unusual for a knowledgeable
builder-contractor to build and lease an office building with its own funds, then
mortgage out for more than the costs. In such a case, the loan security rests as
much on an assignment of the lease income as on the mortgage pledge. With
regard to speculative office buildings, lenders often set rental minimums to protect
their repayments. Buildings with multitenant occupancy usually provide janitorial
service, which can be a separate agreement subject to escalation if costs increase.

Owner-Occupied Building with Space to Lease.   The third type of building loan
in this building category is the owner-occupied with space to lease. In this sit-

uation, there can be a mixture of several types of income, including the owner's normal rental payment, plus rent anticipated from space for speculative lease, as well as from space already pre-leased. But no one source may provide sufficient revenue to assure recovery of a normal ratio loan. The underwriter must analyze the property as a whole and make certain that the full loan has a reasonable chance of recovery before any portion of that loan is permitted to be released.

General Guidelines

The ability to maintain high occupancy in office buildings is less dependent on economic inducements than on such intangible qualities as prestige and status. For example, ground floor space rented to a dignified, prestigious merchant can enhance the value of upper-floor space. The class of tenants can add to a particular building's value; that is, a building known for top-rate law firms, or a medical office building of high-caliber tenancy, will attract other professional people. Companies and business concerns seeking a high-class clientele are often willing to pay a few dollars more each month in rentals for the advertising value of a prestige address.

The expenses of operating an office building must be considered in the total loan picture. Unlike other types of real estate properties, office buildings usually furnish a janitorial service for the tenant as well as for the public areas. There are many companies specializing in contract cleaning services, and competition will allow some control to be exercised over these costs. If a building is new, projected operating costs must be utilized, but actual operating costs should be available in the records kept on existing buildings. Care must be taken in analyzing any cost figures to minimize distortions that might lead to misleading conclusions. For example, expense items may be omitted, maintenance work can be neglected, incidental repairs may sometimes be capitalized to reduce expense figures, and tenant services can be held to a dangerously low level to distort earnings figures in an upward direction. All these factors should become apparent to the experienced underwriter and properly weighed in the final loan analysis.

Like other properties, the operating management is a key ingredient in continuing success. Poor management can discourage occupancy and drive good tenants away.

Example of an Office Building Loan

The impact of high interest costs and the concern of long-term lenders for inflation is most strongly reflected in the loan example illustrated in Table 11–1. The loan itself is a high-ratio (90 percent) commitment for a commercial loan, and the lender felt that a participation in the property income was justified. The terms outlined in the three features of the loan agreement are called *income participation* and are usually limited to the duration of the loan. Another form of participation by lenders is called *equity participation* and is an ownership interest extending beyond the term of the loan.

Following are the three income participation requirements:

1. The land amounting to 100,000 square feet was purchased by the lender for $5 per square foot and then leased back to the owner of the building for a ground rental of $70,000 per year.

2. As additional ground rental, the lender took 3 percent of the gross annual income, which amounted to approximately $30,000 more.

3. With the repayment of the loan calculated on an $11 per square foot rental, the lender demanded 15 percent of any rentals earned in excess of $11 per foot as a hedge against inflation.

With the substantial participation protection available to the lender in this loan agreement, there was no requirement for personal endorsement on the part of the borrower.

TABLE 11–1
Projected Statement for Office Building (based on 100,000 sq. ft. net rentable space costing $54.00 per sq. ft. total—$5,400,000)

Capital Investment		
Equity investment (10%)	$ 540,000	
90% mortgage loan	4,860,000	
Total investment		$5,400,000
Annual Operating Calculations		
Gross scheduled income ($11.00 per sq. ft.)	$1,100,000	
Less 5% vacancy and credit loss	55,000	
Gross operating income		$1,045,000
Less Expenses—		
All operating costs @ 34.5%		
of gross operating income		360,525
Net operating income		$ 684,475
Less debt service—		
12% interest for 30-year term		
Constant—.1234 × 4,860,000		599,724
Cash flow before taxes		$ 84,751

Warehouse Buildings

Another type of income property that is preferred by many investors because of its relatively low maintenance and management requirements is the warehouse building. The demand for warehouse space has grown substantially in the past decade for several reasons. Many types of companies use general warehouse space to store merchandise in peak seasons, to keep a product closer to its ultimate market, or to house an unusually large stock of a particular raw material.

Somewhat like office buildings, this type of facility can be built for use by an owner, such as a grocery chain operator; it can be built for use in part by an owner, such as a light manufacturer, with portions available for lease to others; or it can be built for speculative leasing as commercial warehouse space. It is the speculative warehouse that requires the most careful loan evaluation of the property. Owner-occupied or partially occupied buildings provide an established business with a source of income to substantiate and undergird the loan analysis. Warehouses are built fully pre-leased and partially pre-leased in much the same way as office buildings and shopping centers, so that the analysis of the different types is similar.

There are several basic requirements for effective warehouse space that would make it more easily rentable during the life of a loan. Like all other income properties, location is of paramount importance. The location of a warehouse should include accessibility by roads running in several directions and capable of handling large trucks. The warehouse should also be accessible to rail spurs, if possible. The land need not be in high-density traffic zones as required by shopping centers and some office buildings, but neither should it be locked into small street patterns that limit the size of the truck that can be accommodated. Availability of a rail siding is not essential to every user, but lack of this facility may limit future marketability. Another requirement that must be checked out is the availability of adequate water lines and pressures to support proper fire extinguisher installations. Without adequate fire protection, insurance rates skyrocket and greatly increase storage costs for the prospective tenant.

In the construction design of the building itself, provision should be made for loading docks capable of handling truck and freight-car loadings at the proper heights. The ceilings must be high, generally over 15 feet, for more efficient stack storage of merchandise.

The costs of construction of a warehouse building are similar to those for a shopping center building inasmuch as both are fairly high ceiling buildings with little or no interior finishing provided by the builder. Warehouses require heavier floors to support more weight, but use much less parking space than a shopping center building. Further, the cost of land suitable for a warehouse is much lower than that required for freeway-accessible shopping sites.

Warehouse leases often provide for a net/net return to the owner which means the *tenant* pays all maintenance and operating costs, plus all insurance and taxes on the building. In such a lease, management expenses would be held to a bare minimum. The cash available for debt service is thus very easy to calculate. On general warehouses with multitenant occupancy, the owner may provide some services and, most likely, will be responsible for taxes and insurance costs.

Miniwarehouses

Recently, a relatively new form of investment has grown up in the building of one-story structures partitioned into small rental spaces. The market for such space comes from the more affluent and mobile citizens who accumulate material goods but are unable to accommodate them in small apartments and houses. The structures usually contain from 100 to 300 rental spaces each ranging in size from 5 × 5 to 20 × 20 feet.

The management requirement, depending somewhat on size, ranges from almost nil to full-time administrative personnel and security guards. The returns on investment have been good. Owners have reported that a completed warehouse averages about one-half the cost per square foot as that for an apartment building, and the rental rates *per square foot* are about the same.

Farm and Ranch Loans

Farm and ranch loans are distinctive and should not be classified as commercial loans. They require a very specialized knowledge of both the borrower and the property pledged to make a sound underwriting judgment. Almost all these loans are analyzed in the local area. There are few, if any, national guidelines, as each local area presents its own special soil, weather, crops, and markets. Because of the great importance of agriculture to the national economy, the federal and many state governments have undertaken a number of helpful programs to support some stability within the industry. Government land and crop loans are the single most important source of farm loans. In 1988, federal and related agencies accounted for 44 percent of all farm mortgage debt outstanding. Of the regulated lenders, both commercial banks and life insurance companies are involved with farm loans, but in a much smaller capacity. The addition of Farmer Mac, a new secondary market underwriter of farm loan pools, in 1989, enhanced the willingness of regulated lenders to undertake farm loans.

Some of the major government agencies handling direct farm loans were discussed in Chapter 3, Mortgage Money: The Primary Market. This section comments on some questions that would be involved in underwriting farm and ranch loans.

At the turn of this century, 90 percent of our country's population depended on farm income. Today, farmers make up less than 4 percent of the total population. And the farm loan business has changed, also. Two general categories of farm loans are (1) the family-resident loan and (2) the agricorporate loan.

Family-Resident Farm Loans

The family-resident farm loan has not changed a great deal in the past 30 years. It is still based on the three legs of any good mortgage loan: (1) a credit worthy borrower, (2) a piece of real estate of sufficient value to provide good collateral, and (3) the ability of the property and the borrower to produce an income assuring repayment of the loan. Judgments on farmland value require good knowledge and experience in the local area. A single-crop farm is the most vulnerable to failure and subsequent loan default. A diversified crop operation, plus some livestock, gives the best security. So the ability of the farm to produce a continued income, regardless of an occasional crop failure or a fluctuating market, is a prime consideration in making a sound farm loan. The land value itself may be distorted by outside pressures such as a city growing nearby, a large neighboring farm desiring to expand, or possibly a new freeway providing much frontage acreage. But the farm underwriter should confine the analysis to the producing factors—soil conditions, weather, available irrigation, type of crops, nearness to markets, and condition of the markets—for it is these factors that will produce the income from which the loan can be recovered. To give any substantial weight to the rising land values takes the loan into the category of land development.

Agricorporate Farm Loans

Agricorporate loans show some similarity to special-purpose property loans. Large commercial farm companies control much of the nation's agriculture today and usually provide good business records to assist an underwriter in making an evaluation. Studies of land productivity with various crops and fertilizers, of the most effective methods of breeding and feeding livestock, and of the management techniques of cost control are all helpful in evaluating the operating procedures of commercial farms. These large farms have proved economical in their operations, and they are willing to test new technologies. Equipment can be more fully utilized and better maintained than on smaller holdings. But, along with the advantages, a word of caution: The dependency on hired labor and the management costs of a large commercial farm make them less flexible and more difficult to retrench in periods of lowering prices. The lender should hold the loan-to-value ratio at a conservative level in this type of operation.

The term of a farm loan varies as to need, and may run from 10 to 40 years with 33 years a popular term, partly because the Federal Land Bank formerly used 33 years. More leniency is given in the repayment of farm loans than other real estate loans. A farmer's income is subject to greater variation, and a rigid payment schedule can be self-defeating. But any long-term farm loan should have full amortization as a goal.

Ranch Loans

A ranch presents only slight variations to a farm loan in that it produces livestock as a principal source of revenue. Because ranches are predominantly in the water-short southwestern regions, an underwriter must take care to analyze the water situation. Often water rights can be of greater value than the land since without water the land may be worthless. A common practice in ranching is to lease public lands for grazing. The acreage so leased becomes of value to the ranch only in the productivity the land can add to the ranch, and this can be limited by the term of the lease. But leased land or grazing rights do add value and should be included in the appraisal for loan purposes. Sometimes ranches produce additional revenues from the sale of timber rights, from mineral leasing, and even from hunting leases and dude ranching. All income has its value, but must be considered according to its tenure and stability.

Questions for Discussion

1. Identify the financial statements that may be examined in analyzing a commercial loan applicant.
2. What is a feasibility report?
3. How would you use a present worth table?
4. Why is a land loan considered difficult to obtain?
5. What is a land development loan?
6. Discuss the essential features of a construction loan.
7. List the specialized knowledge needed to make good farm loans.
8. Comment on the problems that can be associated with a mobile home park loan.
9. Why does a special-purpose building present unusual problems for a loan underwriter?

10. Discuss problems that are unique to apartment loans.

11. What is the key feature that supports shopping center loans?

12. What kind of lease is most commonly found in retail store leasing?

13. Discuss the difference between pre-leasing and speculative leasing of an office building.

14. Are there any advantages to owning a warehouse rather than other types of income property?

Settlement Procedures

KEY WORDS AND PHRASES

Settlement agent
Escrow closing
Loan status report
Preliminary title report
Real Estate Settlement Procedures
   Act (RESPA)
Homebuyer's Guide to Settlement
   Costs
Good faith estimate
Designated service providers
Kickbacks
Seller-designated title company

Truth-in-Lending Act
Finance Charge
Annual percentage rate
HUD-designed settlement statement
Loan costs
Prepaid items
Required reserves
Title insurance charges
Recording fees
Additional settlement charges
Mortgagee's closing instructions
Disbursement of funds

Settlement Practices

Since property laws are essentially determined by each state, their diversity is reflected in the methods used to close, or settle, real estate transactions. Customs and practices have developed in every region of the country that best suit its unique business and legal requirements. The person or company selected to bring together the instruments of conveyance, mortgages, promissory notes and, of course, the monetary considerations to be exchanged between the buyer and seller of real estate is most generally known as the *settlement agent*. The agent can be a lender, a real estate broker, a title company, an attorney, or a company specializing in these procedures, called an escrow company. In most parts of the country, the settlement agent arranges for the principals involved in the transaction to meet together at a location where all the documents needed to transfer title and to secure and fund a loan can be reviewed and executed. At the conclusion of this process, if all documents are in order, the documents and the money are then distributed to the various parties entitled to receive them.

Another procedure, called *escrow closing*, is commonly used in some states. In this procedure, however, the parties involved do not meet around a table to sign instruments or exchange any cash or documents. Rather, at the time of entering a contract of sale, the parties sign an escrow agreement. The agreement requires the deposit of certain documents and funds with the escrow agent within an agreed time. The agent is responsible for meeting the requirements of the escrow agreement, which usually include the adjustment of taxes, insurance, and rentals, if any, between the buyer and seller, the payoff of any existing loan, arrangements for hazard insurance coverage, the computing of interest, and any other requirements for a new loan. If all papers and monies are deposited within the agreed time limit, the escrow is considered closed. The appropriate documents are then recorded and delivered to the proper parties along with the money that each is entitled to receive.

It was this area of diverse procedures that Congress focused on in 1974 and began to regulate. The purpose of the proposed legislation, by its own findings, was to protect consumers from "unnecessarily high settlement charges caused by certain abusive practices that have developed in some areas of the country." The result of congressional efforts was the enactment of the Real Estate Settlement Procedures Act (RESPA). Unfortunately, this act in its initial form was vaguely worded and contained a number of ill-defined requirements. Its effect on the real estate industry was one of substantial confusion as it was difficult to determine exactly what activities were considered legal or illegal. A temporary moratorium on the provisions of the act helped to restore normal business and in 1976 an amendment to the act effectively modified it, resulting in more practical legislation. The amended act adds several new requirements to the closing procedures of a residential real estate transaction. It does not change any local practices and sets no prices for settlement services. Mostly, it is directed toward providing better information on the settlement process so that a home buyer can make informed decisions.

Preliminary Procedures

There are two pieces of information closely associated with the settlement of a real estate transaction that are noted separately here because of their special usefulness in any property disposition. These are an existing *loan status report* and a *preliminary title report*. Many good real estate brokers arrange for both pieces of information at the time a property is listed for sale. In this way, if there are problems with either an existing loan or legal title to the property, they are discovered early on, allowing more time for resolution before the seller is faced with an impending closing date. Also, it is very important that the seller or agent have accurate information on these two subjects since they are of intense interest to any prospective buyer.

Loan Status Report

Several different names are used within the industry to describe the information contained in the status report on an existing mortgage loan. Some call it a Mortgagor's Information Letter, some a Mortgagee's Report. Further confusion is added to the nomenclature because in some areas of the country a Mortgagee's Information Letter means a preliminary title report on the land. What is referred to here is a report on the current status of an existing loan prepared by the mortgagee for the mortgagor. It is a statement, usually in letter form, giving the remaining balance due on the loan, the monthly payments required, the reserve held in the escrow account, and the requirements and cost of a loan payoff.

A request for this information must come from the mortgagor, although brokers often use form letters for the request that require only the mortgagor's signature. While this information is very helpful in providing accurate sales information, it is not normally used by the settlement agent in closing a real estate transaction. The agent calls for a current report that reflects the loan status as of the date a settlement actually takes place.

Preliminary Title Report

When an earnest money contract has been signed, it is a good idea to "open title" with whatever title insurance company has been selected to handle the closing. Under the new RESPA procedures, the seller may not require that title insurance be purchased from a particular title company as a condition of the sale, but the mortgage lender still has a right to accept or reject a proposed title company, so it is a good suggestion for buyers to make certain that they are selecting an acceptable title company when they decide. Lending institutions are now required to submit a statement to the borrower listing acceptable title companies and attorneys, along with the anticipated charges the borrower might expect. Also, any business relationship between the lender and *any* settlement service provider must be disclosed. To simplify handling, the title company selected is normally one located in the same county as the property being sold.

The preliminary title report is furnished by the title company to both the real estate agent and the mortgage company. The information contained is a confirmation of the correct legal description, and it also includes the names of the owners of the property according to the county records, any restrictions or liens on the property, any judgments against the owners of record, and a listing of any requirements the title company may have to perfect title and to issue a title insurance policy. The report is for information only; it is not to be confused with a title *binder*, which legally obligates the title company for specific insurance. Title companies normally make no charge for the preliminary report as it is part of their service in anticipation of writing the title insurance policy at closing.

RESPA Requirements

The Real Estate Settlement Procedures Act, as amended in 1976, applies to *residential* mortgage loans. Commercial loans are not included in the provisions of the act. Residential mortgage loans are those used to finance the purchase of one- to four-family housing, a condominium, a cooperative apartment unit, a lot with a mobile home, or a lot on which a house is to be built or a mobile home located. RESPA requirements can be divided into two general categories: (1) information requirements, and (2) prohibited practices.

Information Requirements

Lenders are now required to furnish certain specific information to each loan *applicant* and additional information to the borrower prior to closing a loan.

Information Booklet. At the time of a loan application, or not later than three business days after, the lender must give the applicant a copy of the HUD-prepared booklet entitled "A Homebuyer's Guide to Settlement Costs." The booklet is prepared by the Office of Consumer Affairs and Regulatory Functions of the U.S. Department of Housing and Urban Development. The information provided is discussed in two parts.

1. Part One describes the settlement process and the nature of the charges that are incurred. Questions are suggested for the home buyer to ask that might help clarify charges and procedures. It also lists unfair and illegal practices and gives information on the rights and remedies available to home buyers should they encounter a wrongful practice.

2. Part Two is an item-by-item explanation of settlement services and costs. Sample forms and worksheets are included to help guide the home buyer in making cost comparisons.

Good Faith Estimate. Within three business days of accepting a loan application, a lender is required to submit a *good faith estimate* of settlement costs to the loan applicant. The settlement charges are estimated for each item anticipated, except for prepaid hazard insurance and cash reserves deposited with the lender. (Reserves are subject to RESPA restrictions, which are detailed later.) The estimate may be stated in either a dollar amount or as a range for each charge, and the information must be furnished in a clear and concise manner (no special form is required). A typical Good Faith Estimate is illustrated in Figure 12–1, which uses the terminology and account numbers from Section L of the mandatory Settlement Statement (see Figure 12–3 later).

Designated Service Providers. If a lender designates settlement service providers, who perform such tasks as legal services, title examination, title insurance, or the conduct of the settlement, the normal charges for these specific providers must be used in the good faith estimate. Further, when this designation occurs, the lender must provide as part of the good faith estimate additional information giving the name, address, and telephone number of each designated provider. Any business relationship between the lender and the service provider must be fully disclosed.

Disclosure of Settlement Costs. As a part of the RESPA requirements, the use of a uniform Settlement Statement has been made mandatory for residential loan closings. Account numbers and terminology are standardized on the form, and it is expected that settlement charges, however designated in various parts of the country, be fitted into this form (Figure 12–3). A copy of the completed form must be delivered by the settlement agent to both the buyer and the seller at or before the closing. Since some of the information needed to complete the form may not be available until the time of actual closing, the borrower may waive the right of delivery at closing. However, in such a case, the completed settlement statement must be mailed at the earliest practical date.

Borrower's Right to Disclosure of Costs Prior to Closing. A borrower has the right under RESPA to request an inspection of the Settlement Statement one business day prior to closing. The form is completed by the person who will conduct the settlement procedures. The act does recognize that all costs may not be available one day prior to closing, but there is an obligation to show the borrower what is available, if requested.

Prohibited Practices

The vast majority of settlement procedures have always been conducted in an ethical manner by qualified professionals. However, abuses do occur occasionally,

LENDER: **GOOD FAITH ESTIMATE**   **(RESPA)**
       OF SETTLEMENT CHARGES

Listed below is the Good Faith Estimate of Settlement Charges made pursuant to the requirements of the Real Estate Settlement Procedures Act (RESPA). These figures are only estimates and the actual charges due at settlement, may be different.

This form may not cover all items you will be required to pay in cash at settlement, for example, deposits in escrow for real estate taxes and insurance. You may wish to inquire as to the amounts of such other items. You may be required to pay other additional amounts at settlement.

THIS ESTIMATE IS NOT A LOAN COMMITMENT.

Property To Be Mortgaged _____

Sale Price: $ _____ Estimated Monthly Principal And Interest Payment: $ _____

Down Payment: $ _____ Estimated Monthly Tax And Insurance Reserve: $ _____

Loan Request: $ _____ Mortgage Life Insurance $_____

Maximum Anticipated Interest Charge: _____ % Private Mortgage Insurance: $ _____

Term of Loan: _____ years Total Payment: $ _____

	SETTLEMENT ITEM	Estimated Charge
801	Loan Origination Fee	$ _____
802	Loan Discount	$ _____
803	Appraisal Fee	$ _____
804	Credit Report	$ _____
805	Lender's Inspection Fee	$ _____
806	Mortgage Insurance Application Fee	$ _____
807	Assumption Fee	$ _____
901	Interest	$ _____
902	Mortgage Insurance Premium for _____ mo.	$ _____
903	Hazard Insurance Premium for _____ yrs.	$ _____
1001	Hazard Insurance for _____ mo.	$ _____
1002	Mortgage Insurance for _____ mo.	$ _____
1003/1005	Property Tax for _____ mo.	$ _____
1101	Settlement or Closing Fee	$ _____
1102	Abstract or Title Search	$ _____
1103	Title Examination	$ _____
1105	Document Preparation	$ _____
1106	Notary Fees	$ _____
1107	Attorney Fees	$ _____
1108	Title Insurance	$ _____
1201	Recording Fees	$ _____
1204	Tax Certificates	$ _____
1301	Survey	$ _____
1302	Pest Inspection	$ _____
Other	_____	$ _____
Other	_____	$ _____
	TOTAL ESTIMATED	$ _____

THIS SECTION TO BE COMPLETED BY LENDER ONLY IF A PARTICULAR PROVIDER OF SERVICE IS REQUIRED

Listed below are providers of service which we require you use. The charges or range indicated in the Good Faith Estimate above are based upon the corresponding charge of the below designated providers.

Designated Charge Item No. _____   Item No. _____
Service Provided _____
Providers Name _____
Address and _____
Telephone Number _____

| We do, do not have a business relationship with the above named provider. | We do, do not have a business relationship with the above named provider. |

NOTICE: The Federal Equal Credit Opportunity Act prohibits creditors from discriminating against credit applicants on the basis of race, color, religion, national origin, sex, marital status, age (provided that the applicant has the capacity to enter into a binding contract); because all or part of the applicant's income derives from any public assistance program; or because the applicant has in good faith exercised any right under the Consumer Credit Protection Act. The Federal agency that administers compliance with this law concerning this creditor is: _____

_____

_____

The undersigned applicant hereby acknowledges receipt of the above Good Faith Estimate and Equal Credit Opportunity Notice.

Signature _____ Date _____

FIGURE 12–1 Good Faith Estimate

and it is one of the purposes of RESPA to expose unfair practices and make them illegal. Two such practices are described here.

Kickbacks.   The law specifically prohibits any arrangement by means of which a fee is charged, or accepted, where no services have actually been performed. The requirement does not prevent agents for the lender, attorneys, or others from actually performing a service in connection with the mortgage loan or settlement procedure. Nor does it prohibit cooperative brokerage arrangements such as are normally found in multiple listing services or referral arrangements between real estate agents and brokers. The target for the prohibition is the arrangement wherein one party returns a part of the fee (such as a loan origination fee) to obtain business from the referring party. The abuse involved here, of course, is that such an arrangement can result in a higher settlement fee for the borrower with no increase in the services rendered.

Title Companies.   A *seller* is not permitted to require the use of a specified title insurance company as a condition of sale. The buyer has the right to compare the service and charges of competing title companies. In many states the rates for title insurance come under the regulatory authority of the state and are thus uniform. Also, lenders retain the right to reject title companies that do not meet their minimum requirements of financial strength.

Truth-in-Lending Act

The Truth-in-Lending Act is a federal law that became effective in July 1969, as a part of the Consumer Credit Protection Act. It is implemented by the Federal Reserve Board's Regulation Z. The purpose of the law is to require lenders to give meaningful information to borrowers on the cost of consumer credit, which includes credit extended in real estate transactions. The credit covered must involve a finance charge or be payable in more than four installments. Credit extended for business purposes, which includes dwelling units containing more than four family units, is not covered by the law. No maximum or minimum interest rates or charges for credit are set by the law, for its purpose is primarily one of disclosure.

While the act contains a limited right allowing the borrower to rescind or cancel the credit transaction and covers *all* types of advertising to promote the extension of consumer credit, the principal features considered here are the disclosure of the *Finance Charge* and the *Annual Percentage Rate* (APR).

Finance Charge

The finance charge is the total amount of all costs that the consumer must pay for obtaining credit. These costs include interest, the loan fee, a loan finder's fee, time-price differentials, discount points, and the cost of credit life insurance if it is a condition for granting credit. In a real estate transaction, purchase costs that would be paid regardless of whether or not credit is extended are *not* included in the finance charge, provided these charges are reasonable and bona fide and not included to circumvent the law. Among these excluded purchase costs are legal fees, taxes not included in the cash price, recording fees, title insurance premiums, and credit report charges. However, such charges must be itemized and disclosed to the customer. In the case of first mortgages intended to purchase residential dwellings, the total dollar finance charge need not be stated, although the annual percentage rate must be disclosed.

Annual Percentage Rate

The annual percentage rate as determined under Regulation Z is not an "interest rate." Interest is one of the costs included in the finance charge. The APR is the relationship of the total finance charge to the total amount to be financed and must be computed to the nearest one-quarter percent. Figure 12–2 illustrates a typical form used in a real estate transaction prepared in compliance with Regulation Z.

Settlement Practices and Costs

As noted earlier in this chapter, settlement practices vary considerably in different sections of the country. There is no federal requirement to change any basic practices for residential loans except where it is necessary to add some disclosure procedures and to eliminate any prohibited practices. There are limitations set by RESPA on the amount of reserve, or escrow, accounts that may be held by lenders, and there is one mandatory form to be used in the settlement of residential loans.

The mandatory uniform Settlement Statement form is illustrated in Figure 12–3 and will be used as the basis for the following discussion of the various services involved with a loan closing. While the emphasis is on residential loan practices, the procedures used in closing commercial loans involve most of the same services.

FEDERAL TRUTH IN LENDING DISCLOSURE STATEMENT

Creditor: Borrower(s):

Date:

Property Address:

ANNUAL PERCENTAGE RATE The cost of your credit as a yearly rate. **(APR)**	FINANCE CHARGE The dollar amount the credit will cost you.	AMOUNT FINANCED The amount of credit provided to you or on your behalf.	TOTAL OF PAYMENTS The amount you will have paid after you have made all payments as scheduled.
e %	$ e	$ e	$

Your payment schedule will be:

Number of Payments	Amount of Payments	When Payments are due

☐ Your loan contains a variable-rate feature and variable-rate disclosures have been provided earlier.

☐ ESCROWS: Added to your monthly note payments will be required amounts which will be put into an escrow account to ensure the payment of real estate taxes, hazard insurance premiums, mortgage insurance premiums (if this insurance is required by the lender), etc. The amount of your escrow payments will be determined by the lender and will be enough to ensure that there will be sufficient funds in the account to pay the items when due. The lender will periodically review the account to determine changes that may be required in your escrow payments and you will be notified in writing of the changes and when they are effective. If deficiencies occur in your account, the lender will prorate the deficiencies among your regularly scheduled payments, however, you may clear the deficiency in one lump-sum payment. If surpluses occur in your escrow account, you can decide to have the surpluses credited to your account, or receive a refund. If you fail to pay the escrow payments when due, the lender can immediately require you to pay the entire loan balance and other amounts owed on the loan in full. If the total amounts owed on the loan are not paid, the lender could begin foreclosure proceedings which could ultimately cause a forced sale of your home.

SECURITY: You are giving a security interest in: ☐ The goods or property being purchased ☐ Other collateral
☐ Real property you own located at

LATE CHARGE: If a payment is _____ days late, you will be charged _____ % of the payment.
            Minimum Late Charge $
PREPAYMENT: If you pay off early, you
☐ may   ☐ will not   have to pay a penalty.
☐ may   ☐ will not   be entitled to a refund of part of the finance charge.
☐ ASSUMPTION: Someone buying your property
☐ may, subject to conditions   ☐ cannot   assume the remainder of your loan on the original terms.

CHECK BOX IF APPLICABLE

See your contract documents for any additional information about nonpayment, default, any required repayment in full before the scheduled date, and prepayment refunds and penalties.

e means an estimate

I/We the undersigned Borrower(s) acknowledge that I/we received a copy of this Disclosure Statement on _____

WITNESS	SIGNATURE
	SIGNATURE
	SIGNATURE
	SIGNATURE

CMCA: L P 78006 (9/88)

FIGURE 12–2 Federal Truth-in-Lending Statement

OMB No. 2502-0265 (Exp. 12-31-86)   Page 1

A.

CHICAGO TITLE INSURANCE COMPANY

B. TYPE OF LOAN

| 1. ☐ FHA | 2. ☐ FmHA | 3. ☒ CONV. UNINS. |
| 4. ☐ VA | 5. ☐ CONV. INS. | |

6. File Number: | SAMPLE |
| | SAMPLE   GPS |

7. Loan Number

SETTLEMENT STATEMENT
U.S. DEPARTMENT OF HOUSING AND URBAN DEVELOPMENT

8. Mortgage Insurance Case Number

C. NOTE: This form is furnished to give you a statement of actual settlement costs. Amounts paid to and by the settlement agent are shown. Items marked "(p.o.c.)" were paid outside the closing; they are shown here for informational purposes and are not included in the totals.

D. NAME OF BORROWER: Samuel S. Smith and Sally Smith
ADDRESS: 1234 Main Street
Houston   Texas   77777

E. NAME OF SELLER: Judy Jean Jones
ADDRESS: 24 Lovers Lane
Dallas, TX   75225

F. NAME OF LENDER: Second Mortgages, Inc.
ADDRESS: 55 Greenback Drive
Houston   Texas   77222

G. PROPERTY LOCATION: 1234 Main Street
Houston   Texas   77056

H. SETTLEMENT AGENT: Chicago Title Insurance Company
ADDRESS:

I. SETTLEMENT DATE: 03/15/89

PLACE OF SETTLEMENT: 1001 S. Dairy Ashford
ADDRESS: Houston   Texas   77077

J. SUMMARY OF BORROWER'S TRANSACTION		**K. SUMMARY OF SELLER'S TRANSACTION**	
100. GROSS AMOUNT DUE FROM BORROWER:		**400. GROSS AMOUNT DUE TO SELLER:**	
101. Contract sales price	200,000.00	401. Contract sales price	200,000.00
102. Personal Property		402. Personal Property	
103. Settlement charges to borrower (line 1400)	2,556.42	403.	
104. Escrow Balance	1,156.90	404. Escrow Balance	1,156.90
105.		405.	
Adjustments for items paid by seller in advance		Adjustments for items paid by seller in advance	
106. City/town taxes / / to / /		406. City/town taxes / / to / /	
107. County taxes / / to / /		407. County taxes / / to / /	
108. Assessments 03/16/89 to 01/01/90	114.81	408. Assessments 03/16/89 to 01/01/90	114.81
109. Hazard Insurance 3/16/89 to 7/1/88	244.07	409. Hazard Insurance 3/16/89 to 7/1/88	244.07
110.		410.	
111.		411.	
112.		412.	
120. GROSS AMT DUE FROM BORROWER	204,072.20	**420. GROSS AMT DUE TO SELLER**	201,515.78
200. AMOUNTS PAID BY OR IN BEHALF OF BORROWER		**500. REDUCTIONS IN AMOUNT DUE TO SELLER:**	
201. Deposit or earnest money	10,000.00	501. Excess deposit (see instructions)	
202. Principal amount of new loan(s)	63,000.00	502. Settlement charges to seller (line 1400)	13,872.00
203. Existing loan(s) taken subject to	96,943.00	503. Existing loan(s) taken subject to	96,943.00
		504. Payoff of first mortgage loan	
204.			
205.		505. Payoff of second mortgage loan	
206.		506.	
207.		507.	
208.		508.	
209.		509.	
Adjustments for items unpaid by seller		Adjustments for items unpaid by seller	
210. City/town taxes 01/01/89 to 03/16/89	364.93	510. City/town taxes 01/01/89 to 03/16/89	364.93
211. County taxes / / to / /		511. County taxes / / to / /	
212. Assessments / / to / /		512. Assessments / / to / /	
213. Interest on Existing Loan	484.72	513. Interest on Existing Loan	484.72
214. INTEREST ADJ. FROM / / TO / /		514. INTEREST ADJ. FROM / / TO / /	
215.		515.	
216.		516.	
217.		517.	
218.		518.	
219.		519.	
220. TOTAL PAID BY/FOR BORROWER	170,792.65	**520. TOTAL REDUCTIONS AMT DUE SELLER**	111,664.65
300. CASH AT SETTLEMENT FROM/TO BORROWER		**600. CASH AT SETTLEMENT TO/FROM SELLER**	
301. Gross amt due from borrower (line 120)	204,072.20	601. Gross amt due to seller (line 420)	201,515.78
302. Less amts paid by/for borrower (line 220)	170,792.65	602. Less reductions in amt due seller (line 520)	111,664.65
303. CASH(☒ FROM) (☐ TO) BORROWER	33,279.55	603. CASH(☒ TO) (☐ FROM) SELLER	89,851.13

I have carefully reviewed the HUD-1 Settlement Statement and to the best of my knowledge and belief, it is a true and accurate statement of all receipts and disbursements made on my account or by me in this transaction. I further certify that I have received a copy of the HUD-1 Settlement Statement.

Borrower   Seller

Samuel S. Smith   Judy Jean Jones

Sally Smith

The HUD-1 Settlement Statement which I have prepared is a true and accurate account of this transaction. I have caused or will cause funds to be disbursed in accordance with this statement.

Settlement Agent   Date

WARNING: It is a crime to knowingly make false statements to the United States on this or any other similar form. Penalties upon conviction can include a fine and imprisonment. For details see: Title 18 U.S. Code Section 1001 and Section 1010.

FIGURE 12–3   HUD Settlement Statement for Residential Loans

F-2857-01 4/80	Page 2	OMB No. 2502-0265 (Exp. 12-31-86)

File Number: SAMPLE	L. SETTLEMENT CHARGES		

		PAID FROM BORROWER'S FUNDS AT SETTLEMENT	PAID FROM SELLER'S FUNDS AT SETTLEMENT
700.	TOTAL SALES/BROKER'S COMMISSION based on price $ 200,000.00 @ 6.000 %= 12,000.00		
	Division of Commission (line 700) as follows:		
701.	$ 6,000.00 to Uptown Realty		
702.	$ 6,000.00 to Boomtown Properties		
703.	$ to		
	(Money retained by broker applied to commission $)		
704.	Commission paid at Settlement		12,000.00
705.	Other sales agent charges payable to:		
800.	**ITEMS PAYABLE IN CONNECTION WITH LOAN**		
801.	Loan Origination Fee 1.000 % Second Mortgages, Inc.	630.00	
802.	Loan Discount %		
803.	Appraisal Fee to Second Mortgages, Inc. POC		
804.	Credit Report to Credco	45.00	
805.	Lender's Inspection Fee to		
806.	Mortgage Insurance Application Fee to		
807.	Assumption Fee to E-Z Mortgage	970.00	
808.	Application Fee to E-Z Mortgage	125.00	
809.	Recording of Assignment to Second Liens, Inc.	25.00	
810.			
811.			
900.	**ITEMS REQUIRED BY LENDER TO BE PAID IN ADVANCE**		
901.	Interest from 03/15/89 to 04/01/89 @$ 14.2600 /day	242.42	
902.	Mortgage Insurance Premium for 0 months to		
903.	Hazard Insurance Premium for 0 years to		
904.	0 years to		
905.			
1000.	**RESERVES DEPOSITED WITH LENDER**		
1001.	Hazard insurance 0 month @$ per month		
1002.	Mortgage insurance 0 month @$ per month		
1003.	City property taxes 0 month @$ per month		
1004.	County property taxes 0 month @$ per month		
1005.	Annual assessments 0 month @$ per month		
1006.	0 month @$ per month		
1007.	0 month @$ per month		
1008.	0 month @$ per month		
1100.	**TITLE CHARGES**		
1101.	Settlement or Closing Fee (Escrow Fee) to Chicago Title Insurance	60.00	60.00
1102.	Abstract or title search to		
1103.	Title examination to		
1104.	Title insurance binder to		
1105.	Document preparation to		
1106.	Notary fees to		
1107.	Attorney's fee to Dewey, Cheatem & Howe	150.00	160.00
	(includes above items numbers:)		
1108.	Title insurance to Chicago Title Insurance	120.00	1,518.00
	(includes above items numbers:)		
1109.	Lender's coverage $ 63,000.00		
1110.	Owner's coverage $ 200,000.00		
1111.	State of Texas Policy Guaranty Fees	3.00	3.00
1112.	Messenger Fees	50.00	50.00
1113.			
1200.	**GOVERNMENT RECORDING AND TRANSFER CHARGES**		
1201.	Recording fees: Deed $ 20.00 ; Mortgage $ 32.00 ; Release $	26.00	26.00
1202.	City/county tax/stamps: Deed $; Mortgage $		
1203.	State tax/stamps: Deed $; Mortgage $		
1204.			55.00
1205.			
1300.	**ADDITIONAL SETTLEMENT CHARGES**		
1301.	Survey to		
1302.	Pest inspection to No Bugs, Inc	25.00	
1303.	Structural Inspection to The House Inspector	85.00	
1304.			
1305.			
1306.			
1307.			
1400.	**TOTAL SETTLEMENT CHARGES** (enter on lines 103, Section J and 502, Section K)	2,556.42	13,872.00

I have carefully reviewed the HUD-1 Settlement Statement and to the best of my knowledge and belief, it is a true and accurate statement of all receipts and disbursements made on my account or by me in this transaction. I further certify that I have received a copy of the HUD-1 Settlement Statement.

Borrower
Samuel S. Smith

Seller
Judy Jean Jones

Sally Smith

The HUD-1 Settlement Statement which I have prepared is a true and accurate account of this transaction. I have caused or will cause funds to be disbursed in accordance with this statement.

Settlement Agent _____ Date _____

HUD-1 (3/86) RESPA, HB 4305.2

FIGURE 12–3 (Continued)

Settlement Statement

The design of the Settlement Statement places all the costs chargeable to the buyer, or the seller, on the first page, and a detail of these costs on the second page. A cursory examination of the statement shows that the first section, A through I, contains information concerning the loan and the parties involved. Section J lists the amounts due from, or paid by, the borrower, and Section K details the same for the seller. The bottom line in each column indicates the cash due by the borrower-buyer on the left-hand side, and that due by the seller on the right-hand side. Whatever money must change hands is clearly the result of the two figures. Section L on the second page of the form lists various settlement services that can be involved in a closing with some blank lines for any separate entries not otherwise clearly identified.

This particular form must be completed for the settlement meeting by the person conducting the settlement procedures. A copy of the completed form is either given to both the buyer and seller at the meeting, or mailed as soon as practical after the meeting. If there is no actual meeting of the parties involved for settlement, the agent must still mail the completed forms after the closing has been finalized. This is the same form that a borrower has the right to inspect one business day prior to closing. It is not required that all information be filled in one day prior to closing, but the settlement agent must disclose whatever is available if requested to do so by the borrower.

A Settlement Costs Worksheet is also available and is intended for use by the prospective borrower as a handy guide for making comparisons of the charges quoted by the various service providers.

Sales/Broker's Commission (Item 700)

The sales commission is usually paid by the seller and is listed on the settlement in the total dollar amount, then divided between participating brokers as the sales agreement may provide. The amount is negotiable and may be a flat fee for the sale or a percentage of the sales amount.

Items Payable in Connection with Loan (Item 800)

As identified by RESPA, the costs of the loan are the fees charged by the lenders to process, approve, and make the mortgage loan.

Loan Origination (801). This is the fee charged by the primary lender to assemble information necessary to evaluate a loan application, to determine its acceptability, and to prepare the completed loan package. The charge is negotiable and varies from 1 percent to 1.5 percent of the loan amount.

Loan Discount (802). The loan discount is not truly a fee in that it is not considered payment for services rendered. Rather, the discount, expressed in points or as a percentage of the loan amount, is the procedure used in all financial markets to adjust the yield on a fixed interest rate certificate to a level of return that is commensurate with the current market rate for money loaned. In a practical sense, the discount is interest, or a cost of borrowed money, paid in advance— sometimes explained as a down payment on the cost of borrowed money. As a cost of borrowed money paid at the time of loan settlement, a loan discount must properly be charged as one of the items payable in connection with the loan.

Appraisal Fee (803). An appraisal of the property is necessary to establish the value basis for a mortgage loan. All regulated lenders must have an appraisal prepared by an independent professional appraiser, or by a qualified member of the lender's staff, to provide factual data on the value of the property offered as loan collateral. Since an appraisal is of value to both the buyer and seller of property, it may be paid for by either one. In some cases the cost of an appraisal may be included as a part of the initial application fee (either for the loan, or for the mortgage insurance).

Credit Report Fee (804). All applicants for mortgage loans are required to submit credit reports that are obtained by the lender from local credit bureaus. This report is a necessary verification of information submitted in the loan application plus statistical information on the bill-paying record of the applicant. The credit report is one source of information that a lender uses to determine if the applicant is an acceptable credit risk. Payment for the report is most often made by the borrower.

Lender's Inspection Fee (805). The lender is permitted to assess a charge for an inspection of the property offered as collateral. The inspection can be made by the lender's personnel or by an independent inspector. This inspection is not to be confused with pest inspections, which are discussed later.

Mortgage Insurance Application Fee (806). Private mortgage insurance com- panies charge fees for the processing of a loan application. This fee sometimes covers both an appraisal fee and an application fee.

Assumption Fee (807). An assumption fee is essentially a paper processing fee charged in transactions in which the buyer takes over and assumes liability for payments on a prior loan of the seller.

Items Required by Lender to Be Paid in Advance (Item 900)

There are certain items that must be paid in advance at the closing of a loan.

Interest (901). Since mortgage loans extend for long terms, it is a common practice to adjust the monthly payment to a convenient date each month, most often the first of each month. The normal monthly payment on a mortgage loan includes a charge for interest at the end of the month; that is, *after* the borrower has had the use of the money loaned. So, to adjust the monthly payment to a date other than that of loan closing, the interest charge is computed for the time period from the date of closing to the beginning of the period covered by the first monthly payment. For example, if the settlement takes place on June 16, a prepayment of charges is needed through June 30. The period covered by the regular monthly payment begins on July 1, and the first payment is due on August 1.

Example

Compute the interest charges for 15 days (June 16 through June 30) on a $45,000 loan at 10 percent interest as follows:

$$\$45,000 \times .10 \quad = \$4,500.00 \quad \text{Annual interest cost}$$
$$\$4,500 \div 360 \quad = \$ \quad 12.50 \quad \text{Daily interest cost}$$
$$\$12.50 \times 15 \text{ days} = \$ \quad 187.50 \quad \textit{Prepaid interest due}$$

Mortgage Insurance Premium (902). Almost all lenders now require private mortgage insurance on loans in excess of 80 percent of the property value. The protection is against a borrower default in the payment of the loan. It enables a lender to make higher-ratio (up to 95 percent) loans than would otherwise be possible, and thus allows lower down payments for the borrower. The first premium charge is always higher than the continuing annual payments, as it includes an issuing fee and is payable in full at the loan closing. This type of mortgage insurance should not be confused with mortgage life, credit life, or disability insurance, which are designed to pay off a mortgage in the event of physical disability or death of the borrower.

Hazard Insurance Premium (903). Hazard insurance protects both the lender and the borrower against loss to the building by fire, windstorm, or other natural hazard. Such coverage is a requirement for mortgage loans and includes the naming of the lender as a loss payee (in addition to the homeowner) should a loss be incurred. The normal lender requirement is for insurance coverage in an amount not less than the loan amount. With escalation of home value, coverage in the amount of a loan may quickly prove inadequate. Co-insurance clauses found in most insurance policies require a minimum coverage (usually 80 percent of the building value at the time of loss) to protect the homeowner on full recovery of partial losses. So while the lender may set a minimum requirement, the buyer may elect to take increased coverage with an escalation protection policy. It should be noted that hazard insurance coverage does not necessarily include flood insurance. In certain areas of the country, federally subsidized flood insurance is available under the National Flood Insurance Act. Most lenders require a full first year's premium of hazard insurance paid at the time of closing. Often, the paid-up policy is delivered at the closing table. In addition to the first year's premium, lenders may require a reserve of up to two months of annual premiums deposited with them at closing.

Reserves Deposited with Lenders (Item 1000)

Almost all residential loans require cash deposited with the lender at the time of loan closing to be used for future payment of recurring annual charges such as taxes, insurance, and maintenance assessments. The identification of these accounts differs as they may be referred to as reserves, escrow accounts, impound accounts, or reserve accruals. The purpose of the initial deposits is to give the lender enough cash to make the first annual payment that comes due after the closing date. Because real estate practices differ throughout the country, RESPA leaves the actual calculation of the initial deposit up to the lender. In some areas, taxes are paid for a year in advance; in others, they are paid for at the end of the tax year. The same is true of maintenance assessments. RESPA does place a limit on the deposits that may be required to meet the first year's payments although the amount to be deposited cannot exceed a sum sufficient to pay taxes, insurance premiums, or other charges that would have been paid under normal lending practices *up to the due date* of the first full monthly installment payment.

There is a second restriction in the amount of reserves that may be held by a lender on a *continuing* basis. At the time of closing, a lender can require that the deposit of up to two months of annual charges for taxes, insurance, and other recurring assessments be held by the lender. This is in addition to the deposits that may be needed to handle the first year's charges. Then, each monthly installment payment can include one-twelfth of the annual charges on a continuing basis. RESPA rules restrict the lender to collecting no more than one-twelfth of the annual taxes and other charges, unless a larger payment is necessary to make up a deficit in the reserve account. Further, RESPA restricts the cushion that a lender may hold against a possible deficit in the account to one-sixth of the annual charges. A deficit in the account may be caused, for example, by raises in the taxes and insurance premiums during the loan payment year. These monthly mortgage payment reserve limitations apply to *all* RESPA-covered mortgage loans, whether originated before or after the implementation of RESPA.

Example

Initial Reserve Calculation for a Settlement Date of June 30, 1990

First-mortgage payment due on August 1, 1990
Annual taxes, $900 (monthly = $75.00)
Due date for taxes, December 1 for calendar year
Initial reserve requirement from December 1 to July 30

8 months × $75	= $600.00
Plus two months' cushion	
2 months × $75	= $150.00
Deposit required at closing for taxes	= $750.00

In considering this example, keep in mind that the taxes due for the months prior to the actual sale of the house are the financial responsibility of the seller. So the settlement statement would reflect the proration of the tax liability, and thus most of the reserve deposit for this purpose (taxes) would be from the seller, not the buyer. If the house is newly constructed, the tax assessment during the construction period would most likely be a lesser amount than that for the finished house. In areas where taxes are paid at the beginning of each tax year, the deposit requirement to meet the coming year's taxes would fall to the buyer. Insurance premiums (if an existing policy is continued) and other recurring charges are handled in the same manner.

Hazard Insurance (1001). Since most home buyers elect to purchase new insurance policies to fit their own needs, no adjustment for an initial reserve requirement is needed. The normal lender requirement, approved as being in compliance with RESPA restrictions, is for a one-year premium paid in advance, plus a deposit to a reserve account in the amount of two months of the annual premium. A buyer may purchase hazard insurance from whatever company he or she chooses, so long as the company meets the lender's minimum standards for insurance carriers.

Mortgage Insurance (1002). The premium reserve requirement for mortgage insurance is negotiable with the lender. It may be required that a part of the total annual premium be placed in a reserve account, but no more than one-sixth of the annual premium could be held as a cushion by the lender.

City/County Property Taxes (1003–1004). Initial reserve requirements have been detailed in the earlier example of this section. Lenders do require monthly payments of one-twelfth the annual taxes to be paid into the reserve account.

Annual Assessments (1005).   The reserve that may be required for assessments is for such charges as a homeowner's association fee, a condominium maintenance charge, or a municipal improvement assessment. The same previously described RESPA reserve limitations apply to all forms of reserves.

Title Charges (Item 1100)

In the uniform Settlement Statement, *title charges* designates a variety of services performed to conclude a real estate transaction properly. These include searching records, preparing documents, and acquiring insurance against title failure. While practices and terminology differ in some areas, the services needed are basically similar.

Settlement or Closing Fee (1101).   The charges made by the person or company for the service of handling the settlement procedures. The payment of the fee is negotiable between buyer and seller and is often divided equally between them.

Abstract or Title Search, Title Examination, Title Insurance Binder (1102–1104).   In a real estate transaction, it is reasonable to expect that a seller offer some solid proof of his or her right to convey the property to be purchased. This can be accomplished through a search of all the recorded documents affecting the land title (an abstract of title) culminating in an attorney's opinion as to the quality of the title. More commonly, it is handled through a title insurance company, which continuously searches the records and insures their title opinions. Title to real property is a matter of public record and that record can also contain other instruments or claims that affect the ownership rights of a potential seller. Thus the cost of assuring good title most often is paid by the seller.

Document Preparation (1105).   The charge for preparing the legal documents may be listed separately or may be included with other service fees, most likely as a part of the attorney's fee.

Notary Fee (1106).   Instruments that are to be recorded in the public records usually require that all signatures be witnessed by a notary public. Settlement agents are often licensed for this purpose and may ask a separate charge for their official services in this capacity.

Attorney's Fees (1107).   Few lenders will permit a loan to be closed without the assurance of a qualified attorney that all instruments have been properly prepared and executed. In any real estate transaction, the buyer and the seller may each be represented by their own attorney and, in such case, each may pay the attorney outside the closing procedure. In the handling of residential loans, the title company or settlement agent involved may employ an attorney to handle the legal requirements and, if both parties agree, the charges are allocated equally between buyer and seller.

Title Insurance (1108). Title insurance offers protection to the policyholder against adverse claims to the ownership rights of a landholder. It is issued in two separate policy forms: one to protect the landowner, the other to protect the lender whose mortgage claim is dependent on the landholder's right to dispose of the land.

Lender's Title Policy (1109). The lender's title policy is paid for as a single premium at closing. It is also called a *mortgagee's policy,* and in many areas it is issued simultaneously with an owner's policy, since the same basic risk is covered. Local practice varies as to whether the lender's or the owner's policy must pay the major share of premium cost. If the lender's policy carries the major cost, the owner's policy is usually issued for a nominal amount. Payment for a lender's policy is most likely to be made by a buyer as it is clearly part of the cost of obtaining a loan. There are some differences in a lender's policy as compared with an owner's policy. The lender's policy runs with the loan (the amount of insurance is reduced as the mortgage balance is reduced) and it covers the designated holder of the mortgage note (an owner's policy cannot be assigned). Furthermore, a payoff of the loan automatically cancels the lender's insurance coverage.

Owner's Title Insurance (1110). The owner's policy is purchased at closing with a one-time premium charge and continues to protect the holder up to the face value of the policy for as long as responsibility exists for an adverse claim. The time period for responsibility is determined by each state's limitation statutes on adverse claims. Even though an owner may hold actual title to property for a short period, say, a year or so, at the time the property is sold, the warranty deed normally used to convey title leaves the seller with a responsibility. The wording of the conveyance reads that seller "will warrant and defend generally the title to the property against all claims and demands." So the owner's title policy protects the owner not only while he or she is in possession of the insured premises, but also for the time period after it may be sold during which the seller remains liable for possible adverse claims. Customs vary regionally as to whether or not the buyer or seller pays for owner's title insurance. Since the issuance of such a policy represents a good proof of the validity of the seller's own title to the land to be conveyed, in some areas the cost is paid by the seller. In other areas, if the seller can prove good title to the property through an attorney's opinion based on the abstract of title, or by the issuance of a title binder by a title company, then payment for the owner's policy falls to the buyer—he or she is the one being protected.

Government Recording and Transfer Charges (Item 1200)

Recording and transfer fees are those charged by city, county, or state governments for recording services, or as a tax on the transaction. The fees may be based on the amount of the mortgage loan or on the value of the property being transferred. Payment of these charges is negotiable between buyer and seller but are usually paid by the buyer.

Additional Settlement Charges (Item 1300)

Charges that are not easily classified within the previous categories of costs can be listed under this section of additional charges. Mostly, they include the costs of a survey and any inspections of the property that may be required to determine adequacy of the structure.

Survey (1301). Almost all lenders require that a survey of the property offered as collateral be included in the loan package. A survey, which can only be prepared by a registered surveyor, gives a picture description of the land with an outline of its perimeter boundaries. It should show the precise location of buildings as well as any easements or rights-of-way that may cross the land. The survey can disclose any encroachments on the land that may create a cloud on the ownership rights. It is not unusual for an attorney to require a survey before preparing a deed or mortgage instrument to make sure of the land and the rights being conveyed. Payment for the survey is negotiable—the seller has an obligation to prove exactly what land is to be conveyed while the buyer has a need for the survey to complete the loan requirements.

Pest and Other Inspections (1302). In certain areas of the country where termites or other insects infest buildings and can create damage, it is normal to require a separate pest inspection. In such areas, sales agreements may call for the property to be delivered free of infestation. The pest inspection, with a certified letter of proof, is the seller's method of fulfilling this requirement. Regardless of a sales agreement, lenders may require a pest inspection to assure them that the property offered as collateral is free of pest-caused structural damage. In such a case, the cost may be paid by the buyer as part of the requirements for obtaining a mortgage loan.

Total Settlement Charges (Item 1400)

At the bottom of the page listing the various settlement charges, the totals for the borrower's charges and for the seller's charges are listed, and transferred to the summary section of the first page.

Final Closing Instructions

Mortgagee's Closing Instructions

Once a loan has been approved, the mortgage company prepares a sheet of instructions for delivery to the settlement agent handling closing procedures. The instructions detail such items as the correct legal name of the mortgage note, the name of the trustee for the deed of trust, the terms of the mortgage note, and special requirements to be included in the mortgage or deed of trust (that is, if the mortgage company is not submitting its own forms for a note and mortgage), specific instructions on monthly payments to be given to the borrowers, details of the escrow requirements, and details of disbursement procedures. Along with the instructions, the mortgage company will send the buyer-seller affidavits as may be required, which certify to the actual down payment (cash and/or property exchanged) and to the use of the loan proceeds, which must be acknowledged by the notarized signatures of all buyers and sellers. Also, a truth-in-lending statement is prepared for the purchaser-borrower signature at closing. Some mortgage companies require certifications of occupancy (for homestead information). The forms vary between companies according to how their legal counselors interpret the state laws.

The instructions of the mortgage company invariably call for a certain amount of work on the part of the settlement agent closing the loan, if only as a means of clarifying the loan requirements. This is an addition to the other details of closing that a settlement agent must handle, such as assembling the title information, preparing or reviewing the note and deed of trust, verifying tax requirements, and determining the insurance payments needed.

It is advisable to allow the settlement agent a reasonable time for its work in preparing for a closing. A forced deadline can induce errors and omissions. Figure 12–4 gives an example of typical mortgagee's closing instructions.

Setting the Closing

When the mortgage company has approved the loan and prepared its closing instructions, it is the responsibility of the real estate agent, or agents, involved to arrange a mutually agreeable closing time. Practices vary in different parts of

COMMONWEALTH MORTGAGE COMPANY OF AMERICA, L.P.   SCHEDULE OF CLOSING CHARGES

CMCA Loan Number	Borrower	CMCA Office
Settlement Date		

The sales price and down payment specified are not to be reduced by any credits or allowances. Any changes or adjustments to the financing terms will require CMCA approval prior to execution of the documents and disbursement of the funds.

If applicable, this loan transaction has been approved subject to the following financing terms:

Sales Price $_____   Interest Rate _____

Prepaid Earnest Money Deposit _____

CMCA Mortgage Loan _____

Secondary Financing _____   P & I $_____

Balance of Down Payment _____

☐ Commonwealth will fund this loan upon receiving the instruments later referred to in these instructions, in form and content acceptable to us. **Documents must be returned 24 hours prior to funding.** Prepaid interest is to be computed at a per diem rate of $_____.

☐ Our net check in the amount of $_____ is enclosed. **A funding number must be obtained prior to disbursement of proceeds by calling Commonwealth.** The funding number is _____, obtained from _____ at Commonwealth on _____. The check is not to be deposited in advance of the actual closing. It is to be returned to the branch office within _7_ days in the event of a postponement and immediately if the closer is unable to comply with our instructions.

Our closing charges have been deducted or are to be deducted from the loan funding check and are itemized below and to be charged to the applicable party indicated.

		WITH LOAN – DEDUCTED FROM CHECK	PAID FROM BORROWER'S FUNDS AT SETTLEMENT	PAID FROM SELLER'S FUNDS AT SETTLEMENT
801	LOAN ORIGINATION FEE	%		
802	LOAN DISCOUNT	%		
803	APPRAISAL FEE	"POC" – $ COST – $		
804	CREDIT REPORT	"POC" – $ COST – $		
805	LENDER'S INSPECTION FEE			
807	ASSUMPTION FEE			
808	APPLICATION FEE			
810	UNDERWRITING FEE			
811	BUYDOWN FEE			
812	COMMITMENT FEE			
813	MESSENGER FEE			
814	LONG DISTANCE CALLS			
815	AMORTIZATION FEE			
816	PHOTO FEE			
817	FLOOD CERTIFICATION FEE			
818	REVIEW FEE			
819	TAX SERVICE CONTRACT FEE			
820	DOCUMENT PREPARATION FEE			
821	ATTORNEY'S FEE			
822	DEPARTMENT OF HUD — ONE-TIME MIP/PMI FINANCED			
823	VA FUNDING FEE			
824				
825				
826				
	ITEMS REQUIRED BY COMMONWEALTH MORTGAGE COMPANY OF AMERICA, L.P.			
901	INTEREST FROM TO AT $ DAY			
902	FIRST YEAR'S MORTGAGE INSURANCE PREMIUM			
903	FIRST YEAR'S HAZARD INSURANCE PREMIUM			
904	FIRST YEAR'S FLOOD INSURANCE PREMIUM			
905				
	RESERVES DEPOSITED WITH COMMONWEALTH MORTGAGE COMPANY OF AMERICA, L.P. – TO BE COLLECTED			
1001	HAZARD INSURANCE MONTHS AT $* PER MONTH			
1002	MORTGAGE INSURANCE MONTHS AT $ PER MONTH			
1003	CITY PROPERTY TAXES MONTHS AT $* PER MONTH			
1004	COUNTY PROPERTY TAXES MONTHS AT $* PER MONTH			
1005	ANNUAL ASSESSMENTS MONTHS AT $* PER MONTH			
1006	FLOOD INSURANCE MONTHS AT $* PER MONTH			
1007	MONTHS AT $ PER MONTH			
	*CALCULATE AT 1 12 ANNUAL PREMIUM			
	ADDITIONAL SETTLEMENT CHARGES			
1301				
1302				
1303				

Closing Agent Please Note:

1. Purchaser's costs not to exceed $_____. Seller's costs not to exceed $_____.
2. Purchasers to pay $_____ closing costs.
3. FHA and Conventional Purchasers must pay prepaid items, including preliminary interest and insurance premiums.
4. Purchaser and Seller must not pay more than the discount and closing costs listed above. Any excess will require investor and Commonwealth's approval before funding can take place.
5. Endorsements required: _____

_____

_____

_____

FIGURE 12–4 Mortgagee's Closing Instructions

the country—in some areas all parties meet for the settlement procedures; in other parts, no actual meeting is required, and escrow agents are authorized to request that the necessary instruments be delivered to them for release after all escrow requirements have been met.

Whenever the local practices require a meeting of the parties involved, it is usually held in the offices of the company or person designated to handle the settlement procedures. This may be a title company, an attorney, a real estate agent, an escrow agent, or the lender itself. Whoever handles the loan closing must have the approval of the lender as it is its money that is generally most involved. Closings can be accomplished with separate meetings, the buyer at one time and the seller at another, leaving the settlement agent to escrow the instruments and consideration until the procedure is completed and distribution can be made.

It is easier for the agents involved, and provides greater clarity for both buyer and seller, to arrange for a single meeting. Although a closing is no place for negotiations, if a misunderstanding crops up, it can be more readily resolved if all parties are immediately available for decisions.

Disbursement of Funds

In many parts of the country, a closing is just that; instruments are signed and funds are disbursed before anyone leaves the closing table. In some areas, it is more common to execute and acknowledge the instruments at the closing, but delay the disbursement of funds until later.

The purpose for any delay in releasing funds is twofold: first, to give the lender an opportunity to make a second review of all instruments and to verify proper signatures and acknowledgments; and second, to allow the settlement agent time to clear any checks that may have been submitted by the parties involved before releasing its own disbursement checks. One interpretation of state regulations governing title insurance companies calls *any* check paid to a title company an "escrow receivable," rather than a cash item, until the check has actually cleared the bank. However, there is growing pressure to handle a closing in its proper sequence and not call for the parties to meet until all the loose ends have been accomplished and the money is available for distribution.

The actual disbursement of funds at or following the settlement procedures is usually made to several different individuals and companies as well as the cash due to the seller. One of the reasons an escrow agent is employed in the settlement is to make sure that all parties with claims in the settlement are paid. The mortgage lender wants to be certain that taxes arc paid, that the insurance coverage has been paid for, and that no subsequent claims can be filed that might cloud their right to a first-mortgage lien securing their loan. The sales agents, inspectors, attorneys, and service agents all expect to receive their fees from the closing agent. After all required payments have been made, the necessary instruments are filed on record, the balance due the seller is disbursed, and the transaction is considered closed.

Questions for Discussion

1. Discuss the purpose of the Real Estate Settlement Procedures Act and how it is accomplished.
2. Does RESPA prescribe any limitations on fees that may be charged in closing a loan?
3. Discuss the importance of a survey in the settlement procedure.
4. How does RESPA define its prohibition against a "kickback"?
5. What is the reason for a prepayment of interest at the time of settlement procedures?
6. Where are loan closings normally held in your community? And who is the agent usually selected to represent the mortgage company at the closing procedure?
7. What information is furnished to the settlement agent (closer) by the mortgage lender just prior to closing?
8. Describe at least three RESPA requirements that call for disclosure of information to the borrower.
9. Discuss the requirements of the Truth-in-Lending Act as it relates to mortgage loans.
10. What are the limitations on reserve deposits that may be held by a lender for a residential mortgage loan?

Glossary

The following terms are those most frequently used in real estate financing, and are considered essential in understanding the material presented in this text.

Abstract.   The recorded history of a land title. A compilation of all instruments affecting the title to a tract of land.

Acceleration.   A clause in a mortgage instrument that permits the lender to declare the entire balance due and payable in the event of a default on the mortgage terms.

Acknowledgment.   For real estate purposes, a signature witnessed or notarized in a manner that can be recorded.

Adjustable Rate Mortgage (ARM).   A mortgage design that permits the lender to adjust the interest rate at periodic intervals with the amountof change generally tied to an independent published index of interest rates or yields.

Alienation.   The act of transferring rights in real property. Sometimes used to identify the clause in a mortgage that allows the lender to declare the balance due and payable if the mortaged property is sold.

Alternative Mortgage.   Any mortgage repayment plan other than a fixed-interest, constant-level plan that allows either, or both, a periodic change in the monthly payment amount or an adjustment in the rate of interest.

Amortization.   The systematic and continuous payment of an obligation through installments until such time as that debt has been paid off in full.

Annual Percentage Rate (APR).   The cost of credit expressed as a percentage of the net amount borrowed calculated as required by Regulation Z implementing the Truth-in-Lending Act.

Appraisal.   An estimate of property value by a qualified person.

Appreciation.   An increase in value. In real estate, appreciation is considered the passive increase in property value resulting from population growth, scarcity, and/or the changing value of money.

Assessed Value. Property value as determined by a taxing authority.

Assessment. A charge against a property owner for purposes of taxation; that is, the property owner pays his share of community improvements and maintenance according to the valuation of the property.

Assets. Real and personal property that may be chargeable with the debts of the owner.

Assignment of Mortgage. Transfer by the lender (mortgagee) of the mortgage obligation.

Assumption Agreement. A contract, by deed or other form, through which a buyer undertakes the obligations of an existing mortgage.

Balloon Payment. A debt repayment plan wherein the installments are less than required for a full amortization, with the balance due in a lump sum at maturity. Technically, a final payment greater than two monthly payments.

Basis Points. The movement of interest rates or yields expressed in hundredths of a percent; that is, a change in yield from 7.45 percent to 7.55 percent would be termed an increase of 10 basis points. One one hundreth of 1 percent.

Basket Provision. Regulations applicable to financial institutions that permit a small percentage of total assets to be held in otherwise unauthorized investments.

Beneficiary. The lender in a deed of trust transaction. The lender benefits from the note.

Blanket Mortgage. A type of mortgage that pledges more than one parcel of real estate as collateral.

Blind Pool. A syndicate organized to acquire property, the nature of which is not known or disclosed to the participants at the time of solicitation.

Bond. A type of security that guarantees payment of the face value with interest to the purchaser (lender), and is usually secured with a pledge of property or a commitment of income, such as a tax revenue bond. A debt instrument.

Borrower. A person or company using another's money or property, who has both a legal and moral obligation to repay the loan.

Broker. An intermediary between buyer and seller, or between lender and borrower, usually acting as agent for one or more parties, who arranges loans or sells property in return for a fee or commission.

Buy-down Mortgage. A mortgage repayment design offering lower initial monthly payments achieved through prepayment of a portion of the interest cost. The prepayment of interest is usually limited to the first few years and is normally paid by a seller to help attract buyers and to allow easier borrower qualification.

Capitalization. The conversion of an income stream into a property valuation for purposes of appraisal.

Cash Flow. The amount of cash received over a period of time from an income property.

Certificate of Reasonable Value (CRV). An estimate of property value prepared in accordance with requirements of the Veterans Administration. A VA appraisal.

Chain of Title. The sequence of ownership interests in a tract of land.

Chattel. An article of property that can be moved; personal property.

Chattel Mortgage. A type of lien (legal claim) that applies to personal property as distinguished from real property.

Closer. The individual responsible for making final settlement of the property transaction and disbursement of loan proceeds.

Closing. The consummation of a real estate transaction wherein certain rights of ownership are transferred in exchange for the monetary and other considerations agreed upon. Also called *loan closing*.

Cloud. A defect in the chain of title to property that obstructs, or prevents, good delivery.

Collateral. Any asset acceptable as security for a loan.

Collateralized Mortgage Obligations (CMO). A variation of a mortgage-backed security that segments the cash flows from an underlying block of mortgage loans so as to retire different classes of bonds in a sequence based on the bond's maturity. Bonds with the shortest maturities are retired first, then the next class, until all are paid off.

Commercial Loan. An imprecise term generally applied to an obligation collateralized by real property other than that used as a residence.

Commitment. A promise of loanable funds.

Commitment Fee. Money paid in return for the pledge of a future loan.

Common Areas. That part of a condominium property owned jointly by all unit owners.

Community Property. Property owned in common by a husband and wife.

Compensating Balance. A minimum balance held on deposit in accordance with a loan agreement.

Conditional Sale. An agreement granting title to property after all payments have been made.

Condominium. A unit in a multifamily structure or office building wherein the owner holds a fee simple title to a unit and a tenancy in common in the common elements with the other owners.

Consideration. The cash, services, or token given in exchange for property or services.

Constant Payment. A fixed payment amount, covering the interest due and a partial reduction of principal. Usually calculated in a manner that repays the loan within its term.

Constant Rate. Also called *constant*, is that percentage of the initial loan amount that must be paid periodically to repay the loan within the specified term.

Construction Loan. A type of mortgage loan to finance construction, which is funded by the lender to the builder at periodic intervals as the work progresses.

Contingent Interest. The amount that a lender expects to earn from a share of appreciation as calculated in a shared appreciation mortgage.

Contingent Liability. The responsibility assumed by a third party who accepts liability for an obligation upon the failure of an initial obligor to perform as agreed.

Contract for Deed. An agreement to sell property wherein title to the property is delivered to the buyer after payment has been made.

Contract of Sale. An agreement between a buyer and a seller of real property to deliver good title in return for a consideration.

Conventional Loan.   A loan that is not underwritten by a federal agency.

Conveyance.   The written instrument by which an interest in real property is transferred from one party to another.

Cooperative.   Corporate ownership of real estate wherein the stockholders are also the tenants through leasehold agreement.

Covenant.   An agreement between two or more parties.

Creative Financing.   A generalized term applied to many kinds of unconventional mortgage repayment plans. More specifically, refers to reduction of initial payment amounts with the principal balance coming due in a short term of three to five years.

Creditor.   One who lends something of value to another.

Credit Report.   Information prepared from a credit bureau's files that reveals previous debt payment experience as well as other identifying data on an individual or company.

Debenture Bond.   An unsecured pledge to repay a debt.

Debt.   An obligation to be repaid by a borrower to a lender.

Debt Service.   The periodic payment due on a loan, which includes principal, interest, mortgage insurance, and any other periodic fees required by the loan agreement.

Deed.   A written instrument by which real estate is transferred to another owner. The deed is signed, sealed, and delivered by the seller.

Deed of Trust.   A type of mortgage that conditionally conveys real property to a third party for holding in trust as security for payment of a loan.

Deed Restriction.   A clause in a deed that restricts the use of the land being conveyed.

Default.   The failure to perform on an obligation as agreed in a contract.

Delinquency.   A loan payment that is overdue but within the grace period allowed before actual default is declared.

Depreciation.   The loss in value to property due to wear and tear, obsolescence, or economic factors. To offset depreciation, tax laws permit recovery of the cost of an investment through annual deductions from taxable income.

Development Loan.   Money loaned for the purpose of improving land by the building of streets and utilities so as to make lots suitable for sale or use in construction.

Discount.   The difference between the amount paid for a note and the nominal, or face value, of that note. The reduction in the amount paid is normally expressed in "points" as a percentage of the note amount.

Disintermediation.   The withdrawal of substantial sums from savings accounts held by "intermediaries" such as savings associations, mutual savings banks, or commercial banks, generally for reinvestment in higher yielding investments.

Disposition.   The right of a landowner to sell, lease, give away, mortgage, or otherwise dispose of, his or her land.

Due-on-sale Clause.   A mortgage clause that calls for the payoff of a loan in the event of a sale or conveyance of the collateral prior to maturity of the loan.

Earnest Money.   A portion of the down payment delivered to the seller or an escrow agent as evidence of good faith to bind the purchase.

Encroachment. Any physical intrusion upon the property rights of another.

Encumbrance. A claim against land such as a lien or easement. Anything that affects or limits the fee simple title to, or value of, property; for example, a mortgage.

Equity. The ownership interest—that portion of a property's value beyond any liability therein.

Escalation. The right of a lender to increase the rate of interest in a loan agreement.

Escrow. Property, money, or something of value held in custody by a third party in accordance with an agreement.

Execute. The act of signing a legal instrument by the involved parties, usually witnessed or notarized, so that it may be recorded.

Fair-market Value. The highest monetary price or its equivalent available in a competitive market as determined by negotiation between an informed, willing, and capable buyer and an informed and willing seller.

Fee Simple. A legal term designating the highest interest in land that includes all the rights of ownership.

Federal Home Loan Mortgage Corporation (FHLMC). Also known as "Freddie Mac." A quasi-government agency owned by the Federal Home Loan Bank member savings associations. Its purpose is the purchase and resale of mortgage loans, thus offering greater liquidity for participants' portfolios.

FHA Loan. A loan insured by the Insuring Office of the Department of Housing and Urban Development; the Federal Housing Administration.

Finance Fee. The charge made by a lender for preparing and processing a loan package; also known as an origination fee.

Fixture. Personal property so affixed to the land as to become a part of the realty.

Foreclosure. Legal action to bar a mortgagor's claims to property after default has occurred.

Government National Mortgage Association (GNMA). Also known as "Ginnie Mae." Government agency under HUD created in 1968 to take over certain functions formerly handled by FNMA.

Graduated Payment Adjustable Rate Mortgage (GPARM, also called GPAM). A mortgage repayment plan that provides for lower initial monthly payments, increasing annually for three to five years, then changing to a fully amortized payment amount with interest rate periodically adjusted by the lender.

Graduated Payment Mortgage. A repayment plan popularized by the FHA, but also approved as a conventional loan, that offers first-year monthly payments substantially lower than a constant-level plan permitting easier qualification for a borrower. Payment amounts increase annually at a predetermined rate until reaching a level that fully amortizes the loan within its term.

Gross Income. The total money received from an operating property over a given period of time.

Guarantee (vb). The act of pledging by a third party to assure payment.

Guaranty (n). A pledge by a third party to assume the obligation of another.

Hazard Insurance. The insurance covering physical damage to property.

Homestead. A legal life estate in land created in differing ways by state laws devised to protect the possession and enjoyment of the owner against the claims of certain creditors.

HUD.   The Department of Housing and Urban Development.

Hypothecate.   A pledge of property without delivering possession, such as a mortgage.

Impound Account.   Money held for payment of an obligation due at some future time. Also known as an escrow account.

Income.   Money or other benefit received from the investment of labor or capital.

Income Property.   Real estate capable of producing net revenue.

Instrument.   A legal document in writing.

Interest.   The payment for the use of money.

Interim Loan.   Or *interim financing.* A loan made with the expectation of repayment from the proceeds of another loan. Most often used in reference to a construction loan.

Junior Mortgage.   A mortgage claim of lesser than first-lien priority.

Land Contract.   Another term used to indicate a contract for deed.

Land Loan.   Money loaned for the purchase of raw land.

Late Charge.   A fee added to an installment as a penalty for failure to make a timely payment.

Leasehold.   An estate in real property limited as to time, obtained and held with the consent of and by the payment of a consideration to the owner.

Leverage.   The capacity to borrow an amount greater than the equity in property. The larger the loan in relation to the equity, the greater the leverage.

Lien.   A legal claim or attachment, filed on record, against property as security for payment of an obligation.

Limitation.   A time limit as determined by statute within which periodic litigation may be undertaken.

Liquidity.   The extent to which assets held in other forms can be easily and quickly converted into cash.

Loan.   A granting of the use of money in return for the payment of interest.

Loan Pool.   A block of loans pledged as security for the issuance of a guarantee certificate.

Loan-to-value Ratio (LTVR).   The relationship between the amount of a loan and the value of the property pledged.

Marginal Property.   Capable of making only a very low economic return.

Maturity.   The date that final payment is due on a loan.

Mechanic's Lien.   Also known as mechanic's and materialmen's lien, or M & M lien. A claim for payment for services rendered or materials furnished to a landowner and filed on record in the county where the property is located.

Merchantable title.   That condition of title that is acceptable in the market.

Mortgage.   A conditional conveyance of property as security for a debt.

Mortgagee.   The lender of money and the receiver of the security in the form of a mortgage. (*Note:* Lender and mortgagee both have two "ee"s.)

Mortgage Note.   A description of the debt and a promise to pay—the instrument that is secured by the mortgage.

Mortgage Portfolio.   The aggregate of mortgage loans held by a lender.

Mortgage Release. A disclaimer of further liability on the mortgage note granted by the lender. When used with a trust deed, it is a deed of reconveyance.

Mortgaging out. Securing a loan upon completion of a project that is sufficient to cover all costs: a 100 percent loan.

Mortgagor. The borrower of money and the giver of a mortgage as security.

Multifamily Mortgage. An FHA term designating an apartment or any house with more than four family units.

Mutual Mortgage Insurance Fund. A fund established by the National Housing Act into which all mortgage insurance premiums and other specified revenue of the FHA are paid and from which losses are met.

Negative Amortization. An increase in the principal balance due on a mortgage loan, usually resulting from unpaid interest added to the principal periodically.

Net Income. That portion of gross income remaining after payment of all expenses.

Note. A unilateral instrument containing a promise to pay a sum of money at a specified time.

Open-end Mortgage. A mortgage with a clause permitting additional money to be advanced by the lender secured by the same collateral pledge.

Option. The right to purchase or lease a piece of property at a certain price for a designated period of time.

Origination Fee. The amount charged for services performed by the company handling the initial application and processing of a loan.

Package Mortgage. A mortgage pledge that includes both real and personal property.

Partial Release. The removal of a general mortgage lien from a specific portion of the land that has been pledged.

Participation Loan. A loan funded by more than one lender and serviced by one of them.

Passthrough Security. A bond, certificate, or other form of security collateralized by a block of mortgage loans. The payments on the mortgage loans are passed through a trustee to the holders of the securities as the payments are received.

Permanent Loan. A mortgage loan granted for a long term based on the economic life of a property.

Personal Property. A possession: Any item of value that is not real estate.

PITI. An acronym used to identify the components of a mortgage payment: principal, interest, taxes, insurance.

Planned Unit Development (PUD). A comprehensive land development plan employed primarily in the planning and construction of residential areas.

Pledged Account Mortgage (PAM). A mortgage repayment plan that features lower initial monthly payment amounts. The borrower deposits a portion of the down payment in an escrow account with the lender. Each month the lender withdraws enough money from the escrow account to supplement the borrower's payments so that a constant-level, fully amortized payment amount is applied to the loan each month.

Points. A unit of measure for charges that amounts to 1 percent of a loan. One point is 1 percent of the subject loan.

Possession. Occupancy: the highest form of "notice."

Price-Level–Adjusted Mortgage (PLAM). A mortgage repayment design that ties the mortgage payment amount and the principal balance due to an inflation index.

Principal. The amount of the mortgage debt.

Private Mortgage Insurance (PMI). Insurance against payment default on a mortgage loan as offered by private insurance carriers.

Promissory Note. A written promise to pay someone a given amount of money at a specified time.

Purchase Money Mortgage. A mortgage taken by the seller as all or part of the purchase consideration. Also identifies a mortgage wherein the proceeds of the loan are used to purchase the property.

Real Estate. Land and that attached thereto, including minerals and resources inherent to the land, and any manmade improvements so affixed as to become a part of the land. Also known as *realty* or *real property*.

Realtist. A real estate broker holding an active membership in a real estate board affiliated with the National Association of Real Estate Brokers.

Realtor.® A registered word designating a member in good standing of the National Association of Realtors.

Recording. Filing a legal instrument in the public records of a county.

Refinancing. Obtaining a loan for the purpose of repaying an existing loan.

Rescission. Annulling a contract and placing the parties thereto in status quo.

Reverse Annuity Mortgage. A mortgage form designed to use the equity value of a home as collateral for installment payments made by the lender to the borrower to supplement living costs.

Secondary Financing. Negotiation of a second mortgage, or a junior mortgage.

Secondary Market. Large investors who buy and sell mortgage loans that they do not originate.

Seller/Servicer. Loan originators who service loans as approved by FNMA or FHLMC.

Servicing (Loan Servicing). The work of an agent, usually a mortgage company, comprising the collection of mortgage payments, securing of escrow funds, payment of property taxes and insurance from the escrowed funds, follow-up on delinquencies, accounting for and remitting principal, and interest payments to the lender.

Settlement Procedure. The steps taken to finalize the funding of a loan agreement and a property transfer. Also called a loan closing.

Shared Appreciation Mortgage (SAM). A mortgage repayment plan whereby the lender accepts a reduced interest rate on condition that a share of any property appreciation is given to the lender. For example, a reduction in the interest rate from 15 percent to 10 percent with the requirement that one-third of any appreciation belongs to the lender.

Short-term Loan. In financial markets, a loan that matures in three years or less. When identified as "shorter-term" loans in the mortgage industry, it means one that matures in 20 years or less.

Simple Interest. Interest computed on the principal only.

Single-family Mortgage. A mortgage loan on property occupied by one family.

Spot Loan. Money loaned on individual houses in various neighborhoods, as contrasted to new houses in a single development.

Statutory Redemption. A state law that permits a mortgagor a limited time after foreclosure to pay off the debt and reclaim the mortgage property.

Subordination. To make a claim to real property inferior to that of another by specific agreement.

Survey. The measurement and description of land by a registered surveyor.

Sweat Equity. An ownership interest in property earned by the performance of manual labor on that property.

Syndication. A group of individuals or companies joined together in pursuit of a limited investment purpose.

Takeout Loan. A type of loan commitment—a promise to make a loan at a future specified time. It is most commonly used to designate a higher-cost, shorter-term, backup commitment as a support for construction financing until a suitable permanent loan can be secured.

Tandem Plan. GNMA's Special Assistance Program under which private lenders, backed by mortgage purchase commitments from GNMA, originate below-market-rate loans to be sold to GNMA without discount. GNMA later sells these loans to private investors at a price to yield market rates to the investor and absorbs the difference (the discounted amount) as a subsidy.

Term. The time limit within which a loan must be repaid in full.

Time Deposits. Money held in savings accounts not subject to demand withdrawal.

Title. The right to ownership in land.

Torrens Certificate. A certificate issued by a public authority, known as registrar of titles, establishing an indefeasible title for the registered owner of the land.

Tract Loan. Individual mortgage loan negotiated for houses of similar character located in a new development.

Trade Fixture. Personal property, peculiar to a trade, which remains personal even though affixed to real property.

Trust Deed. An agreement in writing under seal conveying property from the owner to a trustee for the accomplishment of the objectives set forth in the agreement. Sometimes used to describe a deed of trust instrument.

Trustee. One who holds property in trust for another to secure performance of an obligation. The third party holding a conditional title to property as collateral under a deed of trust.

Trustor. One who borrows money under the terms of a deed of trust.

Underwriter. The person or company taking responsibility for approving a mortgage loan.

Unsecured Loan. A loan made without the benefit of a pledge of collateral.

Usury. Interest in excess of that permitted by state law.

Variable Rate Mortgage. A type of mortgage agreement that allows for periodic adjustment of the interest rate in keeping with a fluctuating market.

VA Loan. A loan made by private lenders that is partially guaranteed by the Veterans Administration.

Vendor's Lien. A lien securing the loan by a seller that is used to purchase the property.

Warehousing. The practice, mostly by mortgage bankers, of pledging mortgage notes to a commercial bank for cash used to fund the mortgage loans. A line of credit.

Whole Loan. A term used in the secondary market to indicate the full amount of a loan is available for sale with no portion, or participation, retained by the seller.

Wraparound Mortgage. A junior mortgage that acknowledges and includes an existing mortgage loan in its principal amount due and in its payment conditions. Payment is made to the holder of the wrap, or his or her agent, who in turn makes payment on the existing mortgage. The purpose is to gain some advantages in the lower interest cost on an existing loan, to hold the mortgage priority of the existing loan, and to retain an element of control over the loan payments.

Yield. The total money earned on a loan for the term of the loan computed on an annual percentage basis.

Appendices

RESIDENTIAL LOAN APPLICATION

MORTGAGE APPLIED FOR	☐ Conventional ☐ FHA ☐ VA	Amount $	Interest Rate %	No. of Months	Monthly Payment (Principal & Interest) $	Escrow / Impounds (To be collected monthly) ☐ Taxes ☐ Hazard Insurance ☐ Mtg. Insurance

Prepayment Option

SUBJECT PROPERTY

Property Street Address		City	County	State	Zip

Legal Description (Attach description if necessary)	No. of Units	Year Built

Purpose of Loan ☐ Purchase ☐ Construction-Permanent ☐ Construction ☐ Refinance ☐ Other (Explain)

Complete this line if Construction-Permanent or Construction Loan ▶ LOT VALUE DATA | Year Acquired | Original Cost | Present Value (a) | Cost of Improvements (b) | TOTAL (a + b) | Enter Total as Purchase Price in Details of Purchase
| | $ | $ | $ | $ |

Complete this line if a Refinance Loan | Year Acquired | Original Cost | Amount of Existing Liens | Purpose of Refinance | Describe Improvements ☐ Made ☐ To be Made Cost $

Title Will be Held in What Name(s)	Manner in Which Title Will be Held

Source of Down Payment and Settlement Charges

This application is designed to be completed by the borrower(s) with the lender's assistance. The Co-Borrower Section and all other Co-Borrower questions must be completed and the appropriate box(es) checked if
- ☐ another person will be jointly obligated with the Borrower on the loan, or
- ☐ the Borrower is relying on income from alimony, child support, or separate maintenance, or on the income or assets of another person as a basis for repayment of the loan, or
- ☐ the Borrower is married and resides, or the property is located, in a community property state

BORROWER / CO-BORROWER

BORROWER			CO-BORROWER		
Name	Age	School Yrs	Name	Age	School Yrs
Present Address: Number of Years ☐ Own ☐ Rent			Present Address: Number of Years ☐ Own ☐ Rent		
Street			Street		
City, State & Zip			City, State & Zip		
Former Address: (If less than 2 years at present address)			Former Address: (If less than 2 years at present address)		
Street			Street		
City, State & Zip			City, State & Zip		
Years at Former Address ☐ Own ☐ Rent			Years at Former Address ☐ Own ☐ Rent		

Marital Status ☐ Married ☐ Separated ☐ Unmarried (Include Single, Divorced, and Widowed)	Dependents Other Than Listed by Co-Borrower Number / Ages	Marital Status ☐ Married ☐ Separated ☐ Unmarried (Include Single, Divorced, and Widowed)	Dependents Other Than Listed by Borrower Number / Ages

Name and Address of Employer		Name and Address of Employer	
Years Employed in This Line of Work or Profession	Years on This Job ☐ Self-Employed *	Years Employed in This Line of Work or Profession	Years on This Job ☐ Self-Employed *
Position / Title	Type of Business	Position / Title	Type of Business
Social Security Number ***	Home Phone	Business Phone	Social Security Number ***	Home Phone	Business Phone

GROSS MONTHLY INCOME / MONTHLY HOUSING EXPENSE ** / DETAILS OF PURCHASE

ITEM	BORROWER	CO-BORROWER	TOTAL		PRESENT	PROPOSED	DETAILS OF PURCHASE	Do Not Complete If Refinance
Base Empl. Income	$	$	$	Rent	$		a Purchase Price	$
Overtime				First Mortgage (P & I)		$	b Total Closing Costs (Est.)	
Bonuses				Other Financing (P & I)			c Prepaid Escrows (Est.)	
Commissions				Hazard Insurance			d Total (a + b + c) ▶	$
Dividends / Interest				Real Estate Taxes			e Amount of This Mortgage	( )
Net Rental Income				Mortgage Insurance			f Other Financing	( )
Other † (Before Completing, See Notice Under "Describe Other Income Below"				Homeowner Assn. Dues			g Other Equity	( )
				Other			h Amount of Cash Deposit	( )
				Total Monthly Payment	$	$	i Closing Costs Paid by Seller	( )
				Utilities			j Cash Reqd. for Closing (Est.)	$
TOTAL ▶	$	$	$	TOTAL ▶	$	$		

DESCRIBE OTHER INCOME

☞ B = BORROWER C = CO-BORROWER

NOTICE † Alimony, child support, or separate maintenance income need not be revealed if the Borrower or Co-Borrower does not choose to have it considered as a basis for repaying this loan

MONTHLY AMOUNT

IF EMPLOYED IN CURRENT POSITION FOR LESS THAN TWO YEARS, COMPLETE THE FOLLOWING

B/C	PREVIOUS EMPLOYER / SCHOOL	CITY / STATE	TYPE OF BUSINESS	POSITION / TITLE	DATES FROM / TO	MONTHLY INCOME

THESE QUESTIONS APPLY TO BOTH BORROWER AND CO-BORROWER

If a "yes" answer is given to a question in this column, please explain on an attached sheet.

	Borrower Yes or No	Co-Borrower Yes or No		Borrower Yes or No	Co-Borrower Yes or No
Are there any outstanding judgments against you?					
Have you been declared bankrupt within the past 7 years?					
Have you had property foreclosed upon or given title or deed in lieu thereof in the last 7 years?			Are you a U.S. citizen?		
Are you a party to a law suit?			If "no", are you a resident alien?		
Are you obligated to pay alimony, child support, or separate maintenance?			If "no", are you a non-resident alien?		
Is any part of the down payment borrowed?			Explain Other Financing or Other Equity (if any)		
Are you a co-maker or endorser on a note?					

*FHLMC/FNMA require business credit report, signed Federal Income Tax returns for last two years, and, if available, audited Profit and Loss Statement plus balance sheet for same period
**All Present Monthly Housing Expenses of Borrower and Co-Borrower should be listed on a combined basis
***Optional for FHLMC

304

This Statement and any applicable supporting schedules may be completed jointly by both married and unmarried co-borrowers if their assets and liabilities are sufficiently joined so that the Statement can be meaningfully and fairly presented on a combined basis, otherwise separate Statements and Schedules are required (FHLMC 65A/FNMA 1073A). If the co-borrower section was completed about a spouse, this statement and supporting schedules must be completed about that spouse also.

☐ Completed Jointly   ☐ Not Completed Jointly

Assets — Liabilities and Pledged Assets

Indicated by (*) those liabilities or pledged assets which will be satisfied upon sale of real estate owned or upon refinancing of subject property.

Description	Cash or Market Value	Creditor's Name, Address and Account Number		Acct. Name if Not Borrower's	Mo. Pmt. and Mos. Left to Pay	Unpaid Balance
		Installment Debts (Include "revolving" charge accounts)			$ Pmt /Mos	$
Cash Deposit Toward Purchase Held By	$	Co.	Acct No			
Checking and Savings Accounts (Show Names of Institutions Account Numbers)		Addr				
Bank, S & L or Credit Union		City			/	
		Co.	Acct No			
Addr		Addr				
City		City			/	
Acct. No		Co.	Acct No			
Bank, S & L or Credit Union		Addr				
		City			/	
Addr		Co.	Acct No			
City		Addr				
Acct No		City			/	
Bank, S & L or Credit Union		Co.	Acct No			
		Addr				
Addr		City			/	
City		Other Debts including Stock Pledges				
Acct. No					/	
Stocks and Bonds (No./Description)		Real Estate Loans Co.	Acct No			
		Addr			╳	
		City				
Life Insurance Net Cash Value Face Amount $		Co.	Acct No		╳	
		Addr				
Subtotal Liquid Assets		City				
Real Estate Owned (Enter Market Value from Schedule of Real Estate Owned)		Automobile Loans Co.	Acct No			
		Addr				
Vested Interest in Retirement Fund		City			/	
Net worth of Business Owned (ATTACH FINANCIAL STATEMENT)		Co.	Acct No			
Automobiles Owned (Make and Year)		Addr			/	
		City				
		Alimony/Child Support/Separate Maintenance Payments Owed To			/	╳
Furniture and Personal Property						
Other Assets (Itemize)		Total Monthly Payments			$	
Total Assets	A $	Net Worth (A minus B) $			Total Liabilities	B $

SCHEDULE OF REAL ESTATE OWNED (If Additional Properties Owned Attach Separate Schedule)

Address of Property (Indicate S if Sold, PS if Pending Sale or R if Rental being held for income)	Type of Property	Present Market Value	Amount of Mortgages & Liens	Gross Rental Income	Mortgage Payments	Taxes, Ins. Maintenance and Misc	Net Rental Income
		$	$	$	$	$	$
TOTALS ►		$	$	$	$	$	$

List Previous Credit References

▼ B—Borrower C—Co-Borrower	Creditor's Name and Address	Account Number	Purpose	Highest Balance	Date Paid
				$	

List any additional names under which credit has previously been received ....

AGREEMENT: The undersigned applies for the loan indicated in this application to be secured by a first mortgage or deed of trust on the property described herein, and represents that the property will not be used for any illegal or restricted purpose, and that all statements made in this application are true and are made for the purpose of obtaining the loan. Verification may be obtained from any source named in this application. The original or a copy of this application will be retained by the lender, even if the loan is not granted. The undersigned ☐ intend or ☐ do not intend to occupy the property as their primary residence.

I/We fully understand that it is a federal crime punishable by fine or imprisonment, or both, to knowingly make any false statements concerning any of the above facts as applicable under the provisions of Title 18, United States Code, Section 1014.

_____ Date _____   _____ Date _____
Borrower's Signature   Co-Borrower's Signature

Information for Government Monitoring Purposes

The following information is requested by the Federal Government for certain types of loans related to a dwelling, in order to monitor the lender's compliance with equal credit opportunity and fair housing laws. You are not required to furnish this information, but are encouraged to do so. The law provides that a lender may neither discriminate on the basis of this information, nor on whether you choose to furnish it. However, if you choose not to furnish it, under Federal regulations this lender is required to note race and sex on the basis of visual observation or surname. If you do not wish to furnish the above information, please check the box below. [Lender must review the above material to assure that the disclosures satisfy all requirements to which the Lender is subject under applicable state law for the particular type of loan applied for.]

Borrower: ☐ I do not wish to furnish this information   Co-Borrower: ☐ I do not wish to furnish this information

Race/National Origin: Race/National Origin:
☐ American Indian, Alaskan Native ☐ Asian, Pacific Islander   ☐ American Indian, Alaskan Native ☐ Asian, Pacific Islander
☐ Black ☐ Hispanic ☐ White   ☐ Black ☐ Hispanic ☐ White
☐ Other (specify) _____   ☐ Other (specify) _____
Sex: ☐ Female ☐ Male   Sex: ☐ Female ☐ Male

To Be Completed by Interviewer

This application was taken by: Name of Interviewer's Employer
☐ face to face interview   _____
                                Interviewer
☐ by mail
☐ by telephone   _____   _____
                                Interviewer's Phone Number   Address of Interviewer's Employer

FHLMC 65 Rev 10/86
FNMA 1003 Rev 10/86   REVERSE   1580 (8702)

305

UNIFORM RESIDENTIAL APPRAISAL REPORT   File No. _____

Purpose of Appraisal is to estimate Market Value as defined in the Certification & Statement of Limiting Conditions.

COST APPROACH

BUILDING SKETCH (SHOW GROSS LIVING AREA ABOVE GRADE)
If for Freddie Mac or Fannie Mae, show only square foot calculations and cost approach comments in this space

ESTIMATED REPRODUCTION COST - NEW - OF IMPROVEMENTS:

Dwelling _____ Sq. Ft. @ $ _____	=	$ _____
_____ Sq. Ft. @ $ _____	=	_____
Extras _____	=	_____
	=	_____
Special Energy Efficient Items _____	=	_____
Porches, Patios, etc. _____	=	_____
Garage/Carport _____ Sq. Ft. @ $ _____	=	_____
Total Estimated Cost New	=	$ _____

	Physical	Functional	External
Less			
Depreciation			

Depreciated Value of Improvements	=	$ _____
Site Imp. "as is" (driveway, landscaping, etc.)	=	$ _____
ESTIMATED SITE VALUE	=	$ _____
(If leasehold, show only leasehold value.)		
INDICATED VALUE BY COST APPROACH	=	$ _____

(Not Required by Freddie Mac and Fannie Mae)

Does property conform to applicable HUD/VA property standards? ☐ Yes ☐ No
If No, explain: _____

Construction Warranty ☐ Yes ☐ No
Name of Warranty Program _____
Warranty Coverage Expires _____

The undersigned has recited three recent sales of properties most similar and proximate to subject and has considered these in the market analysis. The description includes a dollar adjustment, reflecting market reaction to those items of significant variation between the subject and comparable properties. If a significant item in the comparable property is superior to, or more favorable than, the subject property, a minus (−) adjustment is made, thus reducing the indicated value of subject; if a significant item in the comparable is inferior to, or less favorable than, the subject property, a plus (+) adjustment is made, thus increasing the indicated value of the subject.

SALES COMPARISON ANALYSIS

ITEM	SUBJECT	COMPARABLE NO. 1		COMPARABLE NO. 2		COMPARABLE NO. 3	
Address							
Proximity to Subject							
Sales Price	$		$		$		$
Price/Gross Liv. Area	$	$		$		$	
Data Source							
VALUE ADJUSTMENTS	DESCRIPTION	DESCRIPTION	+ (−) $ Adjustment	DESCRIPTION	+ (−) $ Adjustment	DESCRIPTION	+ (−) $ Adjustment
Sales or Financing Concessions							
Date of Sale/Time							
Location							
Site/View							
Design and Appeal							
Quality of Construction							
Age							
Condition							
Above Grade Room Count	Total / Bdrms / Baths	Total / Bdrms / Baths		Total / Bdrms / Baths		Total / Bdrms / Baths	
Gross Living Area	Sq. Ft.	Sq. Ft.		Sq. Ft.		Sq. Ft.	
Basement & Finished Rooms Below Grade							
Functional Utility							
Heating/Cooling							
Garage/Carport							
Porches, Patio, Pools, etc.							
Special Energy Efficient Items							
Fireplace(s)							
Other (e.g. kitchen equip., remodeling)							
Net Adj. (total)		☐ + ☐ − $		☐ + ☐ − $		☐ + ☐ − $	
Indicated Value of Subject		$		$		$	

Comments on Sales Comparison: _____

INDICATED VALUE BY SALES COMPARISON APPROACH .... $ _____

INDICATED VALUE BY INCOME APPROACH (If Applicable) Estimated Market Rent $ _____ /Mo. x Gross Rent Multiplier _____ = $ _____

This appraisal is made ☐ "as is" ☐ subject to the repairs, alterations, inspections or conditions listed below ☐ completion per plans and specifications.

Comments and Conditions of Appraisal: _____

RECONCILIATION

Final Reconciliation: _____

This appraisal is based upon the above requirements, the certification, contingent and limiting conditions, and Market Value definition that are stated in

☐ FmHA, HUD &/or VA instructions.
☐ Freddie Mac Form 439 (Rev. 7/86)/Fannie Mae Form 1004B (Rev. 7/86) filed with client _____ 19 ___ ☐ attached.

I (WE) ESTIMATE THE MARKET VALUE, AS DEFINED, OF THE SUBJECT PROPERTY AS OF _____ 19 ___ to be $ _____

I (We) certify: that to the best of my (our) knowledge and belief the facts and data used herein and belief the facts and data used herein and belief are true and correct: that I (we) personally inspected the subject property, both inside and out, and have made an exterior inspection of all comparable sales cited in this report; and that I (we) have no undisclosed interest, present or prospective therein.

APPRAISER(S)   REVIEW APPRAISER (if applicable)

Signature _____   Signature _____   ☐ Did ☐ Did Not

Name _____   Name _____   Inspect Property

Freddie Mac Form 70 10/86 12 CH.   Federal Standard Forms • 1155 Meridian Avenue, Suite 204, San Jose, CA 95125 • (800) 345-1182   Fannie Mae Form 1004 10/86

UNIFORM RESIDENTIAL APPRAISAL REPORT

Property Description & Analysis File No. _____

SUBJECT

Property Address	Census Tract
City	County	State	Zip Code
Legal Description	
Owner/Occupant	Map Reference
Sale Price $	Date of Sale
Loan charges/concessions to be paid by seller $	
R.E. Taxes $	Tax Year	HOA $/Mo
Lender/Client	

PROPERTY RIGHTS APPRAISED
- Fee Simple
- Leasehold
- Condominium (HUD/VA)
- De Minimis PUD

LENDER DISCRETIONARY USE

Sale Price	$
Date	
Mortgage Amount	$
Mortgage Type	
Discount Points and Other Concessions	
Paid by Seller	$
Source	

NEIGHBORHOOD

LOCATION	Urban	Suburban	Rural	
BUILT UP	Over 75%	25-75%	Under 25%	
GROWTH RATE	Rapid	Stable	Slow	
PROPERTY VALUES	Increasing	Stable	Declining	
DEMAND/SUPPLY	Shortage	In Balance	Over Supply	
MARKETING TIME	Under 3 Mos.	3-6 Mos.	Over 6 Mos.	

PRESENT LAND USE	%	LAND USE CHANGE	PREDOMINANT OCCUPANCY	SINGLE FAMILY HOUSING
Single Family		Not Likely	Owner	PRICE $ (000) / AGE (yrs)
2-4 Family		Likely	Tenant	
Multi-family		In process	Vacant (0-5%)	Low
Commercial		To:	Vacant (over 5%)	High
Industrial				Predominant
Vacant				–

NEIGHBORHOOD ANALYSIS — Good / Avg / Fair / Poor
- Employment Stability
- Convenience to Employment
- Convenience to Shopping
- Convenience to Schools
- Adequacy of Public Transportation
- Recreation Facilities
- Adequacy of Utilities
- Property Compatibility
- Protection from Detrimental Cond
- Police & Fire Protection
- General Appearance of Properties
- Appeal to Market

Note: Race or the racial composition of the neighborhood are not considered reliable appraisal factors.

COMMENTS: _____

SITE

Dimensions	Topography
Site Area	Size
Zoning Classification	Shape
HIGHEST & BEST USE: Present Use	Other Use	Drainage

UTILITIES	Public	Other	SITE IMPROVEMENTS	Type	Public	Private	
Electricity			Street				View
Gas			Curb/Gutter				Landscaping
Water			Sidewalk				Driveway
Sanitary Sewer			Street Lights				Apparent Easements
Storm Sewer			Alley				FEMA Flood Hazard Yes* No
							FEMA* Map/Zone

Zoning Compliance

COMMENTS (Apparent adverse easements, encroachments, special assessments, slide areas, etc.): _____

IMPROVEMENTS

GENERAL DESCRIPTION	EXTERIOR DESCRIPTION	FOUNDATION	BASEMENT	INSULATION
Units	Foundation	Slab	Area Sq. Ft	Roof
Stories	Exterior Walls	Crawl Space	% Finished	Ceiling
Type (Det./Att.)	Roof Surface	Basement	Ceiling	Walls
Design (Style)	Gutters & Dwnspts	Sump Pump	Walls	Floor
Existing	Window Type	Dampness	Floor	None
Proposed	Storm Sash	Settlement	Outside Entry	Adequacy
Under Construction	Screens	Infestation		Energy Efficient Items
Age (Yrs.)	Manufactured House			
Effective Age (Yrs.)				

ROOM LIST

ROOMS	Foyer	Living	Dining	Kitchen	Den	Family Rm	Rec. Rm	Bedrooms	# Baths	Laundry	Other	Area Sq. Ft
Basement												
Level 1												
Level 2												

Finished area **above** grade contains: Rooms: ___ Bedroom(s): ___ Bath(s): ___ Square Feet of Gross Living Area

INTERIOR

SURFACES	Materials/Condition	HEATING	KITCHEN EQUIP.	ATTIC
Floors		Type	Refrigerator	None
Walls		Fuel	Range/Oven	Stairs
Trim/Finish		Condition	Disposal	Drop Stair
Bath Floor		Adequacy	Dishwasher	Scuttle
Bath Wainscot		COOLING	Fan/Hood	Floor
Doors		Central	Compactor	Heated
		Other	Washer/Dryer	Finished
		Condition	Microwave	
Fireplace(s)	#	Adequacy	Intercom	

IMPROVEMENT ANALYSIS — Good / Avg / Fair / Poor
- Quality of Construction
- Condition of Improvements
- Room Sizes/Layout
- Closets and Storage
- Energy Efficiency
- Plumbing-Adequacy & Condition
- Electrical-Adequacy & Condition
- Kitchen Cabinets-Adequacy & Cond
- Compatibility to Neighborhood
- Appeal & Marketability
- Estimated Remaining Economic Life ___ Yrs
- Estimated Remaining Physical Life ___ Yrs

AUTOS

CAR STORAGE				
No Cars	Garage	Attached	Adequate	House Entry
Condition	Carport	Detached	Inadequate	Outside Entry
	None	Built-In	Electric Door	Basement Entry

Additional features _____

COMMENTS

Depreciation (Physical, functional and external inadequacies, repairs needed, modernization, etc.): _____

General market conditions and prevalence and impact in subject/market area regarding loan discounts, interest buydowns and concessions: _____

Freddie Mac Form 70 10/86 12 CH.   Federal Standard Forms • 1155 Meridian Avenue, Suite 204, San Jose, CA 95125 • (800) 345-1182   Fannie Mae Form 1004 10/86

307

FannieMae Verification of Deposit

PART I - REQUEST

1. TO (Name and address of depository)	2. FROM (Name and address of lender)

3. SIGNATURE OF LENDER	4. TITLE	5. DATE	6. LENDER'S NUMBER (Optional)

7. INFORMATION TO BE VERIFIED

TYPE OF ACCOUNT	ACCOUNT IN NAME OF	ACCOUNT NUMBER	BALANCE
			$
			$
			$
			$

TO DEPOSITORY: I have applied for a mortgage loan and stated in my financial statement that the balance on deposit with you is as shown above. You are authorized to verify this information and to supply the lender identified above with the information requested in Items 10 thru 12. Your response is solely a matter of courtesy for which no responsibility is attached to your institution or any of your officers.

8. NAME AND ADDRESS OF APPLICANT(s)	9. SIGNATURE OF APPLICANT(s)

TO BE COMPLETED BY DEPOSITORY

PART II - VERIFICATION OF DEPOSITORY

10. DEPOSIT ACCOUNTS OF APPLICANT(s)

TYPE OF ACCOUNT	ACCOUNT NUMBER	CURRENT BALANCE	AVERAGE BALANCE FOR PREVIOUS TWO MONTHS	DATE OPENED
		$	$	
		$	$	
		$	$	
		$	$	

11. LOANS OUTSTANDING TO APPLICANT(s)

LOAN NUMBER	DATE OF LOAN	ORIGINAL AMOUNT	CURRENT BALANCE	INSTALLMENTS (Monthly/Quarterly)	SECURED BY	NUMBER OF LATE PAYMENTS
		$	$	$ per		
		$	$	$ per		
		$	$	$ per		

12. ADDITIONAL INFORMATION WHICH MAY BE OF ASSISTANCE IN DETERMINATION OF CREDIT WORTHINESS:
(Please include information on loans paid-in-full as in Item 11 above)

13. SIGNATURE OF DEPOSITORY	14. TITLE	15. DATE

The confidentiality of the information you have furnished will be preserved except where disclosure of this information is required by applicable law. The form is to be transmitted directly to the lender and is not to be transmitted through the applicant or any other party.

FNMA Form 1006

Federal National Mortgage Association

REQUEST FOR VERIFICATION OF EMPLOYMENT

INSTRUCTIONS: LENDER- Complete items 1 thru 7. Have applicant complete item 8. Forward directly to employer named in item 1.

EMPLOYER-Please complete either Part II or Part III as applicable. Sign and return directly to lender named in item 2.

PART I - REQUEST

1. TO *(Name and address of employer)*	2. FROM*(Name and address of lender)*		
3. SIGNATURE OF LENDER	**4. TITLE**	**5. DATE**	**6. LENDER'S NUMBER** *(optional)*

I have applied for a mortgage loan and stated that I am now or was formerly employed by you. My signature below authorizes verification of this information.

7. NAME AND ADDRESS OF APPLICANT *(Include employee or badge number)*	8. SIGNATURE OF APPLICANT

PART II - VERIFICATION OF PRESENT EMPLOYMENT

EMPLOYMENT DATA	PAY DATA		
9. APPLICANT'S DATE OF EMPLOYMENT	12A. CURRENT BASE PAY (Enter Amount and Check Period) ☐ ANNUAL ☐ HOURLY ☐ MONTHLY ☐ OTHER ☐ WEEKLY *(Specify)* $ _____	12C.FOR MILITARY PERSONNEL ONLY	

10. PRESENT POSITION		PAY GRADE	

	12B. EARNINGS	TYPE	MONTHLY AMOUNT
11. PROBABILITY OF CONTINUED EMPLOYMENT	TYPE / YEAR TO DATE / PAST YEAR	BASE PAY	$
13.IF OVERTIME OR BONUS IS APPLICABLE, IS ITS CONTINUANCE LIKELY?	BASE PAY $ ___ $ ___	RATIONS	$
		FLIGHT OR HAZARD	$
	OVERTIME $ ___ $ ___	CLOTHING	$
		QUARTERS	$
	COMMISSIONS $ ___ $ ___	PRO PAY	$
OVERTIME ☐ YES ☐ NO BONUS ☐ YES ☐ NO	BONUS $ ___ $ ___	OVER SEAS OR COMBAT	$

14. REMARKS *(if paid hourly, please indicate average hours worked each week during current and past year)*

PART III - VERIFICATION OF PREVIOUS EMPLOYMENT

15. DATES OF EMPLOYMENT	16. SALARY/WAGE AT TERMINATION PER (Year) (Month)(Week) BASE _____ OVERTIME _____ COMMISSIONS _____ BONUS _____
17. REASON FOR LEAVING	18. POSITION HELD

19. SIGNATURE OF EMPLOYER	20. TITLE	21. DATE

The confidentiality of the information you have furnished will be preserved except where disclosure of this information is required by applicable law. The form is to be transmitted directly to the lender and is not to be transmitted through the applicant or any other party.

PREVIOUS EDITION WILL BE USED UNTIL STOCK IS EXHAUSTED   FNMA Form 1005

DEED OF TRUST

THIS DEED OF TRUST ("Security Instrument") is made on ....,
19.......... The grantor is ....
.... ("Borrower"). The trustee is ....
.... ("Trustee"). The beneficiary is
...., which is organized and existing
under the laws of ...., and whose address is ....
.... ("Lender").
Borrower owes Lender the principal sum of ....
.... Dollars (U.S. $..................................). This debt is evidenced by Borrower's note
dated the same date as this Security Instrument ("Note"), which provides for monthly payments, with the full debt, if not
paid earlier, due and payable on ....
This Security Instrument secures to Lender: (a) the repayment of the debt evidenced by the Note, with interest, and all
renewals, extensions and modifications; (b) the payment of all other sums, with interest, advanced under paragraph 7 to
protect the security of this Security Instrument; and (c) the performance of Borrower's covenants and agreements under
this Security Instrument and the Note. For this purpose, Borrower irrevocably grants and conveys to Trustee and Trustee's
successors and assigns, in trust, with power of sale, the following described property located in ....
.... County, North Carolina:

which has the address of ...., ...,
                                                    [Street]   [City]
North Carolina .... ("Property Address");
                              [Zip Code]

TO HAVE AND TO HOLD unto Trustee and Trustee's successors and assigns, forever, together with all the
improvements now or hereafter erected on the property, and all easements, rights, appurtenances, rents, royalties, mineral,
oil and gas rights and profits, water rights and stock and all fixtures now or hereafter a part of the property. All
replacements and additions shall also be covered by this Security Instrument. All of the foregoing is referred to in this
Security Instrument as the "Property."

BORROWER COVENANTS that Borrower is lawfully seised of the estate hereby conveyed and has the right to grant
and convey the Property and that the Property is unencumbered, except for encumbrances of record. Borrower warrants
and will defend generally the title to the Property against all claims and demands, subject to any encumbrances of record.

THIS SECURITY INSTRUMENT combines uniform covenants for national use and non-uniform covenants with
limited variations by jurisdiction to constitute a uniform security instrument covering real property.

UNIFORM COVENANTS. Borrower and Lender covenant and agree as follows:
   1. Payment of Principal and Interest; Prepayment and Late Charges. Borrower shall promptly pay when due
the principal of and interest on the debt evidenced by the Note and any prepayment and late charges due under the Note.
   2. Funds for Taxes and Insurance. Subject to applicable law or to a written waiver by Lender, Borrower shall pay
to Lender on the day monthly payments are due under the Note, until the Note is paid in full, a sum ("Funds") equal to
one-twelfth of: (a) yearly taxes and assessments which may attain priority over this Security Instrument; (b) yearly
leasehold payments or ground rents on the Property, if any; (c) yearly hazard insurance premiums; and (d) yearly
mortgage insurance premiums, if any. These items are called "escrow items." Lender may estimate the Funds due on the
basis of current data and reasonable estimates of future escrow items.
   The Funds shall be held in an institution the deposits or accounts of which are insured or guaranteed by a federal or
state agency (including Lender if Lender is such an institution). Lender shall apply the Funds to pay the escrow items.

NORTH CAROLINA—Single Family—FNMA/FHLMC UNIFORM INSTRUMENT   Form 3034 12/83

Lender may not charge for holding and applying the Funds, analyzing the account or verifying the escrow items, unless Lender pays Borrower interest on the Funds and applicable law permits Lender to make such a charge. Borrower and Lender may agree in writing that interest shall be paid on the Funds. Unless an agreement is made or applicable law requires interest to be paid, Lender shall not be required to pay Borrower any interest or earnings on the Funds. Lender shall give to Borrower, without charge, an annual accounting of the Funds showing credits and debits to the Funds and the purpose for which each debit to the Funds was made. The Funds are pledged as additional security for the sums secured by this Security Instrument.

If the amount of the Funds held by Lender, together with the future monthly payments of Funds payable prior to the due dates of the escrow items, shall exceed the amount required to pay the escrow items when due, the excess shall be, at Borrower's option, either promptly repaid to Borrower or credited to Borrower on monthly payments of Funds. If the amount of the Funds held by Lender is not sufficient to pay the escrow items when due, Borrower shall pay to Lender any amount necessary to make up the deficiency in one or more payments as required by Lender.

Upon payment in full of all sums secured by this Security Instrument, Lender shall promptly refund to Borrower any Funds held by Lender. If under paragraph 19 the Property is sold or acquired by Lender, Lender shall apply, no later than immediately prior to the sale of the Property or its acquisition by Lender, any Funds held by Lender at the time of application as a credit against the sums secured by this Security Instrument.

3. Application of Payments. Unless applicable law provides otherwise, all payments received by Lender under paragraphs 1 and 2 shall be applied: first, to late charges due under the Note; second, to prepayment charges due under the Note; third, to amounts payable under paragraph 2; fourth, to interest due; and last, to principal due.

4. Charges; Liens. Borrower shall pay all taxes, assessments, charges, fines and impositions attributable to the Property which may attain priority over this Security Instrument, and leasehold payments or ground rents, if any. Borrower shall pay these obligations in the manner provided in paragraph 2, or if not paid in that manner, Borrower shall pay them on time directly to the person owed payment. Borrower shall promptly furnish to Lender all notices of amounts to be paid under this paragraph. If Borrower makes these payments directly, Borrower shall promptly furnish to Lender receipts evidencing the payments.

Borrower shall promptly discharge any lien which has priority over this Security Instrument unless Borrower: (a) agrees in writing to the payment of the obligation secured by the lien in a manner acceptable to Lender; (b) contests in good faith the lien by, or defends against enforcement of the lien in, legal proceedings which in the Lender's opinion operate to prevent the enforcement of the lien or forfeiture of any part of the Property; or (c) secures from the holder of the lien an agreement satisfactory to Lender subordinating the lien to this Security Instrument. If Lender determines that any part of the Property is subject to a lien which may attain priority over this Security Instrument, Lender may give Borrower a notice identifying the lien. Borrower shall satisfy the lien or take one or more of the actions set forth above within 10 days of the giving of notice.

5. Hazard Insurance. Borrower shall keep the improvements now existing or hereafter erected on the Property insured against loss by fire, hazards included within the term "extended coverage" and any other hazards for which Lender requires insurance. This insurance shall be maintained in the amounts and for the periods that Lender requires. The insurance carrier providing the insurance shall be chosen by Borrower subject to Lender's approval which shall not be unreasonably withheld.

All insurance policies and renewals shall be acceptable to Lender and shall include a standard mortgage clause. Lender shall have the right to hold the policies and renewals. If Lender requires, Borrower shall promptly give to Lender all receipts of paid premiums and renewal notices. In the event of loss, Borrower shall give prompt notice to the insurance carrier and Lender. Lender may make proof of loss if not made promptly by Borrower.

Unless Lender and Borrower otherwise agree in writing, insurance proceeds shall be applied to restoration or repair of the Property damaged, if the restoration or repair is economically feasible and Lender's security is not lessened. If the restoration or repair is not economically feasible or Lender's security would be lessened, the insurance proceeds shall be applied to the sums secured by this Security Instrument, whether or not then due, with any excess paid to Borrower. If Borrower abandons the Property, or does not answer within 30 days a notice from Lender that the insurance carrier has offered to settle a claim, then Lender may collect the insurance proceeds. Lender may use the proceeds to repair or restore the Property or to pay sums secured by this Security Instrument, whether or not then due. The 30-day period will begin when the notice is given.

Unless Lender and Borrower otherwise agree in writing, any application of proceeds to principal shall not extend or postpone the due date of the monthly payments referred to in paragraphs 1 and 2 or change the amount of the payments. If under paragraph 19 the Property is acquired by Lender, Borrower's right to any insurance policies and proceeds resulting from damage to the Property prior to the acquisition shall pass to Lender to the extent of the sums secured by this Security Instrument immediately prior to the acquisition.

6. Preservation and Maintenance of Property; Leaseholds. Borrower shall not destroy, damage or substantially change the Property, allow the Property to deteriorate or commit waste. If this Security Instrument is on a leasehold, Borrower shall comply with the provisions of the lease, and if Borrower acquires fee title to the Property, the leasehold and fee title shall not merge unless Lender agrees to the merger in writing.

7. Protection of Lender's Rights in the Property; Mortgage Insurance. If Borrower fails to perform the covenants and agreements contained in this Security Instrument, or there is a legal proceeding that may significantly affect Lender's rights in the Property (such as a proceeding in bankruptcy, probate, for condemnation or to enforce laws or regulations), then Lender may do and pay for whatever is necessary to protect the value of the Property and Lender's rights in the Property. Lender's actions may include paying any sums secured by a lien which has priority over this Security Instrument, appearing in court, paying reasonable attorneys' fees and entering on the Property to make repairs. Although Lender may take action under this paragraph 7, Lender does not have to do so.

Any amounts disbursed by Lender under this paragraph 7 shall become additional debt of Borrower secured by this Security Instrument. Unless Borrower and Lender agree to other terms of payment, these amounts shall bear interest from the date of disbursement at the Note rate and shall be payable, with interest, upon notice from Lender to Borrower requesting payment.

If Lender required mortgage insurance as a condition of making the loan secured by this Security Instrument, Borrower shall pay the premiums required to maintain the insurance in effect until such time as the requirement for the insurance terminates in accordance with Borrower's and Lender's written agreement or applicable law.

8. Inspection. Lender or its agent may make reasonable entries upon and inspections of the Property. Lender shall give Borrower notice at the time of or prior to an inspection specifying reasonable cause for the inspection.

9. Condemnation. The proceeds of any award or claim for damages, direct or consequential, in connection with any condemnation or other taking of any part of the Property, or for conveyance in lieu of condemnation, are hereby assigned and shall be paid to Lender.

In the event of a total taking of the Property, the proceeds shall be applied to the sums secured by this Security Instrument, whether or not then due, with any excess paid to Borrower. In the event of a partial taking of the Property, unless Borrower and Lender otherwise agree in writing, the sums secured by this Security Instrument shall be reduced by the amount of the proceeds multiplied by the following fraction: (a) the total amount of the sums secured immediately before the taking, divided by (b) the fair market value of the Property immediately before the taking Any balance shall be paid to Borrower.

If the Property is abandoned by Borrower, or if, after notice by Lender to Borrower that the condemnor offers to make an award or settle a claim for damages, Borrower fails to respond to Lender within 30 days after the date the notice is given, Lender is authorized to collect and apply the proceeds, at its option, either to restoration or repair of the Property or to the sums secured by this Security Instrument, whether or not then due.

Unless Lender and Borrower otherwise agree in writing, any application of proceeds to principal shall not extend or postpone the due date of the monthly payments referred to in paragraphs 1 and 2 or change the amount of such payments.

10. Borrower Not Released; Forbearance By Lender Not a Waiver. Extension of the time for payment or modification of amortization of the sums secured by this Security Instrument granted by Lender to any successor in interest of Borrower shall not operate to release the liability of the original Borrower or Borrower's successors in interest. Lender shall not be required to commence proceedings against any successor in interest or refuse to extend time for payment or otherwise modify amortization of the sums secured by this Security Instrument by reason of any demand made by the original Borrower or Borrower's successors in interest. Any forbearance by Lender in exercising any right or remedy shall not be a waiver of or preclude the exercise of any right or remedy.

11. Successors and Assigns Bound; Joint and Several Liability; Co-signers. The covenants and agreements of this Security Instrument shall bind and benefit the successors and assigns of Lender and Borrower, subject to the provisions of paragraph 17. Borrower's covenants and agreements shall be joint and several. Any Borrower who co-signs this Security Instrument but does not execute the Note: (a) is co-signing this Security Instrument only to mortgage, grant and convey that Borrower's interest in the Property under the terms of this Security Instrument; (b) is not personally obligated to pay the sums secured by this Security Instrument; and (c) agrees that Lender and any other Borrower may agree to extend, modify, forbear or make any accommodations with regard to the terms of this Security Instrument or the Note without that Borrower's consent.

12. Loan Charges. If the loan secured by this Security Instrument is subject to a law which sets maximum loan charges, and that law is finally interpreted so that the interest or other loan charges collected or to be collected in connection with the loan exceed the permitted limits, then: (a) any such loan charge shall be reduced by the amount necessary to reduce the charge to the permitted limit; and (b) any sums already collected from Borrower which exceeded permitted limits will be refunded to Borrower. Lender may choose to make this refund by reducing the principal owed under the Note or by making a direct payment to Borrower. If a refund reduces principal, the reduction will be treated as a partial prepayment without any prepayment charge under the Note.

13. Legislation Affecting Lender's Rights. If enactment or expiration of applicable laws has the effect of rendering any provision of the Note or this Security Instrument unenforceable according to its terms, Lender, at its option, may require immediate payment in full of all sums secured by this Security Instrument and may invoke any remedies permitted by paragraph 19. If Lender exercises this option, Lender shall take the steps specified in the second paragraph of paragraph 17.

14. Notices. Any notice to Borrower provided for in this Security Instrument shall be given by delivering it or by mailing it by first class mail unless applicable law requires use of another method. The notice shall be directed to the Property Address or any other address Borrower designates by notice to Lender. Any notice to Lender shall be given by first class mail to Lender's address stated herein or any other address Lender designates by notice to Borrower. Any notice provided for in this Security Instrument shall be deemed to have been given to Borrower or Lender when given as provided in this paragraph.

15. Governing Law; Severability. This Security Instrument shall be governed by federal law and the law of the jurisdiction in which the Property is located. In the event that any provision or clause of this Security Instrument or the Note conflicts with applicable law, such conflict shall not affect other provisions of this Security Instrument or the Note which can be given effect without the conflicting provision. To this end the provisions of this Security Instrument and the Note are declared to be severable.

16. Borrower's Copy. Borrower shall be given one conformed copy of the Note and of this Security Instrument.

17. Transfer of the Property or a Beneficial Interest in Borrower. If all or any part of the Property or any interest in it is sold or transferred (or if a beneficial interest in Borrower is sold or transferred and Borrower is not a natural person) without Lender's prior written consent, Lender may, at its option, require immediate payment in full of all sums secured by this Security Instrument. However, this option shall not be exercised by Lender if exercise is prohibited by federal law as of the date of this Security Instrument.

If Lender exercises this option, Lender shall give Borrower notice of acceleration. The notice shall provide a period of not less than 30 days from the date the notice is delivered or mailed within which Borrower must pay all sums secured by this Security Instrument. If Borrower fails to pay these sums prior to the expiration of this period, Lender may invoke any remedies permitted by this Security Instrument without further notice or demand on Borrower.

18. Borrower's Right to Reinstate. If Borrower meets certain conditions, Borrower shall have the right to have enforcement of this Security Instrument discontinued at any time prior to the earlier of: (a) 5 days (or such other period as applicable law may specify for reinstatement) before sale of the Property pursuant to any power of sale contained in this Security Instrument; or (b) entry of a judgment enforcing this Security Instrument. Those conditions are that Borrower: (a) pays Lender all sums which then would be due under this Security Instrument and the Note had no acceleration occurred; (b) cures any default of any other covenants or agreements; (c) pays all expenses incurred in enforcing this Security Instrument, including, but not limited to, reasonable attorneys' fees; and (d) takes such action as Lender may reasonably require to assure that the lien of this Security Instrument, Lender's rights in the Property and Borrower's obligation to pay the sums secured by this Security Instrument shall continue unchanged. Upon reinstatement by Borrower, this Security Instrument and the obligations secured hereby shall remain fully effective as if no acceleration had occurred. However, this right to reinstate shall not apply in the case of acceleration under paragraphs 13 or 17.

NON-UNIFORM COVENANTS. Borrower and Lender further covenant and agree as follows:

19. Acceleration; Remedies. Lender shall give notice to Borrower prior to acceleration following Borrower's breach of any covenant or agreement in this Security Instrument (but not prior to acceleration under paragraphs 13 and 17 unless applicable law provides otherwise). The notice shall specify: (a) the default; (b) the action required to cure the default; (c) a date, not less than 30 days from the date the notice is given to Borrower, by which the default must be cured; and (d) that failure to cure the default on or before the date specified in the notice may result in acceleration of the sums secured by this Security Instrument and sale of the Property. The notice shall further inform Borrower of the right to reinstate after acceleration and the right to assert in the foreclosure proceeding the non-existence of a default or any other defense of Borrower to acceleration and sale. If the default is not cured on or before the date specified in the notice, Lender at its option may require immediate payment in full of all sums secured by this Security Instrument without further demand and may invoke the power of sale and any other remedies permitted by applicable law. Lender shall be entitled to collect all expenses incurred in pursuing the remedies provided in this paragraph 19, including, but not limited to, reasonable attorneys' fees and costs of title evidence.

If Lender invokes the power of sale, and if it is determined in a hearing held in accordance with applicable law that Trustee can proceed to sale, Trustee shall take such action regarding notice of sale and shall give such notices to Borrower and to other persons as applicable law may require. After the time required by applicable law and after publication of the notice of sale, Trustee, without demand on Borrower, shall sell the Property at public auction to the highest bidder at the time and place and under the terms designated in the notice of sale in one or more parcels and in any order Trustee determines. Lender or its designee may purchase the Property at any sale.

Trustee shall deliver to the purchaser Trustee's deed conveying the Property without any covenant or warranty, expressed or implied. The recitals in the Trustee's deed shall be prima facie evidence of the truth of the statements made therein. Trustee shall apply the proceeds of the sale in the following order: (a) to all expenses of the sale, including, but not limited to, Trustee's fees of ....% of the gross sale price; (b) to all sums secured by this Security Instrument; and (c) any excess to the person or persons legally entitled to it.

20. Lender in Possession. Upon acceleration under paragraph 19 or abandonment of the Property, Lender (in person, by agent or by judicially appointed receiver) shall be entitled to enter upon, take possession of and manage the Property and to collect the rents of the Property including those past due. Any rents collected by Lender or the receiver shall be applied first to payment of the costs of management of the Property and collection of rents, including, but not limited to, receiver's fees, premiums on receiver's bonds and reasonable attorneys' fees, and then to the sums secured by this Security Instrument.

21. Release. Upon payment of all sums secured by this Security Instrument, Lender or Trustee shall cancel this Security Instrument without charge to Borrower. If Trustee is requested to release this Security Instrument, all notes evidencing debt secured by this Security Instrument shall be surrendered to Trustee. Borrower shall pay any recordation costs.

22. Substitute Trustee. Lender may from time to time remove Trustee and appoint a successor trustee to any Trustee appointed hereunder by an instrument recorded in the county in which this Security Instrument is recorded. Without conveyance of the Property, the successor trustee shall succeed to all the title, power and duties conferred upon Trustee herein and by applicable law.

23. Riders to this Security Instrument. If one or more riders are executed by Borrower and recorded together with this Security Instrument, the covenants and agreements of each such rider shall be incorporated into and shall amend and supplement the covenants and agreements of this Security Instrument as if the rider(s) were a part of this Security Instrument. [Check applicable box(es)]

☐ Adjustable Rate Rider ☐ Condominium Rider ☐ 2–4 Family Rider

☐ Graduated Payment Rider ☐ Planned Unit Development Rider

☐ Other(s) [specify]

BY SIGNING UNDER SEAL BELOW, Borrower accepts and agrees to the terms and covenants contained in this Security Instrument and in any rider(s) executed by Borrower and recorded with it.

....(Seal)
—Borrower

....(Seal)
—Borrower

————————————— [Space Below This Line For Acknowledgment] —————————————

313

NOTE

...., 19......... ...., ...
                                                              [City]   [State]

....
[Property Address]

1. BORROWER'S PROMISE TO PAY

In return for a loan that I have received, I promise to pay U.S. $.. (this amount is called "principal"), plus interest, to the order of the Lender. The Lender is .... I understand that the Lender may transfer this Note. The Lender or anyone who takes this Note by transfer and who is entitled to receive payments under this Note is called the "Note Holder."

2. INTEREST

Interest will be charged on unpaid principal until the full amount of principal has been paid. I will pay interest at a yearly rate of ....%.

The interest rate required by this Section 2 is the rate I will pay both before and after any default described in Section 6(B) of this Note.

3. PAYMENTS

(A) Time and Place of Payments

I will pay principal and interest by making payments every month.

I will make my monthly payments on the .... day of each month beginning on ...., 19......... I will make these payments every month until I have paid all of the principal and interest and any other charges described below that I may owe under this Note. My monthly payments will be applied to interest before principal. If, on ...., ..., I still owe amounts under this Note, I will pay those amounts in full on that date, which is called the "maturity date."

I will make my monthly payments at .... or at a different place if required by the Note Holder.

(B) Amount of Monthly Payments

My monthly payment will be in the amount of U.S. $..

4. BORROWER'S RIGHT TO PREPAY

I have the right to make payments of principal at any time before they are due. A payment of principal only is known as a "prepayment." When I make a prepayment, I will tell the Note Holder in writing that I am doing so.

I may make a full prepayment or partial prepayments without paying any prepayment charge. The Note Holder will use all of my prepayments to reduce the amount of principal that I owe under this Note. If I make a partial prepayment, there will be no changes in the due date or in the amount of my monthly payment unless the Note Holder agrees in writing to those changes.

5. LOAN CHARGES

If a law, which applies to this loan and which sets maximum loan charges, is finally interpreted so that the interest or other loan charges collected or to be collected in connection with this loan exceed the permitted limits, then: (i) any such loan charge shall be reduced by the amount necessary to reduce the charge to the permitted limit; and (ii) any sums already collected from me which exceeded permitted limits will be refunded to me. The Note Holder may choose to make this refund by reducing the principal I owe under this Note or by making a direct payment to me. If a refund reduces principal, the reduction will be treated as a partial prepayment.

6. BORROWER'S FAILURE TO PAY AS REQUIRED

(A) Late Charge for Overdue Payments

If the Note Holder has not received the full amount of any monthly payment by the end of .... calendar days after the date it is due, I will pay a late charge to the Note Holder. The amount of the charge will be ....% of my overdue payment of principal and interest. I will pay this late charge promptly but only once on each late payment.

(B) Default

If I do not pay the full amount of each monthly payment on the date it is due, I will be in default.

(C) Notice of Default

If I am in default, the Note Holder may send me a written notice telling me that if I do not pay the overdue amount by a certain date, the Note Holder may require me to pay immediately the full amount of principal which has not been paid and all the interest that I owe on that amount. That date must be at least 30 days after the date on which the notice is delivered or mailed to me.

(D) No Waiver By Note Holder

Even if, at a time when I am in default, the Note Holder does not require me to pay immediately in full as described above, the Note Holder will still have the right to do so if I am in default at a later time.

(E) Payment of Note Holder's Costs and Expenses

If the Note Holder has required me to pay immediately in full as described above, the Note Holder will have the right to be paid back by me for all of its costs and expenses in enforcing this Note to the extent not prohibited by applicable law. Those expenses include, for example, reasonable attorneys' fees.

7. GIVING OF NOTICES

Unless applicable law requires a different method, any notice that must be given to me under this Note will be given by delivering it or by mailing it by first class mail to me at the Property Address above or at a different address if I give the Note Holder a notice of my different address.

Any notice that must be given to the Note Holder under this Note will be given by mailing it by first class mail to the Note Holder at the address stated in Section 3(A) above or at a different address if I am given a notice of that different address.

MULTISTATE FIXED RATE NOTE—Single Family—**FNMA/FHLMC UNIFORM INSTRUMENT**   Form 3200 12/83

8. OBLIGATIONS OF PERSONS UNDER THIS NOTE

If more than one person signs this Note, each person is fully and personally obligated to keep all of the promises made in this Note, including the promise to pay the full amount owed. Any person who is a guarantor, surety or endorser of this Note is also obligated to do these things. Any person who takes over these obligations, including the obligations of a guarantor, surety or endorser of this Note, is also obligated to keep all of the promises made in this Note. The Note Holder may enforce its rights under this Note against each person individually or against all of us together. This means that any one of us may be required to pay all of the amounts owed under this Note.

9. WAIVERS

I and any other person who has obligations under this Note waive the rights of presentment and notice of dishonor. "Presentment" means the right to require the Note Holder to demand payment of amounts due. "Notice of dishonor" means the right to require the Note Holder to give notice to other persons that amounts due have not been paid.

10. UNIFORM SECURED NOTE

This Note is a uniform instrument with limited variations in some jurisdictions. In addition to the protections given to the Note Holder under this Note, a Mortgage, Deed of Trust or Security Deed (the "Security Instrument"), dated the same date as this Note, protects the Note Holder from possible losses which might result if I do not keep the promises which I make in this Note. That Security Instrument describes how and under what conditions I may be required to make immediate payment in full of all amounts I owe under this Note. Some of those conditions are described as follows:

Transfer of the Property or a Beneficial Interest in Borrower. If all or any part of the Property or any interest in it is sold or transferred (or if a beneficial interest in Borrower is sold or transferred and Borrower is not a natural person) without Lender's prior written consent, Lender may, at its option, require immediate payment in full of all sums secured by this Security Instrument. However, this option shall not be exercised by Lender if exercise is prohibited by federal law as of the date of this Security Instrument.

If Lender exercises this option, Lender shall give Borrower notice of acceleration. The notice shall provide a period of not less than 30 days from the date the notice is delivered or mailed within which Borrower must pay all sums secured by this Security Instrument. If Borrower fails to pay these sums prior to the expiration of this period, Lender may invoke any remedies permitted by this Security Instrument without further notice or demand on Borrower.

DUE
ON
SALE
CLAUSE

WITNESS THE HAND(S) AND SEAL(S) OF THE UNDERSIGNED.

....(Seal)
-Borrower

....(Seal)
-Borrower

....(Seal)
-Borrower

[Sign Original Only]

ADJUSTABLE RATE NOTE
(11th District Cost of Funds Index—Rate Caps)

THIS NOTE CONTAINS PROVISIONS ALLOWING FOR CHANGES IN MY INTEREST RATE AND MY MONTHLY PAYMENT. THIS NOTE LIMITS THE AMOUNT MY INTEREST RATE CAN CHANGE AT ANY ONE TIME AND THE MAXIMUM RATE I MUST PAY.

.... , 19............ , ...

[City]   [State]

....

[Property Address]

1. BORROWER'S PROMISE TO PAY

In return for a loan that I have received, I promise to pay U.S. $................................. (this amount is called "principal"), plus interest, to the order of the Lender. The Lender is ....

I understand that the Lender may transfer this Note. The Lender or anyone who takes this Note by transfer and who is entitled to receive payments under this Note is called the "Note Holder."

2. INTEREST

Interest will be charged on unpaid principal until the full amount of principal has been paid. I will pay interest at a yearly rate of ....%. The interest rate I will pay will change in accordance with Section 4 of this Note.

The interest rate required by this Section 2 and Section 4 of this Note is the rate I will pay both before and after any default described in Section 7(B) of this Note.

3. PAYMENTS

(A) Time and Place of Payments

I will pay principal and interest by making payments every month.

I will make my monthly payments on the first day of each month beginning on ....,19........ I will make these payments every month until I have paid all of the principal and interest and any other charges described below that I may owe under this Note. My monthly payments will be applied to interest before principal. If, on ...., 20......., I still owe amounts under this Note, I will pay those amounts in full on that date, which is called the "maturity date."

I will make my monthly payments at .... or at a different place if required by the Note Holder.

(B) Amount of My Initial Monthly Payments

Each of my initial monthly payments will be in the amount of U.S. $........................... This amount may change.

(C) Monthly Payment Changes

Changes in my monthly payment will reflect changes in the unpaid principal of my loan and in the interest rate that I must pay. The Note Holder will determine my new interest rate and the changed amount of my monthly payment in accordance with Section 4 of this Note.

4. INTEREST RATE AND MONTHLY PAYMENT CHANGES

(A) Change Dates

The interest rate I will pay may change on the first day of .... , 19........, and on that day every .... month thereafter. Each date on which my interest rate could change is called a "Change Date."

MULTISTATE ADJUSTABLE RATE NOTE—COF INDEX—Single Family—**Fannie Mae/Freddie Mac Uniform Instrument**   Form 3510 7/88

(B) The Index

Beginning with the first Change Date, my interest rate will be based on an Index. The "Index" is the monthly weighted average cost of savings, borrowings and advances of members of the Federal Home Loan Bank of San Francisco (the "Bank"), as made available by the Bank. The most recent Index figure available as of the date 45 days before each Change Date is called the "Current Index."

If the Index is no longer available, the Note Holder will choose a new index that is based upon comparable information. The Note Holder will give me notice of this choice.

(C) Calculation of Changes

Before each Change Date, the Note Holder will calculate my new interest rate by adding .... percentage points (............%) to the Current Index. The Note Holder will then round the result of this addition to the nearest one-eighth of one percentage point (0.125%). Subject to the limits stated in Section 4(D) below, this rounded amount will be my new interest rate until the next Change Date.

The Note Holder will then determine the amount of the monthly payment that would be sufficient to repay the unpaid principal that I am expected to owe at the Change Date in full on the maturity date at my new interest rate in substantially equal payments. The result of this calculation will be the new amount of my monthly payment.

(D) Limits on Interest Rate Changes

The interest rate I am required to pay at the first Change Date will not be greater than ....% or less than ....%. Thereafter, my interest rate will never be increased or decreased on any single Change Date by more than .... percentage point(s) (............%) from the rate of interest I have been paying for the preceding .... months. My interest rate will never be greater than ....%.

(E) Effective Date of Changes

My new interest rate will become effective on each Change Date. I will pay the amount of my new monthly payment beginning on the first monthly payment date after the Change Date until the amount of my monthly payment changes again.

(F) Notice of Changes

The Note Holder will deliver or mail to me a notice of any changes in my interest rate and the amount of my monthly payment before the effective date of any change. The notice will include information required by law to be given me and also the title and telephone number of a person who will answer any question I may have regarding the notice.

5. BORROWER'S RIGHT TO PREPAY

I have the right to make payments of principal at any time before they are due. A payment of principal only is known as a "prepayment." When I make a prepayment, I will tell the Note Holder in writing that I am doing so.

I may make a full prepayment or partial prepayments without paying any prepayment charge. The Note Holder will use all of my prepayments to reduce the amount of principal that I owe under this Note. If I make a partial prepayment, there will be no changes in the due dates of my monthly payments unless the Note Holder agrees in writing to those changes. My partial prepayment may reduce the amount of my monthly payments after the first Change Date following my partial prepayment. However, any reduction due to my partial prepayment may be offset by an interest rate increase.

6. LOAN CHARGES

If a law, which applies to this loan and which sets maximum loan charges, is finally interpreted so that the interest or other loan charges collected or to be collected in connection with this loan exceed the permitted limits, then: (i) any such loan charge shall be reduced by the amount necessary to reduce the charge to the permitted limit; and (ii) any sums already collected from me which exceeded permitted limits will be refunded to me. The Note Holder may choose to make this refund by reducing the principal I owe under this Note or by making a direct payment to me. If a refund reduces principal, the reduction will be treated as a partial prepayment.

7. BORROWER'S FAILURE TO PAY AS REQUIRED

(A) Late Charges for Overdue Payments

If the Note Holder has not received the full amount of any monthly payment by the end of .... calendar days after the date it is due, I will pay a late charge to the Note Holder. The amount of the charge will be ....% of my overdue payment of principal and interest. I will pay this late charge promptly but only once on each late payment.

(B) Default

If I do not pay the full amount of each monthly payment on the date it is due, I will be in default.

(C) Notice of Default

If I am in default, the Note Holder may send me a written notice telling me that if I do not pay the overdue amount by a certain date, the Note Holder may require me to pay immediately the full amount of principal which has not been paid and all the interest that I owe on that amount. That date must be at least 30 days after the date on which the notice is delivered or mailed to me.

(D) No Waiver by Note Holder

Even if, at a time when I am in default, the Note Holder does not require me to pay immediately in full as described above, the Note Holder will still have the right to do so if I am in default at a later time.

(E) Payment of Note Holder's Costs and Expenses

If the Note Holder has required me to pay immediately in full as described above, the Note Holder will have the right to be paid back by me for all of its costs and expenses in enforcing this Note to the extent not prohibited by applicable law. Those expenses include, for example, reasonable attorneys' fees.

8. GIVING OF NOTICES

Unless applicable law requires a different method, any notice that must be given to me under this Note will be given by delivering it or by mailing it by first class mail to me at the Property Address above or at a different address if I give the Note Holder a notice of my different address.

Any notice that must be given to the Note Holder under this Note will be given by mailing it by first class mail to the Note Holder at the address stated in Section 3(A) above or at a different address if I am given a notice of that different address.

9. OBLIGATIONS OF PERSONS UNDER THIS NOTE

If more than one person signs this Note, each person is fully and personally obligated to keep all of the promises made in this Note, including the promise to pay the full amount owed. Any person who is a guarantor, surety or endorser of this Note is also obligated to do these things. Any person who takes over these obligations, including the obligations of a guarantor, surety or endorser of this Note, is also obligated to keep all of the promises made in this Note. The Note Holder may enforce its rights under this Note against each person individually or against all of us together. This means that any one of us may be required to pay all of the amounts owed under this Note.

10. WAIVERS

I and any other person who has obligations under this Note waive the rights of presentment and notice of dishonor. "Presentment" means the right to require the Note Holder to demand payment of amounts due. "Notice of dishonor" means the right to require the Note Holder to give notice to other persons that amounts due have not been paid.

11. UNIFORM SECURED NOTE

This Note is a uniform instrument with limited variations in some jurisdictions. In addition to the protections given to the Note Holder under this Note, a Mortgage, Deed of Trust or Security Deed (the "Security Instrument"), dated the same date as this Note, protects the Note Holder from possible losses which might result if I do not keep the promises that I make in this Note. That Security Instrument describes how and under what conditions I may be required to make immediate payment in full of all amounts I owe under this Note. Some of those conditions are described as follows:

Transfer of the Property or a Beneficial Interest in Borrower. If all or any part of the Property or any interest in it is sold or transferred (or if a beneficial interest in Borrower is sold or transferred and Borrower is not a natural person) without Lender's prior written consent, Lender may, at its option, require immediate payment in full of all sums secured by this Security Instrument. However, this option shall not be exercised by Lender if exercise is prohibited by federal law as of the date of this Security Instrument. Lender also shall not exercise this option if: (a) Borrower causes to be submitted to Lender information required by Lender to evaluate the intended transferee as if a new loan were being made to the transferee; and (b) Lender reasonably determines that Lender's security will not be impaired by the loan assumption and that the risk of a breach of any covenant or agreement in this Security Instrument is acceptable to Lender.

To the extent permitted by applicable law, Lender may charge a reasonable fee as a condition to Lender's consent to the loan assumption. Lender may also require the transferee to sign an assumption agreement that is acceptable to Lender and that obligates the transferee to keep all the promises and agreements made in the Note and in this Security Instrument. Borrower will continue to be obligated under the Note and this Security Instrument unless Lender releases Borrower in writing.

If Lender exercises the option to require immediate payment in full, Lender shall give Borrower notice of acceleration. The notice shall provide a period of not less than 30 days from the date the notice is delivered or mailed within which Borrower must pay all sums secured by this Security Instrument. If Borrower fails to pay these sums prior to the expiration of this period, Lender may invoke any remedies permitted by this Security Instrument without further notice or demand on Borrower.

WITNESS THE HAND(S) AND SEAL(S) OF THE UNDERSIGNED.

.... (Seal)
—Borrower

.... (Seal)
—Borrower

.... (Seal)
—Borrower

[Sign Original Only]

319

ADJUSTABLE RATE RIDER
(11th District Cost of Funds Index—Rate Caps)

THIS ADJUSTABLE RATE RIDER is made this .... day of..., 19.............., and is incorporated into and shall be deemed to amend and supplement the Mortgage, Deed of Trust or Security Deed (the "Security Instrument") of the same date given by the undersigned (the "Borrower") to secure Borrower's Adjustable Rate Note (the "Note") to ....

....

(the "Lender") of the same date and covering the property described in the Security Instrument and located at:

....
[Property Address]

THE NOTE CONTAINS PROVISIONS ALLOWING FOR CHANGES IN THE INTEREST RATE AND THE MONTHLY PAYMENT. THE NOTE LIMITS THE AMOUNT THE BORROWER'S INTEREST RATE CAN CHANGE AT ANY ONE TIME AND THE MAXIMUM RATE THE BORROWER MUST PAY.

ADDITIONAL COVENANTS. In addition to the covenants and agreements made in the Security Instrument, Borrower and Lender further covenant and agree as follows:

A. INTEREST RATE AND MONTHLY PAYMENT CHANGES

The Note provides for an initial interest rate of............. %. The Note provides for changes in the interest rate and the monthly payments, as follows:

4. INTEREST RATE AND MONTHLY PAYMENT CHANGES

(A) Change Dates

The interest rate I will pay may change on the first day of .... , 19................., and on that day every ...... month thereafter. Each date on which my interest rate could change is called a "Change Date."

(B) The Index

Beginning with the first Change Date, my interest rate will be based on an Index. The "Index" is the monthly weighted average cost of savings, borrowings and advances of members of the Federal Home Loan Bank of San Francisco (the "Bank"), as made available by the Bank. The most recent Index figure available as of the date 45 days before each Change Date is called the "Current Index."

If the Index is no longer available, the Note Holder will choose a new index that is based upon comparable information. The Note Holder will give me notice of this choice.

(C) Calculation of Changes

Before each Change Date, the Note Holder will calculate my new interest rate by adding ....
.... percentage points (................%) to the Current Index. The Note Holder will then round the result of this addition to the nearest one-eighth of one percentage point (0.125%). Subject to the limits stated in Section 4(D) below, this rounded amount will be my new interest rate until the next Change Date.

The Note Holder will then determine the amount of the monthly payment that would be sufficient to repay the unpaid principal that I am expected to owe at the Change Date in full on the maturity date at my new interest rate in substantially equal payments. The result of this calculation will be the new amount of my monthly payment.

(D) Limits on Interest Rate Changes

The interest rate I am required to pay at the first Change Date will not be greater than ....%
or less than ....%. Thereafter, my interest rate will never be increased or decreased on any single Change Date by more than .... percentage point(s) (............ %) from the rate of interest I have been paying for the preceding .... months. My interest rate will never be greater than .... %.

(E) Effective Date of Changes

My new interest rate will become effective on each Change Date. I will pay the amount of my new monthly payment beginning on the first monthly payment date after the Change Date until the amount of my monthly payment changes again.

(F) Notice of Changes

The Note Holder will deliver or mail to me a notice of any changes in my interest rate and the amount of my monthly payment before the effective date of any change. The notice will include information required by law to be given me and also the title and telephone number of a person who will answer any question I may have regarding the notice.

B. TRANSFER OF THE PROPERTY OR A BENEFICIAL INTEREST IN BORROWER

Uniform Covenant 17 of the Security Instrument is amended to read as follows:

Transfer of the Property or a Beneficial Interest in Borrower. If all or any part of the Property or any interest in it is sold or transferred (or if a beneficial interest in Borrower is sold or transferred and Borrower is not a natural person) without Lender's prior written consent, Lender may, at its option, require immediate payment in full of all sums secured by this Security Instrument. However, this option shall not be exercised by Lender if exercise is prohibited by federal law as of the date of this Security Instrument. Lender also shall not exercise this option if: (a) Borrower causes to be submitted to Lender information required by Lender to evaluate the intended transferee as if a new loan were being made to the transferee; and (b) Lender reasonably determines that Lender's security will not be impaired by the loan assumption and that the risk of a breach of any covenant or agreement in this Security Instrument is acceptable to Lender.

MULTISTATE ADJUSTABLE RATE RIDER—COF INDEX—Single Family—Fannie Mae/Freddie Mac Uniform Instrument   Form 3120 7/88

To the extent permitted by applicable law, Lender may charge a reasonable fee as a condition to Lender's consent to the loan assumption. Lender may also require the transferee to sign an assumption agreement that is acceptable to Lender and that obligates the transferee to keep all the promises and agreements made in the Note and in this Security Instrument. Borrower will continue to be obligated under the Note and this Security Instrument unless Lender releases Borrower in writing.

If Lender exercises the option to require immediate payment in full, Lender shall give Borrower notice of acceleration. The notice shall provide a period of not less than 30 days from the date the notice is delivered or mailed within which Borrower must pay all sums secured by this Security Instrument. If Borrower fails to pay these sums prior to the expiration of this period, Lender may invoke any remedies permitted by this Security Instrument without further notice or demand on Borrower.

By SIGNING BELOW, Borrower accepts and agrees to the terms and covenants contained in this Adjustable Rate Rider.

....(Seal)
—Borrower

....(Seal)
—Borrower

Index

328 / *Index*